CW01546246

POWER
PRIDE &
PREJUDICE

*Afrikanerdom is not a loose group
of people like the Americans
with their Poles, their Puerto Ricans,
their Irish ... Afrikanerdom is not
a recipe for chaos like Canada with its
English and French.
We are altogether different.
Afrikanerdom is a closed circle,
complete and perfect. There is
no way in except by birth and no
way out except by death. It is a
perfection that is of God.*

*Colonel Wheelwright in Closed Circle
Wessel Ebersohn*

POWER PRIDE & PREJUDICE

The years of Afrikaner Nationalist rule in South Africa

HENRY KENNEY

JONATHAN BALL PUBLISHERS · JOHANNESBURG

All rights reserved. No part of this publication may be reproduced or transmitted, in any form or by an means, without permission from the publisher.

© Henry Kenney, 1991

First published in 1991 by
Jonathan Ball Publishers
P O Box 2105
Parklands
2121

ISBN 0 947464 48 4

Typesetting and reproduction by Book Productions, Pretoria
Printed and bound by National Book Printers, Goodwood, Cape
Cover design by Michael Barnett

*To my Mother
and the memory
of my Father*

Contents

	Prologue 1
CHAPTER ONE	1948 21
CHAPTER TWO	A Pattern Unfolds 36
CHAPTER THREE	Getting Round the Constitution 53
CHAPTER FOUR	Tomlinson and Bantu Education 68
CHAPTER FIVE	On the Road to Separate Freedoms 84
CHAPTER SIX	New Directions and Some Old Ones 106
CHAPTER SEVEN	Winds of Change 125
CHAPTER EIGHT	Sharpeville 137
CHAPTER NINE	The Republic 152
CHAPTER TEN	The State Ruled by Verwoerd 170
CHAPTER ELEVEN	The First Verkrampte Split 200
CHAPTER TWELVE	Faces of Janus 221
CHAPTER THIRTEEN	Approaching Soweto 237
CHAPTER FOURTEEN	Making Neo-Apartheid Work 253
CHAPTER FIFTEEN	Inertia and Info 272
CHAPTER SIXTEEN	Unfabian Strategies 290
CHAPTER SEVENTEEN	Treurnicht Makes It Final 308
CHAPTER EIGHTEEN	A New Constitution 325
CHAPTER NINETEEN	States of Emergency 340
CHAPTER TWENTY	One Step Forward, Two Steps Back 368
	Notes 398
	Index 408

Preface

A punch-drunk reading public would probably shout, 'Hold, enough!', when faced by yet another book on apartheid. Whatever their evils, the policies of the South African Nationalist Government have been a boon to publishers all over the world. We have had books examining the White Tribe of Africa, the Rise and Decline of Apartheid, Capitalism and Apartheid, Black Power in South Africa and the Rise and Crisis of Afrikaner Power. Books have asked whether South Africa could survive. They have discerned an eleventh hour at which the country seemed somehow to be permanently stuck. There have been recipe books, specifying *the* solution, how to get permanent peace and indicating high roads upon which the country would do well to start travelling. Any new work on apartheid must plainly establish its claim to product differentiation.

This book simply attempts to tell a story: how the Nationalists arrived in power, what they wanted for themselves and did to other South Africans in pursuing their own self-interest, how their policies changed over the years and why. It is, in short, a history of Nationalist rule in South Africa from 1948 till the release of Nelson Mandela in February 1990.

Writers on South Africa and apartheid have inevitably had a point of view, sometimes to the exclusion of anything else. I too have had to interpret, to decide which facts are more important than others. Firstly, I can say how I have not seen apartheid. I have not attempted to explain it as a natural expression of the Afrikaner's brooding Calvinist mentality, obsessed with the distinction between the chosen and the lost. Nor have I found much evidence that apartheid was synonymous with the South African version of capitalism. At one time there was a school of true believers which stridently attempted to rewrite the South African past in such terms. Recently they have been more muted, possibly because the increasingly overt conflicts between state and capital have been so much at odds with what they wanted to believe. A smattering of economics would have helped at the outset.

There is in fact not much of a mystery about apartheid. It was an intensified form of that white supremacy which passed under the name of segregation before 1948 and to which virtually the whole white population of South Africa subscribed, as it continued to support white rule after the Nationalists came to power. Apartheid can most plausibly be seen as a manifestation of what economists have come to call 'rent-seeking': the use of government power by interest groups to obtain special privileges for themselves. It was about the mobilisation of Afrikaners as Afrikaners to confer favours on their own. What is interesting about the South African variety of rent-seeking is the degree to which the overriding imperative of maintaining white supremacy made government independent of specific interest groups.

Another conclusion is in order. Apartheid was destroyed primarily by economic growth. They were incompatible, as liberal critics pronounced at the beginning of Nationalist rule. The future is usually unfathomable, but this was one of the safest predictions ever made. The logic of economic development made a mockery of the schemes of the planners, the controllers, the social engineers. Change came primarily from within. Sanctions had little to do with it.

I wish to thank my friend David Rees for reading the manuscript and giving me the benefit of his often uncomfortably candid comments. I also gained from the detailed, sometimes outraged, but mostly constructive remarks of my publisher's reader. My 'Cape Dutch' colleague, Johann de Villiers, and I had many, often fruitful, discussions about the nature of South Africa's peculiar people. Lastly, there is Jonathan Ball, who was not so much supportive as insistent. This time round I have no complaints about my publisher. He must get full credit – or discredit – for the title.

Prologue

On Sunday, 11 February 1990, the world's most celebrated political prisoner was released. Nelson Mandela was arrested in 1963 for subversive activities aimed at overthrowing the apartheid regime of South Africa. The following year, at the famous Rivonia Treason Trial, he and other colleagues of the African National Congress were sentenced to varying terms of imprisonment. Mandela himself received a life sentence. On that day he was just short of his 46th birthday.

Over the years Mandela had acquired an almost godlike status, the revered cult-object of millions all over the world looking for role models to adore. As a prisoner of a government cast by popular opinion everywhere as one of the most villainous in history, Mandela was exempt from error. For him there was little chance of making the mistakes which come to those who act on the public stage. All he had to do to become a hero of his time was to remain where he was, in prison.

Mandela had plenty of co-operation from the National Party Government of South Africa. As the demands for his release became louder both at home and abroad, the Nationalists took refuge in a sterile legalism: Mandela had been sentenced to life imprisonment and there he would stay – unless he renounced violence as a means of political change. If he refused, he was in actual fact imprisoning himself. It was an unsubtle attempt, doomed to failure, to separate the mythical freedom-fighter from his followers.

Even if Mandela had been tempted to buy his freedom by making the required renunciation, he must have known that it would mean his instant demise as a hero of the liberation movement. But there was no evidence of temptation. For someone who valued his place in history, as Mandela certainly did, it was unthinkable that he should repudiate his past by yielding to the insistence of the South African Government. Taking up arms against oppression had honourable precedents; it was all too plausible that the practices of the Nationalist Government since 1948 had made a resort to violence by Africans both inevitable and justifiable. Afrikaners themselves had been prone to violent means when they considered that they had been ill-used. Mandela knew that history was on his side, that the white minority could not rule South Africa for ever. All Africans had to do was wait and majority rule would fall into their laps.

In a sense then Mandela turned the tables on his prison-keepers. They became his captives as they attempted to escape from the hackneyed formula they had devised for his release. And yet, of the many demands the world outside was making of the rulers of South Africa, the freeing of Mandela was always near the top of the list. Life in prison improved: he was moved from Robben Island to Pollsmoor near Cape Town and later occupied a house in the grounds of the Paarl prison in the Western Cape. In July 1989 the world was astonished to hear that Mandela had met the State President, P W Botha, for tea and discussions in Cape Town. It was all the more surprising as Botha had by then reached the limits of his capacity as a reformer and had turned into a defiant last-ditcher and strict law-and-order man. It was a reflection of the Government's desperation to find a face-saving way to get Mandela not only out of captivity but into the public arena, for it had become evident that he would have to play a commanding role in negotiating a South African future different from the one which had been planned long before by the social engineers of apartheid.

The political situation changed, suddenly and irrevocably, on 2 February 1990. By then there was a new State President, F W de Klerk, who had succeeded the truculent Botha the previous August. De Klerk had a reputation as a grey man, someone who had never strained himself to be identified as one of the more ardent reforming spirits in the National Party. As leader of the party in the Transvaal, the heartland of white reactionary sentiment, and himself the representative of a notably conservative constituency, De Klerk had been maintaining a balancing act between the right and the left, such as it was, in the National Party. Had he lost his equilibrium the chances were that the right would have him. Yet on that memorable day in February, De Klerk grasped the initiative and never let it go. He announced that banned political organisations were now legal. It meant that the African National Congress, its ally, the South African Communist Party, and the Pan Africanist Congress were free to organise and win support in South African itself. The ANC and the PAC had been declared illegal in 1960, and the SACP had been an outlaw for 40 years. De Klerk declared that the Government had 'taken a firm decision to release Mr Mandela unconditionally'. It happened nine days later.

F W de Klerk came as a relief after P W Botha. He had been conciliatory and pragmatic as only someone with feet in both wings of the party could be. His very lack of previous commitment made it easier to respond to rapidly changing circumstances, none of them favourable to continued white supremacy. The previous June, as overall leader of the National Party, an appointment which he had taken up five months before, De Klerk told the *Financial Times* of London that his goal was 'a totally new South Africa free of oppression and domination'. Fine words, but Nationalist leaders had raised expectations in the past and had then proceeded to dash them with little ceremony when they appeared to conflict with the overriding imperative of white rule.

What was different about De Klerk was that he now made firm commitments, set the pace and kept on doing so. A year later he once more surpassed expectations and announced that the Group Areas Act and the Population Registration Act would be repealed. They were laws long regarded as absolutely crucial to the survival of apartheid. The right wing Official Opposition in the House of Assembly, the Conservative Party, made it plain that it had no illusions about the future of white rule in the new South Africa: its members walked out as De Klerk delivered his presidential address. There could have been no more telling comment about times that were changing.

De Klerk was as good as his word. Both laws were scrapped, as were the 1913 and 1936 Land Acts, which had limited African land ownership to small and backward parts of the country. Moreover, Parliament decided to establish a land advisory commission to consider reparations to the victims who had lost land through apartheid.

The familiar complaints of the ANC that 'real change' in the form of universal suffrage had not yet arrived came across more than ever as the sterile carping of an organisation which had been caught off balance a year before and had not yet adapted to a situation where it had to do more than play up to a world gallery with platitudes about the evils of apartheid.

Something drastic had evidently happened since the general election of September 1989. The National Party had gone into that contest on its most reformist platform yet, but it provided little to indicate the total reversal of Nationalist policy less than six months away. There was no sign that the Government line on the ANC differed from the tested vote-catching clichés of previous elections: it was a terrorist organisation which had to turn its back on violence before it could be admitted as a serious participant in shaping the non-oppressive South Africa the Nationalists had come to like talking about. Even less in prospect then was the scrapping of the cornerstone of the whole system of racial classification, the Population Registration Act. What De Klerk did at the beginning of the parliamentary sessions of 1990 and 1991 was simple and ruthless: he stole the programme of the Democratic Party.

The unbanning of black nationalist organisations, the scrapping of racist laws, the adoption of a non-racial franchise in a unitary state, these had for thirty years been the policy of the Progressive Party and its later incarnations, most recently the Democratic Party. They were proposals for which their supporters received nothing but consistent and scurrilous abuse from the Nationalists. For thirteen years, from 1961 to 1974, the only liberal voice in the South African Parliament had been that of the Progressive member for the Johannesburg constituency of Houghton, Helen Suzman. During that time Suzman had to endure vicious attacks on her integrity, her alleged affinity to outlandish doctrines like Communism, her eagerness to swamp 'white civilisation' under a barbarous black flood. In 1974 she was joined by six other Progressives, all of whom received the same treatment from the

Nationalists. Now, in 1990 and 1991, the wheel came full circle: F W de Klerk blandly took over policies he had had no difficulty in condemning only a very short time before. One of the few amusing things in South African politics was watching the Nationalists contort themselves in trying to explain that it was all there in the election manifesto of 1989.

It was of course nothing of the sort. The manifesto had committed itself to broad generalities about reform without giving anything away about particulars. The Nationalists had only managed to restrain themselves from knocking the Democratic Party for being soft on security because they themselves had suddenly become vulnerable to that well-tried smear tactic; De Klerk and Pik Botha, his Foreign Minister, had just visited the President of Zambia in Lusaka, where the ANC had its African headquarters. They were also committed to the notion of 'group rights', at that time inconceivable without the support of the Population Registration Act. The truth was that the Nationalist leadership had suddenly changed its mind but could not be seen to be rejecting policies which had so long provided a rationale for white rule. So it tried to find threads of continuity where none existed.

It was in this vein that F W de Klerk denied in a television interview in February 1991 that he had taken any particular road to Damascus. He had just been implementing established Nationalist policy. In support of his statement he cited a congress in 1986 which accepted the principle of power-sharing. Both his history and his interpretation were shaky. Since the late 1970s the Nationalists had found it fashionable to sound off about the excellences of power-sharing; that after all was why the right wing hard-liners under Treurnicht decided to get out of the party in 1982. But the Government had also found it embarrassing to be identified with Progressive notions of power-sharing: its own version had nothing to do with 'abdication' and handing over power to a black majority. Similarly, the De Klerk course since 1990 has had nothing to do with previous Nationalist policy except in the most broadly vacuous 'reformist' sense. It was a genuine break with the past, to which politicians can hardly ever bear to admit.

There can be no question that De Klerk suddenly, expediently, decided to throw policies overboard which he had once found it in his own interests to defend. But, as Sir William Harcourt once said, 'a man with an unalterable opinion is an unalterable ass'. The important question is not why he made the break but why it took so long, for it had been plain for many years that Nationalist policies were taking all of South Africa down a dead-end where only ruin awaited.

Yet history is cluttered with examples of groups, classes and nations which have seemingly made a point of blatantly ignoring what appears to be their own self-interest. In South Africa apartheid had accumulated vested interests over four decades which made reform tortuous and hard-won, when it came at all. Even if many white South Africans could clearly see that apartheid was not the ideal way of running a country, it was not so simple to find an alternative. It was easy and comforting for pious foreigners to be dismayed by the sins of the white racist regime, but they would not be subject to the black majority rule which they proclaimed so blithely as the obvious and only solution. The post-colonial era in Africa had done little to persuade white South Africans that a black government would result in anything but autocracy, plunder and a different brand of racism. The indifference of the rest of the world to genocide in places like Sudan and Ethiopia, to name but a few, suggested that universal condemnation of apartheid had nothing to do with racism, but simply with that variety which involved white rule over blacks. To most white South Africans it could not have been so difficult a choice after all: if they had to live under an authoritarian racially-based government, it was far better that it should be controlled by their own kind than by blacks who would quite likely be out for revenge and at the very least deprive them of their property.

It was the misfortune of South Africa's whites that when decolonisation came after the Second World War they had nowhere else to go. The colonial powers packed up and went home, even if some of them required plenty of persuasion. They did not have to live under the Asians and Africans whom they had once ruled. The white South Africans found, for the first time, that they had to justify a way of life which they, and the rest of the world, had previously simply taken for granted. When Afrikaner nationalists took over the government of South Africa in 1948 the principle of white supremacy was never at issue: the main difference between the new rulers and their predecessors was in how it was to be applied. Apartheid was a catchy vote-winning slogan but it did not herald the beginning of a new age in which white voters set their faces resolutely against reformist trends which were taking South Africa to a multiracial democracy. For more than four decades after that the majority of the white population of South Africa, Afrikaans- and English-speaking, showed themselves fully determined to keep power in their own hands.

At first, apartheid was not a system. It was an intensified version of that white supremacy which had always been the South African way of life. The Nationalists who gained power in 1948 knew how precarious was their electoral majority: they had 79 seats in the House of Assembly compared with the 74 of the combined Opposition. They only drew a minority of votes in the election but still won due to the over-representation of rural seats. Yet Afrikaners were 60 per cent of the white population. If they could be persuaded to support the National Party it would be plain sailing for the cause of Afrikaner nationalism. Afrikaners would then rule a country they regarded as peculiarly theirs for ever, regardless of the feelings, resentments and protests of English-speaking whites, coloureds, Africans and Asians. Apartheid played a crucial role in furthering the group identity of the Afrikaners. The intensified exclusion of non-whites encouraged the cohesiveness of a group which increasingly knew that it was different from all others. This was why the Nationalists pursued to a point of obsession the removal of coloureds from the Cape voters' roll, long after any possible electoral threat from that source had disappeared. There were high political returns in portraying the coloureds as pawns manipulated by the English-speakers in their obsession to get rid of an Afrikaner government. Until well into the 1960s the main trend of white South African politics was the mobilisation of Afrikaners behind the National Party in response to ethnic appeals well calculated to achieve just that.

Of course apartheid was not always as sophisticated as this. Most of it was just plain old-fashioned greed masquerading at best behind an implausible facade of separate but equal. But so convinced were the Nationalists that they were unassailable that they hardly bothered about facades. They passed laws to suit themselves and did not care who knew it. Under the Group Areas Act hundreds of thousands of coloureds and Indians were thrown out of their homes. Years later a coloured leader in the 'reformed' Tricameral Parliament told Nationalist members that it amounted to legalised theft. He was right, but at the time, when the forced removals happened, supporters of the ruling party could not have cared less. What they did care about was having the votes to rule the country in perpetuity, and they were getting those in a big way.

Apartheid did eventually become a system, for a time. It has become customary to blame Hendrik Verwoerd and his undoubted fanaticism for the obsessive enforcement of racial separation in areas large and small. It was under Verwoerd, in the 1960s, that the Government attempted to control the flow of black workers to the urban areas to the minimum compatible with the economic needs of the white population. The doctrine was old, going back to the 1920s, but it had never before been applied with such rigour and enthusiasm. In their wilder moments Verwoerd and his menials talked about the flow being reversed by 1978: blacks would then be absorbed in ever-larger numbers by the 'homelands' which had been designed for their separate ethnic destinies.

It was of course nothing but exuberant fantasy, an exercise in concerted folly which is permanent testimony to the human capacity for self-delusion. Yet it would be wrong to blame Verwoerd as if the system sprang full-grown from his doctrinaire professorial brain. The truth was that he found a ready market for what he was selling. Verwoerd had an answer for every problem under the sun. Afrikaners were only too eager to believe that the enormous complexity of a multiracial society could be conjured away by wishful rhetoric about 'separate freedoms'. They wished to be seduced by Verwoerd and they were. It only delayed their inevitable rendezvous with reality and made it more painful.

Anyone who doubts the capacity of highly intelligent men to fool themselves need only go back to the editorials written during the Verwoerdian heyday in *Die Burger*, then the leading intellectual mouthpiece of the National Party. Although *Die Burger* had difficulties with what it was pleased to call *klein apartheid* (small apartheid), at once mistranslated as 'petty apartheid'), it had no problems with the bigger variety, involving as it did eventual independence for blacks in 'their own areas'. The end justifying the means, *Die Burger* defended day by day, with impressive sophistication and sophistry, the huge powers the Government took to itself to direct the movements of Africans throughout the 'white' areas, to repatriate those who were 'superfluous' and to ban and imprison political enemies whom it found too uncomfortable and of whom there were plenty.

It is interesting to note that more than 80 years ago the American sociologist William Graham Sumner had already given the lie to this kind of special pleading: 'It is not possible to experiment with a society and just drop the experiment whenever we choose. The experiment enters into the life of the society and can never be got out again'.

Nearly two decades after the death of Verwoerd the editor of *Die Burger* in those stirring times, Piet Cillié, could still not find much to regret about the high days of social engineering:

> Was 'big apartheid' then all in vain? Once more 'as if' scenarios are useless. There was development in the homelands, as there was town development under group areas which would scarcely have been imaginable without the negative spur of racial separation. Compare the futility of the dream: if the billions the world spends on arms could only have been devoted to health, education and economic upliftment. It is impossible and will remain so. The same funds would not have been available for such purposes.

True no doubt, but quite beside the point. The real question was what would have happened had the Nationalists not gone on the kind of racial rampage which they did. They could never claim that they had no idea of what was awaiting them. The most conservative estimates at the time showed that schemes of territorial separation between white and black were a mere pipe-dream which had not the remotest prospect of becoming fact. Shortly before the Nationalists came into power in 1948 the Fagan Commission submitted its report. It recorded in the most telling detail the extent of economic integration between white and black. The commission argued that black urbanisation should be accepted as an irrevocable fact of South African life. The new rulers did not like what they were confronted with and appointed their own commission. The Tomlinson Commission Report of 1954 could not quarrel with the evidence presented by its predecessor, but concluded that substantial territorial separation was still possible if massive resources went into the development of the black rural areas. The Government accepted the end but found specious arguments for rejecting the means, which were bound to be politically unpopular. From the very beginning then, proposals for undoing the economic interdependence of the races were no more than an intellectually dishonest evasion of facts which were staring everyone in the face.

The question of what would have happened had the Nationalists not been in power still remains. Racial equality was not an option. The Official Opposition, the United Party, which had been defeated in 1948 believed as much in white rule as did the Nationalists, but would probably have maintained it in a less crude and doctrinaire manner. During the war years it had largely accepted economic integration as inevitable; the *laissez-faire* policies of the UP turned out to be a major grievance of the Nationalists in the run-up to 1948. More responsive to business interests, the United Party would no doubt have allowed the process of black urbanisation to continue at a more rapid pace. It would not have introduced group areas, nor would it have passed a Population Registration Act which created a national register of race. It would have retained the Land Acts. It did believe in permanent white rule over an undivided South Africa. The United Party would have avoided the worst excesses of the Nationalists, but that would not have been enough to avert a confrontation with a more assertive African nationalism. When white power changed hands in 1948 the ANC claimed that it made no difference: it was really a contest between competing oppressors of Africans. It soon discovered that the Nationalist willingness to use force against campaigners for racial equality was rather more hair-trigger than that of the United Party. Yet the ANC was not so far wrong. Until perhaps fairly recently, the great majority of white South Africans could not contemplate a government in which blacks had a majority. The fate of the Progressive Party and its various successors is a sad commentary on what most of the white population thought about sharing power with those of a different colour.

Apartheid was then a more extreme version of the supremacist policies which any white government would have pursued. It was not only the poor benighted Afrikaners who had to bear the burden of historic guilt for racial injustice. Most white South Africans were as determined that 'civilised standards' should prevail and were just as ready to dismiss foreign criticism as rooted in ignorance and hypocrisy. They were equally intent on refusing to accept the political implications of economic integration, all the more as they managed to find easy rationalisations for their blinkered vision in the disasters of independence in post-colonial Africa.

It remains true that the Nationalist way of remaining on top involved excesses and follies, many of them perpetrated by a thriving apartheid bureaucracy, which would only make it more difficult, if not impossible, to find the bases of a common nationhood. In 1941 a book appeared of which the title at least was to become well-known: *There are no South Africans*. It dealt mainly with relations between the white language groups and their inability to find an encompassing unity as South Africans. It was still early days to think of members of other races as part of a South African nation. The supreme achievement of the Nationalists was that in their pursuit of separatism, their relentless drawing of ethnic dividing lines, they managed to make of South Africa the epitome of a fragmented society where in 1991 it is was even more true than fifty years before to say, 'there are no South Africans'.

If apartheid was ever a system, it did not last for long. In the early 1970s it began to disintegrate and kept on doing so until by 1990 there was nothing left of the house that Verwoerd tried to build. Economic growth destroyed apartheid as a system. The white population had been spoilt by the rising living standards which came in the 1960s and the early 1970s as South Africa was caught up in the growth of the world economy. Only a small band of ideologues was prepared to defend the belt-tightening which serious attempts at territorial separation would bring. With growth came black urbanisation, massive and uncontrollable. The Government gradually accepted a permanent African presence in the urban areas; it began to distinguish between insiders and outsiders, between blacks who had a right to stay in town and those who did not. It was to prove a futile expedient, but at the time was a break with a major tenet of Verwoerdian ideology. From now on it was downhill all the way for 'separate development'.

The 1976 Soweto uprising was a watershed, but not because it came close to overthrowing the Government. That was not the original intent and it did not come close. Yet it marked a new mood of black assertiveness and served final notice that the repression-induced docility of the latter part of the 1960s had finally gone. Towards the end of the decade began the labour reforms which gave new legitimacy and power to black trade unions. The early part of the 1980s saw the Nationalist version of 'power-sharing': supposedly it was of the 'healthy' variety, to distinguish it from the unhealthy package of the Progressive Federal Party, which, according to the Government, just provided a recipe for black takeover. Nationalist reform from above had an obvious and fatal flaw: the new constitution of 1984 had room only for the two minority groups, the coloureds and the Indians, in a Tricameral Parliament which was devised so that the Nationalists would remain in charge. The exclusion of blacks on the grounds that they could enjoy their separate freedoms elsewhere led to bitter and overt resentment. The rest of the decade was turbulent: unrest became endemic as protesters aimed at making the country ungovernable. The Government of P W Botha responded with states of emergency. Partial reform yielded to comprehensive repression.

From 1985 sanctions against South Africa became the fashionable cause of those who competed with one another in demonstrating moral outrage at the apparently unique evil of apartheid. The frenzy of the sanctioneers was misplaced. Historically, the connection between sanctions and what they were supposed to achieve has generally been tenuous. In the case of South Africa the idea was apparently that ruining the economy would force the erring whites to accept majority rule. Or perhaps an impoverished and starving black population would rise against its oppressors and overthrow them in a vast upsurge of anger. The theory behind sanctions was half-baked at best. The practice only contributed to the further barbarisation of South African society as a sluggish economy refused to provide rising standards of living for a fast-growing population. Sanctions were most effective at the beginning and were of the unofficial variety: in July 1985 the Chase Manhattan Bank refused to renew its short-term loans to the Republic and precipitated a huge debt crisis as other creditors followed suit. Official sanctions were far less damaging: the major part of the Republic's exports, gold above all, were difficult, if not impossible, to sanction.

Long before sanctions became a moral crusade, private investment in South Africa had diminished. World commodity markets had turned against the Republic, uncertainty about the political future had become profound. Inflation had increased drastically, from five per cent in 1970 to fourteen per cent in 1989. Revenue from personal and corporate income tax had more than doubled in real terms, while real per capita disposable income declined by fifteen per cent between 1980 and 1989. The state was taking more and individuals were receiving less. The seemingly permanent economic recession which had set in would have at least one predictable effect: white workers who felt threatened would renew their demands for the protection provided by discriminatory laws. Their discontent was reflected in the rapid progress of the Conservative Party after 1982. Other whites rallied to a government which was adamant about rejecting foreign intervention. Contrary to the conventional wisdom of the sanctions lobbies, a poorer economic performance, deepened by sanctions, could be expected to increase the demand for apartheid rather than force white oppressors to repent.

By 1980 however, the damage had been done. The growth of former years had carried within it the seeds of apartheid's destruction by creating an irreversibly integrated economy. No downturn could undo what the past had wrought. The forces for change in South Africa came mainly from within.

Towards the end of his time of power P W Botha had lost interest in further reform. He was an aggrieved man, convinced that he had not received his due for going back on much of the Nationalist past. When at last, grudgingly and spitefully, he gave up the office of State President to which he had clung with such desperation, Botha had painted himself and his government into a corner. Increasingly he had relied on the security forces to take South Africa through its time of troubles. Botha had not bothered to make friends outside the National Party; the tricameral constitution after all did not make that necessary. Within the Party Botha was much detested, but feared. He made his biggest blunder when he resigned the Party leadership in February 1989 after a stroke. Botha hung on to the presidency till 15 August, but he was, in fact, finished.

Botha's successor, F W de Klerk, changed his mind in a hurry between 15 August 1989 and 2 February 1990. That much is certain, although, in his politician's way, De Klerk had claimed consistency all along. It was all there in the National Party's programme of power-sharing, it seemed. He had not really broken with established Nationalist policy at all. The most apt comment on that kind of special pleading was P W Botha's resignation from the National Party, to which he had belonged for more than 50 years, shortly after De Klerk's fateful speech in February. It could only be dismissed in part as the natural response of an embittered old man. There was evidently the world of difference between the power-sharing to which Botha and the National Party had been committed, and the De Klerk version which Nationalists now defended with such energy and sometimes enthusiasm. They still believed in power-sharing, but it was now the 'unhealthy' variety of the former Progressive Federal Party and the current Democratic Party which they once could not find words enough to condemn.

What made De Klerk do it? At present we can only speculate. Most obviously, necessity is the mother of 'real' reform. The Nationalists' efforts at power-sharing fooled no one, except perhaps themselves and the far right. Separate parliamentary representation for the coloured and Indian minorities, half-hearted attempts at co-opting blacks, all subject to ultimate Nationalist control – efforts like these were taking the country nowhere except further down a dead-end.

It had been plain for many years that a black majority government was inevitable, probably sooner rather than later. The sheer demographic imperatives of South Africa could make for no less. The white population had been declining steadily as a proportion of the total. In 1960 whites accounted for nineteen per cent of the population of South Africa; 30 years later it had dropped to fourteen per cent. African urbanisation continued without pause: one estimate of the late 1980s was that by the year 2000 urban blacks would outnumber urban whites by five to one.

What was most likely was that, shortly after he became State President, De Klerk became convinced that he had to come to terms with the future, that it was best to take the initiative before time ran out, rather than yield at the last moment under duress. If he could do it his way, while the Government was still the toughest kid on the block, there remained a chance that white South Africans would not be deprived of their property and that they could perhaps still play a significant although not dominant role in the political future of the country. His past had shown him to be a pragmatist: all he had to do now was to bend once more to circumstance and make-believe that nothing basic had changed.

Probably, it was not just the historic failure of apartheid which induced De Klerk to change his mind so fast. There was another failure, enormously larger and of much greater significance for the future of the world. This was the collapse of socialism in Eastern Europe. The wretched demise of an economic system which had for so long cast a spell over advanced thinkers of the Third World, and the Soviet Union's own decline as a world power meant that Communism ceased to be a viable option for South Africa. Quite likely it never was, but the Nationalists and other white South Africans had always feared the imposition of a Communist dictatorship, African-style. Now, suddenly, that threat had vanished. Coming to terms with black nationalism would not become the first step to a Marxist-Leninist take-over.

So De Klerk and his fellow-Nationalists changed. The former bogeymen of the ANC became respectable. The avuncular figure of Joe Slovo, leader of the South African Communist Party, was seen on the Republic's television screens; he was quoted in all the media and as a top member of the ANC was part of the team which now talked about talks with the Government. White South Africans abroad found that it was no longer an embarrassment to announce where they came from. The new South Africa had arrived.

Fairly soon it became evident that it was the Government and the ANC which would be negotiating a constitutional settlement. Both De Klerk and Mandela liked to make a point of stressing that there was a host of other parties which would have to be drawn into the process of negotiation – the National Party and the ANC were only two in a crowd. But some of these parties announced that they would have no part in negotiating with organisations as infamous as either the National Party or the ANC, while others could at best be fairly minor participants only. The truth was that the Government and the ANC needed one another.

Amongst the whites the far right repeatedly rejected any negotiations with the ANC and its Communist allies, resorting to threats of armed resistance if whites were deprived of their right to self-determination by being subjected to a black majority government. The Democratic Party had no choice but to applaud what the Government was doing so belatedly, but its future was in doubt after De Klerk's appropriation of its policy. It made sense for DP supporters to turn increasingly to the Government, a far more formidable defender of their interests than the DP could ever be.

The blacks were more fragmented than the whites. The Pan Africanist Congress rejected negotiations at the outset and demanded immediate power to the people. Since its beginnings in 1959 the PAC had acquired a doctrinaire attachment to hardline socialism; what happened in Eastern Europe had no lessons for the PAC except perhaps that the job had not been done properly. Even more damning, the PAC had a slogan, 'One settler one bullet', to which it clung with admirable tenacity but which classified it beyond dispute as a bunch of degenerate barbarians. The ANC did its best to deny respectability to the Inkatha Freedom Party of the Chief Minister of KwaZulu, Mangosuthu Buthelezi, by ignoring it. For a long time Mandela found pretexts not to meet Buthelezi, who believed in capitalism, opposed sanctions and had chosen to work within the apartheid structures created by the Government. At last the ANC was compelled to acknowledge Buthelezi's existence and importance because of the unremitting deadliness of the conflict between ANC and Inkatha supporters in Natal. The violence did not end, but spread to the whole country, and Buthelezi's claim to a place at the negotiating table could not be denied. Even so, despite claims to the contrary, he represented Zulus primarily and perhaps even a declining number of them. He could be a major ally of the Nationalists or the ANC, but they were still by far the most formidable players on the field.

The diversity of South Africa, the divisions amongst blacks, the existence of minority groups apprehensive about a first-past-the-post Westminster-type system would place a premium on compromise. It was conceivable that the ANC could win an absolute majority in a one person, one vote election. Yet the fragmentation of South African society made it unlikely that the losers would be willing to accept a government with sweeping autocratic powers. Proportional representation, a bill of rights, division of power between different levels of government, these were some of the devices which could make it possible for South Africans to arrive at a constitutional settlement which was not ideal but an acceptable second-best to most.

That was the best news. The bad news was that it would still be incomparably difficult to arrive at that second-best. On a more fundamental level there was the legacy of a past which had too often been a nightmare. Both the ANC and the Government had excellent reasons for mutual distrust. The elections to the National Executive Committee of the ANC in July 1991 only confirmed what had never been a secret: Communists were exceedingly influential in that organisation. The ANC's refusal to ditch its Marxist allies, or even to identify them individually, intensified white fears that in South Africa the Communists could still gain what they had lost in Eastern Europe: the opportunity of imposing their left-wing version of facism on everyone else. The South African Government however had no ground for moral posturing. The revelation that cabinet ministers had been involved in handing secret funds to Inkatha cast the most basic doubts on the Government's integrity. No one could blame the ANC if it felt that it was faced by a bunch of incorrigible double-dealers, committed to a hidden agenda of white rule by another name. When the Nationalists came to power in 1948 the sense of South African nationhood was virtually absent. As a rough generalisation, English- and Afrikaans-speaking whites thought of themselves as members of their groups first and as South Africans second. During their years in power the Nationalists eventually, after years of resistance, came to propagate the idea of a white South African nation, united by the threat of a hostile world and a still more threatening black majority in its midst. For the rest, the Nationalists set themselves to divide: there were many black 'nations', the coloureds too were seen, except by some conspicuous verligtes ('liberal' Nationalists), as a distinct nation, the Indians were usually disregarded as an uncomfortable and alien presence. After more than four decades of officially-inculcated separatism it is hard to imagine that a South African nation transcending group differences will soon emerge. F W de Klerk as a reformer has been compared with Mikhail Gorbachev of the Soviet Union. Perhaps the analogy is too close for comfort. The question first asked by the Soviet dissident, Andrei Amalrik, years ago, whether the Soviet Union could survive, has acquired a new significance as totalitarian rule has receded. The question in the new South Africa, given appalling relevance by black-on-black violence which refuses to disappear, is whether the ethnic time-bomb will blow the state apart, as the poet Anthony Delius put it many years ago.

Conflict can still be mitigated by a high rate of economic growth, which can produce the resources to make a common society possible. There is however no reason to believe that growth will return to South Africa soon. For a long time the performance of the South African economy has been disappointing; during the 1980s the growth rate barely averaged one per cent per year, while population increased at a rate of between two and three per cent. Pronouncements by the ANC since its unbanning have done little to improve economic prospects. Virtually the first thing Nelson Mandela did after his release was to confirm the ANC's continued commitment to nationalisation. It was an unbelievably foolish statement which the ANC has since done its best to play down. Subsequent pronouncements have suggested a greater sophistication and flexibility. Even so it has continued to call for sanctions, which suggests that it is so caught up by the boycott mentality of the past that it may have little constructive to offer a South Africa which does make its way into the future. The ANC's lack of economic sophistication remains impressive. Yet there are many black South Africans, poor and uneducated, who will have great expectations of majority rule. Most of them are bound to be disappointed, even if the rate of economic growth improves. If it does not there will be increased demands for redistribution by taking away from what are seen to be excessively affluent whites.

Perhaps the best chance South Africa has of defying the past lies in the fact that the main parties have an interest in reaching a settlement. Whatever their disagreements, they can have no doubt that the alternative is not pretty to contemplate.

CHAPTER ONE

1948

The victory of the National Party in the South African general election of 1948 marked a decisive turn in the history of what had always been a troubled land. The reality, however, is more complex. In some ways the years after 1948 were remarkably different. Most obviously, South Africa acquired a government far more authoritarian than any of its predecessors, intent on securing Afrikaner nationalist rule regardless of democratic niceties and constitutional restraints. Doubtless, it amounted to a fundamental change in white South African politics. Yet most South Africans were not white. Those of them who were politically conscious, and more of them were becoming so every day, did not profess to believe that Nationalist rule would make any great difference to their lives. They were politically without rights, or nearly so, before 1948; under the Nationalists they would continue to be deprived.

Later, black leaders would admit to this mistaken judgement on the nature of the new government, and that for Africans it was far worse than its predecessor, led by Jan Smuts. Still, in a crucial sense, their initial insight was correct. South Africa was a country where a white minority ruled a black majority. If the Nationalists had lost the 1948 election, South Africa would still have had a white government which dominated blacks. The post-colonial era of the sixties in Africa was some way off, but political awareness amongst blacks was becoming increasingly powerful. It was manifest in their political organisations and in their demands for self-rule. Black political demands had for most of the century been muted and respectful, but their intensity had been rising before

1948. The United Party Government had responded with a notable lack of sympathy, which underlines that white supremacy was not the creation of Afrikaner nationalists. Whichever political party had been in power would have been confronted with rising black insistence on political rights. There is no reason to suppose that any other South African government would have been successful in satisfying these demands. White South Africans could not walk away from the problem of minority rule in a predominantly black country. Their efforts to do so is one of the strongest continuities between the years before and after 1948.

For Afrikaner nationalists the result of the election meant the triumph of more than a political party. They saw it as the victory of a resurgent nation which had a pre-eminent claim to the land of South Africa. Their joy was unrestrained and prolonged. They could well have echoed the words of the Labour politician who exclaimed after the British general election in 1945, 'We are the masters now!'

But they were in a minority. Many, perhaps most, white South Africans viewed the Nationalist victory as an unmitigated disaster. There was the defeated and stunned United Party of General Smuts. To accuse it of complacency before the election would have been euphemistic. After the resounding win of the United Party in the general election of 1943, when it had won 89 seats to the 43 of the National Party, it seemed inconceivable that the Nationalists could make up the ground to win an election five years later. And had the Government not achieved still more prestige later by participating in the final Allied defeat of Hitler and Mussolini? Was it not led by that illustrious world statesman, General Jan Smuts?

It was small wonder that at first supporters of the United Party were convinced that the new Government, led by Dr D F Malan, with its slight Parliamentary majority of five seats, 79 against the 74 of the combined Opposition, was destined for transience, ephemeral froth on the deeper currents of South African history. Harry Lawrence, Minister of Justice in Smuts's Cabinet, predicted that it could take as much as two years to oust the Nationalists.[1] Certainly, the United Party did not doubt that it would be back in power after the next general election. By then the ungrateful voters would have realised the awful mistake they had made. It was only after increasingly severe trouncings at the ballot-box in later years that the United Party came round to the realisation that 1948 was truly a turning-point in South African history.

Apartheid will always be associated with the advent of the Nationalists to power. The familiar story is that the Nationalists won because they preached apartheid wherever they went and whenever they addressed an audience. They had found a spell-binding slogan which swept them into power on the backs of thousands of impressionable Afrikaner voters convinced of the imminence of the black peril.

There is no doubt that the Nationalists harped obsessively on white racial fears and animosities during the election campaign of 1948. But it is quite likely that apartheid was not as decisive a rallying call as commentators have commonly assumed. The exploitation of the racial issue at election time was after all an established South African political tradition – the 1948 general election was hardly unique.

One of the outstanding Afrikaner journalists of the 1960s and 1970s, Schalk Pienaar, described why he regarded the apartheid explanation as 'nonsense': 'Of course South African politics has always been intertwined with the politics of colour. Also in 1948. But what happened in 1948 was that a long-slumbering yet growing Afrikaner nationalism reached its peak'.[2]

It may have been a growing nationalism but it was not irresistible and its success was hardly inevitable. For Afrikaner nationalists the years of the Second World War were the real watershed, leading to a realignment in South African politics which gave an immense boost to their cause. Till then it had shown little ability to make headway against the government formed by the fusion in 1934 of the National Party of General J B M Hertzog and the South African Party of General Smuts.

Fusion had been followed by the secession of Nationalist hardliners led by the Cape leader, Dr D F Malan. They formed the *Gesuiwerde Nasionale Party* (Purified National Party), but it had only 19 Members of Parliament in a House of Assembly of 150. Faced with the massive preponderance of the United South African Party, or United Party as it came to be known, of Hertzog and Smuts, the future of the Nationalists could only seem bleak, however aggressive their opposition in Parliament and however vigorous their organisation outside it.

The Nationalists did their best to find reasons that fusion could not last, based as it was on an artificial unity which ignored basic differences of principle. Their message was that the time for one white nation had not yet come. Inevitably, they claimed, the Afrikaner would lose his identity in an alliance with English-speakers, leading as it would to a *de facto* acceptance of the values and symbols of the traditional enemy, Britain. After 1934, the Nationalists constantly reiterated the differences between the white language groups and did their level best to intensify them when they could. They insisted on the right of South Africa to remain neutral in any British war, as well as on its right to secede from Britain's Empire. In 1936 the Nationalists adopted republicanism officially as their policy; it was the ultimate affirmation of their quest to be independent of the imperial power which had deprived the Boer republics of their sovereignty in 1902. There was a sudden burgeoning of Afrikaner organisations in the cultural, social and economic fields, all designed to promote Afrikaner self-sufficiency.

Yet when the 1938 general election came around, the fruits were disappointingly meagre. The National Party increased its representation in the House of Assembly from the 19 members of 1934 to 27. But the United Party came back with an unassailable majority of 111.

The Nationalists had indeed cause for concern. It is true that a majority of Afrikaners, an estimated 60 per cent, had supported them.[3] Yet at the current pace it would take them an unconscionable time to gain power. Fusion had in fact been a success, aided largely by a remarkable economic recovery. If the experiment in white unity lasted much longer, the Nationalists would face the unpleasant prospect that their predictions would quite soon become true. Continued prosperity could be expected to erode their economic base as growing numbers of Afrikaners found themselves in material circumstances that softened their enmity towards the Government. Would the passage of time and the continued success of Fusion not make Afrikaners forgetful of their heritage, for which they had fought and suffered so grievously in the past?

Not even the stimulus given to nationalist sentiment by the Great Trek Centenary Celebrations later in 1938, and the emotional glorification of the heroic past could remove the prospect of a long time in the political wilderness for D F Malan and his followers. The detachment of the Afrikaner from his historic roots seemed only a matter of time.

What saved them was a long foreseen external event, the Second World War. The possibility of the country's involvement in one of 'Britain's wars', as in 1914, had been anticipated for years, but had largely been ignored by the Fusion Government. It was the one issue absolutely guaranteed to wreck the whole experiment. Hertzog and his followers were quite sure that participation would flout the principle of South Africa First. Moreover, the right to neutrality was an inherent feature of that national sovereignty Hertzog supposed South Africa had enjoyed since the Statute of Westminster of 1931. Smuts, however, had no doubt that the interests of South Africa were inseparable from those of Britain. He conceded the right to stay neutral, but privately believed that Britain's war would also have to be South Africa's war. Many of his more pro-British followers denied any right of neutrality at all. For them South Africa would automatically be at war when Britain was at war.

Such differences were irreconcilable. The best hope was that Adolf Hitler would eventually abandon the conquest of Eastern Europe which he appeared to be planning. Hitler's invasion of Poland came not a moment too soon for the prospects of D F Malan's National Party.

On 1 September 1939 Members of Parliament had reconvened in Cape Town to extend the life of the Senate. The Cabinet duly split on the question of neutrality; when it went to the House of Assembly the supporters of war led by Smuts defeated the neutralists by 80 votes to 67. The Governor-General, Sir Patrick Duncan, refused Hertzog's request for the dissolution of Parliament, to be followed by a general election, on the grounds that Smuts had a workable majority in the lower House.

South Africa was now at war, but the size of the Opposition had more than doubled, to 67 Members of Parliament. Politically, the most significant domestic development between 1939 and 1948 was the strengthening of Afrikaner nationalism. At first it appeared as if the exact opposite was happening. Internecine feuding between different nationalist groups for the allegiance of Afrikaners created an impression of irretrievable impotence. But, underlying all the squabbles, backbiting and bitterness, there was one persistent trend. It was the unification of Afrikaner nationalism under the leadership of D F Malan and his party.

After the split in the Government, Hertzog and Malan came together again. Malan declared himself willing to serve under the leadership of the defeated Prime Minister. In March a new party emerged, embracing both old and new enemies of the United Party, the *Herenigde Nasionale of Volksparty* (Re-united National or People's Party). Hertzog was to be the leader, with Malan as his deputy.

The initial nationalist euphoria did not last. Hertzog and Malan and their followers had just spent five years abusing one another as political opportunists, enemies of South Africa, and worse. The scars and wounds left by that awful time of Afrikaner disunity were still fresh. They had come to detest one another. They now found that forgiveness and reconciliation did not come so easily, whatever their moving declarations in public about forgetting the past and uniting against the 'handyman of the Empire', Jan Smuts.

Personal animosities were fuelled by differences of principle. The years in opposition had strengthened anti-English sentiment in the National Party. Nationalist hard-liners like the Transvaal leader of the party, J G Strijdom, and the editor of *Die Transvaler,* Hendrik Verwoerd, insisted on the acceptance of republican principles as an essential precondition for membership of the new party. They had no time for Hertzog, who had long ceased being the extreme embodiment of Afrikaner nationalism and who was insisting that the new party make room for non-republicans too.

It was therefore a fragile unity, unstable from the start. For the hard men in the Re-united National Party the unavoidable break could not come too soon. The Orange Free State Congress of the new party met in November 1940 to adopt a programme of principles. Before it were draft programmes issued by both Hertzog and the party's Federal Council. After lengthy debate the Congress accepted by a large majority the party document as a basis for discussion. Just before, Hertzog's candidate for chairman of the Congress had been rejected. The ex-Prime Minister took these decisions as a deliberate snub, a rejection of his leadership. He was right, for the Nationalist leader in the Free State, C R Swart, was as hostile to Hertzog as were Strijdom and Verwoerd. He had in fact stage-managed the public humiliation of Hertzog, who walked out of the Congress with his followers.

Before he left, Hertzog had clouded the issue by alleging that the party programme which had been preferred to his did not guarantee full equality of status and of political rights to English-speakers. The differences were actually not profound, but Hertzog's allegation became widely accepted as the immediate cause of his departure. Bitter opponents like Verwoerd later blamed him for splitting the Afrikaner nation over so unimportant a thing as 'the rights of English-speakers'. But the truth seems to have been that Hertzog was driven out by those who liked their republicanism pure and simple and could only accept unity on their own terms.

Hertzog resigned as leader and member of the National Party in the Free State. Then came a fragmentation of Afrikaner nationalism so extreme as to seem all but irretrievable. The followers of Hertzog formed the Afrikaner Party, led by his close friend and a member of the cabinet before the war, Klaas Havenga. It had a small Parliamentary representation of eight members just before the general election of 1943. After that it had none.

There were also two organisations which proclaimed their National Socialism loudly. The more formidable was the extra-parliamentary *Ossewa Brandwag* (Oxwagon Guard), led by the former Administrator of the Free State, Hans van Rensburg. The OB was founded in 1939 and had its origins in the enthusiasm generated by the centenary celebrations of the Great Trek the previous year. Its purpose was to help sustain the intense feelings of Afrikaner unity aroused by those stirring events. At first the OB confined itself to cultural discussions and semi-military parades. All that changed after South Afrca entered the war and particularly after Van Rensburg became Commandant-General of the OB in January 1941.

Van Rensburg had visited Hitler's Germany in 1936 and became a devoted admirer of the Führer. To split no hairs, he was a dedicated Nazi. It was through Van Rensburg that the OB committed itself to a national socialist future for South Africa. The new leader had no doubt that his country too needed a man of destiny, nor did he have any doubts as to who that saviour should be.

The OB became a mass-based organisation which stood outside politics. At first this seemed a thing which good Afrikaners should welcome, a suitable complement to the role of the National Party as the political embodiment of the *volk*. Yet the alliance soon became uneasy as the OB began to display a propensity for violence which Malan and his followers found incompatible with the parliamentary road to power which they had chosen.

There was another, more ephemeral, organisation which approved of the Nazis and their ways. This was the New Order, led by Oswald Pirow, Minister of Defence under Hertzog and member of the reshaped National Party since the split in 1939. Pirow had admired the Third Reich for some time. After the break with Smuts, he decided that elections and party politics were obsolete. He formed the New Order, a national socialist pressure group within the National Party.

The National Party's road to the 1943 general election is essentially the story of its triumph over all competing organisations which claimed to speak for nationalist Afrikaners.

The party's early amicable relations with the OB broke down after Van Rensburg became that movement's leader. Van Rensburg was a man with imperial aspirations. He believed that the National Party should confine itself to 'party politics', and at the same time was quite sure that the Party had reached the end of the road. He propagated the claims of the OB as a more inclusive body than a mere parliamentary party like the HNP. The OB, he asserted, catered for the whole nation: 'It covers the whole front'.

Malan had no choice but to reject this encroachment on the prerogatives of the National Party. In October 1941 he called on all party members who also belonged to the OB to resign from that body. It was a declaration of war – and it was won by Malan. The attempts to reconcile the HNP and the OB were all futile. The disparities in points of view on the parliamentary system and political parties were fundamental. The OB survived Malan's onslaught, but its vigour as a political force flagged steadily, especially after Hitler began to lose the war. After the 1943 general election it virtually disappeared as a political force.

As for the altogether less formidable New Order, it did not survive the general election of July 1943. By then the sixteen New Order MPs had been thrown out of the Nationalist caucus. They did not stand for re-election, claiming to reject the electoral process, but no doubt also anticipating defeat.

Havenga's Afrikaner Party had eight MPs. It believed in parliamentary politics and actually contested 23 seats, mainly in the Free State, Hertzog's old stamping ground. It did not win any. The parliamentary opposition fell from 66 MPs to 43.

At first sight it seemed like a major victory for Smuts. His majority in the House of Assembly was now 64, compared with 20 before the election. But Malan too had cause for satisfaction. Although the number of Nationalist MPs had only gone up by two, he had effectively destroyed his rivals

As two historians of the war-time opposition observed, 'Malan's long-term policy had obtained its goal. The Hertzogites, the Pirowites, the OB had all challenged the claim that he himself and the HNP were the sole representatives of Afrikanerdom. This challenge had been met, and from the electoral battle the HNP had emerged the victor. It had made good its boasted monopoly. It stood now, the sole effective organ of Afrikanerdom, compact, purified and beyond the reach of revenge'[4].

The 1943 election represented the high tide of the United Party. From now on it ebbed steadily, but not overtly enough for the Government to be anything but wildly over-optimistic when the 1948 election arrived. The HNP made striking gains in the Transvaal provincial elections later in 1943. It won three parliamentary seats from the United Party in by-elections before 1948. Government majorities in other by-elections declined markedly. The evidence suggested that Afrikaner solidarity was reasserting itself after its near-destruction by Fusion.

In his book on Afrikaner politics between 1934 and 1948, Newell Stultz has argued persuasively that it was not the issue and slogan of apartheid which proved decisive in the 1948 election, whatever the verdict of popular mythology. Old cleavages, based on language and culture, and gaining strength from one another, were reasserting themselves in South African life. Temporarily obscured by the 1943 election, they would not afterwards be denied.

The cost for South Africa of the Union's deciding for war in 1939 was nearly all of the electoral margin of safety that sheltered the experiment of Fusion in the middle of the 1930s. Ultimately this cost, when coupled with a mild turn of the political tide against Smuts, meant the return of Afrikaner nationalists to power.[5]

As noted before, race was not a new election issue in 1948. It had been the stock-in-trade of white politicians in earlier elections, including that of 1943. It meant that 'the primary effect of Nationalist agitation on the issue of race after World War II was not that of realigning partisan preferences but rather that of reinforcing and mobilizing existing Nationalist support, although this is not to suggest that no voter shifted his vote to the HNP for this reason'.[6]

The importance of race may have been exaggerated in the 1948 election, but there is no doubt that apartheid became a powerful and emotive slogan in the party struggle. Yet its content was not immediately apparent. The Nationalists themselves were not quite sure what it was all about; they were sure that it was a formidable weapon of assault against what they saw as the excessive liberalism of the Smuts administration.

In its essence apartheid was a response to the Nationalist perception of the breakdown of segregation during the war years, reflected in the *laissez-faire* attitude of the United Party towards the flow of blacks into 'white' towns and cities. Had not Smuts himself announced in 1942, 'I am afraid segregation has fallen on evil days'?[7]

The pragmatic acceptance of economic facts of life was something the Nationalists in those days found intolerable. The Afrikaner workers on whom they depended heavily for votes could not accept so bizarre a notion that they should have to compete on level ground with blacks for jobs in the urban areas. Another crucial part of the Nationalist constituency was white farmers, who saw their labour costs rising when black workers went to the towns in the quest for earnings higher than those the farmers were prepared to pay them.

It was in the 1940s that Afrikaner politicians and intellectuals discovered apartheid. Their dissatisfaction with old-fashioned segregation grew as black urbanisation gathered pace. A *Volkskongres* (People's Congress) held in 1944 'called for an extensive policy of racial apartheid in every sphere of life'.[8]

In 1947 Malan appointed one of his right-hand men, Paul Sauer, to head a committee to devise a feasible programme based on apartheid. The proposals the Sauer Committee came up with were in fact nothing new; it was the slogan which caught on. Essentially, the Committee demanded a more vigorous application of principles laid down years before and known as the Stallard Doctrine, named after the chairman of the Transvaal Local Government Commission of 1922, which insisted that Africans had no place in urban areas except to serve white needs (see next chapter). The Committee insisted on tighter controls over the movements of blacks: 'The ideal which must be aimed at is the gradual elimination of Natives from industries in white areas, but it is realised that it can only be attained over the course of many years'.[9]

If blacks were only visitors in the white areas, their homes had to be elsewhere. Here too the Sauer Committee standardised what had long been the common currency of segregationist thinking. It was very simple. Each ethnic group had its own area of origin; as far as possible it should remain there. As the Committee movingly put it, 'The Native reserve must become the fatherland of the Native. It must be the cradle of his nationhood and the soil on which his love of his fatherland and national pride can grow and flourish. For every Native it must be a spiritual home. It must be the seat of his governmental system'.[10]

The Sauer Committee therefore did little more than systematise the segregationist orthodoxy on the relations between white and black. The black man was a visitor in the white areas, where he could be only on sufferance, but he had the choice of remaining in his homeland where he could find ethnic fulfilment amongst his own kind. It was a theoretical rationale for what was to develop into one of the twentieth century's most drastic ventures into reshaping society.

Apartheid was all set to become the most controversial issue of the 1948 election. But long before the Sauer Committee met, the evidence pointed to an Afrikaner nationalist resurgence. Apartheid only strengthened a current which was by then in full flow.

It was not just the renewed vigour of Afrikaner nationalist sentiment which worked in Malan's favour. The Smuts administration proved remarkably inept after the end of the war in 1945 had deprived it of its main *raison d'être*. Many of the war-time controls remained. Farmers suffered from and resented price controls which lowered their profits. The diversion of resources from their normal peace-time uses had resulted in an acute housing shortage. But the government appeared singularly incapable of reducing the backlog. Food shortages continued, for which the Government inevitably also had to take the blame.

Although the evidence does not suggest that it was decisive, the race issue was at least as prominent as before the war. The appeal to white ethnic anxieties and obsessions had always been a vote-catcher at the ballot-box. It was a tradition honoured by the Nationalists, who milked the last drop of racist sentiment from both the inflow of blacks into towns and Smuts's proposal to give those permanent victims, the Indians of Natal, limited representation in Parliament as a sop for restrictions on the sale and purchase of land by Asians. When sixty to seventy thousand Africans took part in a mineworkers' strike in 1946, which was finally suppressed by the police, the Nationalists ensured that the racial aspects of the confrontation remained at the centre of public attention.

Malan further consolidated Afrikaner unity by forming an agreement in March 1947 with the Afrikaner Party of Havenga, without a parliamentary seat since 1943. The AP came across as losers; plenty of Malan's followers hated the idea of handing out seats to be contested by these no-hopers when it was likely that they could be won by good Nationalists. The most vehement exponents of this line were J G Strijdom and Hendrik Verwoerd in the Transvaal. Their hostility was aroused partly because they were ardent republicans and the leaders of the Afrikaner Party were not, but mainly because many members of the Ossewa Brandwag, cast out by the Nationalists, found a political home in Havenga's party after the 1943 election. Strijdom and Verwoerd were strong believers in the parliamentary road to power; they found it detestable to be linked with a political party now supported by many of those who had only recently adhered to the unparliamentary activities of the Ossewa Brandwag.

But to Malan there were more decisive considerations. Havenga and his followers were the bearers of the Hertzogite flame. They had an appeal not merely to disgruntled OB supporters, but also to a more moderate, less sectarian kind of Afrikaner, of the type that up till then may have had scruples about voting for the kind of party which contained as many firebrands as did Malan's HNP. An alliance with the Afrikaner Party would help to project a long-overdue image of moderation and reasonableness.

Malan had his way. With the utmost reluctance, Strijdom and Verwoerd swallowed their objections and relaxed their principles for the sake of the cause. In terms of the agreement the Afrikaner Party was to contest ten seats. Out of a total number of 150 it seemed fairly insignificant, but it was to prove crucial.

The Nationalist victory on 26 May 1948 was narrow but, as it turned out, irreversible. The Nationalists themselves had their sights set on the 1953 election. At most they only expected to take about twenty seats from the United Party in 1948, while they needed 35 to form a new government. The trend in by-elections had been running strongly in their favour but few, if any, Nationalists expected to find themselves in power after 26 May.

The first results which came in gave no hint that an upheaval was on the way. They showed the familiar huge urban majorities for the United Party. It was only during the afternoon of 27 May that the signs of a possible reversal began to accumulate as seats held by the Government fell to the enemy. Appropriately enough, it was the defeat of Smuts in his constituency of Standerton which told the Nationalists that the spoils of office would soon be theirs.

They emerged from the election with 70 seats and the Afrikaner Party with nine. The United Party had 65 and the Labour Party six. There were three Native Representatives, who would support Smuts, however reluctantly. As the new Speaker of the House of

Assembly would be a Nationalist, Malan had an effective overall majority of four.

It was a minority government. It was so in the obvious sense that all South African regimes since 1910 have been minority governments, drawn from the white fifth of the population. But in addition the new Nationalist government of 1948 only represented a minority of that minority. Of the votes cast, just 42 per cent went to the National and the Afrikaner Parties. It was the outcome of a major peculiarity of the electoral system, namely, the delimitation of seats which gave a disproportionate weighting to the countryside, designed to ensure that rural voters would not be submerged by a growing urban population. All white voters were equal, but some were decidedly more equal than others.

The United Party had gained huge victories in many urban seats, but electorally they proved to be worthless. The Nationalists, however, achieved some very close victories, winning 11 seats with a majority of less than 400. They had also broken through to the urban Afrikaner. With the Afrikaner Party, they gained 21 seats in the Transvaal, six of them on the Witwatersrand.

The National Party that won the 1948 election was for the greater part the political expression of a resurgent Afrikaner nationalism. It was the most overt and the most potent means of Afrikaner self-advancement, but it would scarcely have triumphed if this nationalism had not also expressed itself in the economic, cultural and social fields. And so it did before 1948. In all these fields the drive to Afrikaner self-sufficiency from the late 1920s onwards was powerful indeed. Co-ordinated by the *Afrikaner Broederbond* (League of Brothers), a secret organisation of perhaps unjustly sinister reputation founded in 1918, a variety of organisations emerged which made much of their Afrikaner ethnicity. In 1929 the *Federasie van Afrikaanse Kultuurverenigings* (Federation of Afrikaans Cultural Associations) was established, followed in 1931 by the *Voortrekkers*, the Afrikaans equivalent of the Boy Scouts. Students from Afrikaans universities, repelled by the 'liberalism' of the National Union of South African Students, formed their own volk-orientated body in 1933. Six years later the *Eerste Ekonomiese Volkskongres* (First People's Economic Congress) was held to review the economic situation of the Afrikaners.

From this came the *Reddingsdaadbond* (Rescue Action League) fund, part of which was devoted to Afrikaner poor relief, but which went mostly to investment in Afrikaner businesses.

By 1948 a deeply-felt and deeply-rooted Afrikaner exclusivism had emerged. Many Afrikaners may still have seen themselves as part of a broader white nation, but the trend was strongly in the opposite direction. More and more Afrikaners were thinking of themselves as members of an exclusive group, distinguished from others by unique qualities and in some special sense entitled to the fruits of the South African soil. After the 1948 election they were convinced that at last the fruits were theirs for the taking.

CHAPTER TWO

A Pattern Unfolds

The Nationalists newly in power had only a precarious majority, but if it bothered them they never let on. From the start they behaved as if they had the kind of comfortable margin over their opponents which did not make it necessary to consult with them in matters either large or small. The non-meeting of minds was fundamental. The new government consisted exclusively of Afrikaners, the first since 1910. They were determined that this time nationalist Afrikaners would come into their own. Afrikaner workers would shrug off the chains of poverty and receive protection from the unfair competition of blacks, unborn and unbred to civilised standards of living. Afrikaner business would acquire its rightful place in an economy too long dominated by Jews and English-speakers, whether from abroad or at home. Afrikaans would cease to be the language of a poor relation. The culture of the Afrikaner would gain a new dignity and pride. Eventually, the most cherished of Afrikaner ideals would be realised. South Africa would become a republic.

The white opponents of the new government were at first severely shocked. They never dreamt that so appalling a fate would come their way. They knew that the Smuts government had lost some of its popularity in recent years, but, at worst, they had anticipated that the United Party would be returned with a reduced majority. For them the Nationalists were just a crowd of crypto-Nazis who had been dead keen for Hitler to win the war. When they had partially recovered from their unpleasant surprise, they consoled themselves that it was all a terrible mistake, that it was the merest flash in the pan and that at the next election the voters would decide to end the self-inflicted nightmare of Nationalist rule. Assuming that there would be an election, that is, for the enemies of the Nationalists did not put it past them to do away with the ballot-box altogether in their lust for unchecked power.

That the Nationalists had undemocratic ways, their opponents, both white and black, were soon to discover. But they had no need to jettison the electoral process to get what they wanted. Far from it. Over the years the Nationalists were to show themselves sticklers for doing things by the book. For they knew that they had numbers on their side. The Afrikaners made up about 60 per cent of the white population and were reproducing themselves rather more rapidly than the English-speakers. That the whites only amounted to twenty per cent of the total South African population was quite irrelevant, at least at that time. They had the vote, and the blacks did not. Sheer arithmetic dictated that for the foreseeable future the National Party would continue to rule South Africa. All it had to do was beat the tribal drum, a tactic which had proved so devastatingly effective in 1948, and watch growing numbers of Afrikaner voters come streaming to the polls to rededicate themselves to *Volk* and *Vaderland* (nation and fatherland).

And so the Nationalists set out to reshape South Africa.

From the start they avoided compromise. They were going to do it their way, however unpopular it would make them with non-Nationalists, white or black, but especially black. Their opponents who had voted for the United Party soon found that the new rulers of South Africa did not love cricket. When Parliament met for the first time the Nationalists simply announced their choice of Speaker, ignoring the time-honoured custom of consulting with the Opposition. A straw in the wind perhaps, but here was clearly a different team, playing according to several rules which were entirely its own.

English-speakers had other reasons for concern. British immigrants no longer had automatic preference over those from the European Continent, in so far as immigration was encouraged at all. The Nationalists had no doubt that British immigrants would not only vote for the wrong party but would also cherish the monarchy. Everyone knew that the Nationalists had set their hearts on a republic; they only differed amongst themselves about its continued membership of the British Commonwealth. In 1951 Malan and Strijdom agreed that it was something which could be resolved later, pragmatically, but about the republic itself there was no dispute. For those who saw South Africa as only another outpost of empire such attitudes were bad news, entire and complete.

The full force of the Nationalist fury was however reserved for the lesser breeds with minor, if any, political rights. What apartheid actually meant, few people knew. In principle it paid lip service to the upliftment of Africans and coloureds (the Indians were simply seen as an alien group which should somehow be persuaded to go back to where they, or their ancestors, had came from). In practice apartheid amounted to a massive, prolonged and determined attempt to entrench white domination. Moreover, it aimed at diverting a far larger share of the country's resources than before into deserving Afrikaner hands. Inevitably, it was a policy which could only be enforced at immense human cost. The number of lives it ruined is incalculable, nor can it be known what toll was exacted in terms of distrust and hatred between individuals and groups which had no choice but to continue sharing the same country.

The new government lost no time in attempting to bring nearer its best of all Afrikaner Utopias. A prerequisite was drawing lines which made clear where one race ended and another began. In 1950 a cornerstone of the apartheid regime was laid – the Population Registration Act. South Africans now had to be classified officially into racial groups; later they were required to have identity documents which showed where they stood in the hierarchy of races. Inevitably, much of the classification was subjective, especially when it came to telling coloureds and whites apart. Broken homes abounded and the more grotesque outcomes of bureaucratic fiat received ample publicity, but Population Registration had come to stay.

There were many other laws during these early Nationalist years which aimed both at the separation of the races and the preservation of white privilege; they were indeed difficult to distinguish. One of the most important was the Group Areas Act of 1950. Its goal was an even greater segregation between the races than had existed up till then. The Government could now reserve any area of the country for a particular race group. In a group area for one race, no members of another race could live or own property. In principle it was an impartial law, but in practice it was not. Group Areas were designed by whites for whites. Over the years thousands of coloureds and Indians were forcibly removed from their residential and trading areas and deposited in places which they invariably regarded as inferior. The most spectacular and devastating implementation of the Group Areas Act was the destruction of a coloured settlement area in Cape Town, District Six, which was rezoned for whites. The official rationale, that District Six was a noisome slum, cut no ice with the previous inhabitants who found themselves resettled amongst sand-dunes, with longer distances to travel to work and who often had their families broken up. The anti-white bitterness left as a result of District Six was lasting; years later it was to surface in large-scale civil unrest in Cape Town.

Nor did the Government hesitate to interfere with the most intimate areas of personal life in its pursuit of race purity. In 1949 it passed the Prohibition of Mixed Marriages Act, which outlawed future marriages between whites and members of other races. The following year it amended the Immorality Act to prohibit extra-marital intercourse between white and non-white.

But when it came to matters of race, relations between whites and blacks naturally were of surpassing importance. It was after all the collapse of segregation as manifested in the growing inflow of Africans into 'white' urban areas that had been one of the main issues of the 1948 election. The Nationalists had vowed then that they would enforce segregation with a rigour that in their eyes had been utterly and deplorably absent from the *laissez-faire* policies of the Smuts regime.

Since 1910, all the governments of the Union of South Africa had believed in the preservation of white rule. It was a principle well entrenched in South African history; there would have been no union at all had it not been based on the acceptance of indefinite white supremacy. Much has been made of the conflict at the National Convention in 1908–1909 between the so-called northern and Cape points of view over relations between the races. Union was supposedly possible only because of the agreement to differ between the northern provinces, which rejected any kind of non-white franchise, and the Cape, which did have a non-racial franchise based on property and educational qualifications. The resulting compromise was hardly satisfactory. The Cape was to retain its own system, and the northern provinces were to keep theirs, but only whites were to be eligible for Parliament.

A kind of liberal mythology has grown up around this outcome. Things could supposedly have been rather different had the Cape delegates insisted more vigorously on their own 'colour-blind' franchise. They did indeed feel strongly about 'civilisation' as a test, so the story goes, but they were excessively optimistic in believing that the superiority of their system would come to be recognised by the rest of the country. A splendid opportunity was missed: South Africa could have been spared the enormities of race-obsessed governments which never hesitated to exploit white fears and selfishness at the ballot-box. All the Cape delegates had to do was stand fast and refuse to allow tampering of any kind with the non-white vote. What they settled for instead, was a mess of pottage in the entrenchment of its non-racial franchise in the constitution, only to be alterable by a two-thirds majority of the House of Assembly and the Senate sitting together. Even if the Cape system did not go north, at least it would have remained constant, holding the beacon of civilisation aloft. The Cape would have been a shining example of inter-racial co-operation and goodwill, giving the lie to all those who claimed that segregation was the only way of handling 'race relations'.

This is a moving story. It may even contain some truth. There is no doubt that the Cape delegates at the National Convention did believe in their particular franchise, but then it was not all that incompatible with indefinite white rule. Before Union the Cape franchise qualifications had been raised several times to slow down the growth rate of the non-white electorate. Cape liberal politicians had had little difficulty in persuading themselves that race was not the issue: 'civilisation' was what really mattered. In truth, they were at best white paternalists. Perhaps in the heyday of the British Empire it was difficult to be much else. No doubt they were creatures of their times, like the rest of us, but it should be salutary to remind ourselves that by far the majority of white South Africans has not, until quite recently, had anything but deeply conservative views about giving votes to blacks.

The flimsiness of the South African liberal tradition received no better demonstration than in 1936 when Hertzog achieved one of his deepest heart's desires. With the support of Smuts and most of his followers he removed Cape Africans who had been on the common roll and segregated them on a communal roll, along with blacks in the rest of the country, all of them to be represented in the two Houses of Parliament by seven indirectly elected white members. The entrenched clauses of the constitution were no problem. One hundred and sixty-nine members of the two Houses of Parliament, sitting together, eventually voted for Hertzog's legislation, and eleven voted against. One of the dissenters was the famous liberal, J H Hofmeyr, who had earlier urged that the voting qualifications should be raised continuously so that Africans never amounted to more than ten per cent of the electorate.

The Nationalist Government had no clear idea what it wanted to do with the black majority of South Africans. What it was not hazy about was its resolve to avoid any hint of liberalism in its treatment of Africans. Apartheid amounted to some kind of super-segregation, the drawing of dividing lines between white and black wherever possible. If contact was unavoidable, for after all black labour was indispensable to white employers, from mining to industry to agriculture, it was absolutely essential that any relation involving any kind of equality be avoided. In fact, Africans were least unwelcome in 'white' areas as temporary workers, migrants who had their roots in the rural areas from which they came. It had been put classically as long ago as 1922 when the Stallard Doctrine was formulated: That it should be a recognised principle of government that natives – men, women and children – should only be permitted within municipal areas in so far and for so long as their presence is demanded by the wants of the white population.[1] The Stallard approach was embodied in the Natives (Urban Areas) Act of 1923, which laid the basis for urban segregation. Frequently amended over the years and reflecting the structure of control in its increasing complexity and comprehensiveness, the Act had a simple message for the black man: do not overstay your welcome in white man's land. You are welcome to work for white employers as long as they need you, but afterwards you must return to where you came from. The transient status of Africans in officially white areas was an article of faith for governments long before the Nationalist victory in 1948. Where they differed was in their commitment to enforcing it and the ruthlessness of the means they were prepared to use.

For, inevitably, segregation broke down, especially during the Second World War as thousands of blacks flowed into the cities. It was partly a response to the hot-house industrialisation of a country which found itself suddenly deprived of many of the goods it had previously imported. But it was also partly due to the backwardness of an agricultural sector which could not sustain a growing population except in conditions of increasing poverty. The black rural areas, or reserves as they were called, were poor for many reasons. One of the most important was that the law, especially as expressed in the Native Land Act of 1913, curtailed strictly the area available for black occupation and so, not coincidentally, made more black labour available to white farmers at low rates of pay. But the reserves also suffered from insufficient capital and bad transport. Perhaps most important in explaining their stagnation, was that communal forms of landownership imposed a structure of property rights which provided little incentive for enterprise and innovation. Whatever the reason, it was plain that the economic opportunities on offer to Africans in the cities were better than those in 'their own areas', however forbidding the face of official policy.

Hertzog had attempted to introduce system into Native Policy, as it was called in those distant days. Not only had he provided for limited political representation for Africans on a communal basis, but territorial segregation was supposed to have become more feasible when another Land Act in 1936 provided for additional land for blacks. In 1937 the Native Laws Amendment Act further tightened controls over black mobility, whether within or to the urban areas.

It helped very little. The black proportion of the urban population rose steadily during the war years. By 1946 the number of

Africans actually exceeded the number of whites in the urban areas, 1 810 000 to 1 740 000 according to the official census. Smuts was only stating the obvious four years before when he announced that segregation had fallen on evil days.

Still, the Nationalists had no intention of accepting what economics had wrought. They proclaimed to the world that the feckless ways of the pro big business United Party Government belonged to the past. However, it was only in 1950 that the system and coherence about which the Nationalists had had so much to say made their appearance in the relations between white and black. It was not an accident that this coincided with the appointment of Hendrik Verwoerd as Minister of Native Affairs in October 1950.

The system Verwoerd constructed with dedication and unflagging energy has fallen on such irretrievably hard times that it is difficult to imagine how impressive a figure he cut in his political prime. To the Afrikaners he was quite simply a saviour who would almost miraculously conjure away the complexity of a deeply divided society and replace it with a cut-and-dried world where the different races would be assigned to their own spheres, 'good neighbourliness' as he came to call it, and all conflict would cease. It hardly needs saying that in this best of all South Africas the whites, in fact the Afrikaners, would remain in control. The vision seems bizarre today, yet it made sense to many Afrikaners at the time. So we must attempt to understand Verwoerd's place in the history of South Africa.

The son of Dutch immigrants who came to the country in 1903 when he was two years old, Verwoerd grew up as an Afrikaner. But he discovered that ancestry was important in the making of Afrikaners, who had plenty of glorious forebears to worship. Unfortunately for Verwoerd, he had no Afrikaans ancestors. Like other outsiders who adopt another group, Verwoerd soon became an Afrikaner amongst Afrikaners. His super-Afrikanership is the key to understanding him. It spurred him to extremes of identification which led him to place supreme value on ethnicity. For Verwoerd the survival of the Afrikaners as a distinct nation with a character and culture entirely its own, was the overriding goal of his public career.

It was his identification with the Afrikaners and his conviction that only the conquest of the political kingdom would bring them into their own, that persuaded Verwoerd to abandon what promised to be a brilliant academic future as a professor of psychology and later of sociology at the University of Stellenbosch, then the leading intellectual institution amongst Afrikaners. In 1937 he became the first editor of *Die Transvaler*, a newspaper founded to propagate the cause of Malan's Nationalists in the Transvaal. There he did a splendid job of promoting an uncompromising brand of republican nationalism. His efforts, by common consent, had much to do with the success of the Nationalists in the Transvaal in 1948.

Verwoerd became a member of the Senate, but his energies and his urge to help shape the Afrikaner destiny were largely frustrated in the staid councils of the upper chamber. When he was appointed Minister of Native Affairs in 1950, it was an opportunity which he clasped to himself with hoops of steel.

Whatever the portfolio to which he had been appointed, Verwoerd would have felt a sense of urgency. It was the misfortune of the black people of South Africa that Verwoerd was placed in charge of their destinies. His dynamism, his missionary fervour, and his passion for system were to find an outlet in policies designed to make South Africa safe for the Afrikaner by forcing Africans to develop solely as members of their own separate and unique nations. If the intervention in the lives and hopes of people that was demanded bordered on the totalitarian, it must be said that Verwoerd never shirked from his self-imposed task.

It must also be said that Verwoerd at this stage knew little about Africans. Up till then he had shared the Afrikaner conventional wisdom that blacks were a barbarous lot whose labour was regrettably necessary to the white man, but who had to be kept in their place, which most of the time meant their own tribal areas. Fortunately for him, he had as Secretary of Native Affairs a man who did know a great deal about Africans, the tribal variety anyway, and could impart to his new master some of the surface sophistication desirable for a man in his position. This was Dr Werner Eiselen, a former colleague at Stellenbosch, and an anthropologist whose specialised field was the Bantu-speaking peoples of South Africa.

Eiselen was a man who believed in the integrity of tribal life. Each traditional society amounted to an organic whole with its functionally interdependant parts. Take away one, and the entity itself would change for the worse, as it threatened the entire way of life of a people and its distinctive set of values. Eiselen did not approve of black urbanisation for that very reason. It exposed the black man to alien ways completely antipathetic to the traditions in which he had grown up. It deprived him of the meaning which the tribal culture had conferred on his life, but it did not replace it with a coherent set of values which could serve as a viable alternative. As Eiselen was to put it in 1959 in a much-quoted article:

> The present system of having an unattached mass of Bantu individuals living in cities not subject to any traditional authority or sanctions has proved a dismal failure. It is therefore well worthwhile to establish lines of social, cultural, and educational communication between the city Bantu and the homeland Bantu.[2]

Language such as this was welcome to Verwoerd. He had long believed that nations were fundamental human entities, each with its own uniqueness and, certainly at least in the case of the Afrikaners, with its own high worth. After Fusion in 1934, the Broederbond had concocted a nationalist philosophy designed to cater for Afrikaner exclusiveness. It contained both secular and theological elements and came down to an insistence on the divine origin and purpose of nations. Verwoerd had been a prominent exponent of this ideology for all Afrikaner seasons. It suited him very well, both intellectually and politically, to be told that blacks were quite different from whites. Not only that, but there was no such thing as a homogeneous black group. Blacks were themselves divided into distinct nations. Self-realisation for the Zulu, the Xhosa, the Tswana could only be achieved if they went their own separate tribal ways. Verwoerd discovered a natural empathy with Eiselen and took to him as a mentor. The teacher in turn found his pupil, although at first somewhat ignorant about blacks, 'a fast learner'.[3]

What Verwoerd aimed at in his early days as Minister was to build his policies on a tribal base. By strengthening the tribal system, he also believed he would be weakening the appeal of more modern but unsuitable ways to young and susceptible Africans. He was in effect relying on some form of indirect rule, a colonial device resorted to elsewhere in Africa, but with indifferent success. Verwoerd did not seem to be aware that in most parts of Africa indirect rule had fallen into discredit because of the subservience of the tribal authorities to the colonial rulers. It was also to be a feature of the South African version of roundabout ways of control.

The new Minister of Native Affairs went to some pains to explain his policies to the people over whom he had acquired such vast powers. He travelled a lot, mainly to the rural areas where Africans unspoilt by the white man's urban ways were to be found. The chiefs and headmen were in his eyes the natural leaders of the Africans. He went to elaborate lengths to establish good relations with them, exchanging gifts and listening to their grievances, while playing the role of the Great White Father to the hilt. It was more than just preposterous make-believe. It was all part of his plan to bolster traditional tribal ways.

But there was a problem which made it impossible for Verwoerd to understand, let alone deal with, Africans outside the tribal setting. He was an incorrigible paternalist. To him, adult blacks were really rather large children. His private secretary, Fred Barnard, tells us that Verwoerd told tribal spokesmen to speak to him 'as a child to his father'. When he refused a request it was because he was 'the father who can judge on the desirability of what is good for my children or not'.[4] Verwoerd probably had no more than a superficial understanding of how tribal blacks thought and acted; it is certain that he was totally unqualified to have any kind of empathy with Africans outside the tribal setting. For him, educated blacks in particular, were pathetic, deracinated creatures, caught between two worlds: their natural one which they rejected, and an alien one which they tried vainly to embrace. They were in truth 'black Englishmen' who could never be at home anywhere.

Verwoerd's views help to explain his brief, unhappy relationship with the Native Representative Council. The Council admittedly, had not had a very happy history. Established by Hertzog in 1937, the Native Representative Council contained a majority of elected members and was supposed to be an advisory body to the Government, keeping it informed of what their constituents thought about non-political issues which affected them. The notion of educated blacks who would confine themselves to so limited a role imposed by their white masters, proved an impossible dream. Well before 1948 relations between the Smuts Government and the Council had broken down. Finally, the Native Representative Council decided not to meet with rulers so unsympathetic to black ambitions in a world that had just emerged from a war which had supposedly been fought for human freedom. It went into voluntary recess in 1946.

The Nationalists had vowed to get rid of the Council, composed as it was, in their view, of over-educated upstarts who had entirely the wrong view about how they fitted into the South African scheme of things. Verwoerd himself had condemned it 'as a body by which all dividing lines between various groups of Natives are broken down'.[5] However in December 1950, soon after becoming Minister, he decided to address the Council. Why he decided to do so after his public words of condemnation is not clear. Perhaps he believed that even so unco-operative a group of men could be convinced of the great truths of apartheid. Perhaps he wished to show that in spite of all his sweet reasonableness, the Native Representative Council really had no intention of producing much reason in return.

If that was his wish, Verwoerd must have been pleased with the result. The members of the Council made it plain, with varying degrees of vehemence, that they rejected utterly the separate future which the new Minister of Native Affairs had so carefully explained to them. Their revulsion was perhaps not so surprising after all, for here they were being informed, with a perfectly straight face, that the destiny of the black man in South Africa was to reach self-fulfilment in areas that were exceedingly backward and would obviously remain so for a very long time.

The Native Representative Council adjourned, the deadlock complete. It never met again and ceased to exist in 1952 in terms of the Bantu Authorities Act. Verwoerd could now proceed with a clear conscience to rebuild the entire life of black South Africa on his cherished tribal base. As Albert Luthuli, a member of the Council at the time and later head of the African National Congress, was to comment, 'Worse, much worse, was to come'.[6]

There had been other institutions which were designed to represent black people. Verwoerd found them only marginally more satisfactory than the Native Representative Council. In particular, there had been a system of local government in the Transkei in the Eastern Cape that had developed in the late nineteenth century and still existed. The district councils established there had a majority of elected members. The territorial body, commonly known as the Bunga, consisted of representatives of these councils. For Verwoerd this was all wrong, based as it was on unsound principle: it had committed the supreme sin of bypassing the tribal system.

Right from the start Verwoerd set out to rejuvenate what he conceived of as the black man's traditional way of life. The Bantu Authorities Bill which he introduced in 1951 proposed, apart from getting rid of the Native Representative Council, to restore 'the natural Native democracy' in the form of a three-tier hierarchical system of authority in the reserves. Most important would be what happened down at grass-root level. Here the tribal authority, consisting of the chief or headman and his councillors, would preside. The next tier would be the regional authority, consisting of two or more tribal authorities in charge of matters of common interest. At the top there was to be a territorial authority for each ethnic group, comprising two or more regional authorities.

Verwoerd had spoken of bringing back 'Native democracy.' It was not a resolve to be taken too literally, for the traditional authorities were to receive 'assistance from white Native Commissioners'. In effect, 'guidance' from these helpful officials would ensure that the ways of Native democracy did not diverge too far from what the Minister of Native Affairs believed was in the best interests of Africans.

What emerged from Bantu Authorities was a kind of government admirably suited to the wishes, or rather the indifference, of nearly all the white population, not merely the supporters of the National Party. It amounted to the absolute assertion of a principle, that white and black were separate and never the twain would meet within the ambit of a common political system. That having been done, little else was called for, as neither the political nor the economic development of the reserves was something for which white people, except for some eccentric Negrophiles, could work up enthusiasm. Actual political independence for these backwaters was not contemplated, while their economic advance was liable to deprive white employers of the black labour they could not do without. The watchword was gradualism and so it remained for some considerable time.

The traditional method of rule now implemented in the reserves was in fact not all that 'traditional'. It was tailored to insulate it from those popular pressures which had actually been a feature of the old practices. The Department of Native Affairs admitted naïvely to these 'merits' of Bantu Authorities when, in 1958, it commended the ability of the councillors of tribal authorities to 'perform their task without fear or prejudice, because they are not elected by the majority of votes ...'[7] Nor did the Government hesitate to remove chiefs and headmen who did not prove amenable to the dictates of the Minister. These powers had existed since the Native Administration Act of 1927, but were now wielded with enthusiastic vigour. What Verwoerd found so appealing about Bantu Authorities, in short, was not its reassertion of the tested ways of the past, but that it amounted to a perverted tribalism which inevitably undermined the credibility of traditional leaders among their followers.

There still remained the urban Africans to account for. They had streamed to the urban areas before 1948, a fact the Smuts Government clearly regretted but was not prepared to do much about. Indeed, it had appointed the Native Laws Commission in 1946 to re-examine the role of the African in South African society. Under the chairmanship of a former Minister of Native Affairs, Henry Fagan, it submitted its report only in early 1948. The Fagan Report represented a philosophy which the new government found totally repugnant, for it accepted the urban African as a permanent feature of the population:

It should be clear, firstly, that the idea of total segregation is utterly impracticable; secondly, that the movement from country to town has a background of economic necessity – that it may, so one hopes, be guided and regulated, and may perhaps also be limited, but that it cannot be stopped or turned in the other direction; and thirdly, that in our urban areas there are not only Native migrant labourers, but there is also a settled, permanent Native population.[8]

Verwoerd's answer was to deny any difference between urban and rural Africans. To him they were all the same, ethnic creatures with their roots in the homelands from which they originated. There was no difference in principle between Africans who had spent all their lives in the reserves and those who had never set foot there. In between there was a range of blacks who spent much of their time migrating between the urban and rural areas, temporary workers in white man's land who went back periodically to their families in what became known as the homelands. Verwoerd was naturally aware of these distinctions, but he could not allow them to blur the basic principle that all blacks had their distinct areas of origin, to which they were irrevocably attached and where alone they could enjoy full citizenship.

Once the principle was accepted, the presence of so many thousands of blacks in the urban areas and the white dependence on their labour, did not amount to much of a problem. Their stay was temporary, they were mere visitors, welcome only on sufferance by the white man. So it was simply logical to extend the range of controls over blacks in towns and to limit their right of domicile outside the reserves. There was a gamut of laws in these early years which asserted the transient and alien nature of the black urban presence, an essential but unwelcome accessory in the process of economic development.

In 1952 there was the Native Laws Amendment Act which sought to channel the movement of black workers to and within town through existing labour bureaux, but now adapted to centralised purposes. Ostensibly designed to allocate labour more efficiently by providing work-seekers with information about job opportunities, the bureaux were also a means of directing the flow of African labour. Permission was now required from the nearest labour bureau if an African wished to move from a 'non-prescribed' (mainly rural) area to one which was 'prescribed' (mainly urban), where work opportunities were limited. The Act's restrictions on labour mobility and therefore on the earning capacity of black migrants did not only suit the book of those many whites, especially blue-collar workers, who felt nervous about permanent-seeming Africans in the urban areas, but it was also designed to provide the politically influential farmers with black labour at rates of pay below those which market forces on their own would have produced. As Verwoerd said in the debate on the Bill in the Senate, 'Emigration control must be established to prevent manpower leaving the platteland to become or to create loafers in the cities'.[7] Economically, his remarks were illiterate, but politically they made excellent sense.

The Act also defined more narrowly than did previous legislation the categories of Africans who had the right of permanent residence in urban areas. Those who were so entitled became known as 'Section 10 people', after the relevant section of the Act. Even these fortunates were only relatively so. Permanent residence was limited to those who had been born in a particular town and had then resided there continuously for not less than fifteen years, or those who had been employed continuously in the town for fifteen years, or who had lived in the town and worked for the same employer for not less than ten years.

Also in 1952, Verwoerd gave another indication of what he had in store for Africans when he introduced the Natives (Abolition of Passes and Co-ordination of Documents) Bill. Had he been less humourless and less obsessed with a sense of destiny, Verwoerd might have been suspected of having had his tongue firmly in his cheek when he decided on so odd a choice of words. The measure had nothing to do with abolishing passes; they were simply renamed and became reference books. Previously blacks had had to carry a variety of passes. Now they were consolidated into a single document, which all Africans over the age of sixteen had to produce on demand by the police. Black women had to carry them too, for the first time, which led to widespread but ultimately unavailing protests. In all, it was a measure which fitted perfectly into Verwoerd's scheme of things for it made bureaucratic control over the movements of Africans to urban areas much easier.

In the meantime the groups on which the Government relied primarily for support had no cause for complaint. Not only did farmers benefit from their preferential access to black labour, but they received government subsidies, while marketing boards fixed favourable prices for their produce and agricultural research was funded by the taxpayer on an impressive scale. Unskilled and semi-skilled white workers, that is those most likely to suffer from black competition, were sheltered in a number of forms. Stricter influx control was only one form of protection; there was also job reservation, supposedly designed to protect white workers from 'exploitation' by competition from members of other races with lower standards. The size of the public sector increased steadily after 1948 and the number of Afrikaner civil servants rose still more rapidly. Even Afrikaner capitalism was beginning to thrive. Although some of its success was due to official favours like the award of government contracts and accounts, it can be ascribed largely to the general growth of the economy. In these early days, Afrikaans businessmen were not found to be criticising the Government, although policies which prescribed employment on racial and not meritorious grounds could not have increased the profits of capitalists of any description. But it was still a cost which the Afrikaner capitalist was willing to pay. It was only much later that he became truly concerned over the high price of running an apartheid economy.

CHAPTER THREE

Getting Round the Constitution

At first it seemed that the Nationalist government could not last. Its majority in the House of Assembly was small, a mere five votes, indeed three, if the Speaker of the House and its Chairman of Committees were excluded. The United Party persuaded itself that the 1948 result was an aberration which would inevitably be reversed at the next general election not more than five years away. All it had to do was to sit back and let the Nationalists destroy themselves by their own intemperate deeds, their rashness and their inability to remain within the bounds of reason and restraint.

It was not alone in being shocked. Much as white liberals had disdained the United Party government for its backwardness in matters relating to race, they still saw it as incomparably preferable to the wild men who now found themselves in power. A foremost liberal was Margaret Ballinger, the best-known and perhaps the most able of all the Native Representatives who sat in Parliament. In her political autobiography, *From Union to Apartheid*, she tells of what amounted to a revolution in South African life, the result of the Nationalist accession to power in 1948. Before then it still seemed as if there was hope. The United Party may have been slow, even stick-in-the-mud, but there was no doubt in the minds of people like herself that things were getting better, that the Government was beginning to accept belatedly the requirements of a modern industrial society. The reluctant but genuine admission that black urbanisation could not be turned back was perhaps the most encouraging sign that a more hopeful future was awaiting the underprivileged.

When she wrote, in the late 1960s, it is possible that her views were affected by knowledge of what came after 1948. Certainly, at the time she was not inclined to draw too sharp a distinction between the Nationalists and their predecessors, if some of her comments in Parliament are anything to go by.[1] Even so, it is difficult to avoid the impression that enemies of the Nationalist regime, whatever their surface rhetoric about the horrors of white rule, much preferred having to deal with the United Party. The victims of discrimination were in the habit of saying that there was so little to choose between the Nationalists and the United Party, that they were all so blatantly reactionary, that it hardly mattered who won the 1948 election. But there was a difference. As the ANC leader, Albert Luthuli, later commented: 'The Nationalist win did not either surprise nor extremely interest us, though we did realise that there would probably be an intensification of the hardships and indignities which had always come our way. Nevertheless, I think it is true that very few (if any) of us understood how swift the deterioration was destined to be'.[2]

The Nationalists had been intending to do something about the coloured franchise and had made no secret about it. They objected to coloureds voting on the same electoral roll as whites; when they came into power they quickly set about finding ways of taking them off. However, under the Act of Union the Cape franchise for coloureds was entrenched in the constitution: like the clause safeguarding equal language rights for English and Afrikaans, it could only be altered by a two-thirds majority of both Houses of Parliament sitting together. In turn, the agreed provisions for amending the constitution could also only be amended by a similar majority.

The Nationalist aversion to coloureds voting on the same electoral roll as whites was a fairly recent affair, but had become an article of faith by 1948. Why they should have had these intense feelings about a group which could pose no threat to white, or even Afrikaner, rule is something of a mystery. When Hertzog was Nationalist leader he was as sympathetic to coloured rights as any politician in that white-dominated environment could be. Malan, as Cape leader under Hertzog, had expressed similar sentiments. When Africans in the Cape were removed from the common roll in 1936, the coloured vote had not been an issue. The coloureds were assured that the African fate would not be theirs. They were seen as somehow 'belonging' with the whites in a way that Africans could not.

The Government's policy could least of all be explained in terms of the voting battalions commanded by the coloureds. The non-racial franchise of the Cape had long ceased to be so. After 1910 the franchise had first been extended to all white adult men in the Cape, and then to white adult women. Yet qualifications restricting the vote to a handful of coloured men only, remained entrenched. When the Nationalists came to power in 1948 the coloured franchise had become so diluted that Cape coloureds accounted for less than three per cent of the electorate. There were fewer than 50 000 registered coloured voters, compared with the 1,5 million whites, spread over twelve constituencies. Most of these seats were in any event won by the Nationalists during the 1953 general election.

One common Nationalist rationale was that the coloureds were 'a political football'. They were supposedly exploited by white politicians who had none of their interests at heart, angling for their vote at election time with the bait of large benefits to come, which never materialised.

Had the story been so simple, the coloureds would have had a far better deal. The truth was that the coloureds were by no means a political football, for that metaphor implies exchange of possession. The coloured vote was consistently anti-Nationalist. They were under no illusions about what the Nationalists had in store for them. They may have resented the condescension and paternalism of the United Party, but as the Nationalists made little effort to offer them a better future than the ruling party did, it is hardly a wonder that few coloureds wanted any truck with Malan and his followers.

It would be wrong therefore to suggest, as does Richard van der Ross in his history of coloured politics, that their removal from the common roll 'became essential for the survival of the government'.[3] Even with their initially precarious majority, it was difficult to see the Nationalists being threatened by coloured strength at the polls. The 'threat' receded still further in 1951 when the mandated territory of South West Africa acquired representation in the South

African Parliament and its all-white voters obligingly elected six Nationalist MPs to represent them in the lower House. When the Government came back with a much increased majority after the 1953 general election, its hold on power became effectively entrenched. As long as Afrikaner strength could be mobilised it did not really matter all that much how other groups voted. What is so astonishing is that the Nationalist drive to get the coloureds off the common roll never flagged. Setbacks were seen as merely temporary frustrations of the 'will of the people' as expressed at the ballot-box.

The Nationalists thought they had a foolproof case. The blacks in the Cape had been removed from the common roll in 1936 by an Act of Parliament, by the special procedure prescribed in the constitution. The validity of the law was then challenged in court in the case of *Ndlwana v. Hofmeyr*, 1937. The challenge failed, on the judgment of the Appeal Court that the Statute of Westminster in 1931 had removed all limitations on the sovereignty of the South African Parliament. It followed that whatever Act Parliament decided to pass had the force of law, irrespective of the original entrenched clauses of the constitution.

At first the Government had decided to defer to the scruples of Havenga, leader of the Afrikaner Party and faithful Hertzogite. The votes of his party were still crucial to the alliance and Havenga had doubts about the proper procedure of taking the coloureds off the common roll, although he did not object to the actual principle of doing so. In the meantime the Government went ahead with measures which were constitutionally, if perhaps not morally, beyond reproach. It enforced apartheid on railway lines in the Cape Peninsula and shortly afterwards racial separation appeared in post offices in the Cape.

Havenga came round to seeing the merits of the Nationalist case, a change which may have been influenced by his desire to succeed Malan as Prime Minister. In October 1950 Malan and Havenga came to an agreement whereby they declared themselves satisfied 'that the arrangement will not diminish the existing status of the coloured population and will not conflict with the provisions of the South Africa Act'.[4] They agreed that coloured voters on a separate roll would be able to elect four white MPs and one white Senator, as well as two members of the Cape Provincial Council, the race of whom was not yet specified at that stage.

The Minister of the Interior, T E Dönges, introduced the Separate Representation of Voters Bill in the Assembly on 8 March 1951. Just over a month later the Speaker rejected the argument of the United Party that the Bill had to go before a joint sitting of both Houses. The Bill was passed by a simple majority of each House sitting separately at all stages and received the assent of the Governor-General on 15 June.

Four coloured voters immediately challenged its validity. Although the Cape Provincial Division of the Supreme Court gave judgment in favour of the Government, the Appellate Division unanimously upheld their appeal in March 1952. The Court accepted the 1937 judgment of the Supreme Court that the South African Parliament was indeed sovereign, but held that for the purpose of amending the entrenched clauses Parliament had to sit unicamerally; it could not otherwise be described as Parliament.

It was still the early days of a bitterness and acrimony which hardly had a precedent in the public life of South Africa. From then on the Appellate Division found itself in the midst of a number of manoeuvres by the Government designed to undo that decision of March 1952. These were also the times of the Torch Commando, a body of war veterans formed in April 1951 with the explicit purpose of defeating the coloured vote policy of the Nationalists; at one time it seemed that forces inside and outside Parliament had actually shaped an effective mass movement which could at least prevent the Government from having its way with the constitution.

The official response to the Appellate Division's judgment was prompt. It took the form of the High Court of Parliament. On 22 April Dönges moved a Bill that Parliament reconstitute itself as a High Court which could by a simple majority vote act as the final court of appeal in all constitutional cases. The idea was that the High Court would be a kind of Privy Council which would hear appeals against decisions made by the Appellate Division. The Bill went through all the stages and was finally passed on 3 June.

The same four coloured persons who had contested the validity of the Separate Representation of Voters Act now sought a court order invalidating the High Court of Parliament. In the meantime, the High Court went ahead and reversed the decision of the Appeal Court, so that as far as the Government was concerned its original Act had the force of law once again. On the following day however, 29 August 1952, the Cape Supreme Court declared that the High Court of Parliament Act was itself invalid. The Government disputed the decision before the Appeal Court, but its appeal was dismissed in November 1952.

There, for a while, the matter rested. There was talk amongst Nationalists about the will of the people being frustrated by a bunch of unelected old men on the Supreme Court. There was other talk about how Paul Kruger of revered memory had given short shrift to his own Chief Justice when he was President of the Boer Republic of the Transvaal. But the Government had decided to accept the jurisdiction of the courts. It could not now tamper with the judges because their judgments did not suit Afrikaner populism. This did not mean that it had abandoned the struggle, far from it, but clearly it would have to find more devious ways of depriving coloured voters of their rights in a constitutional manner.

In the meantime there had been blood on the streets as the Torch Commando protested against the Government. In May 1951 it led a procession to Parliament to hand over a petition to the Prime Minister. It culminated with a parade through the streets of Cape Town with lighted torches and ended with baton charges by the police. More than a hundred people were injured. Whether the violence was due to provocateurs or to the Torch Commando's own failure to keep its more enthusiastic followers under control was not clear. But whatever the cause, the incident enabled the Government to label the organisation as an anarchic force, hostile to law and order and worthy of severe police attention.

The Torch Commando quickly reached its peak and then fizzled out. It drew much popular support at first but fell victim to multiple cross-purposes. Some of its members were interested mainly in preventing the constitution from being violated, others saw the Torch Commando as an instrument of social change. Sadly, it also succumbed to the South African disease of racism. In spite of having taken up the issue of coloured rights, the Commando was divided over the issue of coloured people as members. In

November 1951 the coloured ex-servicemen withdrew from the organisation. The Torch Commando was already ceasing to exist as an effective force.

The coloured franchise was a major issue in the general election of April 1953. The United Party had been confident that the 1948 fluke of a Nationalist victory would now be reversed. It was bitterly disappointed. The Government came back with a much enlarged majority. It now had 94 seats, against the 67 of the combined Opposition.

One reason for the Nationalist success was that the economy was doing reasonably well. Since 1948 it had been growing at about five per cent a year. The population was also increasing rapidly so that average real income per capita had gone up at a rate of less than two per cent. But the Government was seen to be furthering the interests of the white race conspicuously, especially those who felt threatened by competition from non-whites. This fear was acute. While a rising proportion of whites was becoming urbanised, so were many of the Africans. In 1948 less than one quarter of the black population had been urbanised; by 1953 it was closer to 30 per cent. Inevitably, many poorer and less-skilled whites in the cities imagined themselves in danger of being submerged by a rising tide of colour.

The Nationalists took care to look after their own. The public sector grew and so did the number of Afrikaners to whom it gave jobs, at higher rates of pay than the blacks whom they often replaced. The Government had tightened the pass laws and increased its controls over the use of black labour. While it did not prohibit black trade unions, it discouraged employers from recognising them.

Under the Smuts Government black wages had risen more rapidly than those of whites. It was a familiar phenomenon in industrialising countries, where income inequalities commonly tend to narrow as economic development takes its course. This trend was now reversed. The ratio of white to black wages began to widen once more, most conspicuously in mining and the public sector, where apartheid was strongest. More Afrikaners had been leaving the working class behind, but many still remained. Nearly 40 per cent of white males were employed in jobs that could be described as of this nature, like working in factories and on the mines. Relatively unskilled, they were conspicuous beneficiaries of Nationalist policies and showed their gratitude in the most tangible way – at the ballot-box.

The Nationalists were now securely in power, with little prospect of being displaced through the electoral process, although the United Party still lived with its illusions for several years to come. Certainly, in terms of their voting strength, there was no possibility of the Cape coloureds amounting to a danger to continued Nationalist rule. But it did not weaken in the slightest the Government's resolve to remove this anomaly from their scheme of things.

Malan had taken the issue to the polls. He and his followers claimed that no less than the sovereignty of Parliament was at stake. It was a sound emotive appeal; there is no reason to believe that the morality of depriving a minority group of already limited rights deterred Nationalist voters. The gratifying outcome at the ballot-box was seen by the Nationalists as an endorsement by the 'people' of the policies they had been pursuing all along.

They had enlarged their majority in Parliament considerably, but it remained short of the two-thirds vote required by the Act of Union. Malan now placed his hopes on more conservative members of the United Party who might have been swayed by the recently-delivered popular verdict. He proceeded in September to hold that Parliamentary joint session clearly held indispensable by the courts. Once more the Government failed to secure a two-thirds majority, coming a tantalising sixteen votes short of its objective.

The Nationalists resorted to a technique with which they were not familiar: persuasion. They knew that the United Party was packed with conservatives whose views differed little, if at all, from those of the Government on matters of race. Malan appealed to dissidents in the Opposition to support the proposed legislation. There was a small group of United Party MPs who were indeed willing to entertain the notion of putting coloured voters on a separate roll. But they would only do so on condition that colcoureds already on the common roll remained there. There were many in the Nationalist caucus, like Strijdom and Verwoerd, who found even this hard to swallow. Malan, however, stood firm. The joint select committee which had been appointed in October 1953 came up with a Bill designed to meet the scruples of the UP rebels. Yet it was of little avail. Another joint sitting was held in May 1954 but, in spite of the support of the dissidents, the Government was still nine votes short of a two-thirds majority when the final vote took place the following month.

Now the way was clear for a more drastic approach, which the Government had at first rejected. This was to pack the Senate with enough Nationalist members to obtain the required majority. This subject had been broached originally when Dönges was busy cooking up the High Court of Parliament. Previous failures could not deter them – now, like Richard III, the Nationalists were 'in so far in blood, that sin would pluck on sin'. There was no turning back.

But Malan himself was not to preside over the final circumvention of the constitution. Already an elderly man when he became Prime Minister in 1948, he left office at the end of November 1954 and was succeeded by the Transvaal leader of the National Party, J G Strijdom, a relentless white supremacist and a man who could be relied upon not to shirk from whatever methods were required to remove the coloured voters from the common roll.

The coloureds were not the only people who had cause for concern about what kind of future they would have under apartheid. Africans soon got the message that whatever prospects they had would have to be realised in 'their own areas', remote from those centres of advancement and civilisation which, it seemed, had been solely the result of the white man's endeavour over three centuries in South Africa. The urban African had now become an official alien presence, only to be tolerated as long as he provided labour which white employers could not do without.

There were protests by many, groups and individuals. The five years between the general elections of 1948 and 1953 were a time of confrontation. Although those who were at the receiving end of discriminatory laws, before and after 1948, proclaimed that there was really nothing to choose between Smuts and Malan, their actions belied their words. They knew that the Nationalists were different.

One result was a renewed call for African unity. Another was closer co-operation between the African National Congress and the South African Communist Party. The ANC had, for lack of anything better, decided in 1949 on a policy of direct action: it would encourage strikes, boycotts and civil disobedience. The Communists were old hands at this game; they were a small conspiratorial group consisting mainly of whites, totally dedicated to the policies of Stalin. The African nationalists found that they could do with the agitational and organisational skills of the Moscow loyalists.

The Government had, however, long intended to do something *kragdadig* (forceful) about 'the Communist menace.' In 1950 the Minister of Justice, C R Swart, introduced the Suppression of Communism Bill, a measure which would give him extremely wide powers to deal both with genuine Communists and all those deemed by him to promote the purposes of Communism. Once it became law, it proved a most potent method of silencing non-Communists who were active against apartheid.

The Nationalists acted against multiracial trade unions. They singled out for special attention both their Communist and ex-Communist members. Most prominent was Solly Sachs, General Secretary of the Garment Workers' Union, who immediately defied a ban imposed on him in May 1952 by addressing a meeting outside the Johannesburg City Hall. Police broke up the gathering violently; Sachs continued to defy the Government for a while but eventually decided that multiracial trade unionism was a lost cause under the Nationalists. He left South Africa in 1953. Sachs was right about the prospects for his kind of unionism. By 1957 all multiracial unions had been compelled to have segregated memberships, under white leadership.

In these early years, however, it was the Defiance Campaign which involved the most concerted and prolonged resistance to the new order descending on South Africa. It had its origins in July 1949 when the Youth League of the ANC published a Programme of Action, rejecting those tired, genteel ways of the past which had brought the black people so little. The document called for a new policy to be carried out by a 'total and complete boycott of all the elections under the Act of 1936'. Strikes, civil disobedience and non-co-operation would now be the methods by which Africans would persuade their white masters to a greater recognition of their rights. The Executive of the ANC adopted the Programme of Action unanimously.

The Defiance Campaign was timed to coincide with the tercentenary celebrations of the founding of white settlement in South Africa in 1652. It had been preceded by other confrontations between the white authorities and their radical opponents. On 1 May 1950 a one-day strike took place in protest against the Unlawful Organisations Bill, milder-mannered and hence abandoned forerunner of the Suppression of Communism Bill. The Communists were mainly responsible for the stay-away as the ANC still suspected them of manipulating African nationalism for Stalinist purposes and was not willing to co-operate. Eighteen Africans died in the area of Johannesburg as the police resorted to incisive measures to break up gatherings. The violence drove the Communists and the ANC together in the realisation that different ends did not preclude co-operation against the common enemy, apartheid.

African nationalism was changing rapidly in the crucible forged by Afrikaner nationalism in a post-war world where the foundations of colonial rule were plainly no longer as secure as they had been before 1939. As Luthuli was to put it: 'The challenge was to be on fundamentals, we were no longer interested in ameliorations and petty adjustments. There was no longer any doubt in our mind that without the vote we are helpless'.[6] The demise of the old cap-in-hand mentality was reflected in a new militancy and a willingness to find allies where they were available, irrespective of ideological differences over such longer-term matters as ownership of the means of production.

The Communists at least came across loud and clear as whites devoid of the paternalistic attitudes which old-fashioned liberals, however sincere, had found so difficult to shed. They were genuinely prepared to accept blacks as equals. What was more, at this time 'socialism' was still widely regarded amongst Africans and Asians as a good thing, or in any event as somehow progressive. Had capitalism not been a feature of colonial rule and had Soviet industrialisation not shown how a backward country could pull itself up by its bootstraps? Considerations such as these made it possible for the ANC and the South African Communist Party to form an alliance based on convenience and a considerable measure of mutual goodwill.

On 6 April 1952, the tercentenary of Jan van Riebeeck's arrival at the Cape, mass protest meetings took place in many parts of South Africa. The ANC and its other ally, the South African Indian Congress, agreed that the enthusiasm generated by these events had to be capitalised upon. On 26 June a deliberate campaign of civil disobedience was to begin. The Defiance Campaign would be a protest against major apartheid legislation, including the pass laws and the Group Areas and Bantu Authorities Acts. It would take the form of passive resistance and would involve the deliberate contravention of a number of apartheid laws.

At the main urban centres on the Witwatersrand and in Port Elizabeth, volunteers were to defy segregation laws and then wait for arrest. Africans were to throw away their passes, 'Whites Only' signs in public facilities were to be flouted, a host of relatively minor offences was to be committed. The intention was not to flood the prisons, for the numbers of the volunteers were supposed to be small. Gradually the campaign was to have a ripple effect till it spread throughout the country, including the rural areas. The design was not to dismantle the system; the time for that was plainly not yet ripe. The purpose was rather to build up mass enthusiasm and lay the basis for an effective movement rooted in popular support. At this time the ANC was still a fairly small organisation with a derisory membership of 7 000, even if it had been increasing.

At first the Defiance Campaign was a success. Volunteer groups informed the police in advance where they intended breaking the law and then allowed themselves to be arrested, in full view of crowds of their supporters. From its original centres the campaign spread to other areas, receiving especially strong support in the industrial regions of the Eastern Cape. In September 2 500 resisters were arrested in 24 centres. That was its peak. In October the campaign began to fizzle out. In spite of official adherence by its organisers to a Gandhian tactic of non-violence, it was conspicuously honoured by its breach. There were riots in the Eastern Cape, followed by predictably harsh police action. Lives were lost: 26 Africans and six whites, including a nun who was murdered, a shocking act which the Government and its press exploited with relish, as they did the violence in general. Whether the ANC was responsible or not, it gave the Government a fine chance both to label the organisation as nothing but a bunch of law-breakers and to portray itself as the only maintainer of the fine line between civilisation and barbarism. It issued a proclamation under which anyone who incited blacks to break any laws could be sentenced to prison for three years or would be fined heavily. None of this was likely to do it much harm in the 1953 general election.

The Defiance Campaign and its failure throw a harsh light on the South Africa of its day. There was the burgeoning black nationalist movement, responding to the challenge of a much more repressive regime than black South Africans had ever known. Before, the ANC had enjoyed little mass support, although its leaders and members were becoming increasingly resentful of white rule. The arrival of apartheid was no watershed, but it clearly accelerated what was already under way. The ANC had launched the campaign to raise the level of black political awareness and so to broaden its own popular base. By the end of 1952 its paid-up membership had risen from 7 000 to 100 000, the largest following it was ever to achieve before it was banned in 1960. But by August 1953 its membership had declined by 40 000.[8]

The ANC had perhaps been excessively optimistic about what the Defiance Campaign could achieve. At that time the longevity of Nationalist rule was not widely appreciated. The Nationalists were far tougher than their predecessors of the United Party, and the organisers of the Defiance Campaign seriously underestimated the determination of the Government to make no concessions.

They seriously overestimated the cohesiveness, self-discipline and long-term commitment of their own followers. There was plenty of enthusiasm at first, individual self-sacrifice was much in evidence, but more is required of a successful mass movement than these often admirable qualities. The organisation of the ANC was notoriously poor; yet good organisation is a prime requisite for effective collective action when it is on the scale of the Defiance Campaign. Confronted by the total intransigence of the Nationalist Government and its readiness, indeed eagerness, to resort to force and intimidation, the Defiance Campaign ended with a whimper.

Even so, for the ANC the campaign was not a complete failure. As a movement rooted in the masses and the wretched of the earth, it had previously been insignificant. Against this background the 100 000 members (out of a total black population of nearly 9 million) which it temporarily acquired were not truly inspiring; membership in any event fell sharply after the demise of the Defiance Campaign. Allowances can be made. The main recruiting ground of the ANC was urban blacks, less than 30 per cent of all Africans. As a proportion of blacks in town, ANC membership was somewhat less unimpressive. However, by 1953, it can truly be said that it had not advanced remarkably as a popular movement. Yet, compared with what it had been before, the advance was real. It had raised the level of political awareness of many thousands of Africans. It had received an infusion of working-class members. The ANC could genuinely claim that it did not merely speak for a small self-conscious middle class elite interested primarily in its own political and economic advancement.

The main problem of the ANC as an organisation was that it lacked a mass base. No one could say that of the National Party. Its victory in 1948 was largely the result of its success in binding together Afrikaners in a national movement, purposeful, cohesive and strongly aware of its own separateness.

Of course, Afrikaner nationalists had advantages African nationalists did not have. For one, they had had an earlier start. The origins of Afrikaner nationalism go back at least to the annexation of the Transvaal by the British in 1877, a time when Africans were still dispersed in their separate tribes, many of them conquered and powerless. The Afrikaner sense of identity derived from sharing a common historical fate and gained strength from the Boer War, and later from the subjection to British rule. Conquest brought resistance and the sharpening of national sentiment. Most important, the Afrikaners had a level playing field. They had the vote and knew how to use it with extreme effectiveness. At an early stage, in 1924, Afrikaner nationalism achieved power in a unified South Africa, even if it needed the support of the English-speaking Labour Party at first, which wanted protection for its working-class constituents from competition by blacks, something their Afrikaner allies were only too happy to give.

Before the 1948 general election the leaders of Afrikaner nationalism knew, like Archilochus' hedgehog, one big thing. This was that Afrikaners were an electoral majority. They had held power before and could hold it again. All they had to do was to stand fast as Afrikaners against other groups. It is what came to pass, through what has aptly been called 'ethnic mobilization'. [9]

Consequently, when Malan resigned toward the end of 1954, Afrikaner and African nationalism confronted one another in different stages of development. The Afrikaners had succeeded in organising themselves into a tightly-knit national movement. The benefits were real and predictably durable, as long as cohesion held. Jobs in an expanding public sector, protection against competition from non-whites, is in practical terms what apartheid came to. The 'distributional coalitions,' as one economist has called them,[10] that benefitted from the system could be relied upon not to abondon it lightly.

Africans, by contrast, had only gone part of the nationalist way. They could also expect that every obstacle would be placed in the path of their progress. The Afrikaners knew what the vote meant. They knew what would happen to their perks and privileges if ever the ANC demand for one-man one-vote were to become a reality. Official force and intimidation were to be an everyday fact of life for African nationalism as long as apartheid remained the foundation of Government policy.

CHAPTER FOUR

Tomlinson and Bantu Education

The Nationalist Government never ceased to proclaim separation between black and white. They also did plenty about it. Segregation signs proliferated. The races were kept apart in most conceivable ways. There were separate entrances to post offices, white and non-white could no longer sit together on buses or trains, and where residential segregation did not exist the Group Areas Act saw to it that eventually it did. If trade unions were still multiracial, there had to be separate branches for whites on the one hand and for coloureds or Indians on the other. Their leaders had to be white as well, however small the number of white members. (African trade unions were not recognised at all, nor could individual blacks belong to officially recognised unions consisting of members of other races.)

As a negative affair, apartheid was an undoubted success. Nor did the Nationalists show any sign of slackening in their separatist offensive. Yet there was a problem. When the slogan of apartheid was first loosed on the world, it came with positive trappings. The message was that separation between the races was of course desirable, yet it was not only whites who benefitted. It was supposed to be for the good of all, offering to each racial group the chance to realise its own unique identity, uncorrupted by alien influences. Yet few saw the positive face of apartheid in these early years. As even Oswald Pirow, Nazi admirer of not so long before, asked in 1949, '... is apartheid advantageous only for the white man?'

For the coloured people the uplifting features of apartheid must have been an especially close secret. What they did know was that the new rulers regarded their presence on a common voters' roll as offensive to whites. Predominantly Afrikaans-speaking, their separate nationhood could hardly have been said to exist. If later the burgeonings of national consciousness seemed to appear, the most obvious cause was the common fate imposed on them by a discrimination more virulent than any they had ever known. The Indians again, concentrated in English-speaking Natal, had been the victims of racist sentiments and practices which owed little to Afrikaners, arising as they did from a typically British imperial contempt for lesser breeds. The Nationalists gave little thought to Indians, regarding them as an alien presence which should be persuaded to go back to the vast impoverished continent whence their forebears came. For Indians too, apartheid was a thing entirely oppressive, manifested most brutally in the application of the Group Areas Act, which forcibly shunted them to remote areas where their trading skills would be less resented by white competitors.

It was Africans who seemed best suited for the upliftment apartheid could provide. Less than a third of them were in the white-controlled urban areas by 1950. Many if not most of these were migrants, who came and went in perpetual movement between town and countryside, partly out of choice, not wishing to abandon their land holdings in the reserves, and partly because it was government policy that they should not establish themselves permanently in the urban areas. It suited the Government to believe that Africans were tribal creatures; but to a large degree it was also the truth. Here, it seemed, was the ideal opportunity for apartheid to prove itself as a policy which offered many good things for Africans. Had the Sauer Committee not proclaimed that 'the Native Reserves must become the fatherland of the native'? Had it not asserted that 'for every Native it must be a spiritual home'?[1] As the rhetoric of apartheid would have it, the sky alone could limit the opportunities open to the black man – as long as he was in his 'own area'.

The black reserves had to be developed, that was certain. As show-pieces of black opportunity and progress they would refute the accusations by the rest of the world that apartheid was an elaborate and obsolete system of racial domination. But, on a less refined level, Afrikaner self-interest demanded that these exceedingly backward rural areas should show some progress. Much as the black man's labour was essential to white comfort and prosperity, the inflow of Africans to the urban areas, unremitting and vast, brought with it awful visions of the whites being submerged beneath a black flood. At the very least the inflow had to be stemmed. It could only happen if the reserves provided a better living for the many thousands of Africans who were forced off the land every year.

The Smuts Government accepted the findings of the Fagan Report of February 1948. The Nationalists could only reject them. The report's conclusions ran counter to the whole racial philosophy which had proved so important, if perhaps not decisive, in their recent electoral success. The Nationalists appointed their own commission.

This was the famous Tomlinson Commission, named after its chairman, the agricultural economist, Prof F R Tomlinson. The Commission was appointed by the first Minister of Native Affairs in the Malan Cabinet, E G Jansen, just before he left office in 1950 to become Governor-General. Its brief was 'to conduct an exhaustive inquiry into and to report on a comprehensive scheme for the rehabilitation of the Native Areas with a view to developing within them a social structure in keeping with the culture of the Native and based on effective socio-economic planning'. The Commission interpreted its terms of reference widely, as it 'very soon realised that the problems relative to the development of the Bantu Areas could only be thoroughly analysed and studied in the light of the wider economic, social and political framework of the Union of South Africa'.[2]

What all the circumlocution came down to was that the Tomlinson Commission saw separate development (by then a common euphemism for the word apartheid, which the Nationalists were beginning to find embarrassing) as the only way for South Africa. It knew that current trends meant that black and white were 'becoming interwoven to an increasing extent'. But this created a 'dilemma' for all South Africans. The whites had 'the unbreakable will to maintain their identity in the national and biological sense', but blacks were being persuaded more and more that they were 'entitled to enjoy the fruits of integration, *inter alia*, by demanding progressively an increased say in the administration of the country as a whole'. The dilemma was to be resolved by separate development 'as the only direction in which racial conflict may possibly be eliminated and racial harmony possibly be maintained'. This required the 'sustained development of the Bantu areas on a large scale'.[3]

One would have expected all this to be sweet music to the ears of Hendrik Verwoerd, Jansen's successor as Minister of Native Affairs. He was after all the most dedicated exponent of separate development in the cabinet. He naturally approved of the basic philosophy of the Tomlinson Commission, but as far as he was concerned there should not have been a commission at all. As it had been appointed by his predecessor, Verwoerd was faced with an accomplished fact. Perforce he had to accept it. But Verwoerd was a man of overweening confidence in his own abilities. He had no desire for advice about what was best for black South Africans. He had no doubt that he already knew.

In fact, he may not have been exhaustively informed about the people of whose future he was so willing to dispose, but it did not matter so much after all. Verwoerd's main concern was not the future of blacks, but that of the Afrikaners. He would do whatever he could and thought necessary to assure that the Afrikaners would control their own destiny. If it meant that the destinies of others had to be manipulated and directed to achieve the greater Afrikaner good, it was a sacrifice Verwoerd was always prepared to impose on them. The last thing he wanted was to be constrained by a commission which he had to pretend at least to take seriously.

The Tomlinson Commission believed in the doctrine of thoroughness. It spent years investigating the social and economic conditions of the reserves. Finally, in 1954, it submitted to the Cabinet a huge report of 3 755 mimeographed pages, later summarised in over 200 printed pages. Verwoerd had in the meantime been complaining in private about the presence of the commission. He was sure that his officials were perfectly adequate on the rare occasions when he wanted advice; what was more he had no doubt that he had learnt enough on visits to the reserves to make up his own mind about what had to be done to develop the black areas.

So the Tomlinson Report was submitted, but for some time nothing happened.

At last, after the Cabinet had sat on it for more than a year, the Tomlinson Report was published, in March 1956. Still the Government did not know its own mind. While it welcomed the Report's conclusion that 'separate development' was the only alternative, it was far less enthusiastic about proposals of substantial financial aid for the development of the reserves. A few months later the Government published a White Paper welcoming the Commission's endorsement of apartheid, but rejecting some of its main recommendations on the grounds that they were not 'a matter of scientific proof but of individual judgment'.[4]

This was the true voice of Verwoerd, for it was the line he was to take later in Parliament. He took from the Tomlinson Report what he wanted and spurned the rest. The reasons he gave were various, but one overriding impression remains. Verwoerd rejected the proposals of the Commission because they were what he least wanted to hear. He had made up his mind already about what to do with the reserves; the Tomlinson Report came to him as a profound irritation which he could simply not ignore as he would have liked to. So in Parliament Verwoerd gave his reasons at length, as was his wont, as to why the Report should not be taken too seriously and then went on to do things his way.

The Tomlinson Report, in spite of its commitment to the Government's policy of racial separation, was an important document, if for one reason only. It provided a wealth of information about conditions in the black rural areas. It recorded in immense detail their economic backwardness and their inability to provide blacks with a living much above the margins of subsistence. No one familiar even with the much abbreviated version of the Report could claim ignorance of the reasons why an increasingly larger percentage of the black population found itself in the urban areas every year. Now no one could propose seriously that the answer to the black inflow was simply to tighten influx controls and send 'superfluous' Africans back to whence they came. Yet, and perhaps not surprisingly, the Verwoerd years (1950–1966) were to be characterised by just such policies.

The report showed why life in the reserves meant a kind of

poverty for its inhabitants which seemed insurmountable. Population density there was far higher than in the rest of South Africa: in 1951 there were on average 63 persons per square mile in the black areas, compared with a figure of 27 for the country as a whole.[5] It was a density which would increase over the Verwoerd era: in 1965 the figures were 79 as opposed to 38.[6]

The reserves, comprising about twelve per cent of the surface area of South Africa, were mainly rural, suffering from acute overstocking and soil erosion. A large number of their able-bodied men left every year to look for work in the 'white' areas; the remittances they sent their families played a major role in helping to sustain living standards in the reserves. Subsistence production predominated in the reserves: only 25 per cent of the agricultural product was being marketed.

Per capita incomes were low and had apparently been declining since 1936. The proportion of the total geographic income of South Africa accounted for by the black areas came to less than four per cent in the years 1950–1951.

The report argued that the land in the reserves should be divided among the inhabitants in economic units. It estimated that 'efficient agricultural development of the Bantu Areas' required the removal of about half the existing population from the land.[7] The land was to be consolidated into economic units which were to be larger than current units. Those who were inevitably forced off the land would have to find jobs in secondary and tertiary activities. The Commission estimated that 50 000 new jobs outside agriculture would have to be created annually for the next 25 years. Initially secondary industry would provide the necessary boost by employing 20 000 workers, with the remaining 30 000 jobs coming from the consequent stimulation of tertiary activities.

All this was fairly optimistic. Industrially the black rural areas were simply 'a desert', as the Commission itself admitted.[8] Even so there was a further dilemma: should industrialisation take place within the reserves or on their borders? Plainly the economic development of the reserves required the first alternative. Yet border area industrialisation had definite advantages purely in economic terms. Border areas had a more advanced infrastructure in the form of communications and transport, they were more urbanised and it would be easier to attract entrepreneurs and skilled workers. A given amount of capital investment would probably have yielded a larger return. But none of this would have amounted to actual development of the reserves themselves, except in so far as they had multiplier effects in these areas and relieved population pressure on the agricultural sector.

Yet the Commission rejected the border areas alternative as it would have involved the perpetuation of the industrial colour bar, applicable in all white areas. It would have made it 'particularly difficult to create a class of skilled workers and entrepreneurs among the Bantu'.[9] Whatever the short-term advantages of border areas, the Commission preferred the internal growth of the reserves, which otherwise would become mere economic dependencies of the white areas, exporters of labour and recipients of the indispensable remittances of black migrant workers.

The Commission supported white capital investment in the reserves strongly. But it left no doubt that white South African taxpayers would have to pay dearly for their super-segregation. Even if other sources of capital investment could be found, the Commission recommended the Government should make R50-million (SA £25-million) available over a period of five years for the purpose of industrial development. The total estimated cost of diversifying the economy of the reserves would come to R208-million over the first ten years. If its proposals were carried out, the Commission estimated that by the end of the century the reserves would accommodate about 70 per cent of the black population. But even on the most optimistic estimate the blacks in the urban areas would continue to outnumber the whites.

The Tomlinson Report was a best-case scenario. Involuntarily, it provided devastating ammunition to the critics of apartheid. It showed that even on the most favourable assumptions, in particular a sense of urgency by the Government about the development of the 'Bantu areas' never displayed before, the white areas would still be so in name only. In fact they would continue to be incorrigibly multiracial, with an absolute majority of black inhabitants. And it would be costly. The report had made it plain that the burden on white taxpayers in achieving even so half-hearted a territorial separation would be enormous. But whether it was practical politics was equally plainly not part of its brief.

Astonishingly perhaps, the Minister of Native Affairs was not the least bit put out by conclusions so adverse to the physical separation of black and white. Verwoerd knew what he was going to do. Pretending to take the Tomlinson Report seriously was simply a distasteful necessity. He was not, however, a man averse to explaining his policies. He did so often, and at length. Verwoerd's reasons for rejecting the substance of the report are an object lesson in the clothing of expediency with the high-flown rationalisations of ideology.

He had already been persuaded that more productive black agriculture required the consolidation of holdings into economic units. Verwoerd accepted that it would mean the removal of many Africans from the land. His solution was the gathering into villages of those landless families dependent upon wage-earning for a living. And it was here that Verwoerd parted company with the Tomlinson Report.

Nearly a year before its publication, Verwoerd had spelt out in the Senate what he had in mind. He opted for border areas. Industrial development in white towns close to the reserves was to be stimulated. It was here that Africans who had been removed from the land would find employment; the reserves would become more economically diversified, but strictly as a by-product of the growth of border industries.[10]

Once this decision had been made, it was a simple matter to reject the recommendations of the Tomlinson Commission. As the reserves would develop only as a result of growth in the white areas, it was no longer necessary, as Verwoerd saw it, to spend those monstrous amounts regarded by the Commission as essential for safeguarding the future of white South Africa. He rejected all this as 'spoon-feeding', a policy that would not encourage those habits of independence and industry so indispensable to a self-respecting people.

Verwoerd's elaborate explanation in the House of Assembly as to why his way was so much better than that of Tomlinson, bore the imprint of an unyielding gradualism. It reflected not only what he found it convenient to believe, but also the instinctive desires of the white electorate. White South Africans did not want their cities and towns swamped by that black flood which was apparently always gaining force in the background. Yet they had no intention of willing the end by willing the means. Even had his inclinations been different, Verwoerd knew that there was no way his fellow-Nationalist politicians would have endangered their popularity with voters by taxing them at swingeing rates to provide funds for black development. It was one thing to keep 'unnecessary' blacks out of the white areas; it was another to make it possible by providing more attractive alternatives in the reserves.

The Tomlinson Commission had emphasised, 'half-hearted efforts will make no impression'.[12] The Government had been making precisely such efforts before 1956. After welcoming the Tomlinson Commission's endorsement of separate development and rejecting its proposals for getting there, the Government proceeded in that same manner which had survived the test of the ballot-box so well.

Its lack of urgency was rationalised splendidly by Verwoerd in Parliament. Indeed, he may even have gone for overkill, for, unlike some of his colleagues, he rejected totally the notion of white capitalists investing their own resources in the reserves. In his familiar didactic, if economically illiterate, style Verwoerd explained that white enterprise in the black areas was incompatible with separate development because 'the whites would pocket everything economically'. Blacks could then not be denied similar rights in white areas, which of course was not the official policy. Nor would the white presence simply be temporary: 'When established rights of this nature are created, it is wishful thinking to believe that after ten or twenty years the industries will pass from the hands of the whites into the hands of the Bantu'.[13]

Hostility to white capitalist investment in the reserves was to be a uniquely Verwoerdian obsession over the years, never to change, despite periodic urgings from other Nationalists that it would really not be so very bad a thing after all. But, at worst, for Nationalists this was a minor aberration. His general message was what they wanted to hear. They would be protected from the *swart gevaar* (black menace) and at hardly any cost to themselves. Blacks would be kept from swamping the urban areas, their labour would continue to be available to white employers, and the development of 'their own areas' would come as a spin-off of the growth of border industries securely inside white South Africa. How white capitalists were to be induced to invest in those border areas, lacking in infrastructure and still subject to the restrictions of the industrial colour bar, was something of little concern to the Minister of Native Affairs.

The supreme imperative at this stage was then not to keep Africans out of those parts of the country officially designated as white. It was rather to slow down the rate of black urbanisation. What mattered was the permanence of black settlement and that, Verwoerd appeared to believe, was mainly an urban problem. In the country areas, or platteland, relations between white and black took on a less disturbing aspect, for there the white man was master and the black man continued to know his place.

As Verwoerd was to put it in Parliament in 1958, in his first speech as Prime Minister:

> Economic integration assumes the simple intermingling of racial groups that cannot later be separated. This is the important point. We say that when a Native drives a tractor on a farm, he is not economically integrated. Merely because he helps the farmer to produce, is such a Native who operates a tractor integrated into the farmer's life and community? Of course he is not, because the concept of integration relates to people, and here we do not have people whose activities are becoming interwoven. They will only become interwoven in this way if the other forms of integration, namely equal social and political rights, result from these activities.[14]

Cities were in effect disturbing places. Here it was more difficult to maintain traditional master-servant relations between white and black. If Africans were allowed into the urban regions it should only be temporarily. The greater the permanence, the greater the risk of them becoming 'interwoven' with the life of the white man as urban ways broke down custom and tradition. The border areas strategy seemed the best possible solution to the problem posed by black urbanisation. The flow of black labour would be diverted from the main industrial areas, but Africans would still be employed on the peripheries of white South Africa. And, above all, blacks would continue to be tribal animals, firmly 'anchored in their homelands' as the Verwoerdian terminology would have it.

To the question of whether apartheid would continue to be a negative phenomenon, the answer that came out of the debate on the Tomlinson Report amounted to an unequivocal 'yes'. Behind all the rhetoric about 'self-development' and the special pleading for not putting resources into the reserves, was the assumption that it was not at all a pressing matter. Economic growth would come in its own good time to these regions; there was no strong reason why natural force should be given a push.

As it was with economics, so it was with politics. Here too, any sense of urgency was absent. As long ago as 1951 Verwoerd had denied that the black areas could ever hope for more than self-government within the borders of a unitary, white-controlled state.[15] Later, in 1959, soon after he became Prime Minister, Verwoerd was to announce his 'new vision' of independent black states excised from the body of the South African state. He and his followers were to make much of the 'moral basis' which this conferred on their race policies, supposedly in contrast to the 'immoral' policies of the Official Opposition, the United Party, which believed in permanent white supremacy, albeit with 'justice', as its spokesmen tried to sugar the pill. Suffice it to say that at this stage of Nationalist rule there was no hint, even theoretically, of independent black states. In short, even as an idea apartheid was as lacking in moral foundation as the execrated policies of the United Party.

Verwoerd did have a vision of the ordering of relations between South Africans. It was based on ethnicity. The races in South Africa were separate groups and had to live their separate lives. This was of course no more than orthodox Nationalist doctrine. What was distinctive about Verwoerd's approach was his attempt to make an all-embracing system of the practice of segregation. In its application to his own special subjects, the black people of South Africa, Verwoerd was to carry the ethnic principle to extremes. For him there were a number of black identities, corresponding to the different black ethnic groups in South Africa, whether Zulu or Xhosa or Tswana or others. As blacks were lost without their tribal identity, it followed that their tribal roots needed reinforcing, which at the same time conveniently fragmented the black population. Hence the establishment of Bantu Authorities and the rejection of permanent black settlement in the urban centres. But Verwoerd knew that the new tribalism would be at risk if the state had no control over the minds of Africans. It made sense that education for blacks should be of a special kind, devoted to inculcating them with pride in their own unique ethnicity. What they needed was Bantu Education.

Before 1948, schools for blacks came under the jurisdiction of the provinces. Most were controlled by a variety of English-speaking church denominations. Although they had a separate primary school syllabus, at the secondary level it was largely the same for all races. Education for blacks had long been an impoverished relation of white education. Till 1945 it had been supported mainly by taxes paid by Africans themselves, but in that year the National Education Finance Act provided for additional funds to come from general taxes. Primary schooling for blacks continued to be characterised by overcrowding and lack of resources, but it grew rapidly. It was at the higher levels that the numbers of black scholars were minuscule and the drop-out rates became alarming.

The Nationalist Government had no objection at all to education for blacks. It even came to congratulate itself on its efforts in the field. Did it not show that separate development was actually beneficent? What it did object to, however, was the kind of education young black people were getting. They were receiving their education mostly from missionaries, unsympathetic to Nationalist policy and instilling in them, the Government was sure, impractical notions about progress in a common Western-orientated society.

One of the first things the Nationalists did was to appoint a Native Education Commission, headed by the ubiquitous Werner Eiselen. It was charged to formulate 'the principles and aims of education for Natives as an independent race, in which their past and present, their inherent social qualities, their distinctive characteristics and aptitudes, and their needs under ever-changing social conditions were taken into consideration'. The explicit aim was to restructure the existing system of black education 'in order to conform to the proposed principles and aims, and to prepare Natives more effectively for their future occupations'.¹⁶

The Commission duly did what it was supposed to do. In 1951 it submitted a report recommending radical changes in black education. It proposed a separate educational system for blacks, centralised under the Department of Native Affairs. Schooling for the other races would continue to be administered by the Department of Education, which could only mean that while all races were different in the ideology of apartheid, blacks were especially different from others.

Even in terms of official doctrine, it made little sense, but in the theory and practice of apartheid it was the practice which invariably proved decisive. The history of the Nationalist Government was to have this common theme: the rulers did whatever they thought necessary for white, especially Afrikaner, privilege; the ideology was basically a self-serving rationalisation for policies that would have been embarked upon in any event. Perhaps the main reason for the unprecedented authority Verwoerd achieved in the National Party was his superlative skill in dressing up courses of action, indefensible by old-fashioned criteria of justice, as really designed in the best interests of the victims.

He was at the top of his form when he steered the Bantu Education Bill through Parliament in 1953. He made it plain that education for blacks 'must not clash with Government policy' and should 'not create wrong expectations on the part of the Native himself'.¹⁷ It was the English-speaking missions which caused blacks to have misguided expectations, teaching them as they did to believe that Africans had a future in common with the white man. As their destinies were in fact separate blacks inevitably acquired hopes which could only be disappointed. They had to advance instead as members of their communities; it was to be the task of Bantu Education to impress upon black scholars that community service was truly a wondrous thing.

The new dispensation in black education meant more emphasis on teaching in the mother tongue. It had been the policy before but had often been disregarded by black teachers, hostile to what they saw as the survival of a backward past, and also by white school inspectors too often ignorant of any African language. From now on mother-tongue instruction was to prevail in all black primary schools.

Yet there was one unavoidable constraint which even the most extreme enthusiast for the new dispensation had to face up to. White prosperity could not survive without black labour. 'Temporary' African workers would still be coming in their thousands each year to find jobs in the white areas. 'For that reason,' Verwoerd was compelled to admit, 'it is essential that Bantu students should receive instruction in both official languages from the beginning so that they can already in the lower primary school develop an ability to speak and understand them'.[18] It was in one sense merely a realistic acceptance of economic necessity. In another sense it was not so very wise: parity between the languages dictated that English could not receive preferential treatment at the expense of Afrikaans, which consequently was forced upon black scholars who were quick to resent it as the tongue of the oppressor and who could see little justification for it anyway. Outside Afrikaner-owned farms, knowledge of English was for the most part perfectly adequate for getting around in the white man's economy.

There can be no doubt that there was widespread resentment among blacks towards the new system that had been imposed upon them. Bantu Education began to operate in April 1955 but was greeted by an attempted boycott organised by younger members of the African National Congress. It was only a partial success, on the Witwatersrand and in the Eastern Cape. Verwoerd, however, always thrived on dealing with blacks who had forgotten their place. He issued an ultimatum that pupils who had not returned to school by a certain date would be excluded altogether. Most did go back, but when the time limit expired there were still 7 000 on the Rand who had not done so. The names of those who had no valid excuse were struck off the rolls. It was only after being presented with signed undertakings from parents not to support any further boycotts that Verwoerd agreed to readmit some black scholars in batches over the next two years.

That the new system of black education was inferior was true in several ways. It was inferior because it involved a differential syllabus, geared to what the Nationalists, more specifically Verwoerd and Eiselen, regarded as suited to the ethnic nature of the different black tribal groups in South Africa. It amounted to cutting blacks off from the culture of the West, which had become a universal culture, on the grounds that it was somehow alien to their 'traditional way of life'.

Even more strikingly, differences in per capita spending by the State on white and black education were not only huge (as of course they had been before) but actually widened. In 1953 per capita annual expenditure by the State on white education came to about R128; for black education it was a mere R18. Ten years later it had declined to R12, while per capita spending on white education had increased. Partly, this reflected the far more rapid increase in the numbers of black pupils, but the differences were still remarkable. Verwoerd was to justify such discrepancies on the grounds that blacks should mainly be responsible for financing their own education. 'Spoon-feeding' after all was the alternative and could only be injurious to black ethnic pride.

Even Verwoerd had to concede that some official assistance to black education was unavoidable. After the adoption of Bantu Education the Government would therefore continue to provide an annual amount of R13-million for this purpose. More funds would have to come from African pockets, which was made possible after 1956 by higher direct taxation of the black community.

By the mid-1950s then the legal framework for a radical restructuring of the lives of black South Africans was in place. Influx control had been tightened, at least on paper. The very notion of a permanent black urban presence had been repudiated in the most vigorous terms. What were seen as traditional tribal structures were being refurbished in the black homelands, under suitable white tutelage. A new educational system had been adopted, designed to indoctrinate black pupils with the ideology of ethnic separatism.

It was neat and tidy, or so it appeared. These were not years of Nationalist self-doubt. For a long time Nationalists would still believe that they were masters of their own fate, and of the fate of others. Yet, in spite of all their best efforts, there was nothing during these years and in the years to come that would belie the earlier insight of C W de Kiewiet, probably South Africa's most outstanding historian, when he wrote, '... it is clear that the leading theme of South African history is the growth of a new society in which white and black are bound together in the closest dependence upon each other'.[19]

CHAPTER FIVE

On the Road to Separate Freedoms

As the 1950s took their course South Africa became a bleaker, harsher place for most of its people. In addition to the laws they had already passed which were designed to make apartheid an encompassing, lasting feature of the South African way of life, the Nationalists produced others, all enforced with unremitting vigour and enthusiasm. Some were of an explicitly racial nature, others were directly repressive, aimed at those who had notions of questioning the new order that was being built in South Africa. The actions of the Government made it plain that it would not tolerate opposition that in any way threatened the permanent supremacy of the white man. The more uncompromising nature of Nationalist rule became apparent under a new leader, Johannes Gerhardus Strijdom, leader of the party in the Transvaal and known to his many admirers in that province as the Lion of the North.

When he became Prime Minister after 1948, D F Malan was already an elderly man. After the general election of 1953, it was widely expected that he would not long remain as leader. Even so, it came as a surprise when Malan suddenly informed his cabinet on 6 October 1954 that he intended resigning at the end of the following month. As the Minister of Labour at the time, Ben Schoeman, put it in his memoirs: 'We were completely taken aback. We knew that he would not continue much longer, but we thought that he would still continue in office for at least another year or two. Our first reaction was therefore to try to persuade him to postpone his resignation, but he made it quite clear that his decision was final'.[1]

Malan's colleagues could live with his departure. By now he was more than 80 years of age. Many Nationalists from the northern provinces had seen him as being excessively biased towards his native Cape Province, both with respect to those who had his ear and his cabinet appointments. They reacted with especial resentment towards the manner in which Malan tried to impose his successor on the Party.

Since 1948 Malan had established a close relationship with the leader of the Afrikaner Party and Minister of Finance, Klaas Havenga. It probably came as a surprise to both, for the alliance between the National Party and the Afrikaner Party had been purely a matter of political expediency, intended to get rid of Smuts, but not rooted in mutual warmth and friendship. There were indeed bitter opponents of the alliance within the National Party, notably Strijdom and Verwoerd. They yielded eventually, but grudgingly and with much ill-feeling. After 1948, however, Malan and Havenga drew closer to one another. They found in one another men of congenial temperament, both relative moderates in a government which included uncompromising asserters of Afrikaner exclusiveness and domination. After the Afrikaner Party merged with the National Party in 1951, Malan became persuaded that Havenga should succeed him as Prime Minister. He believed it was no more than Havenga's due for his contribution to the triumph of 1948. Moreover, Malan had come to have a decidedly strong aversion to Strijdom, going back to the acrimony over the alliance with the Afrikaner Party. They had personalities and temperaments which scratched at one another in all the wrong places. Strijdom had altogether a more unyielding approach to Afrikaner nationalist concerns. In particular, he was an untiring advocate of a South African republic outside the Commonwealth. Neither Malan nor Havenga could get excited over the issue to any comparable extent. It was one reason why Strijdom so vehemently opposed the alliance of 1948. In the eyes of the opposition press he was the 'extremist', Havenga the 'moderate'. It was a distinction which did Strijdom no harm in the eyes of most Nationalists.

For Malan there was a problem. The party constitution did not provide for what Malan now proposed to do, which was to recommend, British-style, to the Governor-General that he ask Havenga to form a new government. As Strijdom immediately pointed out, the correct constitutional procedure was for the party caucus to elect the new leader of the National Party. When Malan eventually realised that he could not persuade the cabinet that Havenga should succeed him, he announced: 'Well, that is then how it will have to be done. The caucus can decide'.[2] He announced his decision to retire the next day.

Malan did not cease from attempting to ensure the premiership for Havenga. He extolled the virtues of the Minister of Finance at a last public meeting on 26 November. The previous week he had tried once more to win his cabinet round, with the same lack of success as before.

Havenga finally realised that he had no chance of succeeding Malan. On 30 November the Nationalist caucus met to choose Malan's successor. Both Strijdom and Havenga were nominated, but there was no contest. Havenga had no desire for the public humiliation he knew awaited him if he stood for the leadership. He stood up and declared that he was not available. Strijdom was unanimously chosen new leader of the National Party, which meant that he would automatically become the next Prime Minister. Havenga followed Malan into retirement.

Under Strijdom there were to be changes in the way the parliamentary National Party handled its affairs. From now on no minister broke ranks by disagreeing in caucus with decisions that had been taken at meetings of the cabinet. Malan's discipline had been lax. When the Nationalist caucus met, members of his cabinet had often spoken out against decisions to which they had earlier agreed. Strijdom himself had been a culprit. In his own cabinet he would brook no such dissent. In part, circumstances favoured him, for during his brief premiership of four years Strijdom's cabinet was not divided on major issues. As it was, a minister knew that he would be laying his career on the line if he committed any such act of disloyalty. Inevitably, the authority of the cabinet was strengthened; the National Party itself became a more disciplined body, united as it had never been in imposing its will on the rest of South Africa.

Strijdom's accession to power meant a marked shift of influence within the National Party. Northern attitudes on Afrikaner nationalist issues came increasingly into their own in the formulation and implementation of policy. Malan and Havenga, conservative as they were, still represented relative moderation and restraint. They were less prepared to push policies to their supposedly logical conclusions; compromise and half-measures were not alien to them. Strijdom, by contrast, was a purist amongst purists. After the break with Hertzog in 1934 he had led the Nationalists in the Transvaal. Once one of the most convivial members of the National Party, Strijdom in those years abandoned his previous *bonhomie* and propensity to socialise for the greater good of restoring Afrikaner unity, which depended so much on a Nationalist revival in his own province. He became a conspicuously austere devotee of the Afrikaner cause. From the lonely years of reconstruction the Transvaal emerged as the province which had made the largest contribution to the victory of 1948. Strijdom himself personified the republican conscience of the National Party and its uncompromising commitment to white racial domination, or *baasskap*. As leader of the National Party it could be expected that Strijdom would continue down the road he had been travelling with such purpose and direction. The republic, supreme symbol of South African independence from Britain, would feature more prominently in the National Party's exhortations to the faithful. The principle of apartheid would be expressed and upheld even more vigorously than before. It also meant that the Nationalists would now take up their unfinished business and finally remove the coloureds from the common roll.

Strijdom's triumph was one for the Minister of Native Affairs as well. For more than ten years Verwoerd and Strijdom had been the closest of allies. In the Transvaal they had collaborated in rebuilding the National Party. Their views on race and the republic were virtually identical. As members of Malan's cabinet they had represented that brand of nationalism associated with the north and commonly denounced by the opposition and its press as a particularly virulent form of Afrikaner extremism, rooted in isolationism and xenophobia. As minister in charge of the fate of by far the majority of South Africans, Verwoerd had made his mark. His considerable abilities, his overriding sense of purpose, his dedication to the cause of his adopted people, the Afrikaners, would have allowed no less. In a mere four years as a member of the cabinet Verwoerd had made the kind of impression that inevitably drew accusations that he was aiming at the supreme power himself. They were far off the mark. Verwoerd was undeniably ambitious, but Strijdom was his leader, to whom he was unfailingly loyal. His time would come, but in the meantime his own standing and influence in the National Party advanced substantially.

Politically close as Strijdom and Verwoerd were, temperamentally they were poles apart. Verwoerd was an ideologue as if to the manner born. Proposing a measure was not for him the relatively straightforward thing it would have been for most of his colleagues. Verwoerd insisted on putting it in its appropriate place in an overall system. It had to be rationalised and justified as an essential part of the proper ordering of the relations between the races in South Africa. Even decisions taken for the most obvious reasons of political self-interest, such as the Government's rejection of the Tomlinson Commission's recommendations for substantial injections of taxpayers' money into the reserves, had to be presented by Verwoerd as for the good of Africans themselves. After all, would such 'spoon-feeding' not destroy self-reliance and pride in one's own efforts? Strijdom disdained such fancy smooth talk. For him the facts of racial confrontation were stark. They had after all their origin in inextinguishable differences of race. Limited development of the reserves was fine by his book, but if blacks demanded more opportunities in the 'white' areas, it could never be theirs. Grandiose visions of complete black self-fulfilment in 'their own areas' were beyond his ken. He had no problems with the notion of permanent black subjection to white rule. If the whites did not dominate then inevitably the blacks would.

The Nationalists had vowed to accept no set-backs in their campaign to remove the coloureds from the common roll. They had lost several battles; they were determined to win the war. Earlier the Government had believed it would not be necessary to enlarge the Senate. But all its other schemes had failed and it was surely intolerable that the will of the people should continue to be frustrated by mere constitutional devices.

Just before the Easter recess of Parliament in 1955, Strijdom announced the appointment of six more judges to the Appellate Division of the Supreme Court. A full quorum of eleven judges was now required for constitutional appeals. The new appointees were not noted for their hostility to the Government's interpretation of the constitution. The Nationalists could now at least expect a sympathetic hearing of any case which might go as far as the Appellate Division.

The Government's real intention became plain only when it introduced the Senate Bill. It provided for the enlargement of the Senate. Representation in the Senate was to be on a proportional basis; the party which had a majority in the electoral college in a province would elect all the Senators for that province. The Nationalists had a majority in three provinces. All now became the plainest of sailing.

There was the inevitable and unseemly scurrying for sinecures by party hacks who knew that all that was required of them was to cast their vote to deprive a minority group of still more of its already limited rights. When the new Senate met it consisted of 89 members, compared with the 48 of before. All but twelve (eight from Natal and four Native Representatives) were Nationalists.

At a new joint session of both Houses of Parliament on 27 February 1956, the Government achieved what it had all along proclaimed it would. The coloureds were removed from the common voters' roll by 174 votes to 68.

This legislation was also tested in the courts. The Cape Supreme Court upheld its validity. It went to the reconstituted Appeal Court, which in November 1956 handed down a judgment. Ten judges confirmed the decision of the Cape Supreme Court. There was one dissenter, Oliver Schreiner. His judgment was to cost him dearly, for the Government later ignored a time-honoured precedent by refusing to appoint Schreiner as Chief Justice when he was next in line to succession by virtue of seniority.

The Nationalists had achieved their goal. They had shown the utmost determination and extreme lack of scruple in getting there. The question recurs: Why did they behave in the way they did? One common answer was that they were afraid of what the coloured vote could do to their electoral chances in a number of marginal constituencies. However true, it ceased to be so after its resounding win in the general election of 1953.

Another notion, seemingly bordering on the self-evident, is that it was sheer unmitigated race prejudice which propelled the Nationalists on their frenzied course. They could not abide the prospect of coloureds being on the same electoral roll as whites; it amounted to racial equality and as such was deeply offensive to a people who inculcated the notion of white superiority into their children from birth.

That most supporters of the Nationalist Government (like indeed most white South Africans) harboured large doses of race prejudice is undoubtedly true. Yet the history of Nationalist rule has shown that the Government and its followers have been quite willing to be pragmatic about apartheid when it suited them. Increasingly from the 1970s onwards, measures which had been held up as sacred matters of principle to the Afrikaners were abandoned, most evidently in sport, but later in many other fields as well. Their disappearance had no obviously adverse effects on the character of the people they were supposed to preserve. Nor had Nationalist policy before 1948 always been overtly hostile to the coloureds. When Hertzog was Nationalist leader he favoured the eventual incorporation of the coloureds into a white South Africa. Malan himself did not then reject such a policy. The change only came when he and his followers rejected Fusion under Hertzog and Smuts.

The Purified National Party of 1935 made a fetish of Afrikaner ethnicity. It was the very principle of its existence, the reason why it repudiated Fusion as a blow aimed at the roots of Afrikaner identity. The new party could only survive by drawing the sharpest possible dividing lines between Afrikaners and other groups. It proceeded to do so. Amongst those it spurned were the coloureds, whose limited presence on the Cape common voters' roll the Nationalists now decided was detestable. They were to find a convenient pretext: the coloureds were allegedly a political football, interchangeable between the political parties, which saw them as pawns in the white political struggle. This was nonsense, for the coloureds knew the enemy. They voted against the National Party because they realised that the Nationalists had assigned them to inferiority in any South Africa in which they attained power. Had the Nationalists built on the foundations laid by Hertzog the outcome might have been very different. But this was something they could not do. Their existence and future success depended on the continuous assertion of Afrikaner separateness. Exclusiveness and xenophobia constituted the soul of the Purified National Party.

It made plenty of electoral sense. The Afrikaners were a comfortable majority of the voters, accounting for about 60 per cent of the white population and reproducing themselves rather more rapidly than the English-speakers. They were also a majority of rural voters, who enjoyed lopsided representation in Parliament because of the vote loading provisions of the South African constitution. Simple arithmetic showed that a modicum of Afrikaner unity must eventually result in rule by the Nationalists. All they had to do was to persuade their potential followers to cast their votes as Afrikaners first and above all else.

What happened in 1948 was a measure of their success in so doing. But as yet there were still many Afrikaners who did not support them. A continued appeal to ethnicity could only yield substantial rewards in ensuring an inbuilt electoral majority, all but irremovable at the polls. The campaign against the Cape coloured franchise was a devastatingly effective means of polarising Afrikaners on the basis of ethnicity. It was a simple matter to portray coloured voters as being manipulated by the United Party to keep Afrikaners out of power for ancient reasons of *Boerehaat* (Boer hatred). It was a well-established vote-catching ploy of the National Party, to resort to allegations that 'the English hated the guts of the Afrikaners' and would stoop to virtually anything to do them political damage. Usually it had the most satisfactory effects. So it was with the Cape coloured franchise. Whatever other purposes it served, it should be seen primarily as a means by which the Government pursued its goal of maximum Afrikaner unity. Apart from preventing a permanent black presence in the urban areas, this was its overriding obsession for the first decade of its rule. Here at least the Government achieved a fair degree of success.

The Nationalists managed to achieve what they wanted with the coloured vote and must have thought their efforts eminently worthwhile. Yet they gave rise to consequences which are with South Africans still. They widened the already large breach between Afrikaners and coloureds to such an extent as to make it all but unbridgable. The Government served notice on the coloureds that their position in a Nationalist-ruled South Africa would be one of permanent and legally-sanctioned inferiority. That was the best for which they could hope. The coloureds would understandably not be appeased by what the Government later did by way of spending on coloured education, housing and welfare. They saw it as paternalistic upliftment, and they were right. It could not be a substitute for political equality, which their rulers had rejected so explicitly and offensively.

Perhaps even worse, the Nationalist willingness to use the means they did to achieve so blatantly selfish an end, debased the standards of public morality. Arguably, these standards were not especially impressive to begin with. A political system designed inherently to maintain white racial domination, as that of South Africa was, whatever the ruling party, could not have had much about it that was admirable. The Africans had after all been removed from the common roll in the Cape as long ago as 1936. Yet, however retrograde a step this may have been, Hertzog had observed old-fashioned proprieties and constraints. He had long been attempting to eliminate the black presence on the voters' roll but could not obtain the required two-thirds majority until he had Smuts's co-operation in the new United Party. He never contemplated going to the lengths to which the Nationalists did. It is an indication of the gulf which separated the Nationalist Government which came to power in 1948, from all its predecessors.

These were years when the Nationalists were consolidating their support, forging an unbreakable coalition of interest groups which, it seemed, would keep them in power for ever. The farmers, desiring cheap labour, were happy with the controls over African labour mobility. So were white workers, especially those with lesser skills, who had reason to be grateful to a government which was doing its level best to protect them from 'unfair' competition by blacks.

One way in which this protection worked was through job reservation. Amendments of the Industrial Conciliation Act in 1956 and 1959 empowered the Minister of Labour to reserve certain kinds of jobs for members of particular races. In practice it was designed to benefit less skilled whites who faced the prospect of their wages being undercut by non-whites who could do the work equally well and at lower cost. More important, however, in providing shelter for deserving Afrikaners who had problems standing on their own two feet in the labour market was the expansion of the civil service. From the 1920s, poor whites fresh from the depopulated countryside and with only rudimentary skills equipping them to survive in a modern economy, had been given employment in the cities by the public sector. The 'civilised labour' policy was made for them. Even before the Second World War well over half the civil service consisted of Afrikaners, although the more senior positions were still held by English-speakers. After 1948 the growth of the public sector became a major vehicle of Afrikaner advancement. Not only did its relative size grow, but the proportion of Afrikaner bureaucrats rose dramatically. It was partly because English-speakers were increasingly attracted to more rewarding posts in the private sector, but to a large degree it was deliberate policy. Bilingualism was more strictly enforced, nor was the Government shy about appointing good Nationalists to top positions in the civil service.

The consequences for all South Africans were profound. Here was a major interest group which stood or fell with the continuation of apartheid. The proliferation of discriminatory legislation after 1948 needed more and more civil servants to ensure that the races were truly kept apart. Tighter pass laws, population registration and group areas, all called into being a bureaucracy which depended on their perpetuation. If apartheid disappeared so would the apartheid bureaucracy. Not only that, there was a whole army of controllers, engaged in the congenial task of ordering the lives of others but contributing hardly anything to productive activity. The rise and development of a civil service with a vested interest in apartheid meant the further entrenchment of Nationalist power and a huge misallocation of potentially productive resources.

While the Nationalists were riding high, their opponents in the African National Congress were not experiencing such good fortune. After the disasters of the Defiance Campaign the ANC had to make difficult choices. Its ultimate goal remained political: equality between white and non-white based on one man, one vote. But the Defiance Campaign had made at least one thing plain. Universal suffrage and majority rule were further away than ever. The Government had demonstrated its willingness to take exceedingly tough measures to suppress extra-parliamentary dissent. It was an intention which became apparent early on when it passed the Supression of Communism Act in 1950, really an excuse to label any opposition it did not like as promoting the aims of Communism. In 1953 it passed measures which would make future protest considerably more uncomfortable. The Public Safety Act provided for the declaration of a state of emergency when security was endangered. The Criminal Law Amendment Act made possible harsh punishment for incitement to break the law.

It was not only that the Government raised the costs of dissent. Even if the ANC was brave enough to ignore the probable consequences to its leaders, it still ran the risk of alienating most of its potential constituency. Seeking a distant political kingdom would not improve the immediate standards of living of the African in the street who was worried about low wages, poor housing and the increasingly stringent enforcement of the pass laws. Yet the ANC could hardly afford to ignore these bread-and-butter issues, not if it wished to prevent a further dwindling of its membership, down from its peak of 100 000 paid-up members in December 1952 to 40 000 a mere six months later. It had to prove to ordinary Africans that they needed the ANC, but it involved the risk that longer-term political goals would increasingly disappear from sight. Nonetheless, the ANC had little choice. It was compelled to demonstrate its relevance to its followers, actual and potential and in so doing, its weaknesses were grievously exposed.

A good example of ANC involvement in such immediate burning issues was its opposition to the Native Resettlement Act of 1954. Hendrik Verwoerd had designed the Act as part of his overall design to provide urban blacks with improved living conditions, but, as usual in these matters, it came with a catch. Under the terms of the Act the Government would remove Africans from pockets in Johannesburg's western areas, known as Sophiatown, and provide them with better housing in the new township of Meadowlands. The catch was that in the western areas a fair number of residents had freehold rights, which they would not enjoy where the Government now proposed to put them.

The ANC decided that this was a splendid opportunity to show that it had a contribution to make in standing up for the interests of ordinary Africans. It announced its opposition to the removal and got a propaganda campaign going which drew the welcome attention of the international media. That, however, was where it ended. The campaign scarcely progressed any further; when the first removals took place in February 1955 there was hardly a sign of disturbance.

It failed most obviously because the Government's willingness to deal with 'agitators' was never in any doubt. Police 'supervised' the removals, which both prevented the ANC from disrupting them and exposed its impotence at a time when it could most do without such publicity. But there was another consideration, which had not entered into the calculations of the ANC. Better housing was really part of the deal, at least for a significant number of those who had to move. The word spread, so that when later removals came, support for the ANC had declined still further. The ANC's efforts to sabotage the removals had foundered on the twin rocks of the certainty of severe Government repression of any resistance, and the definite, however limited, gains from the new dispensation.

Similarly, later in 1955 when the ANC went about organising resistance to the implementation of the Bantu Education Act, it failed signally to achieve any success. However inferior the new system may have been to the one it replaced, it did offer tangible benefits, on the assumption that some kind of education was better than none at all. And once more there was the Government, prepared, as ever, to take an exceedingly tough line if it had to.

There was an occasion when the ANC managed to channel popular discontent and improve its standing among urban blacks. In 1957 the inhabitants of the Alexandra township outside Johannesburg successfully resisted an increase in bus fares. The boycott, which lasted four months, was a spontaneous protest by what had become a closely-knit community against not merely the fare increase but also the way the transport services were being run. The ANC played an important co-ordinating role but it did not lead the boycott and failed to capitalise on the heightened political awareness that came with the protest.

The ANC never, in fact, became much of a mass organisation before its banning in 1960. Resistance was a dangerous business, particularly after the passing of the Public Safety Act and the Criminal Law Amendment Act in 1953. But it was not just government repression which kept the ANC out in the cold. Economic growth in the 1950s was moderately high, of the order of 4,4 per cent per year on average. Africans as a whole probably did not benefit all that much for their rate of population increase came to just over 2,5 per cent annually for the decade. But those who had access to the urban areas were relatively privileged. They could have had no desire to throw away the limited gains they had made. Coupled with ever-present Nationalist willingness to resort to force, it made for a potent disincentive to engage in public protest against apartheid.

The ANC was also badly organised. Political campaigning had led to the neglect of the previous efforts by the leadership to construct a branch network. It was a major source of weakness in a country where the main cities were at considerable distances from one another. Geographic divisions were compounded by ethnic differences, with which they often coincided. There were then good reasons why African nationalism in South Africa was relatively backward. It was to remain so right up until 1960 with the banning of the African National Congress and its offshoot, the Pan Africanist Congress.

These years did, however, produce a document which has acquired a mystique of its own in the history of the ANC. It has been treated as a fundamental blueprint for a new political and economic order in South Africa, a kind of sacred writ which it would be blasphemous to question. This was the Freedom Charter of 1955.

It had its origins in the annual conference of the ANC in December 1953, when Prof Z K Matthews of the black University College of Fort Hare and the organisation's leading intellectual proposed that 'an assembly of the people' be held as a kind of stock-taking after the failures of the Defiance Campaign. It would be a reaffirmation of belief in a South Africa free of apartheid.

Also, it would give a much-needed psychological boost to the whole liberation movement. This was the theory. In practice it did not quite turn out that way.

The Congress of the People eventually met on 25 June 1955 at Kliptown outside Johannesburg. There were 3 000 delegates, of whom more than 2 000 were Africans, the remainder being more or less equally divided between whites, coloureds and Indians. They represented what was known as the Congress Alliance, of which the ANC was by far the most important member. The other constituents of the Alliance were the South African Indian Congress, the South African Coloured People's Organisation, the South African Congress of Trade Unions, and, most significant, even if it had only some hundreds of members, a white organisation calling itself the Congress of Democrats.

The assembly did not meet for long. On the second day it was broken up by those perennial Nationalist watchdogs, the police. But by then the Freedom Charter had been produced. This was a document drafted by the National Action Council, a body representing the Congress Alliance. The Charter affirmed that South Africa belonged to all its people. It also made a number of demands, some of them unexceptionable, which old-fashioned liberals would have had no difficulty in endorsing, like equal protection for all before the law. What gave the Freedom Charter its claim to fame however was its demand for comprehensive state control of the economy: 'The mineral wealth beneath the soil, the banks and monopoly industry shall be transferred to the ownership of the people as a whole ...'.[3]

The ANC carried this ideological baggage with it in the years to come. Yet, apart from its understandable rejection of white rule, it was not a particularly ideological organisation. The man who originally suggested an assembly of the people, Z K Matthews, was himself unsympathetic to socialism. The ANC leadership included many whose views were similar to those of Matthews. The truth seems to be that the ANC let the ideological issue go by default, that it was a price it was willing to pay for co-operation with the South African Communists, in the form of the Congress of Democrats.

For this is what that organisation was, a front for the South African Communist Party. Some of its members may have been white opponents of apartheid with leftish sympathies, but the COD was controlled by Communists and its support for the Moscow line in foreign policy was unwavering, including later the Russian invasion of Hungary in 1956. What it lacked in numbers the COD made up for in terms of enthusiasm and ideological commitment. It was determined to include in the Freedom Charter support for the Stalinist brand of socialism, still the accepted orthodoxy in the Soviet Union and its satellite regimes. For this was a mere two years after the death of Stalin and still a year before Khrushchev denounced his crimes in his Secret Speech. The Freedom Charter's endorsement of nationalisation was the result of the efforts of the Stalinist faithful of the Congress of Democrats to have their version of socialism included in the document.

That the ANC was willing to let them have their way was partly because of its overwhelming concern with quite another issue: race, with the daily oppressions and indignities to which blacks were subjected because of their colour. But 'planning' was also somehow seen as advanced in what came to be known as the Third World. Had the Soviet Union not pulled itself up by its bootstraps because it had got rid of the anarchy of the market and replaced it by conscious control of the system of production? Such ideas, vague, indeed confused, made for a predisposition to accept clauses which in retrospect appear increasingly primitive and economically ignorant.

This did not prevent the ANC from accepting the Freedom Charter officially, with its demand for nationalisation, in March 1956. One notably sympathetic historian has commented: 'It thus became a victory for the left wing which for the first time succeeded in bringing socialism into an ANC programme'.[4]

The Congress of the People did not bring a new dawn of hope to the ANC and its allies. It served as a warning to the Government that African nationalists and white Communists could form a mutually beneficial partnership that could cause much inconvenience to the enforcers of apartheid. On 5 December 1956 the police arrested 156 individuals of all races and from many walks of life, all involved in the Congress Alliance's resistance to white rule. They were later charged with high treason. It was the beginning of an interminable trial, which saw the number of accused steadily dwindle over the years. By November 1960 only 30 remained, all of whom were acquitted in March of the following year.

The Government had been made to look exceedingly foolish and the Treason Trial had cost the taxpayers plenty. But for the Nationalists there were compensations. Many of their leading opponents had been kept out of circulation or had been so harassed that their effectiveness in the struggle against white rule had been much reduced. For this alone, the whole enterprise must have been worthwhile.

The Nationalists had prevented their radical opponents from mobilising the African masses in a movement that would pose a threat to continued white domination. Their efforts to slow down black urbanisation had somewhat more mixed results. Between 1951 and 1960 the urban African population increased by 45 per cent, from 2,4 million to 3,5 million. During this decade influx control was not yet as encompassing as it was to become in the 1960s. It was only then that a truly massive onslaught on the rights of Africans to stay in the urban areas on any kind of permanent basis began. As yet the bureaucratic apparatus was not elaborate enough to exert the kind of sweeping control over the movements of blacks to the cities, and within them, that would later seem commonplace. Prosecutions under the pass laws increased, but so did the African population. Over the decade the rate of prosecutions of the urban metropolitan black population remained essentially unchanged. State control over black labour mobility was still only in its incipiency.

Undeniably, however, the 1950s were times of growing state interference in the lives of Africans. It was reflected not only in the protests of the ANC but also in the intensification of rural violence in the second half of the decade. In Sekhukuneland in the Eastern Transvaal, resistance to the introduction of Bantu Authorities was widespread and vehement. Three hundred were arrested and twenty-one were convicted of murder. In the Western Transvaal there were bitter protests against women being compelled to carry passes, which were burnt in large quantities. In Pondoland in the Eastern Cape, rural violence arrived to stay as Africans seemed determined to reject anything associated with the Government, whether it was Bantu Authorities or agricultural betterment schemes. However expressed, the violence had a common denominator: rejection of a government which had provided much sustenance for the belief that it was hostile to Africans.

The man most responsible for the turmoil in the lives of Africans was the Minister of Native Affairs, Hendrik Verwoerd. His determination to impose racial separation had made him easily the most controversial figure in the Government. His opponents were fond of portraying Verwoerd as a power-hungry fanatic, oblivious to the human cost of his schemes. One opposition newspaper commented typically that he had succeeded in building up his 'Native empire', about which little was known except that it was the scene of rural unrest, as well as of 'banishments, deportations, shootings, burnings, arson, closing of schools'.[5] Another familiar complaint came from the United Party MP, Harry Oppenheimer, later head of the huge Anglo-American Corporation: 'When you have a man prepared to slow down his nation's economic welfare on account of political theories, then you are dealing with an impractical fanatic'.[6]

None of this could have weakened Verwoerd's position in the National Party. Criticism from 'the English' was rather a tribute to the strength of his Nationalist principles and his vigour in implementing them. But still, Verwoerd was not a man to inspire warmth and affection. He was more admired than cherished. His manner was austere and he could not be bothered to spend much time socialising with the Party faithful. Safeguarding the future for an Afrikaner posterity was a time-consuming obsession which did not permit such frivolities.

But Verwoerd's single-mindedness also managed to attract criticism from the wrong kind of people, his own. His cabinet colleague, Ben Schoeman, tells the story of the abrasive dispute they had over race policy. Verwoerd had declared that he realised that total territorial separation was impracticable, but that it must be held up to the Afrikaners as an ideal, inspiring them to support government policy even more enthusiastically. Schoeman, as far from liberalism as Mr Micawber was from making a fortune, was withal a plain, blunt man. He told Verwoerd that preaching an ideal which he knew could not be realised was no less than blatant fraud. Only the intervention of the Prime Minister Strijdom could assuage the bitter quarrel which broke out instantly.⁷

The previous year, 1955, Verwoerd had managed to upset farmers in a large part of the Western and Southern Cape with his proposal that no blacks should be allowed to enter that region, which was to become a Coloured Labour Preference Area. Africans supposedly had no 'historic' claims to the areas, unlike the coloureds, who would now receive preferential treatment at the expense of blacks, while of course whites would continue to be treated preferentially at the expense of the coloureds. The boundary of demarcation became known as the Eiselen Line, after Verwoerd's Secretary of Native Affairs, who had succeeded in persuading his master that this was a thoroughly sound idea. Farmers in the Western Cape could not agree. Many of them employed Africans and did not relish the prospect of paying more for coloured workers just because Verwoerd had decreed that the labour supply be reduced drastically. The farming vote counted for something in the corridors of power. Nonetheless, the Coloured Labour Preference Policy came into effect in 1957, although it had been watered down from Verwoerd's original extreme formulation that no African should be allowed to enter the region in search of work. Instead, the movement of Africans was to be controlled strictly, while those who were 'redundant' were without any further ado to be expelled.

The ideological intransigence of the Minister of Native Affairs received even more notorious illustration in the same year, when yet another Native Laws Amendment Bill appeared before Parliament. The most controversial feature of the Bill was the 'church clause', which made it compulsory for churches in white areas to apply for permission from the minister if they wished to hold services to be attended by both black and white.

The main English-speaking churches announced with much fanfare that they would have to choose martyrdom if the Bill became law. Public protest was intense. Overseas publicity was widespread and totally unfavourable. Verwoerd did what was for him a most unusual thing: he modified his stance. The church clause was amended twice. Even so, the final product remained unpalatable to the outraged men of God. The minister would now exercise his power only after consultation with the local authority concerned, and the church involved would not be liable to prosecution, his fate resting instead with the offending African himself. It was obviously still unsatisfactory, but Verwoerd was sure that he had done quite enough by way of concessions. The Bill was finally enacted in May 1957.

What Verwoerd, a full time super-Afrikaner, must however have found disconcerting was the criticism of Nationalist Afrikaners. There was the Dutch Reformed Church, for many years a docile supporter and rationaliser of apartheid, which still could not approve of state interference in matters spiritual. Some of its leading spokesmen actually said so. There had even been restrained criticism from the normally servile Nationalist press.

Surprisingly, behind the scenes, the far right weighed in with grievances of its own. Whatever its practice, in theory apartheid could not be put across as mere *baasskap*, the simple desire of the whites to dominate blacks forever. It had to have an ethical justification, however specious. This is what Verwoerd's right wing critics could not stomach. The minister had been moving cautiously towards a concept of apartheid which stressed the 'separate freedoms' Africans would one day enjoy in their own areas, where there would be no limit to their advancement and they would be their own masters. Such theorising is easy to portray as so much cant and moonshine, but just to talk in this manner struck at age-old notions of what was good and proper in relations between white and black. Upholders of traditional white domination now began to find that the Minister of Native Affairs was, astonishing as it seemed, showing signs of that stock Nationalist aversion, 'liberalism'. To Verwoerd this must have been the unkindest cut of all.

Outwardly, none of this seemed to put him off his purposeful ideological stride. To the public he continued to come across as a man with a mission, not to be deterred by mere carping and sniping, or who even considered objections from those on the same political wavelength. But behind the supremely confident façade there were indications that all the unpleasant publicity was getting to the man. At the end of the 1957 parliamentary session Verwoerd told the Nationalist caucus that he wished to resign as Minister of Native Affairs as the post had become too closely identified with his own person, while he had in fact been doing no more than carrying out party policy faithfully. His wish, if such it was, was not granted. Verwoerd stayed on and continued to be by far the most controversial member of the Nationalist Government.

A general election took place on 16 April 1958. The Nationalists played a well-worn but entirely successful theme. It was that of Afrikaner unity. They had little difficulty in persuading the *volk* that they could best be protected from the *swart gevaar* (black menace) if they voted early and if they voted Nat, a claim which had more than just a specious plausibility if one contemplated the alternative, namely, the purposeless, characterless and hardly any less racist United Party.

The Government came back with a still bigger majority, winning 103 seats against the United Party's 53. Even now it remained doubtful whether the Nationalists commanded an overall majority among the voters. They did not contest many safe Opposition seats in the urban areas, so that only estimates of voting strength were possible. But, as before, the delimitation system, which gave disproportionate weight to the rural vote, worked in their favour. To all intents and purposes the Nationalists were now irremovably in power.

In August 1958, less than five months after the election, Strijdom died. He had long suffered from poor health and his death did not come as a surprise. For some time there had been speculation about his successor, but no one had emerged as an obvious choice. Three members of the cabinet now announced their candidacy for the leadership of the National Party. One was C R Swart, Minister of Justice and leader of the National Party in the Orange Free State.

As the most senior minister, Swart had been acting Prime Minister since just before Strijdom's death. Then there was T E Dönges, Minister of the Interior and Cape leader of the National Party. He had been responsible for introducing highly controversial legislation, such as that dealing with group areas and the Cape coloured franchise, but was probably more moderate than the other two candidates. The third was Hendrik Verwoerd, the most junior of the three and by far the most controversial.

Of the three candidates, Swart apparently had an excellent

chance of winning. But much of his support was negative, based not so much on his own sterling qualities as on a desire by many to keep Verwoerd out at all costs. Both Ben Schoeman, who nominated him, and Jan de Klerk, Strijdom's brother-in-law, who seconded the nomination, only supported Swart because they wanted no part of Verwoerd. As Schoeman said of Swart: 'I certainly did not think that he was the best of the three to become Prime Minister. I just wanted to keep Verwoerd out at any price'.[8]

Verwoerd did have definite advantages. He came from the Transvaal, the province with the largest number of votes in the caucus. Four years before, when Strijdom became Prime Minister, the result showed that the balance of Nationalist power had shifted to the north. Also, although Verwoerd had become Member of Parliament for the Transvaal constituency of Heidelberg in the last general election, he had for some time before that been leader of a Senate packed with docile hacks who had been put there to vote the coloureds off the Cape common roll. Over them he had established an ascendancy which was to do him a power of good in the race for the top of the greasy pole. And then there were the repeated and strident attacks on Verwoerd by the United Party and its press. Nationalists knew that a man who attracted such a degree of enmity from sources so hostile to the volk and its ideals could not be devoid of many redeeming features. The attempts to destroy him only enhanced his standing among the faithful.

So it proved. Verwoerd was widely expected to win, and he did. But his triumph was no walk-over. It was clear to begin with that Verwoerd had only minority support in the cabinet. Both his opponents were nominated by senior ministers; he had to be satisfied with nomination by one of the most junior members of the cabinet, De Wet Nel. The contest also had to go to two ballots. In the first Verwoerd received 80 votes to the 52 of Dönges and the 41 of Swart, who duly fell out. In the second ballot, Verwoerd won by 98 votes to 75. It was a convincing enough majority, but most MPs had supported Dönges. What proved decisive was the support of the 'enlarged' Senators, who cast their votes faithfully for the former leader. Ironically, it was Dönges who had introduced the legislation to pack the Senate.

What was important was that Verwoerd was elected. In his years as Minister of Native Affairs he had established himself gradually as the dominant figure in the cabinet, but his ascendancy was scarcely undisputed. He was at best the first among equals. Now that he was Prime Minister, Verwoerd could begin to establish a dominance over his cabinet and the National Party, a dominance without precedent. The years between 1960 and 1966, from the inception of his undisputed authority to the time that he was murdered, can most accurately be described as the era of Verwoerd.

CHAPTER SIX

New Directions and Some Old Ones

Hendrik Verwoerd was a marked man when he became Prime Minister. He had a record, and the Opposition and its press did not much like what they believed they saw. They had no doubt that they were looking at an uncompromising extremist, a man determined to achieve his ends and not too scrupulous about how he arrived at them. His recent past as controller-in-chief of the millions of Africans in South Africa had been ominous enough. Yet it was something most English-speakers could live with, committed as they themselves were to white supremacy for as far into the future as the eye could see. Perhaps they did not much care for the way in which Verwoerd kept blacks in their place. Less autocratic, more paternalistic methods often seemed to English-speakers better designed to prevent Natives from getting restless. But about the principle of indefinite white rule there could scarcely be sharp differences between Verwoerd and the supporters of the United Party.

White English-speaking South Africans found Verwoerd's record as a declared exponent of a particularly virulent brand of Afrikaner nationalism disturbing. During the war years, as editor of *Die Transvaler*, a newspaper which unashamedly placed political propaganda ahead of any semblance of objective reporting, Verwoerd had played a major role in the Nationalist resurgence on the Witwatersrand. He was Strijdom's closest ally in propagating that cause cherished by right-thinking Afrikaners: a republic outside the British Commonwealth. Verwoerd was in short, even by Nationalist standards, an extremist, an Afrikaner exclusivist and a republican hardliner who stirred repugnance easily in those who did not share his particular world-view.

In his own party there were those who did not greet Verwoerd's elevation with unrestrained enthusiasm. One of the foremost was the Minister of Transport, Ben Schoeman, a man who had for many years, before and after 1948, been one of the least of Verwoerd's admirers in the National Party. For years they had been at one another's throats: Schoeman, a forthright man of blue-collar origins with no talent or inclination for ideological hairsplitting, and Verwoerd, an ideologue first and foremost, accustomed to having his way and conspicuously unwilling to suffer fools gladly. They were two strong personalities who seemed fated to be engaged in virtually permanent hostilities with one another.

Schoeman's enmity was not based on a contempt for Verwoerd's abilities. By his account it was Schoeman who persuaded D F Malan to appoint Verwoerd as Minister of Native Affairs. As he said to Malan in a comment which also speaks volumes for the Nationalist attitude towards Africans: 'I think, Doctor, that Verwoerd is the right man. It is true that he does not know much about the Natives, but he is extremely able, has tremendous energy and pertinacity and I am sure that he will be a successful Minister'.[1] It was not Verwoerd's competence that bothered Schoeman. It was his dogmatism, his authoritarianism, his conviction that anyone who disagreed with him could only be wrong. Schoeman was to change his mind about Verwoerd eventually, some time after he became Prime Minister. But there were many in the National Party who never managed to hit it off with a man of so autocratic a temperament, addicted as he was to the notion that he had an excellent grasp of what was good for others and not in the least hesitant to act upon it.

Verwoerd addressed the country in a broadcast the evening after his election. Much of what he said was the familiar stuff to be expected of Afrikaner nationalist leaders just arrived in high office. His choice was the will of God. Democracy would be defended. He made a promise about which many were sceptical, with reason as it turned out: 'The right of people with other convictions to express their views will be maintained'.[2]

Verwoerd dwelt on the well-worn theme that the Government's

race policy had been misunderstood. Racial separation was not about oppression, but about 'full opportunity for all'. None of this was new. Indeed, it was tediously familiar to all connoisseurs of Nationalist political rhetoric. But all at once Verwoerd struck an original note. He declared that the attainment of a republic would be at the top of the Government's priorities. But he made it plain that the republic he envisaged would no longer be the realisation of an Afrikaner ethnocentric ideal. For Verwoerd the coming of a republic would be an essential prerequisite for the achievement of unity between the white language groups.

Here was a veritable sea change in the thinking of a man long known as one of the most unbending and determined Afrikaner nationalists of them all. The only plausible explanation is that his years as Minister of Native Affairs had made Verwoerd increasingly aware that the issue of race had now become central to the lives of all South Africans. The world was very different from what it had been ten years before when the Nationalists took office so triumphantly. Then it had been evident, or so it appeared, that the struggle was between Afrikaner nationalism and a somewhat amorphous white South Africanism which stood for nothing in particular except that it was opposed to the kind of 'extremism' represented by Malan and his followers. In 1948 the victors had little doubt that the fruits of power would be theirs for ever.

But in the meantime the world was changing fast, now that it had entered the post-colonial era. It was not something of which many Afrikaners were well aware. They took it for granted that global events affected them little and that traditional master-servant relations between white and non-white were a permanent feature of the South African way of life. Verwoerd's own views hardly differed from those of the Afrikaner nationalist in the street when he became Minister of Native Affairs. Nor did he know much about Africans. But he was a man of considerable ability and sharp intelligence. Between 1950 and 1958 he could not but become acutely aware that the time-honoured squabbles between the white language groups were appearing increasingly anachronistic in the face of the rising nationalisms of Asia and Africa. Verwoerd knew, even if most of his fellow-Afrikaners did not, that an irrevocable change in human relations was taking place. Only the previous year, in 1957, Ghana had become the first colony in black Africa to achieve independence. It was not something he welcomed, but he realised that it would be folly to deny that here was a brand new drama, happening right before his eyes.

Verwoerd became convinced that however divided the white language groups were they had one overriding interest: maintaining their right to rule themselves in a country where they only amounted to a fifth of the total population of nearly 16 million. To him and his fellow-Nationalists, and nearly all white South Africans for that matter, it was unthinkable that the franchise should be extended to millions of largely illiterate Africans in the same political system as themselves. But it was no mere issue of culture, even if cultural differences coincided largely with those of race. In time the coincidence would tend to disappear; there could then be no valid reason for denying political rights to Africans who had attained an 'adequate' level of education. For the Nationalists race was also a criterion of nationhood in some irreducible sense. They were admittedly not too clear about just how this worked. The Afrikaners after all were supposed to be a separate nation, distinct from the English-speakers. Yet in a larger sense, according to Nationalist logic, white South Africans formed one people, irrevocably set apart from all those of other colours.

Evidently much of this was special pleading, and not too coherent at that. South African whites had for so long, both before and after Union, quarrelled with one another over so many issues and with such rancour that it was difficult to detect the underlying bond of common nationhood. But it also made excellent sense. That the Afrikaners were a nation in some meaning of that elusive word there could be little doubt. Nor could there be any doubt that they had won the political struggle against the English-speakers; sheer numbers had done the trick. Verwoerd had come to realise that the Afrikaners would be increasingly under siege for their race policies. The vanquished English-speakers now became their most obvious allies. The internecine squabbles of the past were a luxury neither group could afford in the suddenly more urgent world of decolonisation and Western retreat.

So it was that white unity became one of the main themes of Verwoerd's premiership. As the new leader was to put it two months after assuming office, when addressing the Nationalist congress in the mainly English-speaking province of Natal:

> In a republic, South Africa will have a political set-up as in any other country. In such a system the clash between the two nationalisms – Afrikaner nationalism, founded on South Africa first, and English nationalism, founded on British imperialism – will disappear. The party system will lose one of the main divisive factors and the country will acquire a set-up as in any other country, for example, on the basis of conservatism versus liberalism.[3]

Verwoerd was convinced that by far the most white South Africans agreed on race policy, on the necessity of maintaining white rule. Yet they would remain at odds as long as English-speakers retained their sentimental attachment to monarchical symbols with which Afrikaners could never identify. A republic would eliminate this source of division, Verwoerd anticipated. The two white language groups would grow increasingly close to one another, united by the imperatives of white survival on a hostile continent and in a threatening world.

It is ironic that it was Verwoerd, super-Afrikaner above all, who should have struck out on this new course. In his day no one had done more to heighten Afrikaner ethnocentricity, to persuade the Afrikaner that he belonged to a people like no other, with its own unique destiny. If the barriers of incomprehension and distrust between the white language groups were all but impenetrable it was because men like Verwoerd had laboured long and hard to make them so. Nor did he cease being a totally committed Afrikaner nationalist. What he did was pre-eminently for the Afrikaners, for he continued to identify with them above all others. Verwoerd's situation was tortured and ambiguous, Afrikaner as he was by adoption and not birth. Proving himself was a never-ceasing endeavour. As his more secure colleague, Ben Schoeman, was to put it, 'Before he became Prime Minister, he was a fanatical Afrikaner. He always spoke about *our* ancestors, *our* glorious past and *our* Afrikaner heroes, although he was not born an Afrikaner. It was as if he wanted to convince himself and his supporters of his Afrikanership'.[4]

White unity would then be on the Afrikaner's terms. He would be the senior partner in an ethnic alliance which his English-speaking counterpart would have to accept because of their common fear of the black majority of South Africans on a predominantly black continent. Inevitably, it could only be an uneasy alliance. The immediate memory of past divisions and animosities could not be expunged at a stroke. Being both an Afrikaner nationalist and a South African with white unity at heart, required an effort. If a white nation was to be forged in the crucible of a post-colonial Africa it would take many a long year for the process to reach completion.

This was the first new direction Verwoerd took after he became Prime Minister: the active pursuit of the Nationalist ideal of a republic, which was not to be the exclusivist Afrikaner republic as traditionally conceived but an exclusivist white republic in which Afrikaner and English-speakers would enjoy equal rights, but no one else. As Verwoerd was to make it remarkably clear, however willing he was to deviate from the pursuit of the narrow Afrikaner republic, it would still be in its very essence a white republic, where Africans, coloureds and Indians could never enjoy full citizenship. His inability to think in any categories except those imposed by race was to be a hallmark of all his policies. The far-from-liberal Ben Schoeman observed that 'Verwoerd, with all his exceptional ability, was in many respects unbelievably short-sighted, especially where issues of race were concerned'.[5]

At first Verwoerd had to work at establishing his authority in the cabinet, where most of his colleagues had supported one of his rivals. He himself was not one of the most senior ministers. But he now displayed an unexpected facet of his personality: a willingness to charm and be conciliatory where before he had excelled in taking stands and refusing to budge. Schoeman was one of his most bitter enemies in the cabinet and was quite sure that his last days as a minister had arrived. When Verwoerd asked him to forget the past and remain at his post, assuring him that he was virtually indispensable, no one could have been more astounded than Schoeman. He stayed, at first constantly expecting Verwoerd to commit 'some or other reckless action'. But eventually Schoeman decided that he had been wrong:

I gradually discovered, rather to my surprise, that Verwoerd had much charm and an attractive personality, which all the years I never wanted to notice ... Verwoerd was now a completely different person from the man whom I knew since 1940 and could not bear in my sight. Gradually my antagonism disappeared and it was only now, after all the years of quarrelling, that we would learn to know and appreciate one another.[6]

Verwoerd came to establish his complete ascendancy over his colleagues. He was without rival in the cabinet in combining a superior intelligence, force of personality, ideological conviction and sheer restless energy. It was an unbeatable combination. Then also he appointed new ministers who were beholden to him and who could be relied upon not to be excessively independent (even if they were not all excessively able). The cabinet became little more than his creature, ever ready to follow his dictates.

But that was to come later. As new leader Verwoerd did not only have to cope with possibly recalcitrant colleagues. The Opposition and its press regarded him with bitter hostility and distrust. The *Cape Times* reacted to Verwoerd's election with a typically sour comment: 'As Minister of Native Affairs he has been an autocrat, contemptuous of criticism and public opinion. He is a declared racialist and champion of *baasskap*. He is an advocate of what he calls "strong leadership" ...'.[7] The United Party tried to unsettle Verwoerd, but with little success. When it attacked him for a supposed breach of faith on a relatively minor issue, Verwoerd gave better than he got. Acting on the principle that attack was the best form of defence, a rule which suited him exceptionally well, Verwoerd explained in detail why it was his critics who had made fools of themselves. He accused them of conducting a 'smear campaign' unworthy of decent people. This was the United Party's first full-scale attack on the new Prime Minister. Like all the others which came later, it failed abjectly.

An Opposition journalist who observed Verwoerd from the press gallery has described how he affected his opponents:

Dr Verwoerd – although he did not have a good speaking voice (it often tended to tenseness and too high a pitch) seemed to mesmerize the Opposition with the sheer strength of conviction and the authority of his personality behind his words – physically and politically. Even professional pressmen in the gallery, who had heard him often over the years as Minister of Native Affairs in both the House of Assembly and the Senate, were filled with a new respect and awe for the man's debating abilities. Opposition English language newspaper correspondents, in discussing his performance in the press rooms among themselves, used expressions such as 'talked circles around them' and 'slaughtered' and 'demolished' the Opposition.[8]

Verwoerd, it appears, took to his elevation as if he had been groomed for it all his life. Not only did his opponents fail to unsettle him, but he maintained the same intense work routine as he had when he was Minister of Native Affairs. Members of his cabinet found it disconcerting when he displayed a detailed knowledge, often better than theirs, of what was happening in their own departments. Another facet of his personality became prominent. He insisted on doing things his way. A Nationalist journalist was to comment later: 'If Dr Verwoerd did not wish a thing to be done, fine, then he did not wish it to be done and then it was only by way of high exception that it was done. If he wished a thing to be done, then it had to be done in his time and in his way, and not otherwise'.[9]

The autocratic insistence that his was the only correct way is nowhere better illustrated than in the policy change for which Verwoerd is best remembered. As Minister of Native Affairs Verwoerd had always insisted that it was not the Government's policy to grant independence to the various black 'nations' or ethnic groups. It was enough, he seemed to believe, if traditional authority was consolidated in the reserves and the black migration to the urban areas was controlled. When Afrikaner intellectuals, worried about the patent lack of any moral basis to Nationalist policy, spoke, in the most tentative terms, about greater autonomy for the black areas, they were put in their place smartly.

One such was the Rev. Willem Landman, at the time chairman of the pro-Government South African Bureau of Racial Affairs (Sabra). At the beginning of Verwoerd's premiership, Landman went on a speaking trip through South Africa in which one of his most important themes was that the status of the reserves would grow. He did not exclude the possibility of autonomy (*selfstandigheid*).[10] Landman did not reckon on Verwoerd, who promptly intervened, in a manner which was to become quite familiar. He insisted that what Landman was saying had nothing to do with Nationalist policy. He made awesome threats of what he would do if Landman did not obey. Eventually, and reluctantly, the Reverend abandoned the rest of his journey.

Shortly afterwards, however, Verwoerd announced in the House of Assembly a policy identical to that which he had forbidden Landman to propagate. This was his famous 'new vision', the policy of independent black homelands. All the evidence suggests that Verwoerd had changed his mind in a hurry about what the political future for Africans should be. As late as March 1959 his Secretary of Native Affairs, Werner Eiselen, denied that the 'Bantu areas' would ever become independent. In a widely-cited article Eiselen stated that it seemed to him 'and to most members of the European electorate ... that the maintenance of white political supremacy over the country as a whole' was 'a *sine qua non* for racial peace and prosperity in South Africa'. He believed it unlikely that Parliament would ever grant the reserves a degree of administrative autonomy which would exceed the 'actual surrender of sovereignty by the European trustee.' Still, these were 'problems for the future'.[11]

Eiselen and Verwoerd were the closest of colleagues. They were at one in their vision of the future South Africa, in their acceptance of separation between black and white as the only guarantee of white survival. Up till now there had never been a hint that apartheid could come to mean anything less than continued white control over the lives of blacks. And it is inconceivable that Eiselen would have written what he did if it had not had the approval of Verwoerd himself.

In January 1959 the Prime Minister was talking in somewhat different terms from those of the past about the future of the black areas, but he was keeping his options open by being deliberately vague. It seemed that it could well be a nettle to be grasped by future generations:

> We are giving the Bantu as our wards every opportunity in their areas to move along a road of development by which they can progress in accordance with their ability. And if it should happen that in the future they progress to a very advanced level, the people of those future times will have to consider in what way their relationship must be reorganised.[12]

Yet the tone was unmistakably new. Verwoerd described the territorial authorities which had been created as:

> independent bodies in the first stage of development ... We must ensure that the outside world realises, and that the Bantu realises, that a new period is dawning, a period in which the white man will move away from discrimination against the Bantu as far as his own areas are concerned, that the White man is leading him through the first stage of full development.[13]

Verwoerd's change of course, undefined as it was, caused nothing but trouble for the Opposition, the United Party. For long it had been polarised between conservatives, differing little from the Nationalists in their views on race, and a far smaller group of relative liberals, who had been urging a kind of enlightened paternalism on their colleagues, involving a less rigid application of segregation but not by any means abandoning the principle of white supremacy. The conservatives seized on Verwoerd's statement as a gift from the gods, a splendid opportunity to make racist propaganda at the Government's expense and to portray Verwoerd as that most improbable of all creatures, a dangerous liberal. The already wide rift in the United Party became wider still, hastening the split which Nationalist politicians and journalists had for long been announcing as inevitable.

By now Verwoerd had made up his mind. He had come to accept that black territories could become completely independent. In May 1959 the Government introduced a Promotion of Bantu Self-Government Bill, which proposed to abolish the existing system of representation of blacks by whites in the central Parliament. He had managed to persuade himself that the system of territorial authorities was sufficiently developed to justify the abolition of

Native Representation in Parliament. Verwoerd was displeased with the seven white MPs and Senators whom the Africans had sent to Parliament to represent them. He claimed that they represented only 'small cliques of agitators and their Native friends', a view he might perhaps have modified if they had been less unrelenting in their criticism of him and his government.

There might have been a certain logic in holding that Native Representation was incompatible with the principle of separate development. Yet it was also logical that Native Representation should be retained until the black areas were actually independent. This was the argument of one exceedingly rare specimen, namely, a dissident Nationalist MP, Japie Basson. It was also a view expressed more discreetly by others in the Nationalist caucus, but before a final conclusion had been reached Verwoerd simply announced in Parliament that Native Representation would be abolished. In its high-handedness the statement was typical of Verwoerd, just as its docile acceptance was typical of the Nationalist caucus. The one exception was Basson, who voiced his criticisms in the House of Assembly and was duly expelled from the caucus by his colleagues.

Yet if Native Representation was to go, it could only be because Verwoerd had an alternative and 'better' political deal in store for blacks. The days of old-time *baasskap* were now held to be past. Apartheid had to acquire that moral foundation about which so much had been spoken and written and so little had been done. Verwoerd now embraced the full logic of the course upon which he had set out only such a short time ago: 'If it is within the power of the Bantu, and if the territories in which he now lives can develop to full independence, it will develop in that way.' Confronted with the contradictory words of his underling, Eiselen, he explained that they had been 'written months before the statement I made at the beginning of the year'.[14]

The Promotion of Bantu Self-Government Act provided 'for the gradual development of self-governing Bantu national units,' as well as 'for direct consultation between the Government of the Union and the said national units in regard to matters affecting the interests of such national units'. The Act recognised eight black national units. Economically, all of them were profoundly backward. Most were territorially fragmented. The least unpromising was the Transkei in the Eastern Cape, the national unit of most of the Xhosa; it had the advantage of being large and compact, but was deeply impoverished and likely to remain so for some considerable time. Five white Commissioners-General would serve as links between the Government and the ethnic units, which were reduced to five for administrative and political purposes. For urban Africans too there was no escape from the new dispensation: they would be linked to their territorial authorities through tribal representatives appointed by the new political units.

In years to come the Nationalists were to make much of the supposed moral basis of their policies, in contrast with those of the United Party, which admittedly had nothing to offer Africans except a less harsh version of the white supremacy which Strijdom, Verwoerd and their followers had been enforcing with freewheeling gusto. They went on about it as if they had suddenly been given a new toy of which they could not exhaust the delights. The Nationalists never mentioned that their policies towards the coloureds and the Indians remained exactly that *baasskap* which they now claimed to find so ethically repugnant in the programme of the official Opposition towards Africans. Nor did they ever admit that, in terms of their own logic, apartheid between 1948 and Verwoerd's announcement of his 'new vision' in 1959 was devoid of any moral foundation whatever.

The year 1959 is usually seen as a watershed in the evolution of Nationalist policy. In a sense it clearly was, but the break with the past should not be exaggerated. Government practice changed very little afterwards, except that apartheid during the 1960s was enforced far more harshly than before. Once the principle of eventual political independence for the various black ethnic groups had been accepted, it seemed that the Government felt freer than ever to assert the foreignness of Africans in the 87 per cent of South Africa which was reserved for the white population. The black areas, or homelands as they now came to be called, continued to stagnate economically. The Government made only minimal attempts to redirect investment towards these regions. Verwoerd had of course long before prohibited investment by white capitalists in the reserves, on grounds which revealed only the feeblest grasp of economics. In political terms the homelands fared no better, making scarcely discernible progress. Such independence as they had from Pretoria was mainly exercised by compliant traditional leaders, fully aware that displays of self-reliance could not be carried to extremes if they wished to retain the favour of their white masters.

It was a theoretical break with the past, but hardly more. It did not follow that the 'new vision' was a thing of no account, a mere rationalisation for continued *baasskap*. The official acceptance by the Government that blacks were, in principle, the equals of whites came as a major and disagreeable shock to many, perhaps most, Nationalists. But there could be no reneging on the new policy. Ideas have consequences: once the National Party accepted the principle of equality between black and white, however hedged about with tendentious qualifications concerning the necessity of being equal in separate areas, it was set upon a course which eroded the very foundations of apartheid. For it was plain that if separate areas were not practicable then the logic of the new policy pointed to the acceptance of a common society with racial equality as a cornerstone. It was only reluctantly, belatedly, with the speed of a tortoise and the vision of an ostrich that the National Party moved in this direction. But the new policy and the pressure of economic forces which they could not control pushed the Nationalists inexorably towards an integrated South Africa.

The evidence suggests that the policy of Bantustans, as unfriendly critics described the homelands, had not been gestating for long in the fertile mind of Verwoerd. It seems that after he became Prime Minister he became impressed with the urgency of taking a new direction and did so accordingly. As Minister of Native Affairs Verwoerd had denied emphatically that his policies would lead to independent black states. The article by his mouthpiece Eiselen, also denying the possibility, had been written late in 1958, probably shortly after Verwoerd became Prime Minister. It follows that when he succeeded Strijdom, Verwoerd himself was still thinking along traditional *baasskap* lines.

As old-time supporters of white domination might have put it, it was interfering foreigners at the United Nations that put Verwoerd into such a funk. He had been impressed with the stories told by

Eric Louw, South Africa's truculent Foreign Minister, of the hostility towards apartheid he had to face at the UN. Inevitably, Verwoerd as Prime Minister had to take a wider view of what was needed for Afrikaner survival than he did when he was simply a minister. He came to realise that changing times required changing policies, or at least that old wine required new bottles. In essence, the 'new vision' of Verwoerd was a response to an international environment that had altered beyond recognition since 1948. As he was to say in his earlier speech in January 1959:

> We cannot govern without taking into account the tendencies in the world and in Africa. We must have regard to them. Our policy must take them into account. And we can only take them into account and safeguard the white man's control over our country if we move in the direction of separation – separation in the political sphere at any rate.[15]

In brief, Verwoerd was responding to rapidly changing global circumstances. Bantu homelands were no previously-designed masterplan for the future which could now be sprung on a worshipping party and press simply because he was able to impose his long views on lesser mortals.

Decidedly, the new course had little, if anything, to do with domestic pressures. The average Nationalist voter had limited awareness of what was going on in the wider world. At most there was a generalised resentment of hypocritical foreigners who should have been getting their own houses in order before pointing their fingers at a country attempting to do its Christian duty by primitive people not yet ready for the vote. With no pressure from their own constituents there could be little from Nationalist MPs that apartheid should acquire a more human face. There had, it is true, been protestations from well-meaning members of the Afrikaner intelligentsia that Government race policies should offer its victims rather more than unremitting discrimination. However, they counted for little and could always be told to shut up, like the unfortunate Rev. Landman.

Verwoerd's announcement must have required some courage. The electoral risk could not have appeared negligible, for the United Party was straining at the bit to extract the last drop of racist sentiment from Verwoerd's new-found 'liberalism'. The tone of statements to come had been set after Verwoerd's January statement when Douglas Mitchell, the extreme right wing leader of the United Party in the mainly English-speaking Natal, declared: 'The Government intends selling Oom Piet van der Merwe's farm to the Kaffirs'.[16]

Divided as it was between its large conservative majority and a relatively liberal minority, the United Party finally split at its congress in August 1959. This came about after a determined attempt by the right wing to get rid of its liberal encumbrance, so enabling it to make *swart gevaar* (black menace) propaganda to its heart's content.

The issue was the purchase of more land for black occupation. Douglas Mitchell proposed that the United Party oppose additional land being bought for Bantustans as it would contribute to the eventual 'Balkanisation' of South Africa. When the United Party returned to power there would be nothing wrong with buying land for Africans as it would remain part of a single, undivided South Africa. The 'left' could not swallow such transparent racism and opportunism, as it was not intended to. Eleven MPs resigned and went on to form the Progressive Party.

The Progressives had no doubt taken an admirable moral stand, but if they believed that white South Africans were interested in an enlightened alternative to apartheid they had made a huge mistake. With one exception, they lost all their seats in the 1961 general election. For many years after that their electoral support was derisory, a fitting enough comment on the willingness of English-speaking whites to relinquish any of their privileges. However, if the United Party thought that a splendid opportunity to outbid the Nationalists in the reactionary stakes had now arrived, it too had made a substantial error. It was not really plausible to portray a man with Verwoerd's record of keeping Africans in their place as a leopard who had suddenly changed his spots. Whatever the official rationale of apartheid had become, Nationalist voters were hardly likely to change their allegiance unless confronted with solid evidence that the Government had overnight become less committed to white rule. The evidence was not produced, because it did not exist. The United Party's decline was to continue, reflected in one disastrous election result after another.

In one respect however the United Party's reinvigorated racism probably placed a powerful restraint on the Government's willingness to proceed more rapidly with its homelands policy. Verwoerd himself had always been sensitive to criticism from the strong right wing in the National Party. Indeed, when he contested the Prime Ministership he was widely seen as the candidate of the right, and for this reason expected to win. He, above all, knew to whom he was beholden. His own instincts in any event were to hasten slowly with the political and economic development of the black areas. When he was minister he had plenty to say about the wonders of slow, organic growth. Verwoerd's natural inclinations could only have been reinforced by the possibility of losing conservative votes to the Opposition. There is evidence that he was genuinely concerned about the impact on loyal Nationalists of propaganda that 'he was carving up the country into small Bantu states'.[17] Whatever effects the United Party's agitation about 'Balkanisation' had, it must have retarded even further an already tardy process.

The Bantu Self-Government Act was the major item of apartheid legislation of 1959. It was run a close second by the Extension of University Education Act. As with so many other Government laws, its wording would have been savoured by George Orwell. As long ago as 1955, the Nationalists had announced their intention to enforce racial separation at universities. In spite of public uproar and vehement protests from the English-speaking universities, both segregated and non-segregated, the Nationalist resolve never faltered. In August 1958, just returned with a much enlarged majority and hence still more determined to ignore all dissent, the Government introduced the Extension of University Education Bill.

Up till then South Africa had a few universities which regarded themselves as 'open'. They were the Universities of Cape Town and of the Witwatersrand, each of which had a small minority of non-white students, about three to four hundred out of a total student body of five to six thousand. There was also the University of Natal, which had its own version of 'openness', namely, a campus specially reserved for 'non-Europeans'. UCT and Wits took some pride in not practicing apartheid, but in truth they applied a version of their own. Non-white students could attend lectures, but found that social events and sports facilities were closed to them. These were necessary concessions, the university authorities appeared to believe, to 'the customs and conventions' of the affluent English-speaking communities from where most of their students came. Logically enough, when the Government made known its intention to 'extend university education', the authorites took their stand on university autonomy, not on segregation, which they knew perfectly well how to apply on their own, without instructions from the Government.

The struggle was long and acrimonious, but of course the Government had its way. In addition to Fort Hare in the Eastern Cape, up till then the main source of black university graduates and now reserved for the Xhosa, the new law provided for the establishment of four ethnic university colleges, reserved for coloured, Indian, Zulu and Sotho-Tswana students. Not inappropriately, they came to be known as 'bush colleges.' Once these institutions had been established any non-white student wishing to register at an 'open' university would have to obtain the permission, not lightly granted as it turned out, of the Minister of Education. The Act applied not only to Africans, but to all non-white students. It was however the logical culmination of the policy of educational separateness, pursued with such unremitting zeal since the Bantu Education Act of 1953.

Generally, neither supporters nor opponents of the measure had come off well. The Nationalists had demonstrated anew their obsession with imposing apartheid wherever their ingenuity took them, even in higher education. The 'open' universities, the Opposition and its press protested in the most outraged manner, but the grounds of their outrage had little to do with discrimination. They were offended because English-speaking institutions were under attack, not because they found discrimination so repellent. It was reminiscent of the days of the Torch Commando and the High Court of Parliament. The protesters were also concerned about the circumventing of the constitution and the possibility that the status of the English language might be treated in the same way as the Government was proposing to treat the coloureds. Injustices to victims of apartheid did not feature prominently in the grievances of most white opponents of Government policy.

The 1950s ended with the Nationalists riding high. They were securely in power and were imposing apartheid as if chickens would never come home to roost. They had succeeded in scattering their enemies, both white and black. For it was not only the United Party which had reason to be demoralised when the decade neared its end. The African nationalist movement was also going through hard times. Discontent amongst blacks was overt and continuous, both in the rural and urban areas. Yet the ANC seemed incapable of making any headway against rulers only too eager to turn to force when given an excuse.

Within the ANC the critics of what was known as the Congress Alliance became increasingly outspoken. In particular, they were against the ANC's close links with the Communist Party, in the form of the Congress of Democrats. The Africanists, as they were known, rejected co-operation with other racial groups, nor were they prepared to be diverted by what they regarded as irrelevant issues. In particular, they objected to the commitment to nationalisation which had found its way into the Freedom Charter under the inspiration of the Communists.

Proof of ANC impotence was accumulating all the time. In 1958 the leadership under Albert Luthuli supported a stay-at-home strike of workers, timed to coincide with the general election. Luthuli had allowed himself to be persuaded by the ANC left wing, which imagined that this was the opportunity to recapture some of the prestige that had fled in the previous years. They miscalculated. Few Africans were willing to risk their jobs for an enterprise which promised so meagre a reward. The collapse of the stay-at-home strike provided further evidence, if it was needed, of the ANC's inability to mobilise black masses against the Government.

For the Africanists the fault lay in the failure of nerve of the leadership, which was too flaccid, too caught up in a discredited strategy of multiracialism, to break out on its own with a direct appeal to the oppressed African masses. The militants, drawn mainly from the organisation's youth wing, rejected all co-operation with whites and Communists. Blacks had to achieve their own liberation, which could only be delayed indefinitely by allying themselves with groups whose interests differed so fundamentally from theirs.

In November 1958 the Africanists, led by Robert Sobukwe, walked out of the Transvaal conference of the ANC. In March the following year they formed the Pan Africanist Congress, with Sobukwe as President. Unashamedly exclusivist, the PAC was an entirely more aggressive organisation than its parent body, although it claimed to believe in 'political democracy as understood in the West'. Nor was it inclined to indulge in fancy talk about nonviolence. The guiding principle of the PAC was 'Ourselves alone': only blacks could throw off the bondage of apartheid.

The ANC was at first happy about the exit of these raucous dissidents, but its joy was soon tempered. It found that it was being outbid for support in the black townships by the activism and the demagogy of the PAC. There was just one way for the ANC to go if it wished to avoid losing more support: it had to demonstrate its own radicalism. The uncompromising rhetoric which emerged from the competition between the two African nationalist groups confirmed white convictions that the only alternative to white domination was black domination.

In all, 1960 was shaping up to be a momentous year. It would commemorate the 50th anniversary of the Union of South Africa, the outcome of the deliberations of an exclusively white National Convention. For the white population it was intended to be a year of celebration, although speculation had been growing that Verwoerd would use the occasion to announce a referendum on a republic. For Africans however there was nothing to celebrate. For them 1910 was the year of the great betrayal, when Britain saw fit to entrust the fate of South Africa's black population to a white minority, no more than a fifth of the total population.

The ANC decided in December 1959 to mark the anniversary of Union with massive demonstrations against the pass laws. They were timed for 31 March 1960. But the PAC also had protests to stage. It was determined to get in first and do so in a way which would upstage the ANC totally. Neither the ANC nor the PAC, nor the white population, had any notion of the turbulence that 1960 would bring.

CHAPTER SEVEN

Winds of Change

When he became Prime Minister, Verwoerd had announced that achieving a republic would be one of his top priorities. For him it had become a matter of urgency, linked intimately, as he now saw it, with the settlement of the racial problem along Nationalist lines. As he was to recall later:

> During the last few years before Advocate Strijdom's lamented passing, we had all begun to realise that if the republic was not created within the next five-year period, the time would be lost forever. There were those who considered that greater unity of the people and more progress with the non-white question should be effected first. Advocate Strijdom and I, however, were among those who believed exactly the opposite. We were satisfied that the republic should come first, and then the language groups would grow closer and then tackle the problem together.[1]

It was this sense of urgency which explains why Verwoerd decided to press the issue at a time when it seemed that he could be heading for defeat if the electorate voted on the republic. The results of the 1958 general election suggested that the United Party still had the support of a small majority of the white voters. An enquiry conducted by secretaries of National Party branches throughout the country in the latter half of 1959 only confirmed the impression. Verwoerd had instructed them to calculate, on the available evidence, what would be the likely result of a referendum on a republic. They produced tidings of little joy. Their findings indicated that if 90 per cent of the white voters participated in a referendum the anti-republicans would win by sixty to seventy thousand votes. But Verwoerd was not a bit put out, if the memories of his admirers can be trusted. 'Fellows,' said the leader, 'we are going ahead and we are going to win with a big majority'.[2]

There are republics and republics. Verwoerd was quite sure what kind of republic he preferred. During the heady days of the Second World War he had helped draw up a constitution for an authoritarian Afrikaner republic which would have no truck with that ancient enemy, the British Empire. But, whatever his own preferences, they never became Nationalist policy. Malan was far too astute, and lukewarm about a republic, to endorse so frankly extremist a document. Yet over the years it seemed that Verwoerd's views changed little. At the end of the 1959 parliamentary session Verwoerd told his far-right cabinet colleague, Albert Hertzog, that he himself strongly favoured a republic outside the Commonwealth, but that he knew many Nationalists would be hostile. For the sake of expediency a republic might initially have had to remain in the Commonwealth. Similarly, he had no doubt that the Afrikaners would prefer a president chosen by the people, but he could not be sure that such an elected president would be 'one of our people'.[3] Presumably Verwoerd had in mind the delicate balance between Nationalists and non-Nationalists, who could not be relied upon to help elect a president with the right ideological credentials.

When Verwoerd spoke to Hertzog again, on 10 January the following year, he had made up his mind. The republic could no longer be delayed, he believed, for propaganda against it would only become more intemperate; voters could easily become persuaded that a republic would damage the South African economy. The form of government would at first remain unchanged, for it was probable that a commitment to a republic like that of Paul Kruger would alienate many voters in the Cape. Similarly, whatever the sentiments of Nationalists in the north, the republic should remain in the Commonwealth, certain as it was that English-speakers would be violently hostile to one which proposed to cut this largely symbolic tie with Britain.

The republic had long been debated, but few thought that the issue would be settled in 1960. The Cape Nationalist daily, *Die Burger*, usually well-informed about inner party developments, reported on 14 January that a 'tame' parliamentary session was expected in view of the Union festival later that year. *Die Burger* anticipated that only by 1963 would the republic be feasible.

Verwoerd's decision to proceed with the issue was fully supported by his cabinet. It was agreed that the white voters would be asked to decide in a referendum in which no other issues would be considered. In the Nationalist caucus the news was received with frenzied acclaim. As Verwoerd's hagiographer put it: 'They who had so long yearned for the fulfilment of the greatest ideal of their people, but who had repeatedly been told in the past that the time was not yet 'ripe', were now suddenly given news which filled their hearts with the greatest joy and enthusiasm. Verwoerd's words were truly sweet music to their ears'.[4]

Both the official Opposition, the United Party, and its more liberal offshoot, the Progressive Party, were taken utterly, and disagreeably, by surprise. When the Governor-General opened the session he had not said a word about the prospect of a republican referendum in his speech from the throne. On the day that Verwoerd informed his caucus about the cabinet decision, the leader of the Opposition, Sir De Villiers Graaff, introduced his customary motion of 'no confidence' in the Government. Unlike his motion of the previous year this one contained no reference to a republic. When Verwoerd rose to reply the next day, he proceeded to confound his opponents by asserting: 'The problem which now comes within the realm of practical politics is the attainment of a republic in South Africa.'[5]

The United Party had no desire to make a stand on the republic. Most of its supporters were English-speakers, who could be expected to resist breaking off South Africa's constitutional ties with the British monarchy, but by and large their commitment to the Crown did not match the passionate feelings of Afrikaners about the republic. And many supporters of the United Party were Afrikaans-speaking, traditionalist followers of the party of Smuts. Their loyalties would inevitably face severe strain if the United Party opposed a constitutional change which many of them were bound to welcome. For good reasons, the Official Opposition did not want a fight on the republican issue.

But now it had no choice. The United Party would have to make up its mind, which did not usually come easily. However, even if many of its English-speaking followers did not care especially about the monarchy, they did know that they did not want the kind of republic which it appeared Verwoerd wished to impose on them. Whatever the inclinations of the leadership of the United Party, however apathetic it may have been about the British Crown, it knew that it could do only one thing. It had to oppose the republic as strongly as it could.

Verwoerd naturally saw it differently. As far as he was concerned it was not a political issue at all. He was reasonableness itself. He stressed that the proposed republic would involve at most a change in the head of state. The monarch would be replaced by a president, who, unlike those of the Boer republics of the past, would have no executive power. He stressed that the language rights of the white communities would be fully protected. Although he was not prepared to say whether it was Government policy that South Africa should remain within the Commonwealth, Verwoerd gave 'a clear and unequivocal promise' that he would make it known before the referendum. According to him then, a supporter of the Opposition could vote for the republic and still be in no way committed to Nationalist policies. Similarly, a Nationalist could reject the republic and still remain a perfectly good Nationalist (although it is difficult to imagine that Verwoerd really believed so strange a thing). Such ingratiating talk made sense. He knew that Nationalists would be virtually unanimous in their enthusiasm for the proposed change. It was not so certain that followers of the Opposition would reject a republic uniformly.

It was of course a political matter, inescapably so. Verwoerd had made it quite plain that only whites could decide the constitutional future of South Africa. Theoretically, Africans were heading for separate freedoms, while Indians, traditionally seen by South African whites as an 'alien' element which did not quite belong, had never enjoyed the franchise. Only recently, however, there had been coloured voters on the Cape common roll. Even on fairly conservative assumptions there seemed no good case for them being denied a say in the constitutional fate of their country. Both the United Party and the Progressives had been especially critical of the exclusion of coloureds from the referendum. Verwoerd, however, would have none of it. His reason was that historically the republic had been an issue between the white communities; the coloureds had not been involved. It was scarcely a respectable argument for keeping coloureds out of the referendum, but for Verwoerd and his willing followers it was enough. As he was later to announce in the most explicit and most crass manner, the South African nation was a white nation. And he was undoubtedly aware that the coloureds would have grasped any chance to vote in the referendum as a heaven-sent opportunity to reject the Nationalists and their apartheid.

There was another reason why the republican issue was profoundly political. In spite of Verwoerd's special pleading, there could be no doubt that a rejection of the republic would be a most damaging blow to the Nationalists and, above all, to the prestige of their supremely confident and doctrinaire leader. It was a chance too good to miss. For years the United Party had been complaining about the iniquities of the delimitation system, which had allowed the Nationalists to come to power on a minority vote. It insisted that despite increasing Nationalist majorities at the polls, most voters continued to support the United Party. Verwoerd's own private information was that at the 1958 general election the United Party still commanded majority support. Even if the Government did not fall, the rejection of the republic would be widely interpreted, at home and abroad, as a vote of no-confidence in Nationalist policies. It would be fully exposed as a regime which had only minority support within the white minority. From the start the United Party refused to swallow the 'non-political' bait Verwoerd dangled before its eyes. Nor was there a doubt that the Progressive Party, which looked for its support to the more affluent English-speaking urban constituencies, could take any other course.

Yet Verwoerd had seized the initiative and was to maintain it for the whole of the referendum campaign. The Opposition had been caught off balance. It was not to recover from this body blow and from then on it fought on the defensive. The republic was after all a highly emotive issue to most Afrikaners. Particularly in the Transvaal and the Orange Free State, it represented the culmination of years of striving, the very epitome of realised nationhood and independence of Britain. For English-speakers outside Natal (sometimes described as 'the last outpost of Empire') adherence to the British monarchy could only rarely arouse the same emotional fervour. For them the choice meant more pragmatic issues, like the possible economic consequences of exclusion from the Commonwealth and, of course, that splendid opportunity of 'dishing' a government which over the years had shown scant regard for their institutions and culture.

Amongst the Afrikaners Verwoerd's stature rose to monumental heights. Devoid of populist flair, conspicuously lacking the common touch, addicted to pedantic and long-winded expositions of his invariably correct policies, Verwoerd had until then inspired respect, indeed awe, but little affection. It was ability, force of personality and, let it be said, sheer humourless fanaticism which had brought him to where he was. His initiative on the republic changed all that, immediately and permanently. Verwoerd was now seen as the man who had at a stroke brought the coveted ideal within reach. He became an unlikely figure: a folk hero, no less. He was the subject of popular adulation, a man endowed with virtually super-human qualities. For Verwoerd, as unremitting a super-Afrikaner as only an outsider could be, such ecstatic acceptance by his adopted people must have been supremely gratifying. Yet the risk was great. It was that of total humiliation, which would unavoidably follow defeat in the referendum. The chances of failure were more than even, as Verwoerd well knew after he received the reports from the secretaries of the party branches. His decision to proceed with the referendum was a calculated risk, taken in the full knowledge that his own political future could suffer irreparable damage.

Having decided, Verwoerd still took care to minimise his risk. His predecessor, Strijdom, had been outraged when the *Cape Times* suggested that a republic could be proclaimed on the basis of a majority of one vote. He publicly committed himself to a previously specified majority which was essential to the establishment of a republic. As Verwoerd explained later, it was something about which he and Strijdom could never agree. He believed that:

> ... if one stated a figure, say 20 000 or 40 000, the sceptics and opponents would immediately name something like 100 000. In this way one merely lands in an argument over numbers. Should you propose a two-thirds majority, opponents would begin binding themselves to a three-quarters majority – all to make the achievement impossible. Therefore I always pleaded for the principle of a bare majority, which one would have to admit meant a majority of one.[6]

When he announced the referendum Verwoerd accordingly informed the House of Assembly that a majority of one either way would be decisive.

Not usually noted for his flexibility, Verwoerd now also did an unheard of thing: he changed his mind in response to criticism from a political opponent. On 20 January he made it clear that the voters of the mandated territory of South West Africa would not take part in the referendum, as it was not constitutionally part of South Africa. Sir De Villiers Graaff opportunistically criticised the decision, pleading for the right of South West African voters to help decide their own destiny. Verwoerd promptly declared that he had reconsidered: white South West Africans would indeed be allowed to participate in the referendum. The *Cape Argus*, the only Opposition newspaper in South Africa which suggested that there might be something to say for the republic, commented: 'It is clever politics but dangerously lacking in scruple'.[7]

The stage had been set for an all-white referendum. The country was still deep in acrimonious controversy when it was bluntly confronted with a decision which would directly affect the republican issue and set the stage for the future all South Africans were now entering. The British Prime Minister, Harold Macmillan, arrived in Cape Town at the end of January, on the last leg of an extensive tour of the continent. He had come to make an historic announcement, that the ways of Britain and South Africa must part because to the British the costs of association with apartheid had become a global embarrassment. That was the gist of the message, although a proper British gentleman like Macmillan would not have dreamt of resorting to phraseology so crude.

A crucial feature of Macmillan's whole performance was that it was designed as a most unpleasant surprise for his hosts. They knew nothing about what he was going to tell them. The British went to immense pains to maintain secrecy. The speech had been drafted two months before by the British High Commissioner in South Africa, Sir John Maud, who had visited London for that purpose. It had been rewritten and touched up constantly on Macmillan's tour of Africa. In South Africa the British Prime Minister was the personal guest of his South African counterpart at his official residence of Groote Schuur. Macmillan's determination to cause a sensation was shown in his deliberate flouting of the normal rules of courtesy: he neither gave Verwoerd an advance copy of his speech nor did he give him any idea of what he was going to say. Verwoerd's private secretary made a frantic last-minute attempt to obtain a copy from one of Macmillan's aides, but received a polite brush-off.

When Macmillan stood up to address the combined Houses of Parliament on 3 February 1960, it soon became clear why there had been so obsessive a concern with secrecy. To white South Africans, secure in their conviction that white rule would last forever, it amounted to an abrupt introduction to the harsh realities of international *realpolitik*. In his languid Edwardian manner Macmillan left his audience in no doubt that Britain was dissociating itself from South Africa's policies and was siding instead with the emerging nationalisms of Africa, presumably representing the irresistible currents of history. Afrikaner nationalism, he suggested astutely, was part of this trend, a forerunner of what was now happening in the rest of Africa. He used a phrase which was to become famous:

> The most striking of all the impressions I have formed since I left London a month ago is of the strength of this African national consciousness. In different places it may take different forms, but it is happening everywhere. The wind of change is blowing through the continent. Whether we like it or not, this growth of national consciousness is a political fact. We must all accept it as a fact. Our national policies must take account of it. Of course, you understand this as well as anyone. You

are sprung from Europe, the home of nationalism. And here in Africa you have yourselves created a full nation – a new nation. Indeed, in the history of our times yours will be recorded as the first of the African nationalisms.

Perhaps somewhat misleadingly, Macmillan stated that the following had been British colonial policy:

> Not only to raise the material standards of living but to create a society which respects the rights of individuals – a society in which men are given the opportunity to grow to their full stature, and that must in our view include the opportunity to have an increasing share in political power and responsibility; a society in which individual merit, and individual merit alone, is the criterion for man's advancement whether political or economic.

If white South Africans had not realised it before, they did now, as the distinguished performer then still known as Supermac spelt it out for them: Britain would be guided by a hard-headed sense of its own interests in the councils of the nations. The apartheid regime could no longer count on the kind of British support which had seemed so reliable, if increasingly grudging, in the past. As Macmillan put it in his high-toned way:

> As a fellow member of the Commonwealth, it is our earnest desire to give South Africa our support and encouragement, but I hope you won't mind my saying frankly that there are some aspects of your policies which make it impossible for us to do this without our own deep convictions about the political destinies of free men, to which in our territories we are trying to give effect.[8]

Only those who knew Verwoerd well, like his private secretary, Fred Barnard, could detect signs of strain as he listened. He was now forced to make an impromptu reply to Macmillan's carefully prepared statement. He did so in a manner which impressed even his opponents.

Verwoerd thanked Macmillan for his frank exposition of British policy, but denied that South Africa was flouting a worldwide trend towards colonial emancipation: 'If our policies were rightly understood we believe ... that it would be seen that what we are attempting to do is not at variance with a new direction in Africa, but is in the fullest accord with it'. He questioned whether Britain was actually pursuing its ends in the most effective manner; it was possible 'that there may be great dangers inherent in (British) policies. The very objective at which you are aiming may be defeated by them'.

Verwoerd's response amounted to a statement which by far the most white South Africans would have endorsed:

> The tendency in Africa for nations to become independent and, at the same time, the need to do justice to all, does not only mean being just to the black man of Africa but also being just to the white man of Africa. We call ourselves Europeans but actually we represent the white man of Africa ... We also see ourselves as part of the white world, a true white state in Africa, notwithstanding the possibility of granting a full future to the black man in our midst.[9]

His words captured perfectly the white man's attitude to being in Africa. He may have lived on the continent but he was not of it. The whites in South Africa saw themselves as a fragment of Europe, detached from their countries of origin, whether the Netherlands or Britain or sometimes France and Germany, but still basically Europeans, with hardly a thing in common with the majority of South Africans, an alien presence in their midst which provided only for their material needs. This view of the world was no doubt only too understandable as a product of the past, but it made for an inflexibility in outlook and response ill-designed for circumstances at home and abroad, which were changing all too rapidly.

Verwoerd had in the meantime made many new South African friends. Even his political opponents had to admire the presence of mind with which he responded to Macmillan's calculated shock and his fluency in stating a point of view with which they could scarcely disagree. Many English-speaking whites felt frankly betrayed. They had believed ingenuously that Britain, when push came to shove, would not turn its back on its very own 'kith and kin' in Africa. It was the Natal leader of the United Party, Douglas Mitchell, who best expressed the disillusionment and sense of loss of those white South Africans who had until then regarded Britain as their spiritual home. In Cape Town, shortly after Macmillan's speech, Mitchell referred to 'the reaction by a large section of the public who believed that Mr Macmillan had said something strange and incredible – that he had announced something they did not think could happen'. He added: 'Why do we find it strange? This one thing is certain. Britain is getting out of Africa ... Britain is out for eternity, you cannot bring her back ...' Mitchell then asked a question which had suddenly acquired a new urgency and relevance: 'What matters is: does the white population survive in this southern part of Africa or not?'[10]

For Verwoerd the winds of change speech brought only political gain. It helped raise him above the confines in which he had to operate as a spokesman for a narrow Nationalist point of view. He now came to be seen increasingly as a defender of the white man's presence in South Africa, as the most formidable obstacle to those policies of retreat and indeed capitulation which the colonial powers seemed to be following with such alacrity and which was illustrated so lamentably in the Congolese disaster in that same year of 1960. It could only help the republican cause. Macmillan had made it quite clear that British policies on South Africa would not be affected by its constitutional status or its membership of the Commonwealth. As Verwoerd was to point out in Parliament the following month:

> It was not the Republic of South Africa that was told, 'We are not going to support you in this respect.' Those words were addressed to the monarchy of South Africa, and yet we have the same monarch as this person from Britain who addressed these words to us. It was a warning therefore that was given to all of us, English-speaking and Afrikaans-speaking, republican and anti-republican. It was made clear to all of us that as far as these matters are concerned, we shall have to stand on our own feet.[11]

Verwoerd himself was not as surprised as his English-speaking fellow-South Africans by the shift in British policy, however unaware he had been of the content of Macmillan's speech. His 'new vision' of 1959 had after all been primarily a response to a changing global situation. He knew that the world was entering an era hostile to all forms of white domination of African and Asian peoples. Even before 1960 Britain had begun to be less supportive of South Africa in international forums. When Supermac spoke about the wind of change in Cape Town he repeated an expression used before by British spokesmen. His declaration of policy and intent only placed an official imprimatur on what Britain had already quietly but irrevocably begun to do. The speech did not mark a sharp break with the past. Yet it was of far greater symbolic importance. From now on white South Africans could not claim that they had no idea that Britannia was no longer on their side.

CHAPTER EIGHT

Sharpeville

As white South Africans were shaping up for another year of intense conflict among themselves, they spared little thought for the African majority. They had few reasons to believe that black unrest would be especially overt or troublesome during this 50th anniversary of the Union of South Africa. That Africans were not taking kindly to apartheid was fairly obvious, but attempts to mobilise protest had almost always ended in failure. After the setbacks of the past it seemed that the Government's perennial willingness to repress dissent would once again frustrate the efforts of black nationalists to stage effective and memorable protests against white supremacy.

The prospects were bleak but the ANC could not let it go by default. As a movement claiming to speak for the oppressed black masses it had to show that it had not forfeited their confidence. At its national conference in Durban in December 1959 the ANC voted by an overwhelming majority to demonstrate against the pass laws on 31 March 1960.

Preparations for the campaign were already advanced when the ANC's new rival, the virulently pro-black PAC, decided to upstage an organisation the leaders of which it had previously denounced as 'paid agents of the Indian merchants'. The National President of the PAC, Robert Sobukwe, announced at a press conference on 18 March that his organisation would launch its own campaign against the pass laws, starting on Monday, 21 March. Members and supporters of the PAC all over South Africa would leave their reference books at home and then present themselves for arrest at the nearest police station. Sobukwe made no secret of their intentions, of which he himself informed the Commissioner of Police. Supposedly, the campaign was to be non-violent. The aim was to fill the country's prisons to overflowing with offenders against the pass laws. Eventually, the PAC leaders seem to have thought naïvely, the system would collapse of its own accord. Their slogan was 'no bail, no defence, no fine.' The intention was to bring 'freedom and independence' to South Africa by 1963.

A white radical journalist, an open supporter of the ANC, commented later:

> I remember reading the news with furious impatience. Sobukwe was deliberately jumping the gun. Of course, the campaign would fail, because the PAC commanded little support in the country. But inevitably the ANC would be forced to postpone its own campaign for several weeks, perhaps months, or launch it in an aftermath of dejection and bewilderment.[1]

Sobukwe's announcement was little regarded by the white population. It could not believe that this obscure offshoot of the ANC would be any more effective than its parent body in shaking the foundations of white rule. The PAC had only been in existence for a year and it had no country-wide organisation behind it, which the ANC did have, in its ramshackle way. On 21 March *Die Burger* reported on its front page that the PAC campaign was expected to gain little support, quoting the reassuring words of a 'senior police officer' that the presence of Saracen armoured cars would prevent the protests from getting out of control.

At some places it did seem that everything was indeed under control. At Philippi, near Cape Town, 15 000 Africans went to the local police station and insisted on being arrested. But the police took only the names of ringleaders and warned them to appear in court the following week, upon which they dispersed quietly. In fact, the response to the appeal of the PAC was not widespread. It was only at a few centres in the Transvaal and the Cape that the protests took on any significant proportions. But it was at the black township of Sharpeville, near Vereeniging in the southern Transvaal, where the numbers were sufficient for the making of history.

Here too the police had refused to arrest those who had presented themselves without their passes. The crowd grew; eventually there were about 15 000 to 20 000 Africans gathered outside the police station. After reinforcements arrived the police still only numbered about 150 men. Earlier that year nine policemen had died at the Cato Manor slum near Durban, massacred by thousands of Africans, outraged at the stepped-up frequency of pass and liquor raids by the police. The events at Cato Manor undoubtedly weighed heavily on the minds of the beleaguered policemen.

As the day wore on, the crowd became more aggressive. Stones were thrown and arrests were made. Finally, it all became too much for the nerves of one policeman. He fired a shot in panic, which his colleagues interpreted as a command to open fire as well. What followed was a massacre. The Africans fled immediately, but when the shooting ceased 69 of them lay dead, most of them shot in the back. One hundred and eighty-six had been wounded.

At Langa township near Cape Town there were also deaths, but on a far smaller scale. Later that day a demonstrating crowd of blacks refused to disperse and was duly fired upon by the police. Two were killed and some wounded. Those who had fled went on the rampage, burning cars and buildings. Order only returned by midnight.

In Parliament the news of the events in the Transvaal gradually filtered through on the afternoon of 21 March. It was only the next day that the full extent of the tragedy revealed itself. That did not prevent Verwoerd from announcing that anti-Government propaganda 'necessarily had an inciting effect on the Bantu'.[2] On 22 March he had much more to say. As was his wont, he saw the big picture. Sharpeville, he argued, was merely a symptom of the chaotic times in which they lived. It had nothing to do with apartheid, but was rather one of those periodic disturbances 'which came in cycles as a result of incitement in regard to some or other matter of law'. There had been worse troubles elsewhere in Africa, witness the Congo and Nyasaland. The Smuts Government had experienced its own share of black unrest in 1946 and 1947; exemplary harshness had been the obvious and only remedy. Verwoerd had no doubt that agitation was to blame, arising from sustained attacks on the Government over the previous ten or twelve years by liberals and the sensationalist press.[3]

All this sophistry reduced Sharpeville to a fairly minor happening, quite exceptional in the normally peaceful course of South African events. As an observer from the press gallery, Anthony Delius of the *Cape Times*, commented: 'The Prime Minister looked out over the body-strewn locations of yesterday in his mind's eye, and took a detached, almost academic, view of the tragedy. It had all happened before, he implied – these things come in waves. The main thing was to have a firm police force.'[4]

That was exactly what Verwoerd believed, nor did he hesitate to act upon so strong a conviction. He had blamed both the PAC and the ANC, although the latter had not been involved in the events of 21 March. It was enough that both organisations had attempted to mobilise Africans against white rule. Verwoerd had no doubt that each had contributed more than its fair share to the sudden, recent climate of lawlessness and disorder. The Government took to itself sweeping, in fact dictatorial, powers. Public meetings were banned in specified magisterial districts. On 28 March the Government introduced the Unlawful Organisations Bill, designed to ban the ANC and the PAC. The penalties for intimidation rose tenfold. Two days later the Government declared a state of emergency in 122 of South Africa's electoral districts; 12 000 people of all races were detained in pre-dawn arrests. More than 18 000 were eventually to be held under the emergency regulations.

Overseas condemnation of the massacre was universal and virulent, not only from South Africa's familiar critics in Africa and Asia and in the Communist world, but also from the Western countries with which it had been on relatively good terms and of which it had frequently proclaimed itself an ally in the struggle against 'Communism'. The American Government publicly regretted 'the loss of life' and hoped that 'the African people will be able to obtain redress for legitimate grievances by peaceful means'. Foreign newspapers devoted their front pages to gruesome pictures of the Africans who had died at Sharpeville. As a matter of routine the Security Council of the United Nations condemned South Africa and once more demanded an end to apartheid. The

South African consulate in New York was picketed as well, while a protest meeting outside South Africa House in London drew a crowd 13 000 strong. Gold shares on world stock exchanges slumped.

At home the ANC reasserted itself and proclaimed 28 March as a day of mourning for those who had been killed. In the intervening week violence continued in the form of rioting, the burning of passes, stone-throwing, murder and arson. The Government temporarily suspended the carrying of passes on 26 March. The next day the leader of the ANC, Albert Luthuli, burnt his pass in public and vowed never to carry one again. The day of mourning provided spectacular proof of the economy's vulnerability to a black stay-away. In the major cities of Cape Town, Johannesburg and Port Elizabeth between 85 and 90 per cent of black workers stayed at home. In Durban, where only about 25 per cent did not arrive at work, and in the smaller centres the boycott had a smaller impact, but the day of mourning had made its point: the South African economy could not survive without black labour.

The stock rationalisation of the Government was that intimidators were having their way with basically peace-loving Africans, who wanted nothing better than to turn up at work but were forcibly prevented from doing so. Intimidation there undoubtedly was, but it could hardly explain most of the stay-away, which had its roots deep in African grievances. Any sceptic should have been present when 30 000 Africans marched on Cape Town on 30 March. The ANC had only called for one day of mourning, but the PAC supported a continuing campaign against apartheid. It urged blacks not to return to work after 28 March. Two days later the 23-year old Philip Kgosana of the PAC led his huge crowd of followers to the police headquarters in Cape Town to present themselves for arrest and to demand the release of Sobukwe and other arrested leaders. The march was orderly and disciplined, but white anxiety was intense: any panic reaction could have led to instant anarchy. It did not happen. The Commissioner of Police met Kgosana and promised him a meeting with the Minister of Justice. Upon hearing the news the Africans returned quietly to their homes, but to anyone who saw the march it must have seemed a damned close-run thing. Nor could there be much doubt about the popular support which the PAC enjoyed.

The promise to Kgosana was not honoured. When he later arrived for what he thought was the meeting with the minister, he too was arrested.

The state of emergency was declared on the day of the march. Thousands more were arrested. When further demonstrations followed, the black townships of Langa and Nyanga on the outskirts of Cape Town were cordoned off. Their inhabitants were literally starved out, so that after a week they had no choice but to return to work. All over the country the police rounded up blacks suspected of incitement and intimidation. The Government's methods worked: by the beginning of April it had the situation well under control.

The atmosphere of crisis remained. Talk of reform became increasingly popular, not only amongst opponents of the Government, but also amongst Nationalists who felt that while apartheid may be a fine thing in principle, it could be applied in practice with excessive harshness. There were wishful rumours of a more moderate coalition government consisting of middle-of-the-roaders from both main parties. Even in the cabinet there were ministers who advocated abolishing the reference book system.

Verwoerd would have none of this. For him it all came down to weakness, which made it more difficult for the Government to restore law and order. He became even more intransigent. His watchword was resistance, whatever the cost. His state of mind is illustrated by Mrs Verwoerd's entry in her diary for 3 April: 'He wants to end the situation by drastically limiting the number of Bantu. Manufacturers will complain, but it must force them to border industries. "If I cannot save the country, then I would rather resign. I will *never* be an accomplice to the destruction of our people by abandoning our policy!" '[5]

As a former academic Verwoerd had no trouble in convincing himself of what it suited him to believe. He never doubted that all the sudden upheaval was the fault of ambitious agitators who had somehow persuaded, more often intimidated, basically peace-loving blacks into departing from their daily round. On his first public appearance after Sharpeville, at Meyerton in the Transvaal on 26 March, Verwoerd shared with a gathering of seventy to eighty thousand people the benefits of his training in psychology:

> The black masses of South Africa – and I know the Bantu in all parts of the country – are orderly. They are loyal to the government of the country. The masses are beginning to realise that we are also thinking of their interests, that we too can see what they need, that we know and recognise their rights. The groups of people seeking their own gain are small and they make use of mass psychology at mass gatherings, and by threats and other means are sometimes the cause of trouble.[6]

With beliefs such as these there was never a danger that Verwoerd would swerve from his full-time job of saving the country. Whatever the appearance of black discontent and suffering, reality consisted in the great majority of Africans accepting things as they were. Self-seeking rabble-rousers were behind the troubles; it was the task of a firm police force to prevent them from achieving their ends.

Less than three weeks after Sharpeville Verwoerd narrowly escaped death. He had gone to Johannesburg to open the Rand Easter Show on 9 April. He had just sat down after completing his speech when a slightly built white man approached him and exclaimed, 'Verwoerd!' As the Prime Minister looked up, the man produced a small-calibre revolver and fired two shots point-blank at his face. One bullet fractured his jawbones; the other struck him in the neck. Verwoerd fell back, his face streaming with blood, while security men and bystanders overwhelmed his attacker. Verwoerd was taken to hospital at once, and it was feared that he would not live.

He survived, but the wounds were nearly fatal. Expert medical attention and the man's own remarkable will-power ensured what seemed a miraculous recovery. After nearly a month the bullets were removed. Verwoerd returned home on 15 May and was able to address the country in a radio broadcast five days later.

His attacker was David Pratt, a wealthy Transvaal farmer with a record of mental instability. Pratt later claimed in court that he had not intended to kill Verwoerd. He had instead tried to 'maim' him, which would give his victim, while recovering, 'an opportunity to reconsider some of the things that were going on'.[7] Perhaps not surprisingly, Pratt was committed to a mental hospital, where he killed himself in October the following year.

The absence of Verwoerd's domineering presence meant that reform-minded Nationalists now expressed themselves more freely. Once more there was talk of coalition, even in the Nationalist caucus. The most famous example of submerged ideas rising to the surface was a speech by Paul Sauer, the Minister of Lands and acting chairman of the cabinet in Verwoerd's absence. A product of the Cape, less prone to insist on hard-line enforcement of apartheid in every purist detail, Sauer announced in his constituency of Humansdorp on 19 April that 'the old book of South African history was closed at Sharpeville'. He proposed a new approach, especially with respect to reference books, the prohibition of liquor sales to Africans, their right to a degree of local government in the urban areas, and the raising of their living standards.[8]

Sauer's proposals never had a chance. They were welcomed and rejected by the wrong people. The Opposition acclaimed these fresh and inspiring thoughts from so unexpected a source. Even more ominous for Sauer, he was being cast by his new admirers as a key figure in any political realignment. None of this did his standing in the National Party any good. And it soon became clear that most members of the Nationalist caucus were not much interested in closing old South African history books. Sauer met with strident opposition from his colleagues; it was decided that his suggestions would be discussed no further until the return of the chief.

Verwoerd in fact intervened as soon as he could to eradicate any hint of deviationism. From his home, still unfit to return to Parliament, he prepared a typically lengthy statement which the Cape Nationalist leader, T E Dönges, read to the House of Assembly on 20 May. It amounted to a blunt statement to any Nationalists who were thinking reformist thoughts that they had better stop. The Government, with its access to facts and its opportunity of consulting with experts, knew better than well-meaning but uninformed people what was in the interests of the country. In a palpable hit at Sauer, Verwoerd advised guarding 'against the tendency which has arisen in certain quarters as a result of internal and external propaganda to see the disturbances in the wrong perspective; and in the second place against the attempts of opponents to try to encourage a change to a supposedly altogether new policy or a revision of policy. This in the end appeared to be nothing but an attempt to revitalise the policy of integration which has already failed here and elsewhere in Africa'.

Tougher talk than this there could not be. 'Integration' was about the ultimate term of abuse in the Nationalist lexicon. Once they had been tarred with the integrationist brush there could be no recovery for Sauer and other Nationalists who may have favoured some brand of mild reformism. Having so firmly put non-Verwoerdian thinkers so firmly in their place, the leader triumphantly concluded: 'The Government sees no reason to depart from its policy of separate development as a result of the disturbances. On the contrary, the events have now more than ever emphasised that peace and good order, and friendly relations between the races, can best be achieved through this policy.'

There is no particular mystery about what happened at Sharpeville and after. What were supposed to be peaceful protests against the pass laws did not quite turn out as they had been intended to. Unforeseen events converted peaceful protest into widespread violence and the greatest crisis the Union of South Africa had ever known. The Government took to itself unprecedented powers, which it used in the most robust sense. It quelled the unrest fairly soon and then announced that nothing had happened to make it change its direction.

That, most simply, is the story of Sharpeville. Naturally it is too simple, for it suggests that what happened was a momentary outburst, however spectacular, which had no deep roots in the South African past. That was certainly the stock Nationalist interpretation. For the Government Sharpeville was the work of self-seeking agitators who managed to convince the basically peace-loving black masses that they were the victims of a variety of imaginary grievances. Eager critics have pointed out untiringly how nonsensical such explanations were. Those who are happy with their lot are not so easily aroused to protests which consume plenty of energy and can be exceedingly dangerous to boot.

Unfortunately the critics have not done much better. They knew that Sharpeville was rooted in South African history and that the demonstrators of Sharpeville and Langa had plenty of all-too-real sufferings to complain about. But grievances, however legitimate, and oppression, however severe, do not as such make for outbursts like Sharpeville, let alone for revolutionary situations. Students of revolution have come to accept as one of their few sound generalisations that there is no necessary connection between great hardship and political violence. That there is some correlation is no doubt true, but its nature is hardly self-evident. Between 1910 and 1960 there had been six major protests against the pass laws in South Africa; none had issued in violence comparable to Sharpeville. The question then becomes: what caused Sharpeville? What was so different as to result in violence unique in the fifty-year old history of the South African Union?

That South Africa had for long been on the brink of a revolution was a fashionable thought, accepted by many enemies of Nationalist rule during the years before Sharpeville. Sooner of later, the argument went, the sufferings of the Africans would become so intense that they would rise spontaneously and in a mighty outburst of rage sweep away the whole ghastly apparatus of apartheid. To alter the analogy, it was like sitting on the lid of a pressure cooker: it would not stay in place for ever.

The images may have been vivid and intuitively plausible, yet little tough-minded analysis went into them. Plenty of wishful thinking did. In 1957 a liberal academic from the University of the Witwatersrand, Julius Lewin, wrote an article which harshly exposed the fallacies underlying this kind of argument. Entitled 'No Revolution Round the Corner,' it appeared in the radical journal, *Africa South*. Lewin took as his starting-point *The Anatomy of Revolution* by the Harvard historian, Crane Brinton, who found common features in the English revolution of the seventeenth century, the American and French of the eighteenth, and the Russian of the twentieth. He found that all four revolutions happened in societies which had growing economies and where living standards were in general rising. Material conditions were improving and not declining. All four of them experienced bitter class antagonisms, themselves the mark of rising expectations associated with growth, as many of the more educated and prosperous came up against the exclusive privileges of aristocracies. In all four countries the governmental machinery had been inefficient as institutions found themselves ill-adapted to cope with the strains imposed by economic expansion. Lastly, large sections of the armed forces were disaffected.

Lewin found that only some of these factors were at work in South Africa. The first two were there: the economy was growing fairly rapidly and African living standards were rising, at least the standards of those who had been protesting most loudly against the iniquities of apartheid, namely the small black middle class and the urban working class. But government was not in a state of collapse; indeed, the increasing predominance of Afrikaners in the bureaucracy amounted to a close identity of interest between politicians and civil servants which went far to offset any technical inefficiencies. Lastly, and most decisively, there could be no question of the loyalty of the police and the armed forces to the South African Government. Nor did blacks have the means of armed revolt in their hands. Even if they had had access to modern weapons and been trained in their use there could not have been the slightest chance of a revolutionary overthrow of a regime as well-equipped with military hardware, and willing to use it, as that of South Africa. Moreover, it was a large country with poor communications: the race riots that did occur periodically were localised and unpromising as harbingers of revolution.

Lewin dismissed the possible efficacy of both passive resistance and mass industrial action. The Defiance Campaign of 1952–1953 had never shaken the Government, but had succeeded only in making it pass harsher laws which were a potent disincentive to any further such action. As for urban Africans going on strike, 'their place would be taken and their work carried on somehow by white workers or by other Africans brought, if necessary, from neighbouring territories where Africans are more backward and much less politically conscious than they are in the Union. Add to this the fact that African workers predominate in hardly any service or industry where stoppage or slowing down would at once create a national crisis impossible to resolve. The gold mining industry is not such an industry. Even if it were, the experience of August 1946 showed how a strike could be dealt with and terminated within a week or two'.[9]

Nothing had changed to refute Lewin's analysis by the time of Sharpeville. The Nationalist Government was singularly united in its determination to preserve white domination. That could indeed be said of the white population as a whole, whatever their political differences. The English-speaking whites may have detested the Nationalists, but that was because it was an Afrikaner government which made no bones about treating its own preferentially. They had no problems with the principle of white rule.

There had been an average rate of economic growth of more than four per cent during the previous decade, which could have raised black expectations for an improving future. It is not quite clear, however, whether African living standards, at least those of the middle class and the urban working class, as Lewin suggests, actually did rise. Between 1946 and 1960 the African share of national income rose slightly, from just over 20 per cent to nearly 21 per cent (compared with the white share of more than 70 per cent), while blacks continued to account for about 68 per cent of the total population.[10] Taken with the respectable growth rate and the stricter application of influx control, it is probable that those Africans who did manage to get jobs in the urban areas found that their living standards were rising. But it is also certain that they were not going up remarkably.

This was perhaps not an especially potent recipe for those heightened expectations which appear to precede revolutionary situations, at least not when taken in isolation. But it was of the very essence of the whole period between 1945 and 1960 that South African developments were no mere isolated events. They found their place in a global framework.

As the Second World War neared its end in 1945 more Africans began to feel that for the first time since Union the democratic process could offer them more than the crumbs from the table of which they knew the taste so well. In 1941 the Atlantic Charter had anticipated a peace settlement which would 'afford assurance that all the men in all the lands may live out their lives in freedom from fear and want'. When its principles were later incorporated in the

United Nations Charter of 1945 it appeared to many victims of discrimination that their future was about to take a turn for the better. It coincided with the rapid growth of a black urban working class, one of the major outcomes of war-time industrialisation. The more radical black mood was reflected in the formation in 1944 of the Youth League of the ANC, a body which insisted on the extension of political rights and rejected out of hand any benevolent paternalism which South African governments may have cared to dispense.

Accordingly, in 1945, the ANC published a Bill of Rights, strongly influenced by the Atlantic Charter. It called for universal franchise, the end of the industrial colour bar, and recognition of the right of Africans to collective bargaining. The tone was still moderate, there were no ultimatums, yet the demands were different. The Bill of Rights embodied black hopes and expectations, but by 1948 it had begun to appear to Africans that nothing had changed, except for the worse. The United Party Government had shown itself quite unreceptive to African demands. Indeed, its harsh response to the African mineworkers' strike in 1946 indicated that as far as Jan Smuts was concerned, the Charter of the United Nations did not apply to lesser breeds hardly within the rule of law. Rising black expectations were already taking a downturn when Malan and his followers took over in 1948. The unrelenting racism upon which the Nationalists immediately embarked could only, it seemed, ensure the elimination of any vestiges of black optimism. The failures of the Defiance Campaign, the inability of the ANC to mobilise effective mass protests on particular issues, the constant harassing by the Government of its opponents, all these would have suggested the attrition and ultimate destruction of those African anticipations which appeared so well justified only a short time ago.

That it did not happen was because the international climate had changed irrevocably. Empire was ending in Asia and Africa and being replaced by new countries which claimed all the trappings of nation states. In particular, for Africans on the whole continent, the independence of Ghana in 1957 had immense symbolic significance. It was a statement that blacks could rule themselves, free from white domination. In what was a world trend, South Africa came across as a conspicuous exception, whatever Verwoerd's fine recent talk about separate freedoms for blacks. Despite their current hardships the hopes of blacks were kept alive by events elsewhere. The present might be thoroughly unpleasant but the future could not be denied and it belonged to them.

Sharpeville must not be seen on its own. It was the culmination of a crisis which began before the Nationalists came into power. Africans came to have expectations about the future which they did not have before. They could not but be aware that the United Party and Nationalist Government had no sympathy at all with such expectations and were only too willing to destroy them. Their failure to do so was the result of a change in the course of world history over which South Africa's white politicians had no influence.

Several events triggered Sharpeville. Most important was the arrival of the PAC, militant, unabashedly racist and uncompromising in all its demands. It held out the hope of liberation soon, no later than 1963. In his book, *The True Believer*, Eric Hoffer makes the point well: 'A rising mass movement preaches the immediate hope. It is intent on stirring its followers to action, and it is the around-the-corner brand of hope that prompts people to act'.[11]

There was also Macmillan, who spoke about the wind of change. Nationalists were only too willing to cast the British Prime Minister as the villain of the piece, yet another meddling foreigner who told blacks that they were being oppressed, but that it was all an historical aberration which could not last and that relief was on the way. His speech, Nationalists claimed, heightened discontent and frustration and led to tragedy. Plainly, this was pushing it. At most Macmillan's eloquent rhetoric only made an already tense situation even more so; it did not create the underlying causes which only needed some active prodding to make their effects felt.

What is equally plain is that Sharpeville was no reflection of a state of revolution. South Africa was still remote from so drastic an upheaval, if only because the Government had full control over the armed forces. Its response to the events of 21 March showed that it had relinquished none of its will to rule. It detained many, of whom less than a third were convicted and sentenced for various offences.

Robert Sobukwe received a three-year prison sentence, but was detained for another six years under a special law renewed each year. Albert Luthuli and his ANC colleagues who had burnt their reference books each received a prison sentence of one year or the alternative of a fine of R200. On the face of it, and in fact, the Government had survived the crisis and re-established its authority with little difficulty.

CHAPTER NINE

The Republic

The Government's swift resumption of authority after Sharpeville enabled it to get on with what it knew to be really important: the pursuit of the coveted republic. The driving force behind its campaign was the Prime Minister himself, who had apparently made a miraculous recovery from Pratt's bullets and was soon addressing public meetings with all his familiar conviction and drive.

Verwoerd's stature was immense since his announcement of the referendum in January. The abortive attempt to kill him only intensified the adulation of his followers. A journalist from the Opposition press, a close observer of Verwoerd's career, believed that this event was 'the turning point for Verwoerd as leader of his party. Up until then many in the party had been uncertain about him, his aims and his motives. They had not been able to find in him the personification of their people's struggle ... But now he had suffered grievously in the cause of Afrikanerdom; the onslaught on his life was an onslaught on their cause, and the human sympathy that went out to him became in the case of many an enduring love for a hero who so miraculously survived to lead them on'.[1] A journalist who had worked under Verwoerd on *Die Transvaler* had similar impressions. Verwoerd's wounds and his escape created 'a mystical bond' between him and the Afrikaner people. Many saw his almost inexplicable survival 'as a sign from Above'. His position grew increasingly strong 'until eventually he stood more strongly than any Prime Minister before him'.[2]

Verwoerd himself was quite sure why his life was preserved. In his broadcast to the South African people on 20 May he testified to his conviction 'that the protection of Divine Providence was accorded one with a purpose, a purpose which concerns South Africa too. May it be given to me to fulfill that task faithfully'.[3]

In the same broadcast Verwoerd returned to a theme that was to be a keynote of the remaining years of his premiership: white unity. When convalescing he had received many messages of goodwill and sympathy from members of all language and race groups. He made a point of referring to the messages from those of 'other' races, but it was the good wishes from white non-Afrikaners which clearly impressed him most:

> This proves that South Africa is not nearly as divided or filled with hatred as is so often stated. The realisation that many English- and Afrikaans-speaking people are becoming one nation, that we have to face our problems together ... has perhaps never been felt so clearly by so many. The fundamental consciousness of a real South Africanism which overrules everything else is beginning to predominate over differences of origin, language and outlook.[4]

Never before did Verwoerd so crassly, as at this time of thanksgiving, make it so plain that anyone not white had no claim to membership of what he chose to regard as the emerging 'one nation' of South Africa.

As politicians will, Verwoerd ran horses for courses. He came in two versions. There was the conciliatory Verwoerd, the seeker after a white unity which would make possible the solution of the race problem. On 31 May, speaking to a countrywide constituency at the Bloemfontein celebrations which marked the 50th anniversary of Union, he foresaw a republic 'of the English- and Afrikaans-speaking sections alike, one united white nation governing what is the heritage of South Africa, joined together as one by the very task before them at this time, and through this unity cooperating in solving its special problem of race relations so totally different from problems anywhere else in the world'.[5] But there were also times when the iron fist within the velvet glove made itself felt, when an entirely different Verwoerd, hardly distinguishable from the uncompromising extremist of times past, announced his presence. The week before Sharpeville he told a meeting of Nationalist MPs' wives: 'Our chances of winning are good, provided that we can harness all the forces of the people. If we do not win now, the fight becomes harder, and I am afraid, also more bitter. We are now fighting with gentle means. If we lose, we will fight harder and with more forceful means'.[6]

When confronted with his words in the House of Assembly, Verwoerd claimed that he had been unaware of the presence of the press, which suggested only that the Nationalist wives had been hearing the real Verwoerd, not subject to the constraints of public relations and hence free to express his most genuine thoughts. Typically, he justified himself by blaming the Opposition, which, he stated, had alleged that the exclusion of the coloureds made the referendum a fraud. Accordingly, 'If we do not succeed in the light of this attitude they adopt, and if it should be maintained, I would not be in favour of holding one referendum after another. I would prefer to say frankly that next time we will adopt the normal method adopted by all countries of allowing all decisions to be taken by the majority in Parliament elected for that purpose'.[7]

One thing seemed clear. Whatever the outcome of the referendum, the people of South Africa, whether white or non-white, whether they had voted against the republic or been allowed to vote at all, would soon be living under a new constitution. Much as he preferred to establish a republic after a victorious referendum, Verwoerd was above all determined to have his way. If he could not have his republic through a referendum, Verwoerd would achieve it by whatever other constitutional means suited him best. If he lost the referendum he could call a general election, which would inevitably be won by the Nationalists, and then claim that the electorate had told him to proceed with proclaiming a republic. Or he could dispense with even so face-saving a procedure and simply go ahead to change the constitution by resorting to his current and substantial parliamentary majority. The white unity Verwoerd was making so much of would suffer a decided blow, but that was an unpleasant consequence which had to be accepted. The republic, however attained, was after all, Verwoerd knew, a prerequisite for any such unity, which would at worst only be delayed, but not prevented.

The campaign took place in the midst of a deep economic crisis.

Capital fled South Africa with almost indecent haste after Sharpeville, as foreign investors decided that this was no hospitable environment for healthy returns. The balance of payments deteriorated as gold and foreign exchange reserves fell. The Government responded by imposing severe import and foreign exchange controls. Economic growth fell almost to zero, then still a most unusual experience for the South African economy. Thousands of English-speaking whites, reeling from the successive shocks of the prospect of a 'Verwoerd Republic', Macmillan's 'betrayal', Sharpeville, and the disastrous accession of the Congo to independence, decided that South Africa could no longer offer them the kind of comfortable and secure future they had come to accept as their due. They scurried for what they saw as more hospitable shores, notably those of Britain.

For Verwoerd these were at worst lesser irritations compared with the supreme goal of the republic, which he pursued without deviation. At the beginning of August he announced that the referendum would take place on 5 October. In his broadcast speech he deliberately dealt with the objection most often advanced against the republic, namely, that it would result in South Africa's exclusion from the Commonwealth. Much against his private inclination, Verwoerd gave the white voters an emphatic assurance that he would apply for continued membership of a republic. The precedent set by other members which had remained in the Commonwealth after becoming republics made him confident that his application would be granted. 'An adverse decision,' he pointed out, 'would indicate an important change in the character of the Commonwealth. It would mean interference in the domestic policies of member countries, which in this instance would actually be aimed at the right of the white man in this country to retain control over what he had built up for himself. It would also mean that younger non-white member countries would be exercising a predominating influence in this matter. Such a change would prove a threat to South Africa and her citizens even if she remained a monarchy'.[8]

Few white South Africans could have faulted Verwoerd's analysis, although their intense emotions made it difficult for English-speakers to accept it at the time. Even after Macmillan's marauding visit they still had problems accepting that a white supremacist South Africa, whatever its constitution, would not be treated with warmth and sympathy in a Commonwealth which was becoming more multiracial by the day. For them the Commonwealth still provided an indispensable lifeline without which they would be bereft in a grim world which did not understand the special nature of South Africa's racial problem. They had no doubt that outside the Commonwealth, without its trade preferences and the support of its 'more responsible' white members, namely, Britain, Australia, Canada and New Zealand, a South African republic would have no chance of survival. It was the reflection of an essentially colonial mentality, which would have some difficulty in responding to the challenge of the new and alien world now advancing with bewildering speed.

Opposition propaganda also made much of the frightening prospect of a 'Verwoerd Republic'. Civil liberties and democratic procedures, the propagandists had it, would be peculiarly at risk under such a constitutional dispensation. They never bothered to explain why a Verwoerd Monarchy should have been so preferable from a liberal point of view. Nor did they elaborate on why the continued white supremacy in which they believed as strongly as Verwoerd was compatible with their professed concern with democracy. But no doubt it was a slogan which persuaded many that the status quo was preferable to the change Verwoerd was proposing to make.

Throughout South Africa, Verwoerd addressed large and enthusiastic audiences. His theme was white unity, essential for the preservation of what he chose to regard as 'white civilisation'. But, in spite of his professed intention to conduct a campaign devoted to the discussion of matters of high principle, the temptation to make racist capital out of developments in the rest of Africa proved irresistible. The independence the Belgians had given to an ill-prepared Congo proved even more catastrophic than the most committed pessimists had predicted. This latest addition to the comity of nations erupted into instant chaos, manifested in the secession of Katanga, appalling massacres and the frantic departure of white settlers. It was an opportunity for the Nationalists to make the most of the black menace propaganda which they claimed to deplore when it was employed by the United Party.

Accordingly, towards the end of the campaign, posters appeared in Johannesburg which read: 'To re-unite and keep South Africa white, a republic now.' It was a result of a calculated decision to concentrate on white racial fears, made at a meeting of Nationalist officials in Johannesburg and addressed by Verwoerd himself.[9] From now on the Government's referendum campaign took on a racist slant which must have brought in a fair number of undecided voters. As the *Rand Daily Mail*, the most liberal of all the Opposition newspapers, commented acerbically, Nationalists 'have been given the green light to go ahead on the straight issue of White versus Black. The whole republican referendum is reduced to the simple question of whether you want your daughter to marry an African or, more to the point, to be ravished by a Congolese soldier'.[10]

Verwoerd made the same radical appeal in the letter in his handwriting of which a million printed facsimiles went to voters throughout South Africa. It was dated 21 September 1960 and stressed the 'chaos in the Congo. Internal conflict and the elimination of the White man seem imminent in most other parts of Africa.' In the same vein, the author predicted that, unless South Africa became a republic soon, 'we ourselves may possibly, but our children certainly, will experience all the suffering of the Whites who are being attacked in and driven out of one African territory after the other'.[11]

Outwardly, Verwoerd appeared supremely confident. Privately, he was a worried man. The decision to go ahead with the referendum, even after the poll by the branch secretaries had indicated only minority support for the Nationalists amongst the white voters, might have been brave but it was also foolhardy. He admitted to his extreme right wing cabinet appointee, Albert Hertzog, that 'only a small percentage of the English-speakers would vote for the republic. Therefore he hoped that large numbers of them would fail to vote'.[12]

He was right in his forecast, but disappointed in his hopes. The English-speakers turned out in droves to vote against the Verwoerd Republic. In the predominantly English-speaking Natal the voters' response was the heaviest of that of all four the provinces, with a turn-out of nearly 93 per cent. More than three-quarters of the Natal votes went against the republic. In the Cape Province the turn-out was nearly as high in an exceedingly close race: out of more than 540 000 votes cast, the republican majority came to less than 2 000. The vote in the two northern provinces, where pro-republican support was concentrated, proved decisive. Here the percentage poll was slightly less than 90 per cent. It was enough to ensure a victory for the republicans. After South West Africa had been included, the total republican vote came to 850 458 with 775 878 votes against. The majority was 74 580. Just over 52 per cent had voted for a republic. Verwoerd had been wrong in his initial prediction of a big majority. But for a man who had anticipated defeat shortly before the referendum, it was more than gratifying. It was also a lot better than claiming a mandate for a republic on the basis of a majority of one.

The question of a republic had been ostensibly non-political. In practice it was nothing of the kind. Most voters followed the party line on the day of the referendum. The majority for the republic represented a continuation of a basic trend in South African politics since 1948: increasing adherence to the Government by the white voters. Only two years before, the general election had shown that the Nationalists were close to being supported by an absolute majority of the electorate. The result of the referendum indicated that this had been achieved. Most white voters were now supporters of the Government. Since 1958 there had been a swing of three per cent in favour of the Nationalists.

If anything, the events of 1960 contributed to the republican victory. Macmillan's speech on 3 February could only have contributed to disillusionment with British policy in Africa, intent as it seemed to be on 'selling out' the white man on the continent. It raised doubts about the value of continued membership of a Commonwealth increasingly composed of former colonies bitterly hostile to apartheid and which Britain would clearly prefer not to alienate. Most important were Sharpeville and the Congo. They brought home to white South Africans the terrifying prospect of an ethnic time-bomb about to explode in their midst. The immediate reaction of many, if not most, must have been that its defusion required a strong government, which the Nationalists undoubtedly were. Certainly, the United Party, with its record of indecision and internal squabbling, did not inspire confidence in its ability to maintain that law and order, whatever the cost, which seemed so essential to white South Africans. There had never been any doubt about the ability, or the willingness, of the Nationalists to do so. It was considerations like these which could have done the republican cause no harm in the dramatic year of 1960. But at most they only accentuated a trend towards the Nationalists which had been running strongly since 1948.

The victor Verwoerd could afford to be magnanimous. Two days after the referendum, addressing the nation (in fact, the white population) over the radio, he professed to be encouraged by the spirit in which the voters did their duty: 'This is one of the most encouraging aspects of the referendum contest, since it shows that that fundamental goodwill is present which will make it possible to go forward together in spite of differences.' For him the republic was the start of a new era. He promised to 'lead our nation in such a way that without sacrificing or compromising on principles, either by one party or the other, we need never again feel like two nations in one state'.[13]

Subsequent pronouncements showed that Verwoerd had plainly decided to assume the unfamiliar role of conciliator in the transition to the republic. It was to be made as painless as possible for his opponents to adapt to the new constitutional dispensation that was upon them. Yet the real test was still to come, when he would apply for continued membership of the Commonwealth by the Republic of South Africa. In March of the following year Verwoerd was scheduled to attend the meeting of Commonwealth Prime Ministers in London. The anti-republicans would judge him as statesman and conciliator by what he achieved there.

In the meantime those who led them to defeat were reluctant to accept the result. Sir De Villiers Graaff was impressed with the meagreness of the majority and suggested that a republic created on such a basis would be sectional and not South African. Graaff went on to propose that the Government had no right to introduce legislation to establish a republic unless it was certain that South Africa would remain in the Commonwealth. The leader of the United Party in Natal, Douglas Mitchell, took a delegation to Verwoerd to ask him for greater autonomy for their province, as well as for the entrenchment of a variety of rights in the new constitution. Neither Graaff nor Mitchell achieved the slightest success. Verwoerd had after all made it plain long before that an affirmative vote would lead to a republic, whether inside or outside the Commonwealth. Equally plainly, he had emphasised that the constitution would remain unchanged, except for the replacement of the monarch by a president without executive powers.

In November Verwoerd announced that South Africa would become a republic on 31 May 1961. On 23 January he introduced the Republic of South Africa Constitution Bill in the House of Assembly. As he had promised, there was only one major change, providing for a head of state who symbolised the republic, instead of a Governor-General who represented the British monarch.

In March Verwoerd departed for London. In his New Year message for 1961 he had renewed his undertaking to keep the new republic in the Commonwealth, subject to the familiar proviso that continued membership of that supposedly exclusive club would not be bought by allowing interference in South Africa's domestic policies or by any sacrifice of principle or national honour.

In the British capital Verwoerd immediately established himself as something of a star turn. He held the headlines consistently for the two weeks he was there. The British press soon came to refer to him as 'Dr V'. Here was news value indeed, the representative of a country and a policy the most reviled throughout the world, come to London to confront some of his most bitter critics. As was his wont, Verwoerd appeared imperturbable. He was smiling, he was friendly, and, above all, he was quite inflexible. He made it totally clear right from the start that there would be no compromise on apartheid. What happened at home in South Africa had no bearing on its continued inclusion in the Commonwealth, an association which after all, did not interfere, at least not in principle, in the 'domestic affairs' of its members.

That was Verwoerd's stand and he never budged from it. Not only was apartheid irrelevant to the continued membership of his country, he could not see what all the fuss was about, for, as he informed the hordes of newspapermen, the policy was not about supremacy at all. It was rather, the disbelieving journalists heard, 'a good neighbour policy'.

This statement set the tone for Verwoerd's visit. It symbolised the gulf of incomprehension between himself and his critics. In spite of a common language, they never did manage to communicate with one another. Verwoerd, not distinguished for his ability to see anyone's point of view except his own, was, as usual, absolutely convinced that he was right. His many critics, both at the Commonwealth Conference and outside, could not begin to understand what the man was talking about.

Verwoerd's reasons for expecting success were sound. There were other republics in the Commonwealth. India, Pakistan, Ceylon and Ghana had encountered no objections to their continued membership, nor did their fellow-members raise obstacles about their not always impeccably democratic ways, which were seen as very much their own business. Not only were the precedents solid, but Harold Macmillan had been canvassing Commonwealth Prime Ministers the previous year about continued South African membership. He found little enthusiasm, but also reluctance to force a final break.

That, however, had been a year before. Mighty torrents had passed under the bridge since then. Not only had there been Sharpeville, but the African nationalist movements had been summarily banned, black dissent had been most harshly suppressed and whites only had voted on the republic which now wished to remain in a predominantly non-white Commonwealth. Afro-Asian susceptibilities about the South African version of good neighbourliness had become far more intense. In short, the willingness to put up with a state which had virtually elevated discrimination by white against non-white into an eleventh commandment was no longer much in evidence amongst most members of the Commonwealth. Whatever the rules of the game had been about discussing the internal affairs of member countries at previous Conferences, at this one they were suspended. After Verwoerd agreed to it, in a concession which was wholly untypical and which he must have found thoroughly disagreeable, apartheid took its place on the agenda.

South Africa might still have remained in the Commonwealth

before the decision, and it would have ended with an insincere face-saving formula for membership. But once the discussions had started, it quickly became clear that an apartheid South Africa had no future in a multiracial Commonwealth.

The attacks on South African race policies were bitter and emotional. They were led by Jawaharlal Nehru of India, Kwame Nkrumah of Ghana and, conspicuously, John Diefenbaker of Canada, whose stridently emotional condemnation of apartheid and identification with the Afro-Asian point of view saved the conference from being divided on straight East-West lines, with Britain, Australia and New Zealand siding with South Africa. Verwoerd was now once more back in his favourite role of refusing to bend in the face of intense foreign pressure. He spoke about blacks being materially better off in South Africa than elsewhere on the continent, a possibly true but certainly irrelevant remark, another symptom of the failure of Verwoerd and his critics to establish any common area of discourse. Eventually, in spite of his insistence that apartheid had nothing to do with racism, he refused to accept diplomatic representatives from black Commonwealth members in South Africa. The time for that had not yet come, he suggested. Whatever the susceptibilities of his supporters at home, few things could have come across as a deadlier insult to the African representatives at the Conference. After this there was little prospect of South Africa remaining within the Commonwealth.

Their host, Harold Macmillan, was doing his best to find an acceptable compromise. He thought a communiqué confirming South African membership but recording the rejection of apartheid by the other ten leaders would do the trick. Verwoerd would have accepted, again with utmost reluctance, but other Commonwealth leaders had by now decided that South Africa must be out and told Macmillan so. It meant that if South Africa still wished to remain Verwoerd would have had to make those compromises, such as a softening of race policy, which he had rejected from the outset.

He did the only thing he could do. On 15 March Verwoerd withdrew his country's application to remain a member of the Commonwealth after it became a republic. In his carefully prepared statement he referred to his confidence that 'the great majority of the people of my country' (by which he clearly meant only whites) would appreciate that no other course was open to him. He added, 'I must admit that I was amazed and shocked by the spirit of hostility, and at the last meeting even of vindictiveness towards South Africa shown in the discussions, in spite of the lengths to which we were prepared to go in the various draft communiqués'. For him it meant a total change in the character of the Commonwealth in one short year.[14]

Macmillan, the man in the middle, was exceedingly distressed. All his efforts to find that suitable compromise had yielded nothing. A week later he told the House of Commons that he did not believe that South Africa's exclusion 'would best help all those European people who do not accept the doctrine of apartheid, nor as far as I could see would it help the Africans ... moreover it seemed to me that there was a danger of falling into a somewhat Pharisaical attitude in this.' But, he added, he was convinced 'that had Dr Verwoerd shown the smallest move towards an understanding of the views of his Commonwealth colleagues, or made any concession, I still think the Conference would have looked beyond the immediate difficulties to the possibilities of the future.' Verwoerd however had refused to relax 'the extreme rigidity of his dogma', which left him with no alternative but withdrawal.[15]

South Africa was not the first country to leave the Commonwealth, but it was the first to do so under duress. The news was understandably sensational, both in Britain and in South Africa itself. For Verwoerd there was also a question which must have nagged: how would the English-speakers at home respond to his decision? He had in fact done his very best, in his estimation, to keep South Africa in the Commonwealth. He had even yielded on that principle so dear to his heart that apartheid was South Africa's own private affair by allowing his country's policies to be debated at the Conference. There could be no guarantee that much of this would be appreciated by his English-speaking countrymen.

So it turned out, at first. Verwoerd's critics cast him as the villain whose adamant refusal to make the least concession caused South Africa to be cast out of a truly elite body of nations. Typical of this sort of reaction was that of the *Cape Times*, a newspaper which apparently never had the least difficulty in reconciling its support of the white supremacist United Party with its permanent outrage over apartheid:

> The plain meaning of the events in London last night is that we have been thrown out of the group of the most tolerant, the most civilised, the most fair-minded peoples in the world. And we have been thrown out because of the narrow-minded, inflexible doctrines of racism which began the sabotage of South Africa in 1948 and came to their climax under the direction of Dr Verwoerd.[16]

In Natal there were the familiar threats of secession from people whose views on race would have made Verwoerd look a positive liberal. Both inside and outside Parliament spokesmen for the Opposition made a personal point of it: Verwoerd had blundered and he alone was responsible.

What was tragedy to the English-speakers was the most splendid of triumphs to the Afrikaners. Most of them, certainly in the northern provinces, would have preferred a republic outside the Commonwealth; remaining inside was a sacrifice to that white unity their leaders had been making so much of. Now, unexpectedly, they had given them on a plate what they thought would not soon, if ever, be theirs. Their hearts went out to the man who had made it possible. When Verwoerd arrived on 20 March at Jan Smuts airport near Johannesburg, there were many thousands (ranging from 15 000 to 60 000, depending on the political complexion of those who did the estimating) to give the conquering hero the welcome he deserved. Verwoerd yielded to the spirit of the occasion and spoke about the victory, and not the defeat, which befell him in London: 'We have freed ourselves from the Afro-Asian states'. Years later in a television interview Mrs Verwoerd described the welcome at Jan Smuts as 'probably the highest high point of his life'.

Verwoerd returned to South Africa one day before the first anniversary of Sharpeville. All the indications were that the run-up to the republic would not be smooth. In spite of the Government's severest efforts the previous year, black protest was proving indestructible. At an 'all-in' conference in Pietermaritzburg in Natal towards the end of March, the more than one thousand delegates, mainly members of the banned ANC, demanded a non-racial national convention, to be held not later than 31 May, the day scheduled for the advent of the republic. If the Government refused, blacks would come out in their thousands to reject what had been imposed on them without their consent. A National Action Council was appointed to direct the campaign, which would also attempt to bring in coloureds and Indians to join in opposing 'a regime which is bringing South Africa to disaster'.

The Government responded characteristically. In May they rushed a bill through Parliament which extended security legislation. In massive raids the police detained eight to ten thousand Africans for a variety of supposed offences. The National Action Council reacted by calling upon all Africans to stay at home for three days, starting on 29 May. All police leave was cancelled, and active units of the Defence Force were mobilised.

The appeal of the National Action Council met with a poor response. Only in the Johannesburg did the stay-away not resemble a joke, where 50 to 60 per cent of the workers did not come to work on the first day. Employers had proved unsympathetic, refusing to pay boycotters and sometimes threatening them with dismissal. The ANC's rival, the PAC, had also contributed by distributing leaflets which urged workers to take no part in 'sterile demonstrations'.

For the Government that was the good news. But the first day of the republic could scarcely have been less auspicious. In Pretoria on 31 May 1961, as the first State President, C R Swart, the then Governor-General and former Minister of Justice was sworn in, the skies were heavily overcast and there were intermittent showers. It was a wretched day, but the leader who had made it all possible would allow nothing to stifle his euphoria.

At the banquet which followed, Verwoerd proposed a toast to the new head of state and informed him that he would 'play an essential role in our country because we who must build and fight will inevitably have different ideas about how South Africa's future is to be developed. We shall inevitably from the depths of our convictions quarrel with one another. But notwithstanding all this, there will be the basic unity of one people of the Republic of South Africa and you will have to be the tie to bind us all together'.[17] Fine words no doubt, but the choice of Swart as unifying factor was a poor one. As member of the Nationalist Government he had not been noted for his broad statesmanlike approach to the burning issues of the day. He had been an unashamed partisan, openly pursuing and promoting the interests of the section of the white population upon whose support the Government depended. He was an unlikely symbol of white unity. For that was of course what Verwoerd meant by 'the basic unity of one people of the Republic of South Africa'. For him the South African nation was exclusively white; the rest of the population may have occupied the same territory, but in Verwoerd's book that did not entitle them to membership of his singularly exclusive nation.

The punch-drunk white electorate soon learnt that it would get no respite in the republican era. At the beginning of August Verwoerd informed them that they would have to give judgement at the polls once more, in a general election scheduled for October 1961, nearly three years before it was due. As usual he was at no loss to justify his decision. A strong and stable government in office for the next five years would convey the right message to friends and enemies both at home and abroad. It would give 'national unity' an opportunity to grow, unhampered by partisan electoral conflict. The racial problem could be addressed with the appropriate vigour and determination. Verwoerd's justifications were the prelude to an election which everyone knew the Government would win. All that mattered was how large its majority would be.

One feature of the election was 'the unprecedented number of uncontested seats', 67 out of 150, nearly 45 per cent. Both the National and the United Parties now acknowledged that certain constituencies of their opponents could not be won. Realistically, both decided not to waste energy and resources for the sake of a token show. It confirmed a trend apparent in the 1958 election: 'the electorate was becoming partitioned into two blocks of constituencies, the one composed of safe Nationalist seats, and the other of safe United Party seats, with very few left in the borderland'.[18]

With the conclusion so well known in advance, the election campaign itself was unmemorable. The major parties, and the Progressive Party, now uneasily contesting a general election for the first time, confined themselves to stating and re-stating well-known points of view.

The Government campaigned on the urgency and wonders of that white unity to which it had so recently become a convert. Nothing new came out of this, but at least Verwoerd took the opportunity of setting the record straight for those who may still have had lingering doubts about his, and therefore his government's, notion of South African nationhood. When opening the Transvaal National Party Congress in August he was unequivocal: 'Let me be very clear about this; when I talk of the nation of South Africa I talk of the White people of South Africa. I do not say that in disparagement of any other racial group in South Africa. I do not see us all as one multiracial state descending from various groups'.[19] He came in for plenty of criticism, but it was nothing he had not said before. There was really no room for excessive surprise.

On the Opposition side the main interest lay in how well, or badly, the Progressive Party would do. It had eleven MPs, but they had not yet been tested at the ballot-box after their flight from the United Party two years before. The general expectation was that they would all lose their seats, but could perform respectably in some of the better-heeled constituencies. The United Party itself had little to hope for, apart from eliminating the Progressives. It was still as devoid of policy as before and could offer the voters nothing more definite than what it chose to call 'race federation', which, in so far as it had any content, seemed to be little more than a euphemism for old-fashioned *baasskap*. It had entered into an election pact with the Nationalist dissident, Japie Basson, who had been expelled from the National Party in 1959. Realising that he had no chance of being re-elected as an independent, Basson hastily formed something he called the National Union and persuaded the all-too-gullible UP leader, De Villiers Graaff, that this new 'party' of his would attract many discontented Nationalists who could not yet bring themselves to vote for the United Party with its still strong jingoistic element. Basson's precondition was that he be given a safe United Party seat, which he got.

The results of the election were more or less as predicted. The Government emerged with three more seats than in 1958, namely 105, which gave it a majority over all other parties of 48. The

United Party regained ten constituencies represented by Progressives, losing only the affluent Johannesburg seat of Houghton to the formidable Helen Suzman. Its pact with the National Union had brought it nothing; Basson went back to Parliament, but his seven colleagues all lost, not doing conspicuously better in the seats they contested than the United Party had done in 1958.

The result represented a continuation of the post-1948 trend in favour of the Government, with an average swing since the referendum of two per cent. For the first time the Nationalists could claim that they represented a majority of voters, estimated, after considering the many uncontested seats, at 53,5 per cent of the total. It was reflected in the familiar huge disproportion between seats and votes. On a strictly proportionate basis the Nationalist majority over all other parties would not have been 48, but merely ten.

The Progressives had done surprisingly well in terms of votes, although only one of their 22 candidates was successful. But several of them had come exceptionally close. On average the Progressives had won more than a third of the votes in the constituencies they contested. It was an impressive performance, but misleading, as it turned out. Having expressed their dissatisfaction with the United Party and, perhaps, having been temporarily shocked into an awareness of the urgency of the racial problem by Sharpeville, the flighty English-speaking voters in future elections deserted the uncomfortably liberal Progressives, who were left struggling in the wilderness for well over a decade.

The Government had come out of the election well, but it was evident that Verwoerd's white unity was not around the corner. While the United Party had no capacity for growth, it still offered a safe, if uninspiring, haven for the basically conservative English-speaking electorate. It was all very well for Verwoerd to talk movingly about the need for unity, but the National Party had for too many years been openly and unashamedly an Afrikaner ethnic alliance. From that had come its strength. In that would its strength continue to lie for the foreseeable future. It was too much to expect English-speakers, conservative as most of them undoubtedly were, to be attracted in droves to a party which could do so little to make them feel at home. So they continued to support the slowly dying

United Party, seemingly resigned to the political impotence which was their fate.

CHAPTER TEN

The State Ruled by Verwoerd

No one since 1910 so dominated South Africa as did Hendrik Verwoerd after the coming of the republic. His obsessive drive to impose his own will and his own policies on the country, regardless of opposition, the logic of economic events and, frequently, considerations of humanity, argued that here was a politician out of the ordinary, a man who disdained the everyday pragmatic compromises so typical of those who refuse to rise above the belief that politics is the art of the possible. For Verwoerd humanity was endlessly pliable, to be shaped according to his view of what it should be, to be forced, in fact, into the mould which he had designed for it. In the normal course of events, such a man would not have survived long in politics. But it was a mark of the times in which he lived that in South Africa events were not normal, that is, subject to the familiar give and take of democratic processes. They lent themselves to an autocrat and simplifier, someone who had no doubt that he had the answer to what lesser and more modest creatures saw only as a problem of intolerable complexity. It was the good fortune of Verwoerd, if perhaps the ill fortune of his country, that after the republic his prestige and authority amongst by far the most Afrikaners stood so high that his judgement and his policies went unquestioned, that he gained total acceptance as the leader who had so surely brought them to the passionately-sought promised land.

The decade after the referendum was notable for several reasons. One was that it was a time of exceptionally impressive economic growth. The South African economy had taken the post-

Sharpeville panic in its stride. The instant flight of capital and the continued outflows which, till 1964, exceeded inflows, could only interrupt the expansion of what was clearly a dynamic economy. The manifest determination of the Government to restore order, whatever the cost, carried with it the message that the new republic would be no scene of revolutionary upheaval. Those who wished to resume the business of making money would find the climate for doing so remarkably congenial. It enabled the economy to continue with what it had been doing for most of the century — to grow, but still more rapidly than before, with manufacturing as the most conspicuous achiever, as South Africa was caught up in the advance of the world economy. Between 1960 and 1965 gross domestic product increased on average by six per cent per annum in real terms; in the second half of the decade the growth rate fell only slightly, to an annual average of 5,4 per cent.[1]

The performance of the economy would affect the lives of all South Africans profoundly. Obviously, average per capita incomes rose. It was an advance which affected the races as groups more or less equally; the racial distribution of income changed barely perceptibly as increases in the demand for labour enabled all groups to move forward, with relative disparities remaining in place. Ordinarily, it could have been expected that rising incomes would have been reflected in rising expectations, that an improving present would have led to hopes and demands for a better future. The perhaps too-often-cited case of Britain in the nineteenth century suggested that in the wake of economic progress would shortly come political reform. South African liberals were fond of arguing that the inexorable needs of a modern economy would sooner or later destroy apartheid and lead to the satisfaction of legitimate political aspirations (if perhaps not to the extent of actually leading to majority rule).

It was not, of course, an argument that Verwoerd and his colleagues could accept. They knew that conceding the primacy of the economic would result in the political suicide of the white man (as the terminology of those times was wont to put it). There was naturally no question of undoing the economic expansion which had returned after Sharpeville. Even if they had wished to do so, the political risk would have been too considerable; their constituency could scarcely have been willing to trade off short-term economic gain for long-term political survival, however fond Nationalist politicians were of posing the alternatives facing the volk in just these terms. Verwoerd himself had long been adept at this game. In 1951, in one of his first speeches as Minister of Native Affairs, he had warned against the concentration of black workers in the country's industrial complexes: 'The survival of white civilisation in South Africa is of more importance to me, even more important than expanded industrial development'.[2]

But most Afrikaner voters were little interested in such rarefied issues. Like voters everywhere else, they desired a more comfortable life for themselves and their children; they wasted no time worrying about an abstract posterity which could well look after itself. Verwoerd, a passionate devotee of the long view, could not have been pleased with such short-sightedness, but perforce had to accept for the moment that his followers, however faithful to him as their leader, were only in a limited sense willing to make sacrifices for the grand ideal of apartheid. There was, however, one thing he could do. He could make it plain to Africans that any expectations they might have had about political rights in a common society were totally misconceived. He proceeded to do just that.

Here was another of the notable features of the decade after the referendum, especially under Verwoerd. It was a period of highly authoritarian and often brutally harsh rule. African protest did not disappear after Sharpeville and the banning of the ANC and the PAC. But it would from then on take different, more violent and desperate forms. The Government responded in the only way it knew. It chose the path of repression, no matter what the price. The confrontation between Afrikaner and African nationalism proved bloody, but the struggle was unequal. In the end there could, at this time, be one victor only.

The general strike called to coincide with the proclamation of the republic had failed. To its organiser, Nelson Mandela, and other leaders of the ANC the message was clear. Legal protest was so much wasted effort in the face of official repression. There had to be another way.

Mandela was to explain their decision three years later in his speech from the dock at the Rivonia trial:

It is a fact that for a long time the people had been talking of violence — of the day when they would fight the white man and win back their country — and we, the leaders of the ANC, had prevailed upon them to use peaceful methods. When some of us discussed this in June 1961, it could not be denied that our policy to achieve a non-racial state by non-violent means had achieved nothing, and that our followers were beginning to lose confidence and were developing disturbing ideas of terrorism.[3]

Mandela and his colleagues believed they had found a better, indeed the only, alternative when they decided to form an underground revolutionary movement which embraced violence openly as the only means of overthrowing white rule. They gave it a Zulu name, *Umkhonto we Sizwe*, which meant Spear of the Nation.

Umkhonto had chosen violence, but by the sophisticated standards of a later age it was of a startlingly tame kind. The violence of Umkhonto was not directed at human life, but at government offices, communications and power lines. Eventually public order would so deteriorate, Mandela and his allies imagined, or perhaps just desperately hoped, that the Pretoria regime would be forced to the negotiating table.

Symbolically, Umkhonto chose to launch its new strategy on a sacred day for the Afrikaners, the Day of the Covenant, 16 December 1961, which celebrated the triumph of the Voortrekkers over the Zulus in 1838. Bomb attacks on electric power stations, post offices and other government buildings took place in Johannesburg, Port Elizabeth and Durban. Acts of sabotage over the next three years continued throughout the Republic, most of them committed by Umkhonto.

There was another organisation also committed to violence, but of an entirely more drastic kind. This was an offshoot of the PAC which called itself *Poqo* (Pure). Its main strength was in and near Cape Town and in the Transkei in the Eastern Cape. Bitterly antiwhite, *Poqo* had none of its rival's scruples about taking lives. It killed a number of black 'collaborators' and, apparently in an attempt to terrorise the white community, seven whites as well, all in the Western Cape and in the Transkei.

All this received plenty of publicity in the press, both pro-and anti-Nationalist, as well as on the openly pro-Nationalist South African Broadcasting Corporation. The white population had no doubt that here it was witnessing a determined and credible assault on the levers of power, an impression the Government took care to encourage in every way. It took to itself unprecedented powers to repel what it claimed was largely a Communist-inspired onslaught on white civilisation.

The General Laws Amendment Acts of 1962, 1963 and 1964 made earlier repressive measures seem as if they had been designed for the kindergarten. The first of these laws was generally known as the Sabotage Act. It broadened the definition of sabotage and made it a capital offence. The Minister of Justice now had the power to place anyone under house arrest. A year later the police received the right to detain 'suspects', in fact anyone they chose, for any number of periods of ninety days, without bail, and in solitary confinement. In 1964 the Minister was empowered to extend banning orders before they lapsed; the following year the Attorney-General was given the right to hold witnesses in prison for up to 180 days.

In August 1961 Verwoerd had hit upon the right man to carry out a campaign of mass repression. He was Balthazar Johannes Vorster, a former militant of the Ossewa Brandwag, in which capacity he had been interned by the Smuts Government during the war years. Vorster entered Parliament only in 1953; five years prior to this the Nationalists had still held his OB past against him. But he soon impressed them with his debating abilities, which were of a forceful and aggressive nature. Verwoerd made him a Deputy Minister in 1958, but Vorster found his true *métier* when he became Minister of Justice three years later.

Vorster's predecessor was F C Erasmus, who held the post during Sharpeville and its aftermath. Erasmus had not impressed all his colleagues: they accused him of not being sufficiently *kragdadig* (forceful) in dealing with the many radicals and agitators so eager to destroy civilised standards. Vorster was quite safe from such strictures. He used his vast powers as if they had been designed for him personally and would fall into abeyance if neglected.

When the 90 day measure was suspended in January 1965, 1 095 persons had been detained during the 18 months of its operation. Of these 575 had been charged with special offences, only 272 of whom had been convicted, while 93 were still awaiting trial.[4] In his five years as Minister of Justice Vorster banned 453 persons.

These are only some of the statistics, but they give a flavour of what Vorster was about in his new portfolio. He had a ready explanation for his actions, in which, he claimed, he took no pleasure. The safety of the State was at stake, for the Communist conspiracy was as dangerous as ever: 'With our experience of Communism we have found it necessary to acquire greater powers than are absolutely essential in order to block all loopholes'.[5]

The radical opponents of the Government, of whatever ideological complexion, found that they were no match for a Minister of Justice with such arbitrary and sweeping powers. The most serious of the underground movements, Umkhonto, was soon made powerless, to a large degree because of the highly effective infiltration of the organisation by police informers. Nelson Mandela himself was captured in August 1962. Most of Umkhonto's other leaders were seized in July the following year on a farm at Rivonia, near Johannesburg. The PAC offshoot, Poqo, was crushed by the middle of 1963. There was also an organisation which called itself the African Resistance Movement, really a body of frustrated and mainly white ex-liberals who wished to be part of the vanguard of history. They committed ineffective acts of sabotage in various parts of the country, which merely provided grist for Vorster's mill, for it could all be magnified as part of the revolutionary crisis facing South Africa. Most of the ARM leaders were captured in July 1964, although one of them, John Harris, was still to commit what in those times was an unheard of atrocity by exploding a bomb at the Johannesburg railway station which killed one person and seriously injured fourteen others. Harris was hanged, as were a number of Poqo members. The most important leaders of Umkhonto, including Mandela, received life sentences. By the end of 1964 the South African Government had reasserted its authority beyond all doubt.

It did so at a huge cost in civil liberties. The Republic at its inception acquired a body of still more repressive legislation than it had inherited from the Union and which its leaders would have been superhuman not to abuse. The number of authoritarian laws was to grow steadily over the years.

In spite of all the tension and excitement of those times it was plain enough, even then, that the Communist threat amounted to little and that the State was in no serious danger. Communists were only prominent on Umkhonto, but even so it was not an organisation which they controlled. Their presence amounted to a continuation of the alliance of convenience which had been forged between the ANC and the South African Communist Party during the 1950s. It had persisted, even if it was only because the ANC could not ignore the fact that white Communists were rare specimens indeed who did not look down upon or patronise blacks in any way. And the ANC was happy to accept any allies it could get. To quote Mandela again: 'Theoretical differences amongst those fighting against oppression are a luxury which cannot be afforded'.[6]

The truth was that it suited the Government to claim that it was participating in the Free World's battle against atheistic Communism. Vorster even went so far as to allege that the African Resistance Movement was 'a Communist organisation founded by Bram Fischer', leader of the SACP, a statement which could most charitably be described as rubbish. But, on the principle that any smear will do, some of the filth must have stuck. It did Vorster no harm at all in the eyes of Nationalists, who were wondrously impressed by such unrelenting *kragdadigheid*.

It is difficult to imagine that the operations mounted by Umkhonto, let alone by Poqo and the ARM, could have led to the overthrow of a government as formidably endowed with resources for control and repression as that of South Africa. Nor did the Government, or the white population, panic so easily. The sporadic acts of violence against the State were soon recognised as the desperate and frustrated last resorts of men who did not have the forces, equipment and organisation to do much about the system of apartheid they all hated so much. After the Rivonia arrests the threat was effectively over. The following month, August 1963, Verwoerd let the cat out of the bag when he said in a newspaper interview: 'I see no sign of any major upheaval coming in South

Africa ... internally this country, I believe, is more stable than it has been for years'. He recognised the revolutionaries for what they were: 'We have our instigators and saboteurs but they are, in fact, relatively few in numbers'. He added: 'Our real threat comes from outside'.[7] This explains his concern with foreign policy after 1961.

Most of Vorster's announcements about the dangers of Communism simply amounted to lurid and unsophisticated scaremongering. Yet, from the Government's perspective, there were definite gains from going about the business of suppression the way it did. As long as an organisation like Umkhonto was around to express its defiance by attacking government property, black hopes of not having to live under apartheid for ever remained alive. Mandela has described the response of the black population to the initial acts of sabotage by Umkhonto: 'Suddenly there was hope again. Things were happening. People in the townships became eager for political news. A great deal of enthusiasm was generated by initial successes, and people began to speculate on how soon freedom would be obtained'.[8]

It was black expectations of a future without apartheid that the Government had to disappoint, particularly at a time when rapid economic growth and the rising incomes which went with it could only have heightened frustrations with the racial status quo. The Government's swift and savage response to the violence of the resistance groups made excellent sense from this point of view. It cleared the decks for a period of high and sustained economic growth, which would scarcely have been possible if businessmen began to have doubts about the stability of the Republic's political system. For a while black aspirations were contained. In no way could this be permanent, as later events showed time and again, but for the moment it was enough.

The Government's success in putting down revolutionary dissent gave it plenty of room for getting on with its proclaimed objectives: white unity and separate development. Until the advent of Verwoerd the party faithful had not bothered much about either. White unity seemed superfluous as long as Afrikaners stood together to return ever-larger Nationalist majorities at the polls. Separate development in the sense of separate states for the different black 'nations' was an even headier concept which many good Nationalists found difficult to assimilate. It is perhaps not surprising that Verwoerd's success in moving closer to these goals was not as marked as he could have wished.

Appeals for unity reflected Verwoerd's realisation that it was white, and not merely Afrikaner rule in South Africa which was the focus of bitter international enmity. Both the white language groups were travelling in the same boat on a turbulent sea. Also, Afrikaner power was no longer threatened at the ballot-box, as every election since 1948 had shown more convincingly. Now that the republic had come, the Afrikaners could afford to make peace with the English-speakers, a group which had no distinct political will of its own, or any coherent policies to set against those of the Nationalists, except that it was just as enamoured of the privileges of a white skin. In any united white front against 'Communism' the English-speakers would willy-nilly be the junior partners. All they required was more tactful and considerate treatment than they had received in the past.

Undeniably, the Government made an effort. Towards the end of 1961 Verwoerd took the unprecedented step of appointing two English-speakers to the cabinet. They were the former United Party MPs, Alfred Trollip and Frank Waring. Trollip had been Administrator of Natal as well, so that his appointment could also be seen as an attempt to conciliate the English-speaking majority of the voters of that province, so right wing in their racial attitudes but so traditionally anti-Afrikaans in their political sympathies.

After 1948 the Government had put a virtual stop to the rapid post-war immigration from Europe to South Africa. White the immigrants may have been, but members of the volk they were not. At first the Nationalists, sitting on top of their tenuous parliamentary majority, were entitled to be nervous about 'the Afrikaner being ploughed under' by large inflows of foreigners. But in 1961 Afrikaners had cause to feel secure about their political dominance within the white population. There was still more cause to feel insecure about the place of South Africa's white population in a world which appeared every day to be turning more hostile to the Republic and its peculiar political system. From then on the Government encouraged white immigration. It established a Department of Immigration, of which, aptly enough, Trollip became the head. No longer would white immigrants be seen as underminers of the Afrikaner; they would rather strengthen an embattled white population, the lone defenders of 'civilised standards' on a continent which seemed only too prone to chaos.

There was another side to the coin of white unity. No one who was not white could be a member of the nation. As Verwoerd had emphasised repeatedly before, most controversially and insensitively at the Transvaal National Party Congress in August 1961, the South African nation was a white nation. It meant that the Cape coloured people, whose history was as old as that of white settlement in South Africa, would remain what they had always been: second-class citizens – but with a difference. When the coloureds were on the common roll, even subject as they were to restrictions which did not apply to whites, it was still possible to believe that they had a common future with white South Africans. Verwoerd's pronouncements made it plain that under his government's dispensation the coloureds would always be an officially certified subject group, without even the theoretical separate freedoms awaiting the Africans.

Nationalist policy towards the coloured people at this time throws a sharp light on the nature of the South African regime as it was under Verwoerd: its authoritarianism, its obsessive racial intransigence, its centralisation of decision-making in the hands of one man.

Many Nationalists, especially those of the supposedly more enlightened variety to be found in the Cape, had a conscience about the coloureds. They knew that in spite of all the standard rationalisations about the coloureds being a political football, which supposedly made them political arbiters between the white language groups and which could only arouse extreme Afrikaner animosity, and so forth, there was something not quite right about the way they had been removed from the common roll. These Nationalists were aware than an injustice had been committed and were looking for ways to salve their consciences. But it was not only a moral issue. There were excellent practical reasons for being more accommodating towards the coloureds, who, it was felt, belonged historically and culturally with the whites, and should not be driven by their grievances to make common cause with the blacks.

Surprisingly, there was even a Verwoerdian logic for greater liberalism towards the coloureds. After Verwoerd had his 'new vision' in 1959 and announced his policy of independent black homelands, Nationalists became fond of posing the alternatives for South Africa as between 'separate development' or 'integration'. If blacks could not develop separately in their own states, then the only alternative had to be the unthinkable, namely, equal rights with the white population in a common society. Nationalists now could have endless and sanctimonious fun at the expense of the stick-in-the-mud United Party, advocate of permanent white rule over blacks. What these recent moralists never did was to argue that this kind of logic pointed to a policy of equal rights for the coloureds, and the Indians too, for that matter, as there never was any question of a separate state for either group.

Some Nationalists got the point. Most conspicuously, the Nationalist daily in Cape Town, *Die Burger*, at that time still noted for a degree of thinking independent of the latest party line, decided that the new republican era called for a better deal for the coloureds. Even before the referendum it cautiously began to push the idea in its columns that perhaps the time had come for the four white 'coloured' MPs elected on a separate roll to the House of Assembly to be replaced by members who were themselves coloured.

After the referendum this kind of talk became increasingly fashionable. Earlier that year the pro-Government South African Bureau of Racial Affairs (Sabra) had appointed a commission to investigate the situation of the coloured people. Its report was submitted in January 1961, but it was widely known before then that it contained 'integrationist' proposals about the future of the coloureds. It only confirmed Verwoerd's own suspicions of Sabra for its unhealthy 'liberalistic' tendencies, although most outsiders would have regarded the organisation as almost embarrassingly conformist to the Nationalist party line. Verwoerd, however, had resigned from Sabra years before, in 1958, when still Minister of Native Affairs.

Verwoerd liked none of the fashionable new thinking. He was after all the sole arbiter of policy for the Government. In the words of a prominent Nationalist journalist, 'He simply did not like others discussing possible policy'.⁹ Had it contained any flaws he himself would have removed them long before. So in November 1960 he spelt out in a press interview how little was going to change in policy towards the coloureds. He hauled out a favourite argument: 'small concessions' would lead to big ones; coloureds in Parliament would only be the first step, the last was liable to be the ultimate horror of biological integration. If the coloureds did not know it already, they now discovered from the mouth of the Prime Minister that their immediate priorities were not political at all, but economic and educational. What the Nationalist revisionists had been suggesting amounted to 'multiracialism', always akin to original sin in Verwoerd's eyes. It would lead to continuous 'civil war' as each group attempted to ensure its own existence. Ultimate justice for all would only come through 'separate, parallel development'.¹⁰

Verwoerd's statement was succeeded by a veritable orgy of polemics in the letter columns of *Die Burger*. It was clear that plenty of Nationalists found it painful to swallow their leader's intransigent laying down of the law. But the battle had already been won and lost. Verwoerd was just the man to take a position and staunchly never budge. A week after the press interview he spelt out his own irrevocable intent in one of his most notorious statements. He informed a Nationalist conference on the Witwatersrand that party leaders would have to stand like 'walls of granite' on colour policy: the existence of a nation was at stake.¹¹

Verwoerd's concern about 'multiracial' tendencies in his party undoubtedly went deep. It was reflected in his summoning of a meeting of the Federal Council of the National Party, a rare event, for in practice the federal structure of the party gave autonomy to its provincial branches. The Council was in principle the supreme authority of the National Party; it now did what it had to do by duly giving Verwoerd the rubber stamp he wanted for his dictates on policy towards the coloureds.

The Prime Minister's victory was complete. A few weeks later, on 6 February 1961, Sabra announced that its conference on 'The Position of the Coloured People' would be postponed indefinitely. The report of its commission on the position of the coloureds never appeared. As for Sabra, it was 'purged'. As the Nationalist journalist, Schalk Pienaar, was to write years later, Verwoerd broke it down 'from a first-class venture to a third-rate organisation which was prepared for any genuflection before him'.[12]

The whole disagreeable episode over coloured policy epitomises official decision-making under Verwoerd. Its authoritarian and centralised nature derived from the nature of the man himself. Another quote from the acerbic Pienaar: 'It was once and for all so that Dr Verwoerd accepted that his voice would be decisive when and where he made it heard'.[13] Certainly, in his cabinet there was no such thing as collective leadership. Just as his predecessor, Strijdom, would not perpetuate the indulgent ways of Dr Malan towards fellow-ministers who chose to break cabinet solidarity, so would Verwoerd not allow colleagues even the degree of independence Strijdom had given them. As one of his 'white unity' appointments to the cabinet, Frank Waring, was to say:

> Verwoerd was a man who would listen, ask you questions and show that he knew a great deal about your portfolio. But then he said, "This is what we will do." And that was that. Verwoerd wanted to make all the decisions. Verwoerd was a very strong character and he dominated the cabinet completely... Verwoerd was so overwhelming and dominating as Prime Minister that it was simply inconceivable that the time would arrive when he was not there.[14]

Verwoerd's successor was to display a more relaxed approach to decision-making by his cabinet colleagues. But the power at the top was still there, only more diffused. The cabinet under the Nationalist Government enjoyed substantial autonomy from the pressures of interest groups and lobbies. It was no mere passive reflector of the interests of organised classes and pressure groups. Those Nationalists who pushed for a less illiberal policy towards the coloureds were on particularly shaky ground. As numbers went, they were relatively few, if fairly vocal. The electoral cost to the Government of disregarding them could only be slight.

In so far as the Government did respond to the push and pull of interest groups, the pressure came from the right. It had come to power largely as a representative of white workers and white farmers. One group desired protection from black competition for jobs, the other wanted privileged access to black labour. By and large, neither had reason to complain: tighter influx control over black migration to the cities suited both parties. In practice it came down to the pursuit of racial policies which could only be described as right wing.

By 1966, when Verwoerd died, much had changed since 1948. The economic development of those years had resulted in a more heterogeneous Afrikaner population. Afrikaners were becoming increasingly urbanised, hence more exposed, as many traditionalists feared, to the deracinating and corrupting influences of the environment of the city. In particular, an Afrikaner business class was emerging, larger and more self-assured than the small group of capitalists of 1948 beholden for favours to a government of their own kind.

Afrikaners in the mid-sixties had come to understand what private enterprise could do for them. The condemnations of 'British-Jewish capitalism' so common amongst Nationalist politicians before 1948 had long gone, to be replaced by an appreciation of the resources which economic growth under capitalist auspices could place in the hands of a good Afrikaner government. In effect, capitalist development was used to promote what has been described as a kind of ethnic socialism.[15]

The antagonism between apartheid regulation of the labour market and businessmen's pursuit of profit is by now well known,[16] in spite of the earnest and, at one time, incessant attempts by neo-Marxist and radical writers to show that 'apartheid is a particular mode of class exploitation developed by South African capitalists'.[17] In this respect rising Afrikaner capitalists were as adversely affected as their English-speaking counterparts by the interventions of politicians and bureaucrats who served their own self-interest by imposing and extending apartheid. Yet at a time of high growth the tensions inherent between political policy and economic efficiency could be contained readily. It meant that Afrikaner businessmen still felt close ties between themselves and a government which had done so much for the Afrikaners as a group, and not least for them in particular by way of contracts, subsidies and protection. Here was one interest group which could not, in the 1960s, much shape the theory and practice of apartheid, even if it had the will to do so.

The Afrikaner community was becoming more diversified and in some respects less attached to the values of the past. But in one respect at least this trend strengthened apartheid, for after 1948 another powerful group emerged which had a strong vested interest in the system. It took the form, as one economist has put it, of 'a massive bureaucracy whose *raison d'être* was the production of market regulation designed to effect wealth redistributions away from blacks and white industrial and commercial capitalists in favour of white workers and agricultural capitalists'.[18]

After 1948 Afrikaners took over the civil service rapidly, especially the senior positions, which they found occupied mainly by English-speaking supporters of the United Party, who also tended to be more liberal on matters of race than their supplanters. It was Verwoerd who, assisted by the indispensable Werner Eiselen, was largely responsible for the flowering of a huge apartheid bureaucracy, imbued with its master's own especial world-view. As one of Verwoerd's top underlings later observed, 'he attracted not pliable servants but like-minded ideologues'.[19] Whether concerned with stricter enforcement of influx control, the administration of the black townships, or removing 'redundant' Africans from the officially white areas, here was a group which had acquired immense power, with a clearly identifiable interest not simply in the entrenchment of apartheid but in its extension.

During the Verwoerd years rapid economic growth had only begun to eat at the foundations of white supremacy. Those groups which most needed apartheid in order to prosper were well-established and showed no signs of losing their influence with the Government. By contrast, Afrikaner critics of some aspects of apartheid, like the enthusiasts for a new deal for the coloureds, or those who might have been hurt by specific measures, like Afrikaner capitalists, were simply not strong enough to push the policy in a more 'liberal' direction.

It was to pressures from the right that the Government responded, even when it chose not to yield to them. For instance, Verwoerd had to endure constant criticism from within his party for going too far in wishing to give 'separate freedoms' to blacks.

His reaction was entirely more respectful than it had been to critics of his policies towards the coloureds, as when he opened the Orange Free State National Party Congress in 1962. Ostensibly paying special attention to criticisms made by the leader of the Opposition, De Villiers Graaff, but in fact to the issues for discussion which had been submitted by the various branches of the party, Verwoerd did not refute the popular complaint that his government was doing too much for blacks. He justified his policies rather as essential for white survival. It was a defence which worked, especially as it took a wild flight of the imagination to see Verwoerd as a liberal of any kind.

His success in handling this kind of grievance was triumphantly shown in the fate of the Republican Party in the general election of 1966. Standing on a platform of 'white *baasskap* over the whole of South Africa', it made the disastrous error of believing that strong right wing sentiment would translate into voting behaviour. Instead, all 22 candidates of the Republican Party lost their deposits. It was a convincing demonstration that right-wingers still felt quite at home in the National Party of Verwoerd.

Surprisingly, there was one feature of the Verwoerd era which was more typical of the man himself than of the government which he so dominated. This was his obsession with race. Verwoerd, more than anyone in his cabinet, insisted on the most rigid separation of the races. Whether it concerned coloured MPs in Parliament, integrated sport or professional associations, Verwoerd was always adamant that yielding on such apparently minor issues would amount to the thin end of the wedge, mere preparation for the submerging of the Afrikaner by a conglomerate chaos. During the controversy over possible coloured MPs, Verwoerd repeatedly told his wife: 'I am not going down in history as the man who led the Afrikaner people to bastardisation. If the majority is in favour of it then I will resign'.[20] Even more extraordinary was his reaction at a private showing in August 1966, the month before his death, to the film version of *Othello*, with a blackened-up Laurence Olivier in the title role. After the screening was over Verwoerd at once declared his 'outspoken' opposition to the film being shown to South African audiences; in the circumstances of the Republic it was unthinkable.[21] His cabinet colleague, former enemy and later admirer, Ben Schoeman, himself no liberal, observed that colour was Verwoerd's Achilles' heel: 'Verwoerd, with all his exceptional ability, was in many respects unbelievably short-sighted, especially when issues of race were concerned'.[22]

Of all the Nationalist leaders since 1948 Verwoerd was the most persistent ideologue. He truly made a fetish of race. For him apartheid was a genuine ideology, which stood or fell as a system; tampering with the parts meant changing the very essence of the whole. Some of his colleagues, as Schoeman's remarks suggest, were somewhat more pragmatic. For them, and for Nationalists in general, apartheid was a convenient device to keep the Afrikaners on top. They did not have apocalyptic visions of the end of Afrikanerdom if All Black rugby teams from New Zealand with a few Maoris in them toured South Africa. If adaptations had to be made, if age-old prejudices had to be abandoned, then so it had to be, as long as Afrikaner survival was not endangered. This is what happened increasingly, if slowly and belatedly, after Verwoerd's death. For the Afrikaners, but not for Verwoerd, apartheid was not an ideology where everything had to fit properly. Verwoerd, the immigrant, worked obsessively all his life at being an Afrikaner among Afrikaners. Ironically, it was his very success in making the system of apartheid that measured his failure to understand the people he so badly wished to identify with.

System or no, apartheid still had to be seen to work. It had to keep blacks out of the 'white' areas except when their labour was absolutely necessary. 'Separate freedoms' had to become more than a vague slogan designed to convince a hostile and unimpressionable world that apartheid was actually a doctrine and practice of liberation.

The Government had conveyed its message to black dissidents in the post-Sharpeville repression. Blacks would never have the vote in a common political system with the whites. But in 'their own areas' they could be as free as they chose. The sky would truly be the limit to the constitutional development of the various black 'nations' of South Africa.

For many Africans, especially those who had tasted the delights of Western education, this could only be a repellent message; paternalistic, backward-looking and disregardful of the most up-to-date political thought. But, for the immediate times ahead, there was no alternative. It was a choice between making the most of limited rights in backward areas or taking the long haul, in the hope and expectation that the incoming tide of history would at last sweep Africans to what was rightfully theirs. Perhaps not surprisingly, the Government found that its 'collaborators' in the various Bantu homelands did not all turn out to be quite as docile as their mentors wished them to be.

Even by the unexacting standards of the United Nations Organisation the homelands were not promising material for nationhood. The areas of the ten regions eventually designated as homelands were mostly so scattered and fragmented that self-government, let alone independence, could for them only be a theoretical notion. As one study of homeland development expressed it, they were 'direct legacies of the haphazard system of reserving certain lands for African use during the final stages of white settlement in the late nineteenth and early twentieth centuries'.[23] Nor, in spite of the Government's claims about their distinctness as nations, were they all homogeneous. In designating them the criteria were 'tradition, propinquity, practicality, and political expediency'.[24] Economically, the backwardness of these rural areas was encompassing. They served primarily as reservoirs of labour for the white areas of the Republic. Well over half of the black population lived outside the homelands, which constituted about thirteen per cent of the land area of South Africa.

The least unprepossessing of these compulsory candidates for nationhood was the Transkei, the main (if, somewhat illogically, not the only) homeland of the Xhosa of the Eastern Cape. Its tradition of local government had been strong until the imposition of Bantu Authorities, going back to the previous century. Territorially, the Transkei was a single entity. Even if its economic backwardness was conspicuous, the Transkei hardly differed in this respect from the other homelands.

Bantu Authorities had developed rapidly in the Transkei, building on the foundations laid down before. But there was plenty of resistance. In Pondoland in the eastern part of the territory, unrest had come to stay after 1959. Tribesmen made known their rejection of the new system and other official policies by assaulting and even murdering leaders suspected of being Government 'stooges', refusing to pay their taxes and rioting and burning huts and kraals. The Government responded in its familiar and thorough way by issuing a proclamation for the whole Transkei late in 1960 which, *inter alia*, gave the police and the chiefs extensive powers of arrest and banishment. By the end of May the revolt had been suppressed, but only after thousands of troops had been rushed in. There was a semblance of order, yet unrest continued and the emergency proclamation remained in force until 1965.

The Government appears to have been surprised when the Transkei Territorial Authority decided in April 1961 to take separate development seriously: it demanded complete freedom and independence for the Transkei. Verwoerd could not refuse. He was as good as his word of 1959 and indicated that he had no objection to self-government; in January 1962 he announced that the Transkei would acquire a constitution before the end of 1963 which would eventually give it full domestic control.

The Transkei Constitution Act of that year was in the well-known mould of the constitutions Britain and France had given their colonies in the 1950s. The official majorities of the British and French had as their Transkeian counterpart a majority of chiefs sitting *ex officio* in the Legislative Assembly, 64 out of a total of 109. Only the remaining 45 members would have to thank the voters of Transkei for their seats.

Verwoerd had always advocated the merits of a suitably guided traditionalism. The results of the first elections under the Act, in December 1963, must have convinced him how right he had been all along. The Government's man, Chief Kaiser Matanzima, was elected Chief Minister by 54 votes to the 49 which went to Paramount Chief Victor Poto. But Matanzima had behind him most of the chiefs; it was his opponent who had the support of most of the democratically chosen members. After all the official pressure exerted behind the scenes for Matanzima's election it was, in fact, a surprisingly small majority.

The most obtrusive feature of the Transkeian venture into separate freedom was that Pretoria would remain in charge. The first election took place against the background of the emergency proclamation. The South African Government took care to reserve to itself defence, foreign affairs, internal security, customs and excise, postal services, banking and currency, and railways and harbours. The cabinet of the Transkei would control, *inter alia,* direct taxation of the citizens of the territory, agriculture, education, the maintenance of law and order, and public works. All laws passed by the Legislative Assembly were subject to the approval of the South African Parliament and needed the approval of the State President.

It was in keeping with the minimal role Transkeians themselves played in drafting the constitution. Verwoerd and his colleagues had emphasised the contribution of the recess committee appointed by the Transkei Territorial Authority in jointly drawing up the constitution with the Government. The truth was that Verwoerd substantially had his own way. As the Secretary of Bantu Administration and Development, C B Young, told the Transkei Territorial Assembly in May 1962 when it met to discuss the draft constitution: 'It rests in the hands of the Government of South Africa to decide what it will concede to the Transkei in the form of self-government. The committee has been consulting with the Government for a long time and the basis of agreement, you might say, has already been reached'. Young in effect advised the members to take what they could get 'and be thankful for this great step forward in the historical and constitutional development of the Transkei Territories'.[25]

It was not an auspicious beginning, although hardly ill-suited to a continent where democratic institutions appeared to survive only by way of exception. At first Matanzima was seen as a 'stooge' of the apartheid regime, but this was to oversimplify. However much the Nationalists wished for suitably docile homeland rulers, such an outcome could only destroy the already suspect credibility of 'separate freedoms'. Men like Matanzima had to be given room in which to manoeuvre, they had to be seen to place successful pressure on the supposed puppet-masters in Pretoria. Matanzima did so conspicuously after Verwoerd's death when he persuaded the Government to reverse the ban imposed on white capital investment in the Transkei. Here was a fluid situation, always liable to find its way into channels which the Government had not constructed.

In one respect at least the homelands policy seemed to be going according to design. The banning of the ANC and the PAC, the post-Sharpeville repression, left Africans with few political alternatives. Temporarily, the homelands route must have seemed the only one open to many politically conscious blacks. And there were the substantial perquisites and patronage which successful homelands politicians would be able to lay their hands upon. The well-informed American observer, Edwin Munger, writing a year after Verwoerd's death, discerned the emergence of a different, tribally based, kind of black nationalism: 'This infant nationalism is not really African nationalism in the sense of the last three decades ... What is developing in the rural areas is a Xhosa, Zulu, and a Sotho nationalism'.[26]

That was how it could be seen at the time. But distinct tribal nationalisms were not enough to assure the success of the homelands policy. As a viable nation-state, the Transkei was probably the least unpromising of these areas. The others were so economically backward, so scattered and fragmented, that even by the standards of Africa it was difficult to see in them future members of the comity of nations. They were in truth little more than economic appendages of white South Africa. At Verwoerd's death the total product of the homelands accounted for less than two per cent of that of the Republic. Average output per head was R34, compared with R611 for the rest of the country. In the larger towns black family incomes were on average three to four times the average homeland income.[27] Nor had the prospects of the homelands been improved by Verwoerd's ban on the presence of white capital in these areas. Their failure to provide opportunities for most of their people had to have an impact elsewhere. It was in the cities of South Africa that the success or failure of apartheid would be measured.

In the 1960s the Government came close to a superhuman effort to control black access to the urban areas. If there was a time which could be called the 'heroic' period of apartheid, it was this. Existing laws found more stringent applications. New ones spelt out in fine print the Stallard Doctrine that blacks should only enter urban areas to look after the economic needs of the white population. In all, the years after Sharpeville were a more repressive time for Africans in the towns and cities.

Blacks who had felt reasonably secure because of their 'Section 10 rights' under the Natives (Urban Areas) Consolidation Act of 1945 and its various amendments, now discovered that they had been mistaken. Previously, the Government had relied upon 'Section 10' to keep blacks out, but the law did not do what it was supposed to. Far too many Africans, by the Government's lights, were crowding into the cities, attracted by the prospect of becoming 'Section 10 Bantu'. The official response was to make it increasingly difficult for Africans to acquire such rights. More and more, they became temporary workers, only able to find work as transients. Migrant labour acquired a new lease of life, even less than before a natural outcome of development in an economy sharply divided into modern and traditional sectors, still more a reflection of the visions of social engineers who had no doubt at all that they knew what was good for others.

One year after Verwoerd's death, an interdepartmental inquiry into the pass laws concluded that the policies of the past had not worked as they should have: the 'flood of Bantu to the cities' remained excessive.[28] Labour controls became still more restrictive and, to a point, they did work. The growth rate of black urbanisation declined in the 1960s to 3,9 per cent, compared with the 6,4 per cent of 1946–1950. The absolute number of Africans in the white areas increased, but at a slower rate. In 1970, 54 per cent of the total black population lived in these areas. Ten years before it had been 63 per cent. To quote Merle Lipton, 'In the absence of the controls, rising population growth in the Bantustans, and the growing gap between rural and urban wages, would normally have led to *increased* migration into the white areas, particularly the towns'.[29] The apartheid bureaucracy had done itself proud, and would continue to do so for some time still.

Even so, it was not enough. Verwoerd had identified 1978 as the turning point, the year when the black inflow into the urban areas would turn around. 'White' cities would become genuinely white, in the special sense that they would have no settled black population.[30] But as Schalk Pienaar commented about that special date: 'With the passing of the years and the visible flow of events, this story became thinner and thinner, or should one say a bit much to swallow. The good Lord did after all give us eyesight, even if not always understanding'.[31] The total number of blacks in the white areas was increasing every day, despite its relative decline. Stricter influx control and the greater emphasis on the temporary nature of the African urban presence could not conceal that economic growth was eroding apartheid at its foundations.

It remained true that the Government during these years was unassailable at home. Verwoerd found that foreign policy was taking up more of his time. Unlike most of his colleagues, he was sharply aware of the problems for South Africa arising from global condemnation of apartheid. It was the main reason for his sudden 'new vision' of separate freedoms in 1959, which he announced without having so much as mentioned it in the Nationalist caucus. He knew that in a decolonising world South Africa could get away with no less than at least nominal adherence to the principles of the United Nations.

Verwoerd could only condemn what he saw as the headlong rush by Western colonial powers to abdicate their responsibilities and hand power over to adolescent regimes which had all the trappings but none of the essence of statehood. Increasingly, the new world order, or lack of it, was reflected in annual majorities at the United Nations condemning apartheid. Equally routinely, the Government rejected such 'interference in South Africa's domestic affairs'. But it could not simply be ignored. There was the disturbing prospect that Western countries would be pressurised into casting their vote against South Africa at the United Nations. Macmillan's speech on the winds of change had clearly prepared the way for a more arm's-length relationship with the apartheid government. Verwoerd's main aim in foreign policy became to prevent international action against his country and its policies.

Verwoerd had two official Ministers of Foreign Affairs: the aggressive and petty Eric Louw and, from 1964, the Oxford-trained and far smoother Hilgard Muller, but they were both merely his mouthpieces. Verwoerd was effectively his own foreign minister. Surprisingly perhaps, he displayed qualities which were quite different from those his fellow South Africans had come to know so well. At home Verwoerd was an unbending ideologue. In his dealings with the outside world another man made his appearance, someone who did not yield on what he saw as issues crucial to white survival, but who was withal conciliatory and apparently the soul of reason. He could afford to take a hard line when confronting his domestic opponents; the Government after all had an intimidating command of superior firing power. Abroad, South Africa was only one state, and a fairly small one at that, amongst many others – such abrasive ways would hardly endear it to a world in which it needed all the Western friends it could hang on to.

There were considerable successes. During his premiership, talk of mandatory sanctions against so villainous a regime became increasingly fashionable, but went no further. In 1965 the General Assembly of the United Nations passed a motion recommending just such a step. The Republic's main friends, the United States and Britain, abstained, in itself a disturbing sign, as three years before they had voted against such a motion. But it was a resolution which could not be enforced. In 1963 the Security Council of the United Nations had unanimously adopted a resolution calling for an arms embargo. That, provisionally, was as far as the United States and Britain were prepared to go. They continued to trade with South Africa and to invest in its expanding economy. West Germany and Japan joined them in acquiring a substantial economic stake in the Republic. Profits were high from such activities during the 1960s. The Government in turn stressed the benefits which economic development would bring to all South Africans, whatever their colour. If capitalists needed further reasons for investing in the land of apartheid, in addition to the material rewards it brought them, here they had one which was very difficult to refute.

The Republic was more vulnerable to international pressure on the question of South West Africa, the mandated territory it had acquired after the First World War. When the League of Nations became defunct, South Africa held that the mandate had lapsed. It refused to accept the authority of the United Nations, which regarded South West Africa as one of its trust territories.

In 1950 the International Court of Justice gave its advisory opinion that South Africa remained bound by the mandate, but that it was not legally obliged to place the territory under United

Nations trusteeship. The international body did, however, have the right, according to the Court, to supervise the administration of South West Africa, within the limits imposed upon the Mandates Commission. Both parties took from the opinion what they liked and rejected the rest. From then on dispute between them was endless as the General Assembly passed resolutions annually condemning the South African presence in South West. While it rejected United Nations authority, the South African Government could not afford the cavalier dismissal of these resolutions which it instinctively preferred. They did, after all, not amount to interference with the country's own domestic affairs, but with those of a territory which was decidedly not part of South Africa.

Instead of preparing its white inhabitants for a future which could not but differ from that of South Africa, Verwoerd irresponsibly assured them in 1962 that their destiny was inextricably linked with that of the Republic.[32] He even appointed a commission which in 1964 duly came out with the desired recommendations, namely that this backward and thinly populated territory should be divided into ten homelands, as well as a 'white' area comprising the most developed parts of South West. It was an impressive exercise in outright lunacy; it did not prevent the South African Government from later going some way to implement it.

Verwoerd of course had a grand vision of the future, but such scenarios have a habit of soon making their inventors look absurd. His strength lay in the daily manoeuvring of politics. In 1961 he invited the Secretary-General of the United Nations, Dag Hammarskjöld, to come to South Africa to acquire first-hand knowledge of the country's policies. It was a visit so successful that another was being contemplated at the time when Hammarskjöld died in a plane crash. Verwoerd came out of it well. He had shown that he was prepared to talk to foreign critics of his policies and even seemed willing to listen to what they had to say.

The following year Verwoerd displayed similar flexibility when he invited the chairman and vice-chairman of the UN Committee on South West Africa to visit the territory. These men came to highly favourable conclusions about the South African administration of the mandate, which they later repudiated when they discovered how unpopular they had become at the United Nations.

Once more Verwoerd emerged with an enhanced reputation for adroit diplomatic skills.

In July 1966 the South West African issue ended in a triumphant conclusion for the Republic, or so it seemed at the time, when the International Court decided by eight votes to seven that it could not pronounce on the legality of the South African presence in South West. The plaintiffs, Ethiopia and Liberia, former members of the League of Nations, had no *locus standi* in the case, the Court found. It was an exceedingly strange decision, all the more as it had rejected the South African arguments to that effect four years earlier. But undoubtedly Verwoerd was right in hailing it as 'a major victory'.

He had handled the United Nations with some ease. Nor was there any sign that the Republic's main trading partners had any interest in the sanctions for which the Afro-Asians at the international body had been clamouring. The only other threat facing South Africa could be from independent African countries to the north. But plainly this was negligible, confined to the frustrated rhetoric about the horrors of apartheid which provided a common bond between a disparate collection of dictatorships at meetings of the Organisation of African Unity. Neither their military nor their economic strength was of a kind that could inspire terror in the rulers of South Africa. What they and their Asian collaborators could do was to secure the exclusion of the Republic from a number of international bodies, like the World Health Organisation, and, far more disagreeable to its sports-fanatical whites, from the Olympic Games. South African planes and ships found themselves denied the air space and harbours of most independent African states. But none of this could be a serious threat to the survival of the apartheid government.

In November 1965 Rhodesia issued its unilateral declaration of independence from Britain. Verwoerd had never been enthusiastic about the policy of 'racial partnership' pursued in this self-governing British colony on its northern borders, based as it was, in principle, on multiracialism. In practice, it differed little from apartheid. The window-dressing provided by an ostensibly colour-blind franchise enabled a white minority of 200 000 to rule a black population of two million with little difficulty.

Whatever his philosophical differences with the illegal regime of Ian Smith, Verwoerd knew the advantages to South Africa of continued white rule in Rhodesia. He was also under intense pressure from his own white population to recognise the Smith government. His policy of 'neutrality' was to give Rhodesia the kind of aid which was essential to its survival, without extending to it the official recognition it craved.

Verwoerd refused to join in the international sanctions campaign against Rhodesia, which meant that it could readily be circumvented. Any other decision by a country which was itself being singled out as a target for sanctions would have been extraordinary. As an open sanctions-buster, South Africa's image abroad as an unrepentant upholder of white domination was less endearing than ever, but it was probably the decision by Verwoerd which was most widely supported by the country's white inhabitants.

Most fundamentally, the Nationalist Government knew there was no substitute for strength. Defence spending grew steadily under Verwoerd. In 1959 to 1960 it accounted for seven per cent of the budget; seven years later it had gone up to seventeen per cent. The armed forces were enlarged and military training for all white youths became compulsory. It reflected the determination of the Republic's white population to survive. As Verwoerd put it in 1964: 'We will fight with our economic power against boycotts and with our sons and daughters if there are threats of violence. I give this assurance because for us it is the life or suicide of a nation'.[33]

At the height of his power and prestige, Verwoerd died, shockingly and suddenly.

In March 1966 Verwoerd had led the National Party to its greatest electoral triumph. It won 126 seats out of 166, increasing its share of the vote from the 53,5 per cent of 1961 to 58,6 per cent. For the first time the Nationalists had won the support of a significant number of English-speaking voters. It looked as if the endless harping on white unity was beginning to show dividends.

Peace had been restored to the Republic, even if it came at a substantial cost. Economic growth was continuing at an exuberant rate. The return on foreign investment reflected the new-found overseas confidence in the future of the South African economy; in 1965 net capital inflows came to R235-million. The sanctions campaign against apartheid appeared to be going nowhere. For the moment all things seemed possible in this best of all white republics.

To his fellow white South Africans Verwoerd was the symbol and guarantor of the achievement. He had established an unequalled ascendancy over his colleagues and the electorate. He became the object of a personality cult: it showed itself in the Hendrik Verwoerd schools and streets to be found all over the Republic.

Withal, the object of this adulation showed no sign of mellowing with success. His obsession with race never left him. In 1965 he went out of his way to affront the United States in a series of unpleasant incidents arising from the Government's insistence that American diplomats in South Africa and seamen from visiting US ships comply with the official racial norms of the country. Later that year Verwoerd took a decision which even some hero-worshipping Afrikaners were unhappy with, for it involved their idolised sport of rugby. In the past New Zealand rugby teams touring South Africa had not included Maoris, in deference to white prejudices. By 1965 opposition in New Zealand to such appeasement of racism had become acute: it was agreed that in future only fully representative teams would tour South Africa. It seemed, however, that for the sake of something as important as rugby even the Nationalist Government would be prepared to compromise, but no one had reckoned with Verwoerd. At a Nationalist meeting in the Transvaal, while a Springbok rugby side was actually in New Zealand, he announced that South Africans overseas respected the customs of others; they expected that foreigners visiting South Africa would respect theirs as well. That was the end of the planned New Zealand tour of South Africa. For Verwoerd Maoris in an All Black rugby side would be as dangerous to white survival as universal suffrage on a common voters' roll. His fellow Afrikaners could not have been happy, but they had got into the habit of not questioning Verwoerd's judgement. They duly swallowed what they were told to.

In the first five weeks of the parliamentary session which began on 29 July 1966, Verwoerd spoke only twice, as if he was resting on his laurels. But the Prime Minister's budget vote was up for discussion on 6 September and Verwoerd was then expected to make a major speech. A few days before he had met with Chief Leabua Jonathan, designated Prime Minister of the soon-to-be independent Lesotho. It was the first meeting on South African soil between the country's Prime Minister and the leader of a black state. Verwoerd was expected to report to the House of Assembly on their discussions, as well as to give his view about the Republic's international position and the future of the coloureds.

Public interest was intense. When the House of Assembly met after lunch-time its galleries were packed. Verwoerd entered the House at about 2.15 p.m. as the bells were ringing to summon MPs for the debate. He had just sat down in the Prime Minister's seat and the House was filling up when a uniformed parliamentary messenger approached him in a great hurry. The man pulled out a knife, threw himself upon Verwoerd and in quick succession stabbed him four times in the neck and chest. At first his victim appeared to think it was an accident and smiled as if to indicate that it did not matter. His expression changed when he saw the blood which had suddenly appeared on his chest. He pulled together the lapels of his jacket but by then he was already beyond help. He gave a sigh and slumped forward in his seat.

Verwoerd's assailant was overpowered by MPs, with much difficulty, as he slashed away with his knife. He was removed by the police. Verwoerd himself was given artificial respiration, but it was futile. His heart stopped beating five minutes after the attack, but he was in fact a dead man one minute after being assaulted. Less than an hour later it was announced that Verwoerd had been dead on arrival at Groote Schuur hospital. He would have been 65 years old two days later.

Verwoerd's assassin turned out to be a lunatic, acting entirely on his own. He was Demetrio Tsafendas, the 38-year old illegitimate son of a Greek father and a half-breed Portuguese-African mother. Born in Lourenço Marques, Tsafendas had attended a school for white children in the Transvaal, but had spent most of his life in Mozambique. He returned to South Africa in 1965, by the oversight of a minor official, as he was on the list of prohibited immigrants into the Republic. He was due for deportation, but in the meanwhile managed, through another oversight, to obtain a

F Malan

J G Strijdom

F Verwoerd

B J Vorster

W Botha

F W de Klerk

(SA Communications Service)

Opposite (top): The early days of Nationalist power. Dealing with a Torch Commando recalcitrant. *(Africana Museum)*

Opposite (bottom): 'We Afrikaners are not the work of man, but a creation of God.' D F Malan spelling out the new order. *(Bailey's Archives)*

Left: The launch of the Defiance Campaign. *(Bailey's Archives)*

Below: Sniffing out the traitors. Nelson Mandela and supporters at the Treason Trial in Pretoria, 1958. *(Bailey's Archives)*

Left: 'Cleaning up' slums. Sophiatown during the fifties. *(The Star)*

Below: 'Supermac', (Harold Macmillan) telling South Africans that the winds of change were blowing hard. *(The Star)*

Opposite (top): Pass raid at the entrance to Johannesburg Station, March 1961. *(The Star)*

Opposite (bottom): A queue outside the Bantu Administration office in Market Street, Johannesburg for the renewal of work permits. *(The Star)*

Opposite (top): Aftermath of Sharpeville. Coffins on their way to the mass funeral. *(The Star)*

Opposite (bottom): The coffin of Dr H F Verwoerd in transit to the funeral in Pretoria, 10 September 1966. *(The Star)*

Above: The newly elected leader of the National Party, Balthazar John Vorster. His disgruntled rival, Ben Schoeman, is immediately behind him. *Sunday Times)*

Above: On a clear day you can see forever – Soweto from the air. *(The Star)*

Below: An award-winning composite photograph commemorating 16 June 1976, Soweto. *(Star Africa – Alf Kumalo)*

Opposite (top): P W Botha on the steps of Parliament after his election as the leader of the National Party. *(The Argus)*

Opposite (bottom): Before old friends fall out. P W Botha takes the traditional seat reserved for the Prime Minister in the House of Assembly. On his left are Lourens Muller and Connie Mulder who were to become his bitter enemies. *(The Star)*

Above: 'This is how it is going to be!' The National Party's imperious master P W Botha, in his element. *(The Star)*

Opposite (top): Violent reaction to a state of emergency. *(The Star)*

Opposite (bottom): 'You can always trust me.' Andries Treurnicht and friends during the 1987 general election campaign. *(The Star)*

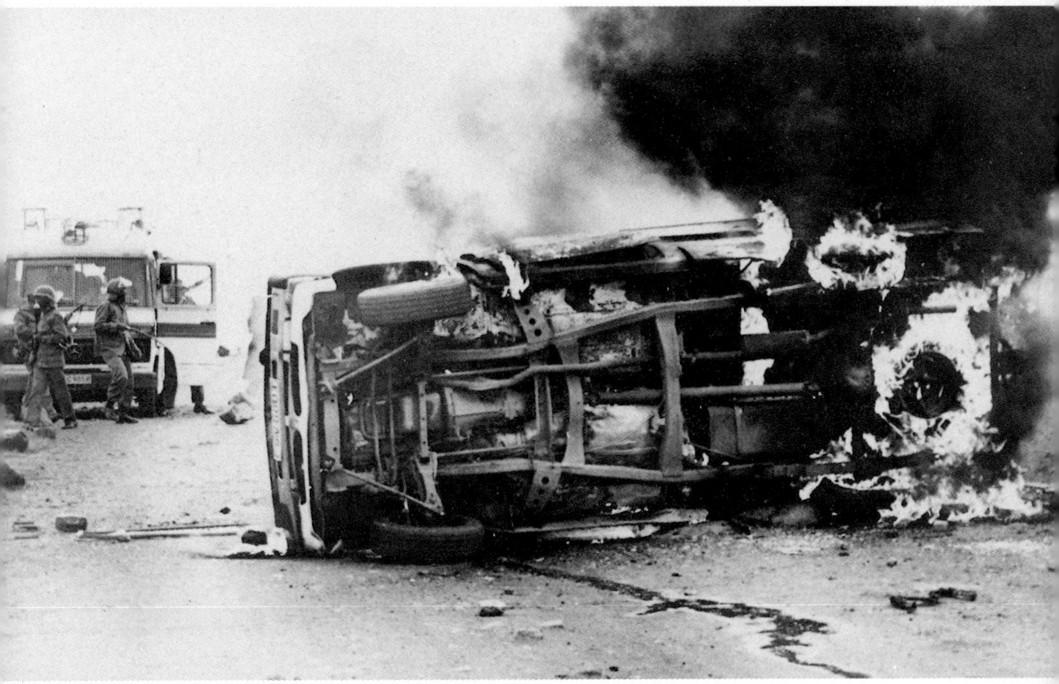

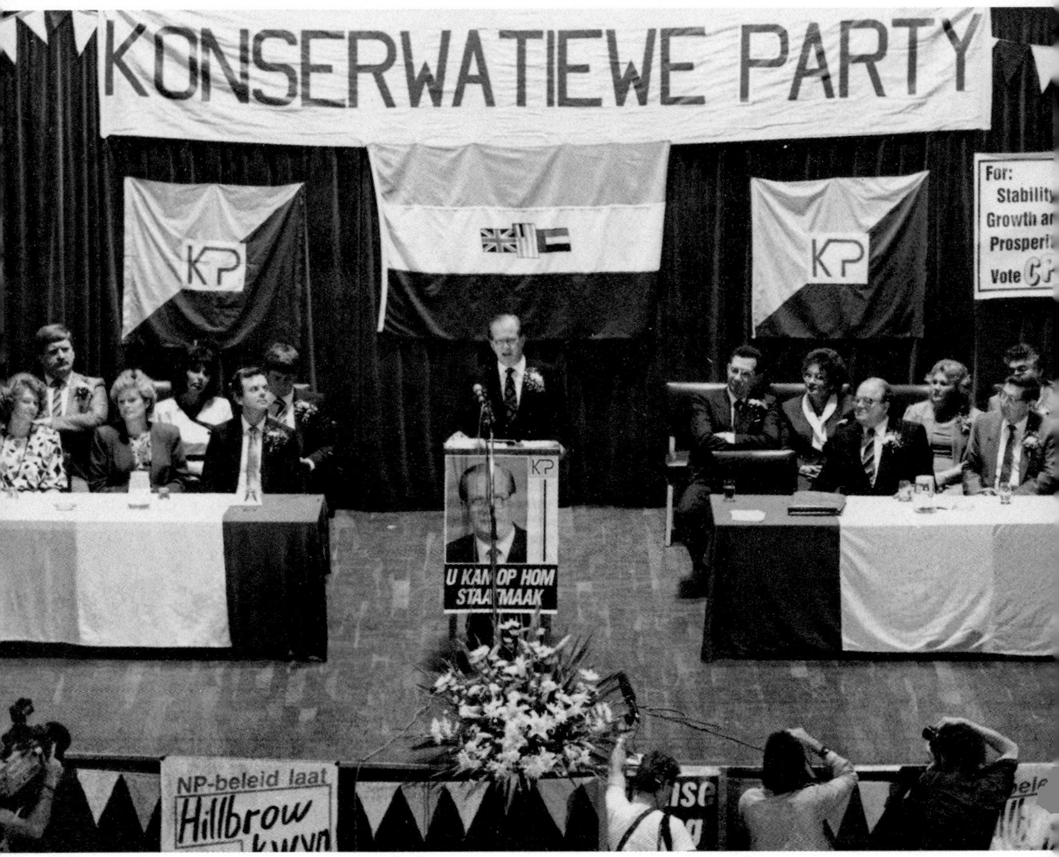
KONSERWATIEWE PARTY
KP
KP
For:
Stability
Vote
KP
U KAN OP HOM STAATMAAK
NP-beleid laat
Hillbrow

Top: Nelson Mandela arriving at the Welcome Home rally, Soweto. On his left is his renowned consort, Winnie. *(Gill de Vlieg)*

Bottom: Entering the new South Africa. F W de Klerk and Nelson Mandela at Groote Schuur, 4 May 1990. *(S A Communications Service)*

job as temporary messenger in Parliament. At his trial it was revealed that Tsafendas had been in eight mental institutions in four different countries. He gave as his reason for killing Verwoerd the presence of a huge tapeworm within his body which tormented him and compelled him to act as he did. Tsafendas was found mentally disturbed and committed to an institution.

On 10 September Verwoerd was laid to rest in Heroes' Acre, the cemetery in Pretoria where some of the most illustrious leaders of the Afrikaners are buried. At the state funeral service, 250 000 people crowded into the amphitheatre of the Union buildings in Pretoria.

During his lifetime Verwoerd had seemed all but irreplaceable. He was the man who took all the decisions and from whom all policy flowed. But his was a stultifying presence and soon there would be signs that his own followers were beginning to breathe more easily. Writing in the late 1970s, Schalk Pienaar recounted the pointed remark made to him by a friend on the evening of the day on which Verwoerd was murdered: 'We all feel now as we do. But tell me, how long still could South Africa have endured Verwoerd?'

'With that,' added Pienaar, 'she shocked me out of my state of shock.

'Nearly the whole of South Africa is asking that question today'.[34]

CHAPTER ELEVEN

The First Verkrampte Split

Verwoerd had hardly died when the canvassing began for his successor. It soon appeared that only two of his former colleagues had a chance. One was Ben Schoeman, Minister of Transport and a member of the cabinet since 1948. A man of forceful but dour personality, Schoeman had been an extremely efficient minister, within the constraints imposed by the policy of apartheid. The other prospective leader was the Minister of Justice, John Vorster, a member of the cabinet only since 1961 and indeed only a Member of Parliament since 1953. At the age of 50, he was also fifteen years younger than Schoeman. During the war years Vorster had been a 'General' in the Ossewa Brandwag and had disdained the tame parliamentary ways of the National Party. Since then he had had other insights, but his performance as Minister of Justice showed that pussy-footing was still not the style he preferred.

Both men had their canvassers, but it soon became evident that Vorster's were better organised and more dynamic. They drew up lists of MPs and Senators and actively cultivated those who were doubtful. Schoeman's organisation was looser, but at first it appeared that he was in with a chance. By the calculations of Vorster's own campaigners, Schoeman had the support of most of the cabinet. There was also a popular notion that Schoeman, although he had never expressed the least doubt about the correctness or wisdom of apartheid, was somehow the 'moderate' candidate. Vorster was counted the 'extremist,' undoubtedly because of his exceedingly rough approach to 'Communists' and other dissidents during his tenure as minister. The sustained attacks on him over the years by the English-language press had only confirmed the impression. It was a reputation that enhanced his standing with the rank and file of the Nationalist caucus, which included about 40 new and impressionable MPs. For this reason too he had the active support of that small group of ultra right wingers in the caucus who were led by the cabinet minister Albert Hertzog. They saw Vorster very much as 'their man'.

As Nationalist parliamentarians began to get feedback from their constituencies, the tide came sweeping in for Vorster. It was clearly the Minister of Justice who had captured the popular imagination in recent years. He had grabbed the headlines constantly as he announced and acted upon his unyielding resolve to settle with the Communists and their allies. Now that Verwoerd was dead, Vorster seemed to most Nationalists to be his logical successor: one strong man would truly succeed another. Schoeman, by contrast, had done nothing similar. He had just been there, an efficient minister who had been doing his job and, after Dönges, the most senior member of the cabinet. He was a natural contender for the succession; his claims could not be denied, but there it stopped. Schoeman appeared more a man of the past than of the confident future which still seemed to be awaiting white South Africa in the buoyant days of the mid-1960s. He did not come across as the natural heir to Verwoerd.

One day before the election of the new leader, on 13 September, some of the Vorster organisers went to see Schoeman. They told him that he did not have the votes to win. Schoeman, by his own account,[1] had not relished the prospect of a showdown. He believed the choice should be unanimous. In the interests of party unity, and no doubt also of his own sensitivities, he decided to withdraw as a candidate.

The next day the Nationalist caucus elected Vorster unanimously as its new leader, which meant that he would become the seventh Prime Minister of South Africa. He was both proposed and seconded by members of what came to be known as the 'Hertzog group', which only confirmed their impression that they had some kind of claim on Vorster and that he was peculiarly one of their own. But the truth was that Vorster, however dictatorial he had been as minister, was not especially right wing in the context of

Nationalist politics. He had the backing not only of the far right, but also of the National Party in the Cape and of its official organ, *Die Burger*, never notably enthusiastic about what they saw as the lunatic fringe excesses of some of their colleagues from the north. It was they who would not regret their support of Vorster.

The new man brought a new style. In his first speech as supreme Nationalist leader, Vorster vowed on the steps of Parliament that he would maintain an unbroken chain of continuity: 'My role is to walk further along the road set by Hendrik Verwoerd'. He could of course express no other sentiment and he was certainly sincere, although Verwoerd would have repudiated in the most emphatic way many of the steps Vorster later took down that supposed road. But the two men had totally different personalities and it had to rub off on their exercise of power. Verwoerd was the natural autocrat who wished to centralise decision-making into the hands of the man who knew best — himself. Vorster had no such illusions about his knowledge and insight, nor did he have any desire to be an encompassing controller. At his first cabinet meeting he reportedly said: 'I will only be John Vorster. Dr Verwoerd was an intellectual giant. He thought for each of us. That is why I cannot be a second Verwoerd. From now on everyone must know his own field, immerse himself in it and be in command of it'.[2]

As Prime Minister, where general policy was at issue, Vorster resembled what a historian has described as 'a chairman of the board whose government did not run unless there was a great measure of consensus'.[3] In departmental matters, he delegated power. Ministers had plenty of autonomy; Vorster assumed that they knew what they were doing. He was also a pragmatist. To quote the same authority, 'If serious divisions arose, the issue was shelved or delaying tactics were employed as far as possible. The overriding concern in the decision-making process was always the maintenance of unity'.[4]

A member of both the Verwoerd and Vorster cabinets, Frank Waring, has described the differences between the two approaches:

> Vorster would not hand down decisions, he would listen to his ministers, question them, make suggestions ... never give or-

ders. While Verwoerd was largely a dictator, Vorster brought us back to true cabinet rule and true cabinet responsibility. Vorster never said 'You are wrong.' He always said 'Don't you think you should consider this or that, don't you think you should do it this way.' Verwoerd made you feel you were a child, Vorster did just the opposite ...[5]

It was not only the style of rule which changed. Many English-speaking whites met Vorster's accession to the premiership with the fear and hostility they had accorded his predecessors. His dictatorial sway as Minister of Justice was all too fresh in the memory. Once more they hauled out his wartime record as Ossewa Brandwag extremist and wondered what the future would bring under such a man.

They, if not the non-white population, were to be pleasantly surprised. The emphasis on white unity was to be one of the main themes of his premiership — in this respect Vorster did travel much further along the road of Verwoerd. In the face of continuous carping by far right-wingers, who began to crawl out of the woodwork after 1966, Vorster stressed the urgency of the need for unity repeatedly and reaffirmed his resolve that English-speakers would not be cheated of their full equality with Afrikaners.

Ironically, as these things had a habit of doing in South Africa, such declarations came at a cost in terms of civil liberties. The Government felt the more obliged to demonstrate that it had not gone soft on such essentials as the threat posed by the ubiquitous Communists and their 'liberalistic' dupes. Here was an ambiguity of the early Vorster years. They were a time of relaxation after the removal of the Verwoerdian strait-jacket, but they were also a time of unrelieved toughness on ideological dissenters, on those who passed beyond the easily reached limits of 'legitimate' criticism.

As Prime Minister, Vorster at first suffered from more than just the obvious disadvantages of a novice. When he became leader he had been one of the most junior members of the cabinet. Nearly all his colleagues had the edge on him in years and experience. There was the disgruntled presence of Ben Schoeman, according to Waring 'still obviously sore about the fact that he had to make way for Vorster in the race for the premiership'.[6] Vorster himself admitted, 'I was totally unprepared for the job. I did not know what the job was all about ... By the very nature of Dr Verwoerd's premiership, so much was centralised in the Prime Minister himself that this made it extremely difficult for his successor'.[7] But Vorster survived and gradually established his ascendancy. Partly this was because in prime ministerial systems power naturally gravitates to the man at the top; the mere passage of time will do him a power of good. But partly it was the result of Vorster's personal qualities and efforts. Waring believed that 'he tackled the transition stage with great skill and tact ... As far as I, and many of my colleagues, was concerned his status grew with every cabinet meeting. Even when I felt that, had I been Vorster, my patience with Ben Schoeman would have been tested to its limit, Vorster took it all in his stride until Ben must have realised that he had underrated Vorster and that he must accept Vorster's leadership fully ... which I really think he did do'.[8]

Soon after Vorster took charge rumours about disunity in the National Party became common. This was a particularly serious matter for the Nationalists. For years the Opposition had looked assiduously for cracks in the apparent Government monolith, convinced, with sound reason, that it was a break in Afrikaner unity that would give it much the best chance of regaining power. Over the years the wishful optimism of the Nationalists' opponents would inflate any semblance of division within the governing party into a crisis that had the enemy on the brink of the abyss. By 1966 'waiting for the Nats to split' had become the most dynamic thing of which the United Party was capable. By the same token the Nationalists always made a point of denying outright that their unity was less than perfect. Each side exaggerated, but the Nationalists were somewhat closer to the truth.

Until the mid-sixties the unity of the National Party had in fact been little tested. The most conspicuous public farewell of a Nationalist to his fellows in arms had been that of Japie Basson in 1959, when he rebelled against the abolition of Natives' Representation in Parliament. But the high hopes of the United Party were bitterly disappointed. Basson was a lone maverick, representing nobody but himself, as the United Party discovered when it was foolish enough to enter into a pact with Basson's National Union.

The disillusioned Nationalists who were supposed to be waiting so eagerly to vote for an Afrikaans alternative to the Government, proved to be no more than a figment of Basson's creative imagination. Other Nationalists who dared to break ranks found a fate far more ignominious. The twenty-odd Republican Party candidates from the extreme right all lost their deposits in the 1961 general election. Thirteen academics from the Universities of South Africa and Pretoria who were brave enough to protest against the Senate Act in 1955 had to endure years of execration for their defiance. It seemed as if the most important thing an Afrikaner could do in those times was to toe, and keep on toeing, the party line.

There were excellent reasons for all this conformity. It was only towards the end of the first decade of Nationalist rule, in the 1958 general election, that it became evident that the United Party could never return to power. Until then any deviation smacked of the cardinal sin, namely, endangering the political supremacy of the volk. The individual was truly a minor cog in the ethnic machine. It was only after the achievement of the republic and the definitive triumph in the 1961 election that some margin of slack appeared, and only after Verwoerd's death that hints of nonconformity would not automatically be seen as evidence of inner turpitude.

The Government had in addition been more responsive to pressures from the right than from the left. The few from the latter source it could handle easily: liberal sentiment had always proved an artificial growth in the stony soil of South Africa. It needed constant cultivation and careful tending to show any signs of life at all. Right wing attitudes were another matter. They required hardly any prompting to flourish. For a party founded on ethnic exclusivism, and which had thrived upon it, complaints that the very nature of the Afrikaner was being eroded by changes in the party line had to be taken seriously. Inevitably, after the adoption of white unity and separate freedoms for blacks as central planks of the Nationalist platform, the grievances started pouring in. There were, for instance, the cultural leaders who feared for the future of the Afrikaner if the protection of Afrikaans culture ceased to be a priority of Nationalist policy. During his lifetime Verwoerd managed, by and large, to assuage the aggrieved. White survival was his justification; in particular, while separate freedoms may have sounded uncomfortably radical to conservative opinion, there was the obtrusive fact that the Government's treatment of Africans, when it came to their daily movements and their political activities in 'white' South Africa, was uncompromisingly illiberal.

There was also the impression of extreme right-wingers within the National Party that Verwoerd was decidedly sympathetic to them and their cause of Afrikaner separateness. Certainly, he made little attempt to prevent their constant sniping at what they regarded as dangerous liberals within the National Party. That, and his autocratic personality which brooked no dissent, were probably the main reasons why divisions amongst Afrikaners did not then lead to a split within the National Party. For divisions there were, and they had long been in the making.

On 6 October 1966 Professor Willem de Klerk of the professedly Calvinist University of Potchefstroom and son of the cabinet minister, Jan de Klerk, made what was to become a famous speech. Addressing a Youth Congress convened by the SA Bureau of Racial Affairs, De Klerk spoke about different kinds of Afrikaners. The distinction he made was between *verligtes* and *verkramptes*. At the time De Klerk attached pejorative connotations to both. While verkramptes were to him reactionaries stuck in the past, obdurately hostile to all change, he saw verligtes as shallow and fashionable radicals who promoted 'liberalistic' tendencies amongst Afrikaners. De Klerk admired what he described as 'positive' Afrikaners, who remained true to their heritage but were still willing to adapt to change. Over time, however, the label of 'verligte' became attached to the positive variety of Afrikaner, a transmutation that De Klerk himself came to accept. It was a kind of Nationalist synonym for liberal, without the sinister implications that term had acquired in party mythology. The expressions caught on. From then on, political commentators and the public saw divisions within the National Party increasingly in terms of a struggle between verligtes and verkramptes for the right to chart the Afrikaner future, and it became a game to classify politicians as one or the other.

Shortly after Vorster became Prime Minister, Schalk Pienaar, without any doubt a verligte among verligtes, who had then just been appointed editor of the recently founded Transvaal Sunday newspaper *Die Beeld*, went to congratulate him on his election. But he proceeded further. Pienaar asked Vorster whether he knew of the massive campaign to undermine him that was being waged in the Transvaal. When Vorster professed ignorance, Pienaar identified two of the campaign leaders: Albert Hertzog, a member of Vorster's cabinet, and Jaap Marais, the ultra-conservative MP for Innesdal.

As Pienaar wrote later:

> There is no doubt that such undermining was taking place: to a large degree organised, meticulously and nation-wide, although its focal point was the Transvaal. Those of us from *Die Beeld* arrived hopelessly ignorant of all this in Johannesburg, but it soon became clear to us that it was more than just the normal resistance of established enterprises to an intruder from outside. Clearly it also took in far more than business interests. Church, party, cultural organisations turned out to be involved. If not officially, then via members, with or without the knowledge of the organisations themselves — or perhaps one should say with varying degrees of knowledge.
>
> It involved no less than a resistance action on all fronts against 'liberalistic influences' from the South. Fortunately we were not alone in this matter. There were others within and outside the Afrikaner organisations, some deep within, who found themselves in their own way and in their own fields at the receiving end of this resistance action in the Transvaal. They often filled us in.
>
> But by far the most people quietly went their way, unaware of all the sinister doings around them. That went for the Party too.[9]

Pienaar had been right in his identification of the leaders of the right wing movement, particularly when it came to Albert Hertzog. The ultra-conservatives in the National Party in fact soon became known as the Hertzog group, or *Hertzogiete* (Hertzogites). Albert Hertzog was the son of the former Prime Minister. He had caused his father much embarrassment and annoyance by his identification, when still a young man, with ultra right wing causes. In 1948 Hertzog entered Parliament as MP for the Eastern Transvaal constituency of Ermelo. After ten years of frustration because neither Malan nor Strijdom recognised his talents, Hertzog eventually got no more than he thought he deserved when Verwoerd appointed him to the cabinet as Minister of Posts and Telegraphs and of Health, much to the disgust of Ben Schoeman, who told Verwoerd that he was making a huge mistake.[10]

In 1942 Hertzog had established an organisation called the *Afrikaner Orde,* designed to promote what it saw as Afrikaner interests. At first its chief goals were fairly limited: it aimed to take over the city council of Pretoria, which had till then been controlled by English-speakers, and to eliminate left wing influences in trade unions. After 1948 the Afrikaner Orde acquired broader interests: its members infiltrated many Afrikaner organisations and institutions, as well as the civil service. From 1961 the Orde made special efforts to infiltrate and control National Party branches and cultural bodies. All this was in accord with Albert Hertzog's strategy of keeping out of no man's land. He preferred operating behind the scenes. Ben Schoeman described the tactics of his colleague: 'Albert never differed on grounds of principle from the rest of the cabinet on any racial issue. He did frequently have his own view on such a matter and expressed it, but he always accepted the decision of the cabinet'.[11]

Under Verwoerd the Hertzog group had a field day. The supreme leader allowed the ultra-right to spread rumours and suspicion about 'liberalists' to its heart's content. He never attempted to inhibit the verkramptes' particular style, which, in a way, was odd, for his own policies were a major, if indirect, target. The urgency of white unity, proclaimed constantly from official platforms after Verwoerd became Prime Minister, was an abomination to Hertzog and his followers. To them it meant the inevitable dilution of the national character of the Afrikaner and its absorption into a broad cosmopolitan stream of which the culture of the English-speakers was so worthy a representative. It would end, they had no doubt, with the Afrikaner's loss of his identity, based as it was on a powerful sense of Calvinist and racial exclusiveness. Nor did the verkramptes approve of independent homelands for blacks; they thought that this was taking ideas of democracy and freedom far too seriously.

After 1960 Hertzog approached several of his colleagues in the cabinet unobtrusively in an attempt to establish a common front against Verwoerd's 'liberal' course.[12] The Prime Minister knew what Hertzog was up to, but never acted against him. Perhaps he thought Hertzog less of a threat inside than outside the cabinet. Perhaps Verwoerd did nothing because the typical targets of the Hertzogites also coincided with many of his own pet aversions in the struggle for power within the National Party. In particular, there were the verligte newspapers, *Die Burger* and *Die Beeld*, and the men who controlled them.

Both these publications strongly supported the policies of white unity and black homelands, but they were members of Nasionale Pers, the Cape-based newspaper group which Verwoerd disliked powerfully. Verwoerd himself was chairman of the rival group, Afrikaanse Pers and ex-editor of its flagship, *Die Transvaler*. In 1965 he had vigorously opposed the introduction by Nasionale Pers of a Sunday newspaper in the Transvaal on the grounds that it would be 'politically undesirable'.[13] He did not mention that for his own group it would also be economically undesirable, for the established Afrikaans Sunday newspaper in the Transvaal, and in the country, was *Dagbreek*, one of its own.

For once, Verwoerd did not have his way. *Die Beeld* arrived in Johannesburg and soon became a deadly rival to *Dagbreek*. For reasons mainly to do with *realpolitik* Verwoerd saw the verligtes of Nasionale Pers as his enemies. While they may have supported the 'liberal' aspects of his policies, they were not amenable to his control, which the newspapers of Afrikaanse Pers most decidedly were. Just a short while before, *Die Burger* had made it plain that Verwoerd's policy towards the coloureds had its limitations. Both *Die Burger* and *Die Beeld* helped to further a critical spirit towards Afrikaner institutions and values, and criticism had been rare during the decade of the 1950s. It could not have been surprising that Verwoerd extended his sympathetic tolerance to the verkramptes in their ideological attacks on what he chose to regard as his personal foes.

All this changed with the advent of Vorster. The new man had none of his predecessor's antipathies towards some of the most prominent verligtes. He was on excellent personal terms with Pienaar of *Die Beeld*, who had not got on at all with Verwoerd. Nasionale Pers had indeed supported Vorster for the premiership, believing that the ultra-right was quite wrong in its assessment of him as a kindred spirit.

The journalist J H P Serfontein, author of a basic work on what he called *Die Verkrampte Aanslag* (The Verkrampte Onslaught), has described the differences between the Verwoerd and Vorster eras well:

> Under the former the verkramptes had the green light to wage war on their verligte opponents. If they did not actually have Dr Verwoerd's full support, he did create a kind of intellectual climate in which their thinking could flourish and enjoy considerable protection. *Die Burger* and other verligte groups and individuals were regarded as a kind of opposition group within the NP — apparently on the losing side.
>
> Under Mr Vorster the position was reversed. Then it was the verligtes who enjoyed the freedom of the land, and apparently the tacit support of the Prime Minister in most of the controversies.[14]

The verkramptes soon began to doubt whether Vorster was the man they thought he was. The first sign came over the proposed abolition of representation for coloureds in Parliament and in the Cape Provincial Council. This was designed to prevent the Progressive Party from getting into these assemblies as representatives of the coloureds. In 1966, when Verwoerd was still alive, the Government duly produced a measure with yet another Orwellian title – the Prohibition of Improper Interference Bill.

But it went much further than merely prohibiting 'improper interference' in the form of mixed political parties: any mixed racial organisation involving any kind of politics, including political discussion, was to be outside the law. Coloured representation in its current form would also be abolished. Predictable public outrage greeted the introduction of the measure. This was the situation inherited by Vorster, who decided on a compromise of sorts. After consultation with the Opposition leader, De Villiers Graaff, it was agreed to refer the matter to a select committee.

This apparently innocuous arrangement disturbed the extreme right within the National Party. Verwoerd had promised that the legislation would go through that session. Its postponement stirred doubts. That was the first straw in the wind, yet the ultra-conservatives continued to hope that it was only the blunder of a beginner still finding his way.

By February 1967 the verkramptes knew they had backed the wrong horse. Vorster proposed to change the sports policy which Verwoerd had proclaimed crucial to the survival of the Afrikaner. He first raised it at a cabinet meeting, where he argued that the identity of the white man would continue unscathed even if Maoris were included in visiting New Zealand rugby teams. Ben Schoeman, who was present, commented in his memoirs that it 'was of course a deviation from Verwoerd's sports policy as he expounded it in 1965'.[15] He warned Vorster that he could expect trouble from some MPs and that he should first discuss it in the caucus before making a public statement. As it happened, no minister, including Hertzog, objected to Vorster's proposal.

Schoeman was right about what Vorster could expect from some MPs. At the caucus Vorster took a line which later became familiar. He spoke about the importance of sport in South Africa and the danger of the country's total isolation because of its rejection of multiracial teams from abroad. However, he said nothing about Maoris, although that was evidently the point of it all. There were immediate objections, particularly from the far-right, Jaap Marais, the right-winger from Innesdale. Vorster had his defenders, but the caucus ended in confusion as many MPs still found it difficult to assimilate that the sacred writ of Verwoerd was being abandoned.

From this time forth the Nationalists never had a peaceful moment amongst themselves. Their latent divisions now burst uncontrollably into the open. Vorster, it is true, did supposedly assure a deputation of thirteen MPs that he was not departing from anything essential. A later gathering of the caucus approved of the policy, but it was more an affirmation of hope and expediency. The fact was that Vorster had so fudged the issue that it was open to interpretations which differed a good deal. Provisionally it suited the Hertzogites to go along, or to pretend to go along, with what passed for the policy on sport, as they jockeyed and manoeuvred for advantage within the National Party.

But they had got Vorster's number by now. They would be unrelenting in their animosity towards the man they regarded as a turncoat and a traitor. There would be no let-up in their undermining of Vorster and no weakening in their determination to rid the National Party of its verligtes. Their strategy was to remain in the party at all costs. Their goal was to take it over from within.

At first the verkramptes seemed justified in their optimism. In 1967 they did most of the running and finished strongly. In June the Hertzogites failed narrowly in their attempt to take control of the Afrikaans cultural body which had the most prestige and authority, the *Suid-Afrikaanse Akademie vir Wetenskap en Kuns* (South African Academy of Science and Art). It seemed only a matter of time before they succeeded. They had on their side the chairman of the South African Broadcasting Corporation, Piet Meyer, who also happened to be chairman of the Afrikaner secret society, the Broederbond, an organisation that was a power in the land when Verwoerd was Prime Minister. They even managed to obtain the protection of Ben Schoeman, who had become the leader of the National Party in the Transvaal after the death of Verwoerd. Schoeman had declared as late as October that year that to be verkramp and conservative was to accept the principles of the National Party.[16]

The Hertzogites were assisted no end by the curiously passive attitude of Vorster. He had long denied that there could be such a thing as a split within the party, as if the polemics rising in the air around him, the accusations and counter-accusations of treason to the Afrikaner cause which were filling the editorial and letter columns of the Nationalist press, were simply much ado about nothing. With the benefit of hindsight, Vorster put as good a face as possible on his leniency towards the verkramptes:

> In view of their continued protestations of loyalty, I, as party leader, had to accept these declarations, no matter how I felt deep down. Naturally I hoped that they were being sincere and I gave them the benefit of the doubt. However, deep

down, I suppose I knew that the time would come for a showdown. But I also knew deep down that I would choose my own time and place for that showdown. But, genuinely, at that time I accepted their declarations of loyalty because I wanted to accept them. When it became clear that they were disloyal, then I acted ... All I can say about this eagerness of mine to accept their declarations of loyalty is that I fought one civil war with my fellow-Afrikaners — and I did not want to become involved in another. But, when it was forced on me, I met it head-on ...[17]

Schoeman recalls a somewhat less resolute Vorster, a man on the brink of resignation. As he tells it: 'By the middle of 1967 there was a smear campaign against Vorster which was repulsive. It was directed at his person and not his policy. I received letters, signed by fictitious persons, which made the most libellous and vilest accusations against Vorster'.[18]

Early in August Schoeman heard from his cabinet colleague, P W Botha, that Vorster intended resigning and leaving politics as he could no longer stomach the horror stories about him. When confronted by Schoeman, Vorster confirmed the rumour: 'I can no longer take it.' He clearly did not trust Albert Hertzog and suspected him of subtle undermining through the Afrikaner Orde.

By his account, Schoeman dissuaded Vorster by pointing to the disastrous effect it would have on the National Party, for his departure would only seem to confirm the truth of the unflattering stories about him. Schoeman promised to deal with the 'underminers' himself.[19]

The trouble was that they were not so easy to find. The Hertzogites took shelter behind anonymity or point-blank denials that they rejected party policy, which had in the meantime gradually widened to include not just the acceptance of multiracial touring sides in South Africa, but of black diplomats as well. This was all part of what came to be known as the 'outward-going' policy. When Schoeman summoned all the Pretoria MPs individually, with the exception of Hertzog, and inquired how they felt about the more controversial aspects of party policy, they all assured him of their support and of their loyalty to the Prime Minister.

Schoeman believed them and concluded that they deserved his protection against the continued assaults of Nationalist newspapers taking a verligte line, among which those from Nasionale Pers were especially prominent. Little wonder the extreme right ended 1967 riding as high as it did.

The tactics of hit-and-run, suspicion-mongering and brinkmanship were most effective, but their success depended on those responsible remaining undetected. Evidence, however, began to present itself that Nationalists right at the core of the party were guiding the verkrampte onslaught. This was fatal to their cause. Once Vorster realised that the party was deeply divided and that the ultra-right was aiming at a take-over, he shook off his lethargy and began to fight back.

Hertzog was a man he distrusted. At the beginning of 1968 Hertzog's Afrikaner Orde officially ceased to exist, at Vorster's instructions. In February Vorster deprived him of his more important portfolio of Posts and Telegraphs. Hertzog took it hard. Immediately after his dismissal he vented his spite in Parliament by bitterly attacking two Nationalist newspaper editors of the verligte variety who had been critical of his more extreme public pronouncements.

The Nationalist press had by then become actively involved in the whole verligte-verkrampte quarrel: *Die Burger* and *Die Beeld* of Nasionale Pers were most diligent in flushing out the Hertzogites, but *Dagbreek* of Afrikaanse Pers also, on occasion, incurred the enmity of the right. Often they drew sharp criticism from people like Vorster and Schoeman, who wanted to believe that the party division did not run as deep as these newspapers alleged. There was one Nationalist newspaper which supported the conservatives. This was *Hoofstad* (Capital), which first appeared in April 1968 and was edited by a former minister of the Dutch Reformed Church, Andries Treurnicht, a wily man who, when the final break came, would leave his spiritual kin in the lurch.

There were other publications which backed the verkrampte cause. They did so vociferously, indeed scurrilously, but outside the National Party. One was *The South African Observer*, edited by an English-speaker of far-right persuasions, S E D Brown, a firm believer in the universality of the Jewish-Communist conspiracy and its manifestation in such unlikely forms as multi-racial sports sides touring the land of apartheid. It was the 'official organ' of the Hertzogites and had once been subsidised by the National Party. *The Observer* was to prove a convenient handle for the verligtes with which they could assault their ideological enemies. Another publication was named *Veg* (Fight) and was started late in 1968 by young ex-Nationalists who had been expelled from the party.

The Hertzogites had been sticking to the guerrilla tactics which had served them so well, but a break came in June 1968 when some younger Nationalists from Pretoria published what came to be known in verligte circles as 'smear letters'. For the first time Vorster was attacked directly by active, if still anonymous, members of the National Party. Serfontein comments: 'And now it was for the first time possible for NP leaders to hit back in a determined attempt to pin down the Hertzog group itself'.[20]

It was the second letter in particular which brought trouble for both its writers and their elder role models. Ostensibly written in praise of Vorster's 'outward-looking' policy, it was in fact designed to cast suspicion on what he had been trying to do. Well-known verligte Afrikaners found themselves grouped with well-known liberals totally out of sympathy with Nationalist policy. It was the worst possible slur on their political characters.

The identity of the authors soon became public. In August the seven composers of the letters were expelled from the Transvaal National Party. Three days before, on 9 August, Vorster had dropped Albert Hertzog from the cabinet, after he had refused to resign. From then on, their cover blown, the Hertzogites who remained within the National Party were invidiously placed, subject both to the pressures from fellow-Nationalists to conform to the party line, and to the demands of those who had been expelled that they defy Vorster the 'liberalist' openly.

At about this time the Hertzogites suffered another setback. The party leadership discovered that the Afrikaner Orde, which had supposedly disbanded, still existed as a pressure group. The discovery gave further backbone to Vorster and helped cause a decisive change in the attitude of Schoeman towards the virtues of being conservative and verkramp.

For a time the ultra-right continued in its old ways, convinced that they could still be made to work and that the National Party could still be taken over from within. They had the assistance of Treurnicht, who wrote cleverly worded editorials in *Hoofstad*, indirectly attacking Vorster, about the threats posed to the Afrikaner's Calvinist identity by such outlandish things as 'adaptation' and 'renewal'. Hertzog himself made a speech in April 1969 in which he affirmed the Afrikaner's Calvinist nature and questioned the reliability of the English-speakers in maintaining 'white civilisation'. In spite of an ostensible peace declared afterwards, whereby Hertzog bound himself to conform to party policy and clear up confusions aroused by his speech, he and his followers continued to make declarations which extolled the wonders of Afrikaner exclusivism. When confronted they always swore that they had been misunderstood and that they remained loyal to the National Party.

The verkramptes were finally caught by surprise. Suddenly they found that they were no longer members of the party they had been designing to make theirs. It was Ben Schoeman who decided to flush them out. He had concluded that, 'Hertzog, Jaap Marais and one or two other Members of Parliament were not worthy of my confidence'. Schoeman believed that they were involved in the unrest in Nationalist ranks in the Transvaal, especially in Pretoria, and that they gave 'moral support to the smear sheets *The Observer* and *Veg*. I realised that the time for action had come and that I would have to call them to account on a suitable occasion'.[21]

The occasion was the Transvaal Congress of the National Party in Pretoria in September 1969. As Transvaal leader of the Party Ben Schoeman sprung his carefully prepared trap. He asked the more than 1 000 delegates to express full confidence in the Government on four issues, each a bone of verkrampte contention in the past. They were official policy on immigration, Afrikaans-English co-operation, the acceptance of black diplomats, and sport.

Hertzog and his followers had not expected so public a confrontation. They tried to do what they had done so effectively before: lie low and live to hit and run another day. They even managed to vote for the resolutions on black diplomats and Afrikaans-English relations. But Schoeman was determined to force them out into the open. When the sports policy came up for discussion he insisted from the platform that any dissenters make their views known. It worked. Hertzog stood up to reject Maoris in an All Black touring side as it would mean 'social integration', with Maoris dancing at social functions, presumably with good Afrikaans girls. He continued, he claimed correctly, to support the policy of Verwoerd.[22] Another now compelled to commit himself was Jaap Marais.

Schoeman's tactics proved devastatingly effective. When it came to the vote, only eleven opposed the resolution, including Hertzog. Seven abstained, including, surprisingly, Jaap Marais. Schoeman had both succeeded in isolating the ultra-right and minimising the extent of the split. It was truly a famous victory.

Within weeks Albert Hertzog and Jaap Marais were expelled from the National Party. Two other MPs resigned. Treurnicht of *Hoofstad* decided that it was safer to remain a Nationalist, much to the chagrin and disdain of the former allies he had supported so enthusiastically. In October the Hertzogites formed their own political party, the *Herstigte Nasionale Party* (Re-established National Party), an attempt to capitalise on the initials of the old *Herenigde Nasionale Party* of Malan. Hertzog was its leader, with Jaap Marais as his deputy.

The new party started with high optimism, expecting to profit substantially from the undoubtedly conservative sentiments of most Nationalist voters, especially those in the rural areas. Its disappointment was to be bitter and permanent.

The Government called a general election for April 1970, a year in advance. Ben Schoeman told his constituents that the purpose was to act before the HNP could build an adequate election organisation.[23] If that was true, it came at a price, for the Nationalists lost ground to the United Party, the first time since 1948. In 1966 they had won 126 seats and the Official Opposition 39. Now the figures were 118 and 47. That represented a swing of just over four per cent to the United Party, mainly the result of fickle English-speakers changing their allegiance. It was enough to give the Opposition absurdly inflated ideas about returning to power one day, an illusion which lasted only until the next general election in 1974.

But the Government did succeed in crushing the HNP in its infancy. The Herstigtes put up 78 candidates. All but three lost their deposits, with the new party attracting less than four per cent of the vote. Over the years it was to show little capacity for growth. Plainly, conservative Afrikaners did not feel so threatened at the very core of their being as to turn against the government which had for so long been the political embodiment of their nationhood.

The departure of the Hertzogites was the most serious split in the National Party since it had come to power. Commentators agree that the whole verligte-verkrampte quarrel was a reflection of profound changes that were taking place amongst the Afrikaners. There is less agreement about what the changes were.

One explanation is that ideological differences were a symptom of the rapid urbanisation of the Afrikaners. The noted Afrikaner and South African historian F A van Jaarsveld, has argued that in effect city air made Afrikaners free, or at least more independent and less ideologically hidebound. The republic was the last great ideal the Afrikaners had to achieve. After 1961 there was no new political ideal which could serve as a binding force. Centrifugal forces now asserted themselves. Urban ways tended to be more liberal ways. In the cities Afrikaners were becoming more prosperous, more exposed to cosmopolitan influences, less in need of government protection against the competition of other groups:

> The urge to renewal led to a struggle between the traditional isolationist Afrikanerdom and the group which was moving 'outwards'. In the mind of the Afrikaner conflict fermented and reached boiling point. It shot to the surface in 1965 and since 1966 the Afrikaner has been divided into two ideological camps ... Whichever word is used, 'liberal' or 'verlig', it remains a fact that the Afrikaner's experience in the cities had separated him by 1965 into two ideological camps ...[24]

There is another interpretation, which would situate the whole conflict squarely in the class struggle. The flavour of this kind of argument can best be given by a quotation from one of its leading proponents:

> The verligte phenomenon was a response to the emergence of a class of aggressive, self-confident Afrikaner capitalists

whose interests now went beyond those of the narrow class alliance out of which they had emerged. By the late 1960s, the verligte element was no longer confined to the Cape, but was a powerful force in the Transvaal, as businessmen began to pursue policies independent of the interests to which they were previously tied.[25]

Each argument ignores the fact that during the later 1960s the Government was pursuing policies that were both profoundly illiberal and anti-capitalist. After Verwoerd's death the Nationalists came forth with laws aimed at yet more comprehensive control of the black labour market. African access to the urban areas became further restricted, at least in terms of the law. It became increasingly difficult for blacks to acquire the Section 10 rights that would give relative permanence to their stay in the cities. Employers met with greater frustrations in employing the number and kinds of African workers they needed. Prosecutions and convictions under the pass laws grew immensely at just this time.

If the triumph of the verligtes in the National Party reflected the arrival of 'a class of aggressive, self-confident capitalists', it is difficult to see why the Government was so aggressively and self-confidently following policies that could do capitalists so little good. Nor is it clear, if class was such a decisive factor, why Afrikaner capitalists did not make common political cause with English-speaking capitalists. Of course, they did not: Afrikaner businessmen were usually loyal, if sometimes mildly critical, Nationalists, while most of their English-speaking counterparts supported the United Party.

Van Jaarsveld's explanation is more plausible, but it exaggerates the liberal nature of the verligte phenomenon. By far the majority of Afrikaners, and of the white population for that matter, had little difficulty in living with laws and practices that increasingly restricted the lives and the opportunities of the African population.

It was not so much the urge to renewal that accounts for the rise of the verligtes. It was rather the desire to enjoy the spoils of victory. During nearly two decades of impressive economic growth Afrikaner living standards had gone up conspicuously. Most Afrikaners had become urbanised, a natural outcome of economic development, and hence more exposed both to up-to-date materialistic influences and, though travel and books, to the outside world and other cultures. The tourism industry grew. After the formation of the Republic and the 1961 general election, the Afrikaners could not but think that they had finally arrived, that South Africa was theirs to be enjoyed in perpetuity. They had become more diverse as urbanisation encouraged the emergence of a variety of interest groups. For many, perhaps most, Afrikaners the end of ideology had come. They wished to be left alone to enjoy their new-found prosperity without the continual ideological exhortation of self-consciously super-Afrikaners like Verwoerd. The verligtes won, not because they were so especially liberal or enlightened, but because the verkramptes had a message which simply no longer interested enough members of the volk.

CHAPTER TWELVE

Faces of Janus

When he became Prime Minister, Vorster committed himself to go further down the path charted by his predecessor. Verwoerd had been so dominant a figure that Vorster could do nothing else, even had he so wished. At first it was no more than the style of leadership which changed. But then Vorster started playing golf with businessmen and cracking after-dinner jokes at functions, displaying a common touch and a joviality which had always been foreign to Verwoerd. English-speakers began to wonder whether they had not excessively maligned the man who had been so ferocious a Minister of Justice. In their pleased surprise, they, and the Opposition press, began to speak favourably of Vorster. All in all, the arrival to power of the former Ossewa Brandwag general heralded more relaxed and pragmatic times for most white South Africans.

As noted in the previous chapter, the early Vorster years saw a continued emphasis on the importance of white unity. It caused grave offence to the ultra-right, who did not trust English-speakers, irredeemably infected by 'liberalism' as they were, not to impart the contagion to the Afrikaners as well. They could only be untrustworthy partners in the preservation of 'white civilisation'. As Albert Hertzog put it in his 'Calvinist' speech of 14 April 1969: 'We as a white nation would have collapsed if our English-speaking friends had had to stand alone'.[1]

Hertzog's words were stragglers from a less confident era. But now, if propagation of white unity meant some dilution of their previously vaunted exclusiveness, they could well afford it. In the heady days after 1966, with the Verwoerdian hoops of steel removed and an economy growing at what was later remembered as the astonishing rate of five per cent per year, it seemed as if there was a new world waiting out there for the Afrikaners, fraught with possibilities and merely awaiting occupation. A less defensive attitude to the rest of Africa also seemed long overdue. It came to take a high place on the verligte agenda.

In practice, despite appeals for white unity, the National Party remained an ethnic party. Afrikaners continued to be appointed to the important public posts. Hardly any English-speakers were chosen or made themselves available as candidates for the National Party. It was as if acceptance of the principle of white unity was enough; the day-to-day running of the state could only be entrusted to Afrikaners. If there was to be 'co-operation' between Afrikaners and English-speakers then it would be on the basis of each according to his own. The Afrikaners would continue to be in political charge and dominate the civil service; the English would stick to making money. Each group would retain its own schools and cultural institutions. Separate identities would persist and indeed be encouraged.

There was nothing especially contradictory about this. It was one thing to reject Afrikaner domination as it was preached by the Herstigte Nasionale Party, with Afrikaans as the sole official language. It was another to abandon that Afrikaner cohesiveness which had since 1948 been the foundation of Nationalist rule. The Afrikaners could claim to be a distinct political entity, highly conscious of themselves as a group. The English-speakers could do no such thing. Their ties to the British Crown had only recently been cut; time alone could bring a substitute in the form of a common loyalty to a white-ruled republic under siege to a sanctimonious and meddling world. Moreover, as voters the English-speakers were unreliable. Sizeable numbers would vote for the Government in one general election, as in 1966, only to abandon it in another, as in 1970. If there were to be white unity it would be on the premise that the South African nation consisted of distinct groups defined primarily by the language they spoke. Nor would there be any doubt about which would be the dominant group.

The novelty about what came to be known as the outward policy was that it meant looking beyond the borders of South Africa. Verwoerd had handled interfering foreigners astutely and diplomatically, but had gone to no great lengths to ingratiate the Republic with the world outside. It was nearly enough, it seemed, to remain on speaking terms with the leading industrial countries and to stress the high returns waiting for foreign businessmen who committed themselves to this anti-Communist bastion on a turbulent continent. That was the other main theme of official propaganda for overseas consumption: anti-Communism. Government spokesmen spoke habitually of the dangers of Communist expansionism. They shook their heads when they deplored the inability of the West to recognise that the Republic was its sole reliable ally in Africa against the encroaching red menace. They liked to talk about the strategic value of South Africa to the West. Apart from that, the Government relied on strength. Facing enemies from outside, there was no substitute for a powerful defence force, which South Africa indubitably had. It was rapidly building up its own arms industry. The permanent posture of defiance went well with the Afrikaners' view of themselves as a small beleaguered nation misunderstood and persecuted by a world bereft of its senses.

But Vorster realised that South African foreign policy could do with less defiance and more conciliation, at least of some carefully chosen countries. The Republic had made few friends abroad by the aid and comfort it had given to the government of Ian Smith in Rhodesia. There was also South West Africa. Although Prime Minister Verwoerd had foolishly assured its white inhabitants that their fate was indissolubly tied to that of the Republic, the fact remained that the territory was not part of South Africa, that there was little chance of its becoming so, and that the United Nations was annually passing resolutions condemning the 'illegal' occupation by the apartheid regime. It was becoming apparent too that not all African governments had those pro-Soviet sympathies which the Nationalists had so readily ascribed to them. Some were notably less radical than others. There could be advantages in establishing friendly relations with these more 'responsible' countries. In a variety of ways South Africa could improve its standing in the world, and its relations with the West. There were more sophisticated ways of defending white rule than merely offering defiance to troublesome outsiders. This was the essence of the outward policy.

South African governments enjoyed considerable independence in their pursuit of foreign policy, even greater than their freedom from restraint at home. The ultimate compulsion was the maintenance of white supremacy. Any government which was seen to be committed to this principle could largely decide for itself how to manage its foreign affairs. In this sensitive area Opposition spokesmen knew that trenchant criticism was liable to be labelled as unpatriotic; it was a standard, but unfailingly effective, Nationalist ploy. They knew also that their own constituents shared many of the Nationalists' convictions about an ignorant and sanctimonious world which had no understanding of the dangers of being white on an overwhelmingly black continent. In foreign affairs, more than in any other sphere of policy, bipartisanship was the rule and not the exception. But it was bipartisanship by default, for the Government usually made scant effort to brief the Opposition about its foreign policy stances.

The Government's own supporters, the Afrikaners, knew little about the outside world and only wished to be left alone to run their own affairs and those of other South Africans as they saw fit. As long as they trusted their rulers they would allow them plenty of latitude in the conduct of foreign policy, which accordingly became personalised, dependent on the insight or lack of it of those at the top. When Verwoerd was Prime Minister he made his own policy; his foreign ministers were merely his errand boys. Vorster's style was different. Consultation and discussion were a feature of this way of doing things, although he too often bypassed the cabinet, preferring to rely on the judgement of confidants.

Verwoerd had done little to improve relations with Africa. At the 1961 Commonwealth Conference, he had rejected the suggestion of diplomatic ties with African states on the unusual grounds that an exchange of ambassadors implied friendship between the countries involved, which was incompatible with the outspoken hostility of African Commonwealth members to apartheid. The most he was willing to concede was that South Africa could appoint a travelling ambassador to Africa. But even Verwoerd did not reject the principle of diplomatic links or of high-level contacts with African countries. A few days before his death he held discussions with Chief Leabua Jonathan, designated Prime Minister of the soon-to-be independent Lesotho. It afforded a precedent for Vorster's own policy of dialogue with African countries.

The new man aimed first at 'normalising' relations with southern African countries, at least with those which were sufficiently amenable. He was to explain the thinking underlying his approach:

> Once there is normalisation of relations, I think the problem of future relationships will take care of itself. One thing I know is this: the whole area lends itself well to a closer relationship because the different countries complement each other so well. I know that it will be difficult to achieve the close relationship I envisage because you are dealing with people of different cultural insights, people of different backgrounds and with widely differing levels of education and development. But I believe that it can be done. All that it will require is a degree of responsibility and clear-sightedness on the part of the leaders of the area ...[2]

The new policy required some rationalising at home, even to an audience not given to questioning the foreign policy decisions of those at the centre of the stage. The Hertzogites in the National Party, then at the height of their anti-Vorster frenzy, could be relied upon to extract the ultimate drop of racist sentiment from the presence of black diplomats in the Republic, seen by them as the harbinger of 'integration' between black and white. The Government felt compelled to go back a long way by explaining that normalising was really not all that strange; it was actually quite in accord with the precedent established by the Voortrekkers of sacrosanct memory, who apparently believed in peaceful coexistence with black tribes. It was in any event absolutely essential to the interests of South Africa that it establish friendly relations with African states.

After all the special pleading it was incongruous that the outward policy yielded so little. One difficulty was that the Government did not itself seem quite sure what it wanted. It had gone to some trouble to justify diplomatic ties with black states, even to the extent of maintaining that they did not have to involve warm feelings of friendship. However, having incurred some pain in establishing the principle, the Government suggested that there were adequate substitutes for the exchange of ambassadors between the Republic and the other countries of Southern Africa: the most important was ongoing dialogue.[3] It was as if the Government could not quite bring itself to take the step, so profoundly disturbing to many Afrikaner susceptibilities, of treating blacks, even in official capacities, as the absolute equals of whites. It looked for alternatives, found excuses and managed to dissipate the limited opportunities it had for a diplomatic breakthrough in Africa.

At first, however, the outward policy seemed set on a fair way to success. In January 1967 Leabua Jonathan once more came to the Republic, but by now his country was independent. It was the first official visit to South Africa by the leader of an independent black African state. It could not have gone better, according to the joint communiqué Vorster and Jonathan released to the press, which expressed the enthusiasm of both countries for 'peaceful co-existence on the basis of equality, mutual respect and non-interference in one another's affairs'. They agreed also that they 'should remain constantly vigilant against the dangers of international communism …' Jonathan himself described the meeting in terms he would later regret as 'a milestone on the road to international co-operation'.[4] At the time he had cause for euphoria, even if only because the customs union agreement between South Africa and Lesotho, in which Swaziland and Botswana also participated, was revised favourably to his country.

Vorster also had amicable but unofficial meetings with the President of Botswana in 1968 and with the Prime Minister of Swaziland in 1971. Perhaps all this strengthened his conviction that dialogue could be a proper substitute for diplomatic ties. Certainly, these countries had little choice, given the facts of geography and their substantial economic dependence on South Africa, but to remain on reasonably friendly terms with their powerful and potentially dangerous neighbour. As it was, the first (and only) black African country to enter into diplomatic relations with South Africa was Malawi, ruled by the conservative and autocratic Hastings Banda, who obligingly sent a white representative to the Republic in 1967.

'Going outward', in the desired form of dialogue, was in its heyday in the early 1970s, proceeding from apparent strength to strength. Conservative African states outside the Republic's immediate sphere of influence now began to test the waters. In November 1970 the Ivory Coast announced that it would call a meeting of other African states to consider direct dialogue with South Africa. A number of other, mainly Francophone, countries declared their interest in talking to the increasingly respectable government of Vorster.

But, in spite of appearances, the policy of dialogue was running aground. It had struck an immovable object in the form of the Organisation of African Unity. At its summit conference in June 1971 the OAU rejected the proposals for dialogue by 28 votes to 6. There were several abstentions, which, along with dissenting votes, showed that the OAU was fairly divided about talking to South Africa. In fact, after the conference Vorster paid dramatic visits to the Ivory Coast and Liberia, highlighting once more his willingness to talk to any African leader on an equal footing. But the official policy of the OAU remained the rejection of dialogue with the Republic as long as apartheid was in force. By the end of 1972 South Africa was engaging hardly any African state in dialogue except those belonging to its captive audience in Southern Africa, and even there relations with Lesotho had sharply deteriorated.

The Vorster Government had forfeited the opportunities which came its way. It realised the urgency of a Rhodesian settlement which did not concede Ian Smith's demand of white rule for ever, but did nothing to bring it closer. In September 1967 Vorster had sent police to Rhodesia to combat South African 'terrorists' who were trying to reach the Republic through that country. Britain, as the legal sovereign, immediately demanded their withdrawal, but they stayed until 1975. Vorster's defiance brought him much emotional applause from his electorate, but his scarcely veiled backing for the Smith regime did nothing to advance the outward policy.

Then too there was the issue of South West Africa. Once more it was only towards the middle of the seventies that the South African Government began to change course, when it at last threw off the dead hand of Verwoerd and committed itself to a separate destiny for South West Africa, as distinct from the 'separate development' which had previously been mapped out for the territory. But by then plenty of damage had been done.

There was a basic difficulty with the outward policy. Vorster had stressed repeatedly that dialogue with African countries was only possible if the participants did not interfere in one another's internal affairs. What he apparently did not realise, or possibly set much store by, was that dialogue would only be acceptable to African states beyond the Republic's direct sphere of influence if it yielded tangible results by way of furthering 'self-determination' in colonial territories like Rhodesia and South West Africa or a softening of apartheid itself in South Africa. The failure of dialogue to achieve anything of the kind only strengthened the hard-liners in the OAU and enabled them to have their way. This amounted to complete rejection of official links with South Africa, support of anti-apartheid 'liberation movements', and the demand for mandatory economic sanctions against the Republic. By the end of 1972 the outward policy had come to a halt. Dialogue had ended. Furthermore, South Africa's ambivalence about diplomatic ties meant that it had failed to press harder for such relationships when they might have been possible. With the maverick exception of Malawi, South Africa's diplomatic isolation on the African continent remained complete.

One seemingly paradoxical feature of the first half of Vorster's premiership was that the promotion of verligte causes went hand in hand with actions the most benighted verkrampte would have applauded. White unity, moving outward, multiracial sport, (white) immigration to South Africa – these were causes which gladdened any verligte heart. At the same time the Government tightened control over black labour mobility, abolished the remaining political representation of the coloureds in Parliament, and tried to wipe out the vestiges of liberalism in the English-speaking community. The obvious question is whether the Government knew what it was about, whether it was simply acting haphazardly and responding in an *ad hoc* manner to circumstances, or whether all these apparent contradictions could be reconciled in a consistent design. The most plausible answer is that there was a certain logic to the Government's behaviour. There were undoubtedly genuine contradictions between the theory and practice of apartheid. However, the supposed discrepancy between the aspirations of verligtes and the authoritarian ways of the Government was largely imaginary. The verligtes had little difficulty in living with what Vorster and his colleagues were doing. All were at one in their rejection of 'liberalism'.

The 1960s and the first half of the 1970s were times of steadily growing control over the movements of Africans within the white areas. The death of Verwoerd in 1966 brought no easing up; on the contrary, it was his successors who made the most drastic attempts yet to demonstrate that here was no mere ideological blueprint, but a feasible plan to restructure South African society.

For the Government and its apartheid bureaucracy the number of Africans with 'Section 10 rights' had become an eyesore, a blot on the apartheid landscape which could not be allowed to persist. The relative permanence in the cities enjoyed by the holders of these rights amounted to a daily negation of the Verwoerdian tenet that all blacks were rooted in their homelands, the ultimate sources of their identity. Short of abolishing Section 10 rights summarily, the Government could make it far more difficult for Africans to acquire them. In 1968 a change in the Bantu Labour Regulations compelled blacks without Section 10 rights to return to their homelands after being employed for a year. They could seek employment again, indeed return to their old jobs, but as they had not been employed 'continuously' they were plainly not entitled to permanent residence in the towns. As part of the new controls labour bureaux in the homelands theoretically had to register African workseekers; without the approval of a bureau no African could take up employment legally outside his homeland.

The total onslaught on black urban rights continued in other ways. The Government cut back on expenditure for black housing. In 1968 it announced that it would no longer provide new accommodation for black families in white areas. The number of housing units erected for Africans declined sharply. The Physical Planning and Utilisation of Resources Act of 1967 attempted to control industrial expansion. Businessmen now required ministerial approval if they wished to expand their black labour force. There was a permissible ratio of African to white labour for firms in the principal industrial areas of the Transvaal and the Cape. Originally it was 2,5 Africans for every white employee, but in 1973 it was reduced to 2 to 1 for new factories. A uniform structure of labour control took shape. In terms of the Bantu Affairs Administration Act of 1971 administration boards, each controlling an area, took to themselves powers over blacks throughout South Africa, superseding municipalities and other local authorities which had sometimes, especially in Johannesburg, implemented official policy with less than apostolic zeal. It was a most natural concomitant of all this stepped-up rigour that prosecutions under the pass laws rose substantially, from an average of 318 700 in the 1950s to an average of 541 500 for the years 1970–1975.[5] What black middle class there was came up against entrenched obstacles to its growth in the form of insecurity of property rights and the bureaucratic red tape which made it virtually impossible for black business enterprises to get started.

To a large degree, the policy worked. It slowed down the rate of black urbanisation. It perpetuated the system of migrant labour far beyond its normal limits. It made the cities much less attractive to Africans looking for jobs.

It was, in its way, a monstrously impressive performance, but it succeeded only in a highly qualified sense. It was not enough to reverse the flow of Africans entering the white areas, where the absolute number of blacks continued to rise. In the 1960s Africans legally entitled to be in the white areas rose from 6,8 million to 8 million.[6] The actual number was probably far more, as even the intensified controls could not keep out the thousands of blacks who preferred to take their chances in the cities rather than stagnate in the homelands.

Paradoxically, the success of Nationalist policy in reducing the pace of black urbanisation only pushed the ultimate goal of territorial separation further into the distance. By far the majority of the inhabitants of the homelands still lived in the subsistence sector, where output growth scarcely kept up with population increase. If most Africans in the white areas were 'surplus appendages' to be deported to the homelands, as one Deputy Minister of Bantu Administration and Development put it in the 1960s,[7] pressure on an unproductive agriculture would only grow, and so would pressure to evade the controls over labour mobility. At the same time, the problem of surplus labour was becoming more acute, for employers were increasingly taking to mechanisation. It was one way at least of overcoming the government-imposed difficulties in attracting the black workers they wanted.

What happened during these years is often seen as a refutation of the familiar and persuasive argument that, in the words of the West Indian economist and Nobel Prize winner, Arthur Lewis, the 'most effective destroyer of discrimination is fast economic growth'. Lewis explained why growth should be such a pervasive solvent:

> This creates a shortage of skilled workers and incites employers to upgrade persons and jobs – unless white labor can be imported from abroad. Tightness in the labor market also reassures skilled workers, making them more willing to accept liberal policies ... The disadvantaged and the subordinate have a vested interest in fast economic growth. Every reduction in the target rate for economic growth is also a reduction in the strength of equalising forces.[8]

On the face of it, the argument finds no immediate support in the South African experience. The author of a recent book on the economics of apartheid has explained why: 'The period of most rapid economic growth, in the 1950s and 1960s, coincided with the consolidation of the basic elements of the apartheid system, some of the worst political repression, and an increase in white per capita income relative to black'. He also points out that 'on the other hand, 'reform' in some apartheid institutions and practices – such as the new labor policies towards unions, reduced restrictions on movements of black South Africans, increased expenditure on black education and training, and the abolition of most legal job reservation – as well as the substantial narrowing of the gap between black and white wage and income levels has taken place in the context of the relatively stagnant economy since the early 1970s'.[9]

The contradiction is however only superficial. If we accept that the consequences of economic growth, as reflected in eroding discriminatory institutions and practices, only come with a lag, then there is nothing puzzling about the evidence, especially if we consider the powerful vested interests, like the hordes of apartheid civil servants, that were upholding the practices of white supremacy till the very last ditch. The upgrading of persons and jobs referred to by Lewis did come, but in the wake of economic growth and at a time when it had lost its momentum. Even so, in the 1960s job reservation was becoming a practice of the past, retained on the statute book as a last resort to protect white workers during recession, but otherwise of little account.

Still, this whole period, from about 1960 to the mid-seventies, was the heyday of Verwoerdian hubris, when politicians befuddled by the doctrines of the architect of apartheid and bureaucrats cast in his mould believed that South Africa could be remade according to his vision of the future. For a time, even the economic growth which was so steadily eating away at the foundations of apartheid seemed to be working in their favour. They found themselves with resources which could be devoted to the supremely unproductive use of imposing and extending a veritable plethora of racial laws and restrictions. Undoubtedly, they made the most of what fell into their laps.

The assault on African rights in the white areas was something which little exercised the verligtes. Their causes were white unity, 'moving outward' and a farewell to Verwoerd's awe-inspiring insistence on the niceties of racial separation wherever it was feasible. This to them was 'small' (usually mistranslated as 'petty') apartheid, something not at all essential to 'grand' apartheid in the shape of separate homelands, in which they did believe and in the name of which blacks were being moved and disposed of all over the Republic. They were embarrassed by the more savage aspects of apartheid, especially when their visibility was high, such as forced removals of Africans from white areas to barren rural regions. It eased the consciences of the verligtes of the National Party to support such obvious good things as multiracial sports teams from abroad; it made it less difficult for them to accept the experiment in social engineering which was taking place right around them, but about which they preferred to know as little as possible.

To be fair to the verligtes, they were not happy about the ending of coloured representation in Parliament, but it was something they managed to swallow, as the leading articles in *Die Burger*, their most articulate mouthpiece, showed only too well. The decision by the Government to end the separate representation of coloureds in Parliament was not something which flowed naturally from the apartheid blueprint. It could be, and was, rationalised on the grounds that such representation was incompatible with 'separate development', but as the coloureds did not have a distinct homeland of their own such arguments never rose above special pleading. The logic of apartheid as a doctrine in fact pointed in the other direction: full equality of the coloureds with whites in a common society.

The removal of the coloured representatives from Parliament is best seen as an act of authoritarian intolerance by a government which had never learnt to respond to criticism as part of the normal cut-and-thrust of politics. The Progressive Party had been a particular irritant since its formation in 1959, committed as it was to a liberal, 'integrationist' alternative to apartheid which differed glaringly from the unceasing commitment to white supremacy of the Official Opposition, the United Party. The Nationalists were happy when the general election of 1961 left the Progressives with only one representative in the House of Assembly, but that was the redoubtable Helen Suzman, whose role as the lone liberal in a body otherwise crammed with official supporters of some kind of discrimination or other made for high drama and international acclaim. The Nationalists detested Suzman and her all-too-well-informed and scathing criticisms of their policies. The prospect of Progressives entering Parliament as representatives of the coloureds was one they could not accept easily. But when the coloureds elected two Progressives to the Cape Provincial Council, it became evident that more of them sitting in Parliament was actually only a matter of time — unless the Government could concoct reasons to keep them out, which it did.

The final shape of the concoction was the Prohibition of Political Interference Act and the Separate Representation of Voters Amendment Act, which in 1968 made racially mixed political parties illegal and abolished coloured representation in the House of Assembly and the Cape Provincial Council before the next elections. As a substitute, the Government established a Coloured

Persons' Representative Council which differed from the Transkeian constitution in that it allowed for 40 elected members as against 20 official nominees. The Council got off to a wretched start, symbolic of what seemed to have become permanently soured relations between the Nationalists and the coloured people. The first elections to the Council took place in September 1969. Most voters boycotted them. Those who did vote mainly supported opponents of apartheid. However, with the help of its nominees which included thirteen defeated candidates from the election, the Government managed to place in office a party which favoured apartheid. The Council could not recover from such unpromising beginnings. It never gained acceptance among coloured voters. When the opposition Labour Party finally gained a majority in 1975 it effectively ceased to function.

The coloured people, as well as the Indians, continued to be at the receiving end of one of the most drastic measures of apartheid legislation. This was the Group Areas Act. From its inception to the end of 1972 nearly 45 000 coloured and 28 000 Indian families had been compelled to move in terms of this measure, compared with just over 1 500 white families. At that date more than 27 000 coloured and nearly 11 000 Indian families were still to be moved; the number of white families came to 135.[10] Here was the starkest evidence possible that apartheid was not letting up, that all South Africans who were not white remained potential victims of policies still largely designed to benefit members of the white race.

It did not follow that all whites could feel secure. The Vorster administration was no more enthusiastic about displays of liberalism from the English-speaking press, universities and churches than Verwoerd had been. The Nationalists were particularly agitated about the 'unpatriotic English press', which they regularly threatened to bring to heel.

Mostly it had been bluster, serving the role of letting off steam, but it helped to keep the non-patriots off balance and insecure. There was also a Publications Control board, established in 1963, which had the power to ban books and periodicals and used it without excessive diffidence. Originally the board was subject to judicial review, but it came up against too many adverse judgments. In 1974 the Government placed it beyond the reach of the courts in a cumbersome system which left the last appeal in the hands of a minister.

In February 1972 Vorster appointed a Select Committee, later a Commission, under the chairmanship of the aspiring Nationalist MP, Alwyn Schlebusch. Its thinly veiled task was to investigate four organisations of a liberal cast which the Government disliked and to produce conclusions that would make action against them appear justified. The Commission would sit in camera. Representatives and members of the organisations under investigation would not be able to cross-examine witnesses, refute allegations made without their knowledge, or lead evidence of their own.

The Commission, on which the United Party, aware of a conservative electorate, chose to serve, did its job well. Early in 1973 it tabled a unanimous interim report on the National Union of South African Students (Nusas) which identified eight 'activists' in that organisation who endangered internal security. All of them, including the president of Nusas, immediately found themselves served with banning orders under the Suppression of Communism Act. In its final report in 1975 the Commission strongly censured the inter-denominational Christian Institute; it contributed to the suspicion-mongering which gave the Government the pretext to ban the institute's director, Beyers Naudé, in 1977 and the organisation itself later that year.

The Vorster years were authoritarian years. The issues the verligtes liked to get excited about — white unity, moving outward, less 'small' apartheid — did not carry within them the seeds of a much more liberal society. On the contrary, to the Government and its verligte supporters the 'liberalists' remained a top public enemy, second only to the Communists. The Vorster regime persecuted them with relish, all the more as it felt compelled to refute HNP claims that it had gone soft on Afrikaner survival. Being verlig was largely a state of mind typical of Afrikaners who had arrived and wished to be free to enjoy the fruits of economic advance, political supremacy and the attainment of the republic. Wider libertarian issues tended to pass the verligtes by. They little noted the near-totalitarian controls over the movements of blacks within South Africa. When they did it was always possible to justify them as being essential to the attainment of separate freedoms.

The contradiction between verligte professions and authoritarian performance was only superficial. They were really two sides of the same apartheid coin.

CHAPTER THIRTEEN

Approaching Soweto

During the sixties African political activity posed no threat to apartheid. After their banning in 1960 and the failure of their resort to arms over the next few years, the ANC and the PAC had regrouped outside South Africa. The PAC never had much success in starting again: it was divided into rival factions, its leadership was unstable and it established no bases of any importance in South Africa itself. The ANC had similar problems, but not in so acute a form. For most of its first decade in exile its leaders were noted more for their propensity for comfortable living than for their austere commitment to the liberation of the masses. It was only towards the late 1970s that the ANC began to succeed in infiltrating the Republic from the north. The resumed 'armed struggle' was reflected in attacks on police stations and the explosion of bombs in public places. It was proof that the ANC still existed, but such acts were no worse than a nuisance to the Nationalist Government, which knew how weak the organisation remained on the ground. It did not fail to extract the last drop of propaganda value from the new willingness of the ANC to kill and maim civilians even if 90 per cent of its actions were still aimed at military and industrial targets. White South Africans saw the ANC increasingly as a Communist-dominated terrorist organisation.

Within the Republic black opponents of apartheid found it no easier to organise resistance. The police were only nominally subject to legal restraints in dealing with African dissidents. They could arrest and detain as they pleased. The number of detainees who 'committed suicide' suggests that there were few limits on the methods police used to extract information and confessions. They had a host of informers who contributed to an atmosphere of fear and distrust in the organisations which they infiltrated.

Police intimidation and violence went hand in hand with the Government's onslaught on the permanence of blacks in the urban areas. More controls over the movement of Africans to the cities, the deliberate encouragement of a work force based primarily on migrant labour – these too made it more difficult for Africans to organise themselves politically.

Yet black political activity could not be submerged indefinitely. It surfaced in the shape of the Black Consciousness movement. Black Consciousness was originally a movement of black students who felt that the liberal, but primarily white, National Union of South African Students could in no way understand the experiences of blacks, the victims of a common oppression in which even the most sympathetic white South Africans could not share. Being black, which theoretically included coloureds and Indians, meant a common servitude, a common fate, and a consciousness that in South Africa at least blackness was more important than similarities of class and education.

The legislation of 1959 had established separate ethnic universities, derogatorily but accurately described as 'tribal colleges', for Africans, coloureds and Indians. A decade later they had enough students who felt that the comfortable once-a-year liberalism of Nusas conferences was not for them. In 1969 Steve Biko led a secession to form the South African Students' Organisation.

Biko became a student at the University of Natal (Non-European Section) in 1966. Originally he had been a supporter of Nusas and 'accepted fully their non-racist approach'.[1] Disillusionment began to take hold at the 1967 Nusas conference at Rhodes University in Grahamstown when black delegates found themselves compelled by the University Council to accept segregated residential facilities. Biko was one of the delegates who blamed Nusas for its willingness, however reluctant, to continue with its conference under such demeaning conditions. He introduced a motion, which was not accepted, proposing that the conference adjourn until 'a non-racist venue' could be found.

It was during the debate that he 'began to feel there was a lot lacking in the proponents of the non-racist idea, that much as they were adhering to this impressive idea they were in fact subject to their own experiences back home, they had the problem ... of superiority, and they tended to take us for granted and wanted us to accept things that were second-class'.[2] Increasingly Biko and other black students began to feel that they faced problems unique to themselves as black students which a wider organisation like Nusas could not grasp or cope with.

In July 1969 the first conference of the South African Students' Organisation (Saso) was held at the University College of the North. It recognised Nusas as the national student organisation but decided against affiliation. Attitudes towards Nusas hardened as the new organisation found that it had to compete with the larger body for support amongst black students. In 1970 Saso decided to go it alone and withdrew its recognition of Nusas.

The final break confirmed a stance expressed in a Saso resolution which emphasised the overriding importance of blackness: 'Saso is a black student organisation working for the liberation of blacks first from psychological oppression by themselves through an inferiority complex, and secondly from the physical oppression accruing out of living in a white racist society'.[3]

For Biko, and other preachers of black consciousness, it was psychological liberation which was decisive: 'The black man in himself has developed a certain state of alienation, he rejects himself precisely because he attaches the meaning white to all that is good, in other words he equates good with white'.[4] As a philosophy black consciousness had clear if disparate forerunners in the Black Power notions of Stokely Carmichael in the United States, the *négritude* of French-speaking black intellectuals like Senegal's president Leopold Senghor, the assertions of the intrinsic worth of Africans by the Algerian revolutionary theorist, Frantz Fanon, and, not least, the Pan Africanist strain manifest in the past of the ANC itself, which led to the founding of the PAC. It was not especially original, but it expressed the conviction of an increasing number of blacks in South Africa that freedom would only come through their own efforts and not at all through attempts to forge alliances across a racial divide that was unbreachable as long as apartheid existed. It was a state of mind best conveyed by the slogan: 'Black man, you are on your own!'

Saso was the forerunner. Three years later, in July 1972, Saso and four other organisations, primarily religious, launched the Black People's Convention (BPC). Its goals were:
- To help the black community become aware of its identity.
- To help the black community create a sense of its own power.
- To enable the black community to organise itself, analyse its needs and problems and also mobilise its resources to meet these needs.
- To develop black leadership capable of guiding the development of the black community.[5]

The BPC rejected violence. It intended to free blacks from psychological oppression through a nationwide campaign for community involvement in health projects, the elimination of illiteracy and the encouragement of cultural activities. Once black consciousness had developed sufficiently blacks would have the inner reserves that were an essential precondition for a change in the status quo.

The philosophy was vague, nor was it to take shape in much that was concrete. The truth was that, however appealing its message of black self-reliance, the Black Consciousness movement never had deep roots in the masses which it wished to free from their supposed inferiority complex. At its formation the Black People's Convention had announced its aim of recruiting a million members in three years. However, as one authority on the black politics of the 1970s, Baruch Hirson, has commented, 'The objective was unreal. It is doubtful whether the organisation on its own ever achieved a membership of 3 000 or, together with SASO, a total enrolment of 7 000 members. The BPC remained an organisation of students, a few clerics, and some professional men and women'.[6]

Hirson is no doubt right when he describes many statements by Saso leaders as obscurantist, as witness Biko's appeal '... to reduce the hold of technology over man and to reduce the materialistic element that is slowly creeping into the African character'.[7] But while romantic longings for an idealised past would not bring liberation any closer, it remained true that the message of the Black Consciousness movement had a considerable emotional force. For the BPC or Saso to have an emancipating impact, they did not have to command large battalions of paid-up members. It was enough that the Black Consciousness movement should proclaim sentiments whose time had come. Whatever the intellectual inconsistencies and confusions of its doctrines, like those of similar ideas preached in other parts of the world, they helped to create a climate of black opinion that would promote self-confidence and raise expectations, so drastically shattered after Sharpeville, that apartheid was not part of the eternal scheme of things. The Black Consciousness movement had no coherent design for ending white supremacy. To its critics in the ANC it was, at best, ambiguous about 'the armed struggle'. The greatest contribution of Saso and the BPC was that notions of black independence and self-reliance became an inescapable part of the air breathed by urbanised and literate Africans.

It was in the decade of the seventies that the apartheid dam began to break at predictable points. The exceedingly rapid economic growth of the 1960s now began to demonstrate that it came at a cost. It would take the shape of reforms in labour relations which were unthinkable in the days of high apartheid and a striking increase in the share of national income going to blacks, matched by an equally remarkable decline in the white share. Businessmen, who normally would have preferred to be apolitical seekers of profit, became increasingly restless under a system which was doing them and the economy visibly little good. The experience of South Africa in the 1970s is a case study of the conflict between discrimination and economic growth.

The South African economy entered the decade facing a quite different scenario from that of the previous twenty years. The country's main earner of foreign exchange had been, and continued to be, gold, which accounted for between 40 to 50 per cent of all exports. Between 1950 and 1971 however, the price of gold had been fixed. It was an essential part of the Bretton Woods system of fixed exchange rates on which the international economy was based. Bretton Woods collapsed in 1971, unable to cope with persistent United States inflation and balance of payments deficits. In its aftermath came a fluctuating gold price. Not only did it escalate rapidly, but it became highly variable, both in rand and dollar terms. The uncoupling of gold created new opportunities for the South African economy, but it also increased the uncertainty under which businessmen had to operate.

The growth of the economy during the 1970s also differed conspicuously from that of the decade before. During the 1960s it had averaged between five and six per cent a year. Between 1970 and 1975 growth declined to an annual average of four per cent. It was however still respectable compared with the 2,8 per cent of the following five years.[8] After 1975 the South African economy entered a period of sustained low growth in which the primacy of the political continued to overshadow the best efforts of businessmen to make profits.

It was in a still growing economy that black workers withdrew their labour. Between 1962 and 1968 there had been little strike action by Africans. In April 1969 about 2 000 Durban dockers went on strike, unsuccessfully, and rates of pay remained unaltered. When they threatened to go on strike later in September 1971 they did receive an increase, which they regarded as inadequate. The watershed strikes, which initiated fundamental changes in the Republic's system of industrial relations, came in 1973.

Once more they happened in Natal, for a variety of reasons. One was that Durban-Pinetown was the largest industrial area in South Africa after the Witwatersrand. An obvious reason advanced by the strikers themselves was low wages, which may have been less plausible than it appeared as several Durban firms at the receiving end of industrial action were known as relatively enlightened and high-paying employers. A conjunction of circumstances peculiar to the region seems the most plausible explanation. There had been a sudden and sharp rise in transport costs. A powerful sense of ethnic identity probably made its own special contribution. A contemporary account in *Race Relations News* provides a handy summary:

> The development of black consciousness, the stature and articulate utterances of prominent Zulu leaders using separate development platforms, the inauguration of Prince Goodwill (as Zulu Paramount Chief), the celebration of Shaka Day and the commemoration of Chief Luthuli's life and ideals may be

all interacting to create a renewed self-awareness among rank-and-file Zulu workers.[9]

Also, the effects of economic growth had strengthened the bargaining power of Africans doing certain kinds of work. Whatever official policy may have been, the needs of industry had been eroding job reservation all over the country, with blacks moving into positions for which whites could not be found. If 'white' vacancies, involving skilled and semi-skilled work, could not be filled by members of the appropriate race, there was no alternative but to resort to the second-best solution of employing Africans, coloureds and Indians. Natal was no exception to what had been happening elsewhere.

Paradoxically, labour shortages were accompanied by widespread unemployment, both in Durban-Pinetown and the rest of South Africa. Both were a direct outcome of Government policy. The shortages were for skilled workers, who in principle should have been white but in practice increasingly turned out to be black. The unemployment was concentrated amongst unskilled blacks, unable to find work because apartheid insisted that as few Africans as possible should be employed in the white urban areas. A measure like the Physical Planning Act, by making it inordinately troublesome for employers to recruit the kind and quantities of black labour they wanted, raised the relative price of unskilled workers. Capitalists had few options but to turn to increasingly capital intensive techniques as a substitute for the factor of production about which the Government was being so difficult.

On two counts did capital intensification improve the leverage of blacks working with the new techniques. They acquired skills which could not at once be imparted to potential replacements. Labour costs became a smaller component of total costs: a wage increase would now be easier to absorb.

The strikes began in January 1973 and at once established themselves as something unprecedented in the history of Nationalist rule. They were huge, widespread and did not go away. They started at a brick and tile company, but it was in the textile industry that thousands of blacks went on strike from the end of January, first in Natal and then spreading to the Transvaal and the Eastern

Cape, bringing out large numbers of Indians and coloureds as well.

There was little organisation. The knowledge that one group had gone on strike acted as a spur for others to do so as well. Trade unions played a negligible role. Black unions scarcely existed and were in any event not officially recognised. The strikers were however highly organised. They took to the streets in huge marches, the first since Sharpeville. The strikers made a point of not having official leaders: the police could not victimise ring leaders whom they could not identify. It was the birth of modern mass action that later helped to inspire the Soweto students' revolt.

The absence of a formal union structure also had its costs. There were no strike funds, so that individual stoppages had limited staying power. Those which went on for four days or longer were the exception. But the extent of the strike wave was exceedingly wide, and when one strike ended another would begin elsewhere.

Between January and the end of March 1973 more than 60 000 Africans had been involved on 160 occasions in strikes and stoppages. On 118 occasions the strikers received wage increases, although in general they were not especially large. In only seven cases did employers dismiss the strikers.[10] Strikes and work stoppages continued for the rest of the year. They went as far as the mining industry, where, at Carletonville in the Transvaal, eleven black miners were killed by the police in September when a strike passed into a riot. Between mid-January and mid-October about 70 000 mainly African workers were involved in strikes and work stoppages.[11]

The events which began in Durban had their effect on the Government. Till then Africans did not have the right to strike. The law in fact prohibited all strikes and lock-outs by Africans. In June Parliament passed the Bantu Labour Relations Regulation Amendment Act, which, in a highly qualified form, legalised the right to strike. It excluded black employees employed by a local authority and in 'essential services' such as the provision of light and sanitation. But the Act was, for all that, a landmark. It accepted the principle that Africans too had the right to withhold their labour. It was without precedent in South African history and constituted the beginning of the transformation of the Republic's system of industrial relations.

Strikes and work stoppages continued in the years between 1973 and 1976, although eventually at a declining rate. From January 1973 to the middle of 1976 more than 200 000 African, coloured and Indian workers went on strike. The great majority of strikers were Africans.[12]

The Black Consciousness movement and the strikes of these years were part of a mood of rising black unrest after the relative quiescence of the 1960s. It was to reach a climax in the Soweto uprising of 1976. From his Trotskyite perspective Baruch Hirson argues that the wave of black strikes was a direct forerunner of Soweto, but that the contribution of Black Consciousness was quite minor. He finds the 'greatest weakness' of the strikes 'in the fact that there was no political group that could offer a lead and make the strikes part of the political struggle against the government'. Hirson concludes however that the strikes 'helped create the atmosphere of revolt and showed that the blacks were not powerless. It was by the multitude of strikes, small and large, that the example of resistance was taken into the townships. The ability to resist the terror of government action was demonstrated repeatedly. Although they have received little attention since the Soweto Revolt, these strikes must be seen as constituting the beginning of the Revolt, and as having affected a far wider section of the population than was ever reached by members of SASO-BPC'.[13]

It is tempting to find a direct line of progression from the strike wave to the Soweto uprising. On closer observation the links appear more tenuous. If Hirson is correct, it is puzzling that by the end of the violent year of 1976 the urban African communities of Natal, where the strikes had been so prominent, were the only ones, as one historian of black politics puts it, 'relatively unaffected by the disturbances.'[14] The strikes should probably be seen more as part of a turbulent background to the events of Soweto, adding to a climate of discontent, unrest and heightened but frustrated expectations. In this respect they did not differ so much from the Black Consciousness movement, which made its own contribution to the psychological tensions to which urban Africans were subject in the first half of the 1970s.

Certainly, it is difficult to discern the immediate origins of what came to be known as the Revolt in anything except the educational policies of the Nationalist Government. Soweto began as a protest by African schoolchildren and ended as a rebellion which encompassed nearly the whole of urban black society.

As the representative of a people which resented bitterly having 'the language of the conqueror' imposed upon Afrikaans schools after the Boer War, the Government proved remarkably insensitive in what it tried to do to the captives of Bantu Education. Under Vorster, it is true, the Government had exanded secondary schooling for Africans in the urban areas considerably. It began in 1970 and was to continue throughout the decade, a response to the realisation that the white population alone could not supply all the skilled workers needed by the economy. But with it went the insistence that African pupils be equally exposed to both official languages.

In 1974 the Department of Bantu Education had sent out a circular stating that half the subjects in secondary schools should be taught in Afrikaans, namely, arithmetic and the social sciences. For an Afrikaner Nationalist the rationale was simple: the education of black children was paid for by the white taxpayers; even-handedness required that each official language receive the same treatment in black schools. The appointment of Andries Treurnicht, in Parliament since 1971 and the foremost right wing ideologue in the National Party, as Deputy Minister of Bantu Administration and Development at the beginning of 1976 only led to the stricter enforcement of this policy. As Treurnicht was to put it with crass insensitivity, 'In the white area of South Africa, where the Government provides the buildings, gives the subsidies and pays the teachers, it is surely our right to be able to determine the choice of language. Why are pupils sent to schools if the choice of language does not suit them?'[15]

The ruling was extremely unpopular amongst both black pupils and their teachers. Afrikaans was unacceptable as the language of the oppressor. English was an international language and seen by blacks as an indispensable vehicle for access to better-paid jobs. Few black teachers had a good command of Afrikaans. But protests by black school boards brought no satisfaction and earned dismissal instead for several of their members.

In May and June 1976 students from seven schools in Soweto, Johannesburg's labour reservoir with its million inhabitants, started boycotting classes. There were of course other reasons for their discontent. They rejected Bantu Education as a preparation for inferiority. The recent expansion of secondary schooling in the urban areas had resulted in huge overcrowding in class-rooms. The number of qualified teachers had not grown at the same rate. Forced subjection to Afrikaans now brought into the open a resentment which had long been building up.

On 16 June 10 000 schoolchildren marched to the Orlando West Junior Secondary School, where the first pupil strike had occurred a month before. Riot police attempted to remove posters which protested against the use of Afrikaans. In the confrontation that followed the police opened fire. They claimed that they were compelled to retaliate because they had been stoned; according to the pupils the police began to shoot without provocation. When the firing ceased one pupil was dead and several had been wounded. The rioting spread; by the end of the day 23 people had died, including three whites killed by outraged mobs.

The violence continued in Soweto, with buses, beer halls and eventually schools being set alight as symbols of white authority. The Government closed all schools while gangsters looted shops and robbed people both in Soweto and in the other black townships to which the protests had spread. The revolt affected urban communities throughout South Africa, especially Cape Town and Port Elizabeth, as well as some of the homelands. In Cape Town thousands of coloured pupils, as well as Africans, took to the streets to protest against what had become more than just the compulsory use of Afrikaans in black schools. The initial protests broadened out into attacks on Bantu Education, segregated education and the principle of apartheid itself.

The Government had in the meantime rescinded the ruling on the teaching of Afrikaans. It announced that black schools would formally reopen on 26 July. Unknown to itself, the Government had taken a decision which divided the leadership of the revolt and compelled it to find other ways of protest.

The South African Students' Movement (SASM) was founded in 1972. It was an organisation which had links with the Black Consciousness movement and devoted itself to assisting senior school students in a number of impeccably respectable ways, such as improving their study techniques and providing career guidance. This had not earned it exemption from harassment by the police. On 13 June SASM formed the Soweto Students' Representative Council (SSRC), which consisted of delegates from the parent body, two from each secondary school in Soweto. It was the SSRC which planned the momentous demonstrations of 16 June.

The tactics of the SSRC consisted in organising class boycotts, which were only possible when the schools were open. When the Government did reopen the schools, the SSRC called on pupils to return but gave no full explanation of their decision, namely, that they should come back so that they could start boycotting again. The response was half-hearted; shortly after that the first schools were burnt down. From August the schools remained empty for the rest of the year.

The SSRC had to find an alternative, which it did in the form of stay-aways. Africans were to be persuaded, by reasoning or by force, not to go to work. The first stay-at-home was on 4 August and was marked by plenty of coercion from stone-throwing youths and the abstention from work of 60 per cent of the African employees of Johannesburg. There were two more stay-aways. The first was jointly called by the SSRC and the ANC, which got into the act belatedly, partly because it had to operate underground. On 23 August 70 to 80 per cent of black workers did not turn up, an absentee rate which held firm for the rest of the week. The last successful use of this method was on 13 to 15 September, when once more large, if varying, numbers of Africans remained at home over the three days of the strike. Also, in an unusual display of solidarity, on 15 September 200 000 coloured workers, representing about 80 per cent of the work force of Cape Town, refused to go to work.

It was all exceedingly impressive, but as a technique the general strike had its limits, the same as those experienced by the ANC fifteen years before. Stay-aways had no staying power, as workers who were not paid for being at home soon discovered. Those who were already impoverished could afford nothing as quixotic as responding interminably to appeals, even when supported by force, that they should stay away from work for the sake of objectives which were far from clearly spelled out. There were also the police, who were patently eager to uphold the right of strike-breakers to opt out of the freedom struggle. Amongst African workers themselves there were divisions, exploited by the authorities: migrants proved less susceptible to political appeals than their more settled brothers. Stay-aways had considerable nuisance value, but they could not come close to shaking any regime which had the white population, the police and the army on its side.

At the end of October the SSRC called for a five-day strike from 1 November. The slogan was to be: 'Blacks are going into mourning for their dead.' The outcome is best summarised by Hirson, an extreme sympathiser with the frustrations of the youthful rebels:

> The strike call and the demands made were unrealistic. Families did not mourn for the dead by starving — and that would have been the consequence of a whole week's stoppage. Nor could workers be expected to respond again and again when the strikes achieved nothing. The call was ignored.[16]

By then the revolt had subsided. The police had now reached full stride and were arresting anyone who was suspected of involvement in the uprising. The SSRC organised partially successful campaigns against the consumption of alcohol, seen as a diversion from more socially useful activities, and the celebration of Christmas. Schools remained virtually closed during 1977, but plainly protest had lost its force and drive long before. Estimates have varied, depending on the source, but possibly a thousand Africans and coloureds lost their lives in the uprising. Many also fled the country.

There has been controversy over the causes of the Soweto uprising, but it is unlikely that it would have happened had it not been preceded by fifteen years of virtually uninterrupted economic growth. One economist has estimated that African real wages grew at 3,9 per cent per annum from 1960 to 1970. The so-called gap between the average wages of white and black widened at the same time, but narrowed slightly between 1970 and 1975.[17] However low the incomes of blacks were by comparison with those of whites, they were noticeably improving, both absolutely and relatively. It has become a trite argument that the roots of revolt need the nourishment of better material circumstances, only for the beneficiaries to be confronted by barriers to further advance. This however was what was happening to urban Africans before Soweto.

The Government had done its level best after Sharpeville to leave blacks with no illusions about what was in store for them in the 'white' areas of the Republic. For a time, through its transparent willingness to use force, it had succeeded. But not even force can keep expectations down indefinitely if there is a sustained improvement in economic conditions. Memories of previous repression fade, while a new generation emerges to which that repression is only a tale told by its elders. Inevitably, it would seem, there had to be another outburst of black protest and discontent, on a far larger scale than Sharpeville. All that it required were the ingredients of continued white rule and economic progress.

Rapid growth had to lead to heightened expectations if only because it had to mean more education for Africans. Rising living standards for the white population demanded continued growth, which could only result in more blacks doing skilled and semi-skilled work. That the Government got the message is evident from the rapid expansion of black secondary education, which trebled its intake between 1970 and 1975.

It was a potent recipe for unrest. Increasing numbers of young Africans acquired basic skills as well as the realisation that they faced a limited and regimented future in white South Africa. They did so in conditions of overcrowding, frequently poor teaching and finally submission to the language of their detested rulers. As with Sharpeville, there was also the knowledge that the tide of history was going their way: decolonisation had at last reached the borders of South Africa and South West Africa. The Portuguese colony of Mozambique had become independent in 1974. Two years later it was the turn of the other Portuguese territory, Angola, but only after a South African invasion to secure non-Marxists in power had ended in failure. It all made for a combination of hope and frustration which had to find an outlet.

The precursors of Soweto were no more than that. There is little evidence that the Black Consciousness movement played a significant role in the revolt. The South African Students' Movement had black consciousness origins and affiliations, but that is where it seems to have ended. The concerns of its offshoot, the SSRC, were somewhat different from those self-help schemes which had been the favourite preoccupations of black consciousness spokesmen. It does not follow that its influence was negligible, but it was rather by way of contributing to a climate of opinion, to a mood of black self-assertiveness and independence which had not been there before.

The same goes for the strike wave of the previous years. Baruch Hirson has called the strikes 'the beginning of the Revolt', but this seems to be little more than a die-hard Marxist determination to find room for the proletariat. His argument has been criticised aptly by Tom Lodge in his history of black politics in South Africa, where he argues that 'in 1976 any memories of events in 1973 would have been dimmed by three years, that subsequent strikes were accorded very little press publicity, and that the strike movement as a whole developed mainly in Natal, the East Rand, the East London conurbation, not in Johannesburg. It is also relevant to point out that Soweto was not a predominantly industrial working-class community; it had a disproportionately large white collar or petty bourgeois group – numbering 50 000 – and the township's population had been left virtually untouched by the revival of working-class consciousness and trade unionism that had begun elsewhere.'[18] Again it seems that the influences were more indirect. The strikes were part of a whole background of renewed confidence and unwillingness to accept white dictates about the future of blacks.

One powerful impression of the Soweto revolt is its spontaneity. Its exceedingly young leaders responded largely to circumstance. They had no master plan for the future. What they planned to do next was the result of what had happened before. They began with the limited goal of improved schooling. As events unfolded they became more ambitious, at least as far as their plans for mass action were concerned. In their more euphoric moods they must have easily believed that they had the Boers on the run. But they had no blueprint for a new society, which could hardly have been expected of them. Even if they had, it would have made little difference: white rule was not yet for the taking and would not be for a long time to come. It remains true that Soweto is one of the watersheds in South African history. The uprising must be judged by its consequences: after 1976 both white and black politics resembled only remotely what had gone before.

CHAPTER FOURTEEN

Making Neo-Apartheid Work

The Vorster Government had not done well in the 1970 general election. For the first time since 1948 the Nationalists had come back with a reduced majority. They still had a huge preponderance in the House of Assembly, with more than 70 per cent of the members, compared with 55 per cent of the total votes cast in the election. But it was an unmistakable reverse, due largely to the Government's efforts to eliminate its Hertzogite enemies on the extreme right. The United Party picked up eight seats by default and once more began to persuade itself that the Nationalist tide had turned and that power was within reach. The Nationalists would take no chances next time the white voters went to the polls.

In a parliamentary by-election in the Transvaal constituency of Brakpan, one of their urban strongholds, the Nationalists had won with a much reduced majority in February 1972. Extreme circumstances called for extreme measures. Despite the call for white unity of the previous years, they decided that life remained in a rested but proven war-horse: the pounding of the Afrikaner ethnic drum. Appeals to Afrikaners as Afrikaners to vote Nationalist had come to resemble a somewhat embarrassing relic of the past, like the response of the *nouveau riche* who does not care to be reminded of his origins on the wrong side of the railway track. They were decidedly unsuited to the more conciliatory times of white unity which the Nationalists insisted had arrived with the Republic. But another parliamentary by-election was due in April, in the Cape rural constituency of Oudtshoorn. The war-horse was brought out of retirement.

The United Party had provided the Government with a bonus the year before: it had once more rehashed its policy and come up with the usual hotch-potch which could please no one except Nationalist propagandists, who regarded as a veritable godsend the Opposition proposals of sixteen representatives (six of them actually coloured) for the different non-white population groups in the House of Assembly. The Nationalists chose to regard them as yet another of those thin ends of the wedge which would cause the Afrikaner to lose his rightful place in the South African sun. As one minister put it with fine simulated outrage in Parliament: 'One cannot get away from the fact that the NP consists chiefly of the Afrikaners and the UP chiefly of the English-speaking, and you are going to use those sixteen to keep the Afrikaner out of power ... If you do that you will create a simply unprecedented situation of hatred in South Africa'.[1] In his characteristic vituperative manner, the Minister of Defence, P W Botha, claimed, truthfully enough, that several members of the United Party did not speak Afrikaans and went on to announce that 'there are elements, both inside and outside this House, that hate the Afrikaner'.[2]

Playing the theme of Afrikaner hatred had been an infallible tactic for electoral success in the past. It was no different at Oudtshoorn. The official organ of the Cape National Party and its leading verligte newspaper, *Die Burger*, waged a strident campaign along these lines and had every reason to be pleased with the result. The Nationalists retained the seat with a substantially enlarged majority. The next month they tried it again at another by-election at Brakpan, this time for the provincial council. Once more the Nationalists increased their majority, but not as impressively as they did in April. Even so, the Brakpan result could be explained away as the expression of local Nationalist grievances, reflected in the low percentage poll of 63 per cent. What the Nationalists had shown once more was that when they set their minds to it they were masters at winning elections, not over-scrupulous as to their methods and perfectly willing to put into cold storage their moving pronouncements about the unity of the white language groups.

At the next general election in April 1974, it became plain that what had happened four years before was no more than a brief hiccup in the trend of Nationalist advance. In an enlarged House of Assembly the Official Opposition now resumed its long-term decline. It came back with 43 members, four less than before, while the Government increased its representation from the 118 of 1970 to 122. The Progressive Party made the largest proportionate gains; from the one member of the previous thirteen years it went up to six, all elected by voters of affluent English-speaking constituencies.

The Herstigte Nasionale Party had once more failed to make any impression. None of its candidates won a seat and many lost their deposits. It was not because their message of white supremacy and apartheid for all time and at all costs did not appeal to Nationalist voters. Many of them, especially in the rural areas, could find no fault with the racial policy of the Herstigtes. It was just that they had no particular reason to abandon the National Party when it was providing so little proof that the interests of the Afrikaner were not close to its heart. It was simply not plausible that a man with a record like Vorster's should suddenly have become a 'liberalist', the standard Nationalist term of abuse for anyone with liberal views on race. Most Nationalist voters were without question not 'liberalists'. They did not believe in giving the vote to blacks except in 'their own areas', and they believed firmly in segregation between the races when territorial separation was not feasible, which mostly it was not.

The Government was committed to these policies. There were the odd pragmatic exceptions, most conspicuously when sport was involved. Four years before an All Black rugby team which included some Maoris had toured South Africa. But the Afrikaners were passionate about their rugby and could not really be bothered with the announcements of the Herstigtes that the beginning of the end had now come. The first All Black tour in a decade was a huge success, especially as South Africa won the test series. Afrikaners were mostly willing to trust the judgement of a government which had shown few signs of misreading the desires of the volk.

But, slowly, cumulatively, changes were taking place over the years of the seventies which added up to a quite different apartheid by the end of the decade. There were several causes. One was that the National Party was becoming more responsive to interest groups which wanted to abandon some of the more obscurantist features of the past. Another was overseas pressure, which could be accommodated within well-defined and readily-reached limits, for the Nationalist government was always obsessed about not being seen to be too compliant towards troublesome foreigners. But probably most important, was the sheer relentless weight of the nature of things. The system constructed with such care, devotion and disregard of economic logic and the weaknesses of human nature, was visibly coming unstuck in crucial places, most obviously in the numbers of Africans who were entering the urban areas in search of jobs, and often finding them successfully. The vital date of 1978, when the black inflow would reverse itself and the white areas would become whiter, came and went, with no noticeable effect on the direction of black migration. By the end of the decade the grand apartheid of Verwoerd had gone. In its place had arisen a more sophisticated version, which accepted the fact of black urbanisation, but still attempted to control and channel it in the interests of white survival and supremacy — 'neo-apartheid' had arrived.

It was economic growth which put the Nationalists into such a state of confusion about tried ways of keeping Africans in their place. Rapid growth had been eroding the original Nationalist coalition based mainly on Afrikaans workers and farmers. It brought with it a more diversified class structure and a more prosperous Afrikaner population, less willing than ever to incur material loss for the sake of posterity or ideological purity.

White agriculture had been declining in political and economic influence as other sectors of the economy expanded. In 1970 thirteen per cent of the white population lived in the rural areas, compared with the twenty-two per cent of twenty years before.[3] The political influence of white farmers remained substantial, and disproportionate, reflected in the one third of Nationalist Members of Parliament who still gave farming as their main occupation in the 1970s.[4] But it was not what it had been, and the Government now felt able to take decisions which farmers would not applaud, such as measures to prevent overstocking. Also, farmers were increasingly abandoning their stake in a system of labour control which had done its best to provide them with plentiful supplies of cheap and unskilled African labour. Their need for workers of this kind declined as low interest rates gave them an incentive to adopt more mechanised techniques of production which required a smaller and more skilled work-force.

The white workers had been the fly in the ointment. Under the apartheid regime they had done well for themselves as the most potent of the distributional coalitions which gained from discrimination. They had played a major role in upholding a system which had treated them so generously. In his wide-ranging book, *The Rise and Decline of Nations*, the American economist Mancur Olson has explained why white labour was so especially effective in pursuing its interests at the expense of others. White workers were organised and their competitors were other workers who were black and unorganised:

> ... the employers would have been just as interested in excluding competitors as the workers were, and would as small groups have been better able to organise to do so than the workers. But the competitors of the employers were other firms or capitalists, often in other lands; the employers were not competing against African labourers, as the white workers were, so the employers were not a principal source of the racial exclusion and discrimination that the Africans suffered. South African consumers of all races paid higher prices because of the higher costs growing out of the discriminatory policy, but, as in other countries, they were not organised.[5]

White workers had benefited from economic growth. During the 1960s their incomes had not only risen but had done so more rapidly than those of blacks. But they were also its victims, for there were simply not enough of them to do all the skilled work in an expanding economy. In 1948 whites accounted for nearly 21 per cent of the South African population, compared with the nearly 69 per cent of Africans. By 1970 only 17,4 per cent of the population consisted of whites; ten years later they amounted to 15,4 per cent. The corresponding figures for Africans were 70,3 and 72,9 per cent.[6] Further advance had to mean removal of the barriers to acquiring skills; a more competitive labour market had to emerge. It also meant that times of recession could add immeasurably to the fears, insecurities and, not least, resentments of white employees. As early as the 1960s coloureds and Asians, better placed than Africans to evade the restrictions of discrimination, were increasing their share of national income as pressure on the supply of skilled white labour made job reservation a practice of the past. It was because of their advance that the white share declined slightly, for the African share also went down.[7] After 1970 Africans began to increase their percentage of total national income as well. The early 1970s were watershed years as the ratio of white wages to those of all other racial groups began to decline in a process that lasted through the next decade.[8] As long as growth continued it could be expected that white workers would not complain excessively about the upward mobility of members of other races. But the kind of slump which arrived after 1974 would be bad news for a government confronted by inevitable demands from some of its most faithful constituents for a renewed dose of apartheid regulation and protection.

Right-wingers had worried about the implications of economic growth. They knew only too well that the expansion of the economy would make a joke of separate development. So when the Government decided to go for more growth in the early 1970s it decisively, if unofficially and perhaps unconsciously, turned its back on the blueprint of Hendrik Verwoerd. At a meeting in 1972 of the Prime Minister's Economic Advisory Council in Pretoria to 'determine' the country's growth rate for the next five years, the target of the Economic Development Plan was raised from 5,5 per cent to 5,75 per cent. It was only a small increase, and there are strict limits on what planners can actually do to stimulate growth, but it spoke volumes about what Government policy had become: growth would be the priority even if the heavens of Verwoerdian apartheid were to fall. As one commentator put it: 'It had always been a cardinal article of the apartheid faith that Nationalism's economic gurus would settle on a growth rate which would create skilled jobs no faster than the ability of the white workers to fill them'.[9]

Ironically, the commitment to growth came at a time when the sustained expansion which dated back to the early 1960s had only a few more years to run. But it was the commitment that was all. It meant the official acceptance of the principle that Africans, where necessary, would have to be allowed and hence trained to do skilled work in the white areas. A grudging admission of the inevitable it may have been. Africans would only move up the skilled job ladder in the wake of whites, coloureds and Indians. But there could be no doubt that it was essential for continued economic growth. The Economic Development Programme said as much, in suitably hedged bureaucratic prose: 'In order to attain the higher growth rates (that is 5,75 or 6 per cent per annum) it would, therefore, be necessary to give non-whites, within the framework of Government policy, improved training and to utilise their services more effectively by giving them work of a more advanced nature'.[10] Nor could there be any doubt that Verwoerd would have disapproved.

And it did come to pass that there was accelerated growth for a time, before a prolonged downturn. In 1974 gross domestic product rose by more than eight per cent in real terms, the result of a much higher gold price and sustained, if not always well-targeted, public sector investment over the previous four years. Recession came the next year as South Africa caught up with a world economy shaken by the rise in oil prices. It was aggravated by a fall in the all-important gold price, a decline in domestic investment after the Soweto uprising, and a flight of private capital to more hospitable climes. But by then the die had been cast. There could be no return to the principle that skilled work was the special preserve of the white race.

The Government had little idea of where it was going. It made scant effort, at first, to hasten African access to more skilled jobs. Instead of actively attempting to set the clock back, its initial response was rather to combine the best of both worlds, which in itself was an advance. It accepted the *de facto* disappearance of job reservation, but kept the machinery for its enforcement, hoping for an escape clause if white unemployment should ever become serious. It reassured white workers that their future was safe in the hands of a caring government. In 1972 the Minister of Labour could still declare piously that the NP 'stands between the survival and doom of the white worker, for if the white worker fails, the National Party too will fail'.[11]

At the start of the 1970s it was still the official labour policy that there was no need for a fundamental overhaul of existing practices. Better use of labour was undeniably a good thing, but only within the framework of the status quo. When the Government expressed itself in 1971 as in favour of the training of homeland Africans for employment not only in the homelands themselves but in the border areas as well, critics saw it as a significant departure from the official stance, as the border areas were technically 'white areas'. For the rest, the Government did its best to avoid recognising that the future would not resemble the past. It would encourage both increased white immigration and the use of white labour in more productive jobs, training schemes would be extended, and white female labour would be encouraged to do more productive work so that white males could be released for yet more productive employment. Indians and coloureds, not Africans, would be trained for skilled and semi-skilled work.[12] The following year it even appeared as if official attitudes had retrogressed, for the Minister of Labour stated that industrialists would not be allowed to train Africans for skilled work in industry in 'white South Africa', which included the border areas: 'The policy of this Government ... is to refrain from training and using them as skilled workers in white areas. That is and remains Government policy'.[13]

South Africa entered a new age in 1973 with the massive strikes by Africans in Durban. They accelerated trends which were already in motion and compelled the Government to make decisions which it had been trying to avoid. In October of that year the Prime Minister, John Vorster, treading uncertainly into the unfamiliar era, told the Motor Industries Federation that '... it should be clear in terms of Government policy there is nothing to prevent employers, with the co-operation of the trade unions, taking the necessary steps to bring about improvements in the productive use of non-white labour'.[14]

Originally, the more productive use of black labour involved what the head of the Anglo-American Corporation, Harry Oppenheimer, called the 'floating colour bar'. Existing skilled jobs were fragmented and reclassified so that their new components could be done by Africans. That was the easy way of getting the agreement of those distributional coalitions, the white trade unions; it was in fact the continuation of a trend that had begun in the late 1960s. Their members moved upwards into better paid, more skilled, or at least more highly rated, jobs with supervisory and managerial duties, so that the principle of racial differentiation remained intact. The rate for the job was the watchword, secure as its proponents were that it would protect white workers from the competition of Africans prepared to accept lower wages.

But the floating colour bar required continued economic growth. When the economy ceased to provide opportunities for white workers to move upwards while blacks moved in below them, hard choices became unavoidable. Once more the issue became whether white privilege should be maintained at the expense of the economy, which now needed all the help it could get.

In the private sector, white protection went only in 1979. The Government scrapped job reservation officially, with the apparently perennial exception of the mining industry, where the white Mine Workers' Union continued to have political leverage disproportionate to its numbers. But in practice racial restrictions in the rest of the private sector had already gone by the board. At first there was some pretence at 'productivity bargaining' with the white trade unions, which amounted to allowing the colour bar to keep floating upwards. Yet it was an obviously wasteful second-best, only affordable in an expanding economy. After recession arrived in the mid-seventies, employers, already hard-pressed by official restrictions on the mobility and use of black labour, increasingly dispensed with the consent of the white unions. They had made a large investment in more capital intensive techniques, partly the result of their inability to use black workers more productively. Those Africans they did employ would have to be skilled enough to use the new methods. Waiting for the permission of the white unions could only further lower profits in an economy which had ceased to boom. So, at varying rates, depending on the nature of the economic activity and the composition of the labour force, the colour bar in the labour market was eroded, the victim of the logic inherent in economic development.

While this was happening, Government expenditure on black education rose remarkably. In 1972 it abandoned the Verwoerdian principle that the education of Africans had to be financed from direct taxes paid by themselves. General revenue now financed black education; the huge disparities between spending on the education of white and black gradually began to narrow. Between 1977 and 1982 spending on African education increased in real terms by 200 per cent.[15] Education remained segregated and the absolute differences between per capita spending on white education and that for other race groups continued to be substantial. It would take time before more educational opportunities would result in higher incomes for blacks. Yet the previous trend of growing relative inequality between white and black educational expenditures had clearly been reversed.

The white workers lost out, or at least those with the fewest skills did. The more highly qualified white employees felt less threatened by black advance; the more poorly qualified knew that black competition was a threat to their own advance. They were the most exercised by the new labour policies, especially during the recession of 1974 to 1978. When recovery began in 1979 their anxieties abated somewhat, but the most they could do was to stage holding actions. During times good and bad African advance in the labour market continued.

It was reflected in a striking redistribution of income from white to black. According to Merle Lipton, 'from 1970 to 1982, real wages for Africans in manufacturing and construction rose by over 60 per cent, compared with 18 per cent for whites; on gold mines real wages for Africans quadrupled, while those for white miners rose by 3 per cent; on white farms, real wages for Africans doubled between 1968 to 1969 and 1976. As a result the white share of personal income declined from over 70 to under 60 per cent, while the African share rose from 19 to 29 per cent'.[16]

Two radical historians, S Marks and S Trapido, have concluded that urban African wages rose more rapidly than those of white wages because of the strike wave of 1972 to 1973.[17] This is hardly plausible. If the strikes were so effective in raising black wages it is puzzling that more strike waves did not come rolling in to raise wages still further. Also, black wages in general went up, which cannot be explained by successful strikes in particular industries. A strike only gets results for particular workers because their union has managed to restrict competition for their jobs. By keeping other workers out it increases the numbers of those who are seeking jobs elsewhere. It follows that a successful strike would, in fact, tend to depress wages in other occupations.

What really happened was that the general demand for black labour increased, while an important component of the labour supply disappeared. Most fundamentally, economic growth in the early and later parts of the 1970s expanded the demand for black workers. At the same time, the recruitment of black mineworkers from outside the Republic declined drastically after the collapse of Portuguese rule, which meant a higher demand by the mines for South African labour: between 1973 and 1982 the proportion of foreign workers on the gold mines declined from 79 to 42 per cent.[18] The rapid rise in the gold price after 1971 enabled the mines to offer conditions of employment which compared favourably with those of other sectors of the economy, which now found themselves in the unusual situation of having to compete with the mining industry for black labour.

The strikes did not cause the sustained rise in African wages. They did initiate basic changes in a system of industrial relations which had till then ignored African employees by defining them out of existence. The most peculiar feature of the South African way of handling relations between labour and capital was that the official definition of employee excluded 'pass bearers', that is Africans. Unlike whites, and even coloureds and Indians, they could have no part in collective bargaining, nor did they have representation on the industrial councils which administered the agreements between employers and registered trade unions. Black unions were not illegal but had no official recognition, nor could blacks go on strike without breaking the law. The Durban strikes and the Soweto uprising showed that the cosy industrial council system, primarily designed to protect the interests of white workers, would no longer survive if it maintained the pretence that most of the country's labour force was somehow too childlike, impulsive and susceptible to left wing agitation to participate in the usual procedures of collective bargaining.

Faced with the inevitable, the Government reacted typically by attempting to continue paternalism under a new guise. Works committees as an alternative to trade unions were supposed to do the trick. From 1973 Africans in establishments employing more than twenty workers could elect works committees which would represent their interests. In the next few years many committees were elected, sometimes with the support of black unions which intended taking them over. But the works committees never did catch on as an alternative to independent and officially recognised black unions.

Employers themselves had come to live with the idea of African trade unions. Admittedly they were divided about the kind of black unions they would least dislike. The Associated Chamber of Commerce wanted the same trade union rights for all workers and an end to discrimination in the labour market. The Afrikaanse Handelsinstituut (The Afrikaans Chamber of Commerce), representing Afrikaans businessmen and with close links to the Government, was more reluctant to rock official boats: it wished to exclude migrant workers from unions and believed that the bargaining power of all trade unions should be 'subordinate ... to the national interest'.[19] But, whatever their differences, employers were beginning to agree that there was no substitute for officially recognised African trade unions of some sort.

The Government adopted a tried remedy, or at least a palliative one. In 1977 it appointed a commission, in fact two. One was the Commission of Inquiry into Labour Legislation under the chairmanship of a university professor, Nic Wiehahn. The other was the Commission on Utilisation of Manpower. Its sole member was Piet Riekert, Economic Adviser to the Prime Minister. Between them these commissions would come up with proposals for a more sophisticated form of apartheid, streamlined for a post-Verwoerdian era where a permanent black presence in the 'white' areas had come to be accepted as part of the normal order of things.

Wiehahn submitted the first of a series of reports in February 1979, a year after the expected date. One of the chairman's problems was that he had thirteen fellow-commissioners of widely disparate backgrounds. There had to be African, coloured and Indian members, however token their presence. Inevitably, conservative white trade unions had to be represented. It was a mix which did not make for unanimity, or achievement of deadlines:

there were minority reports on most of the important points.

The majority recommendations of the Wiehahn Commission were clear enough. They added up to a simple message: the South African system of industrial relations could not survive on the principle of black exclusion. It had to find room for African trade unions and give them the kind of respectability which the most reactionary white unions enjoyed as a matter of course. The unpleasant alternative was increased exposure of black unions to what were seen as alien foreign influences and the establishment of other negotiating channels at plant level which would undermine the whole industrial council system.

The Government's own sense of urgency was reflected in its swift response in the form of a White Paper which accepted some of the main recommendations of Wiehahn.[20] They were embodied in a new Industrial Conciliation Amendment Act which came into force on 1 November 1979.

In the White Paper the Government accepted the Commission's recommendation of freedom of association, with qualifications. Wiehahn had argued that migrant workers should be eligible for union membership. The Government attempted instead to uphold one of the fundamental principles of neo-apartheid, namely, the distinction between insiders and outsiders, by deciding that only Africans with permanent residence in South Africa and with fixed employment should have this right. It was a decision widely and effectively criticised: the following year the Minister of Manpower decided that membership by migrants would after all not be so harmful to the revamped system of industrial relations.

What was crucial to both Wiehahn and the Government was the matter of registration. Registered black unions would have the same rights as any other unions. It would give them the right to strike after the official 30-day notification period; they would participate in all the other conciliation procedures and become part of the industrial council system. It would give them access to the newly constituted Industrial Court if they felt their members had been victimised by their employers. But registration came at a price. It depended on approval by the Government, which naturally imposed fairly tough requirements: unions had to be 'acceptable' to black workers within a firm, they could not engage in political activities and should be free of those sinister and ubiquitous foreign influences. The Government's viewpoint was simple: if there had to be black trade unions, they had to bring with them at least the trappings of respectability. To use terminology which became fashionable, the official intent was to divert the radical anti-apartheid thrust of any black unions by 'co-opting them into the system'. By the same token, African unions would face an agonising choice: registration would bring benefits as yet only dreamt of, but it would also bring the all-too-real prospect of being absorbed into a status quo which could readily accommodate new aspirers to the fruits of capitalist growth. To many the price of apparent emasculation by the 'system' could only seem excessive.

The distinction between economic and political activities of trade unions was no doubt theoretically sound. The Government's obsession with the prospect of black unions using their economic leverage for political purposes was perfectly understandable, but in a country where other means of political expression had been denied Africans with iron determination, it was perhaps ingenuous to hope or believe that the distinction would be rigidly observed by those who had until then been unaccustomed to any power at all.

There were also white fears about what the new dispensation would hold for the former automatic beneficiaries of privilege. The Government went some way to dispel them. It accepted the Commission's recommendation that on industrial councils there should be a statutory requirement of strict parity in the representation of the employee parties. Moreover, existing members of an industrial council, in effect white unions, would be able to veto the admission of new ones.

This was not good enough for many unions, who felt they had reason to fear black advance. There was the predictable outright rejection of the Wiehahn proposals by the Mine Workers' Union. The unions representing the white workers in the building and iron and steel industries mounted the same platform, demanding continued job reservation and a ban on the training of Africans in white areas.

Their opposition split the conservative umbrella organisation, the South African Confederation of Labour, for some of its members felt that it was useless to resist so powerful an incoming tide. Far better, they believed, to make the best of it by promoting 'parallel' black unions which were committed to working within the new system. They were joined by the relatively liberal Trade Union Council of South Africa, white-dominated but with many coloured members, which preferred going with Wiehahn into an admittedly uncertain future than to remain trapped in a racist status quo which had no future at all.

The reformists won. For some it was a question of adapting to the inevitable, for others it was a genuine improvement. There were unions whose skilled members did not feel directly threatened by black advance; there were those who believed that much could be salvaged if such advance could find its course through the proper channels. The Government, secure in the continued support, however reluctant, of white labour, was prepared to isolate and alienate the unions of the far right, rightly convinced that their enmity could not endanger the continued rule of the National Party over South Africa.

The Wiehahn report was no document in the tradition of classical liberalism. It proposed that black workers be placed on the same legal footing as whites, provided they were suitably registered. They would obtain many benefits, but also become formally subject to state control. They would have to follow proper procedures; they would decidedly not be able to pursue political objectives through economic means.

Yet it was too much to expect that in the peculiar circumstances of South Africa the problem of militancy would disappear simply because black unions had been 'co-opted' into the existing system of industrial relations. In particular, and this was the objection to registration, there was the hazard that black parallel unions which had suddenly acquired respectability might find themselves removed from shop-floor pressures. The pressures would not however vanish; they would find other means of expression. Registration was not the answer to black worker militancy.

Ironically, the proposals of the Riekert Commission, published in May 1979, could only add to the bargaining power of Africans who had become urban insiders. The Riekert recommendations, accepted in the main by the Goverment in a White Paper,[21] were less liberal than those of Wiehahn, for they aimed at improving the living conditions of urban Africans by drawing the most emphatic of dividing lines between those with and those without rights of permanent residence in the white areas. Africans with Section 10 rights under what was originally the Natives (Urban Areas) Act of 1945, since then renamed and frequently amended, would have prior rights when it came to existing job opportunities, housing and facilities. There would be insiders whose enjoyment of their rights would depend on the stricter enforcement of influx control, and there would be outsiders from the rural areas, who would be at the receiving end of the tighter controls. Employers would have an incentive not to employ illegal workers: if they were caught doing so they would have to pay higher fines, and the fining process itself would also be more strictly enforced.

The Riekert proposals were a curious blend of attachment to and departure from the principles of Verwoerd. Stricter enforcement of influx control was in the tradition of the Master. Purism could go little further. But nothing could have conformed less to orthodoxy than the acceptance of a permanent black urban population. It amounted to a return to the recommendations of the Fagan Report of 1948 which were spurned with such disdain by the newly-arrived Nationalists in power. The wheel had come at least half-circle. Yet in their insistence on more vigorous control over black access to urban areas the Riekert proposals were in a straight line from 1948. The greater powers they would bring to the apartheid bureaucracy could only be bad news to reformers.

Even so it was not evident that they had much chance of perpetuating the divisions between insiders and outsiders on which their success depended. In fact, the Riekert proposals carried within them the seeds of their own destruction. They required the erection and maintenance of high and solid barriers at the entrance to those preserves of relative privilege conferred by insidership. The more successful they were the greater became the advantages of being an insider, the more tempting became the incentives for outsiders to break out of impoverished rural regions of rapid population growth and to gain access to the cities by evading the controls.

Nor could businessmen, a constituency whose power was supposedly growing at just this time, be too happy about the implications. Their interest was in a large labour supply, from which they could pick and choose as they pleased. In so far as the Riekert proposals were enforced, businessmen were facing exactly the opposite. Labour costs would rise and they would have a further incentive to mechanise. Africans working with more advanced techniques would acquire skills which would make them difficult to replace. Inherent in the Riekert scheme of things was greater bargaining power for urban Africans and their trade unions.

The changing policies of the National Party from the early 1970s, conveniently described as 'neo-apartheid', have usually been explained as a result of shifts in the interest group coalition on which it depended for support. One typical formulation has been that of the sociologist Heribert Adam: 'a mature Afrikaner bourgeoisie in full control of state power has now identified itself once more with the *laissez-faire* labour policies of English capitalists with whom it shares similar interests in curbing the historical monopoly of expensive white labor'.[22] Without a doubt, it would have been surprising had the original coalition remained intact. Historically economic growth has been a solvent for change; South Africa was no exception. The important question is to what degree the Government merely responded to the self-seeking behaviour of the interest groups on which it depended. Alternatively, to what degree were changes in Nationalist policy independent of the often vociferous demands of interest and pressure groups?

The change of course of the 1970s and the emergence of neo-apartheid were the outcome not so much of the decline of the traditional members of the Nationalist coalition, namely, the farmers and the Afrikaner workers, and the simultaneous rise to prominence of business interests, but of a more complex process. What was decisive was that the Afrikaner ethnic machine had remained largely intact. During the previous twenty-odd years the Afrikaner class structure had indeed become transformed, moving from relative homogeneity to greater heterogeneity. Broad social groups had become more fragmented. It became increasingly difficult to speak of *the* working class as the relative numbers of Afrikaans blue-collar workers declined and those in white-collar jobs rose. But, changes withal, Afrikaners retained a powerful sense of group identity, as their willingness to respond to deliberately tribal appeals at election time continued to demonstrate.

The fragmentation of the Afrikaner class structure meant that on specific issues there was often little unity of resolve. The Government could afford to incur the enduring hostility of sections of Afrikaner labour, like the mineworkers, knowing that others would not follow them. It was not Afrikaner workers as a whole which rejected the labour reforms of the 1970s, but particular groups which felt especially threatened. Part of the explanation for neo-apartheid is that Afrikaner labour's influence with Nationalist politicians had declined.

It is not so evident that the growing influence of businessmen, Afrikaans and English, within official circles had much to do with the new policies. That they had some influence is certain. The Wiehahn proposals were close to what businessmen had been demanding for years. The Government's reversal of its decision not to accept migrant workers as members of registered black unions came after loud protests by many, including capitalists. Ironically, it was the Afrikaanse Handelsinstituut, the federation of organised business closest to the Government, which had taken the most conservative stance on African trade unions before Wiehahn and now found itself outflanked by official policy. Yet it is true that crucial features of neo-apartheid were not in line with capitalist interests, which did not prevent the Government from pushing ahead regardless. In particular, the Riekert proposals for tighter influx control were not designed to reduce the labour costs of businessmen. Riekert's acceptance of permanent blacks in the urban areas was welcome to employers, but, taken all in all, they would have designed a very different package for themselves.

What happened, quite simply, was that white South Africans had got hooked on economic growth. By the early 1970s they had gone through a decade of uninterrupted and unprecedented expansion. They were delighted with what had happened to them and wanted more. Appeals by right wing trade unionists that growth should adapt to the amount of skilled labour which could be supplied by the white population simply cut no ice with a materialistic electorate. When the Government in the early 1970s refused to lower the growth target of the Economic Development Programme, the policies of neo-apartheid followed irresistibly from that decision. A permanent black presence became an inevitable feature of the urban landscape. Official policy accepted increasingly the principle that blacks should do skilled work and have opportunities to acquire the necessary skills. Once these decisions had been made, black trade unions co-opted into the official system of industrial relations could not be far behind.

The essence of neo-apartheid was thus the pursuit of economic growth within the constraint imposed by continued white control, seen as essential to white survival. It was not so much the result of a new coalition of class forces. The continued strength of Afrikaner sentiment and the resounding victories of the National Party in the general elections of 1974 and, even more strikingly, in 1977 when 30 per cent of the English-speaking voters supported it, effectively placed the Government above the pressures of particular interest groups. Because it was committed to growth, some of its policies naturally suited capitalists remarkably well. But it was growth within an apartheid framework: as ever, white supremacy came first. Some of the Government's policies could in no way suit businessmen. It mattered little to John Vorster, who was willing enough to play golf with the captains of industry, but resented their advice about how to run the economy. It was left to his successor, P W Botha, to attempt a rapprochement with businessmen. His ultimate failure to do so showed beyond doubt that the refurbished apartheid which came after 1970 was not designed primarily to make capitalists, or any other interest group, happy. It was the survival of the white population as a whole which remained the name of the game.

CHAPTER FIFTEEN

Inertia and Info

After he became Prime Minister in 1966 John Vorster sprang several surprises. He was not only a different man from the fearsome Minister of Justice of all-too-recent memory, but he also differed from his overwhelming and autocratic predecessor. His willingness to 'move outwards', to conciliate the apprehensive English-speakers, to take a hard line with the Hertzogite extremists in the National Party and, even more, with radical dissent, made most white South Africans come to see Vorster as the best man to guide them through what was becoming an increasingly troubled decade. He came across as a reassuring and formidable figure. The Republic's white electorate bore witness to their faith in the man by returning him to power with huge majorities in the general elections of 1974 and 1977.

Yet the second half of Vorster's dozen years at the top increasingly carried with it the smell of failure. When he resigned in 1978 Africans had long ceased to be the cowed post-Sharpeville masses which he had inherited from Verwoerd. They knew that they were at the receiving end of a system which would always deny them the 'liberation' they believed had come to the rest of Africa. In the violent events of 1973 and 1976 blacks had made their feelings plain. To a degree, the Government had adapted, but much of its response was so constrained by circumstance that it could claim little credit for wisdom or foresight. If it regarded economic growth as desirable, as patently it did, then it could hardly keep blacks out of skilled jobs, even had it attempted to do so. 'Co-opting' Africans into the existing system of industrial relations then not only made good sense, but became inevitable. However, reform of the labour market was the furthest Vorster's revisionism took him. Politically, his government would offer nothing beyond the homelands promises of Verwoerd. In so far as political reform found a place on the Nationalist agenda, it involved tentative gropings towards the notion that the outnumbered coloureds and Indians should acquire some form of representation in the same system as the whites. Yet, Alan Paton, probably South Africa's most famous writer said in an appeal to Vorster in 1974: 'People like myself have long believed that the only hope for an evolutionary solution lies with the Afrikaner and the black man. The Indians, the coloured people, the English-speaking, we are not the leading actors in this drama'.[1]

When the Government did not stagnate in its own political inertia, it notched up defeat and scandal. What was left of the outwards policy met with final ignominy when South Africa invaded the former Portuguese colony and newly independent Angola in 1975, to be compelled to withdraw shortly afterwards. But most humiliating of all for Vorster was the infamous Information scandal, the immediate cause of his resignation as Prime Minister and the ultimate cause of his departure from public life.

Much of the failure of the later Vorster years was the result of chickens coming home to roost. It is true that Vorster's style of leadership came as an incomparable relief to those accustomed to the overbearing ways of Verwoerd. Whether he was best described as chairman of the board, leader of the team, or first among equals, Vorster did not presume to know better than his colleagues about what was going on in their departments. He assumed that they had a grasp of what they were about and let them get on with the job. His style was based on consensus rather than on pronouncements from Olympus about what had to be done. Departmental autonomy was a feature of his rule. For all this Vorster got his appropriate share of kudos at the time. Yet, as events were to show, excessive decentralisation can result in loss of control. It was Vorster's misfortune that by his leadership style he forfeited control over what some of his most prominent subordinates were doing; at the same time he could not claim that he was ignorant of how they had abused his trust.

Nationalist unity was also part of Vorster's stock-in-trade. Vorster was not the man to split the Afrikaners. Ironically, the events of 1969 had confirmed his unwillingness to do so. They only came after years of verkrampte undermining of his leadership, which he had done his best to ignore in spite of the vociferous and public war of words going on around him. It was his disappointed rival for the premiership, Ben Schoeman, who eventually insisted on bringing matters to their final resolution at the Transvaal Congress of the National Party in 1969. The exit of the rebels only confirmed Vorster's strong urge to inertia: he knew that far more reactionaries remained within the National Party than departed with Albert Hertzog and Jaap Marais. Andries Treurnicht, editor of *Hoofstad*, was the most conspicuous of them and the obvious rallying-point of right wing sentiment. Vorster's response to Treurnicht was typical of his approach to Afrikaner unity: after the firebrand entered Parliament himself in 1971 and showed no sign of moving towards the expedient centre, his leader attempted to induce tamer ways by corrupting him with a taste of power in the form of a deputy ministership. It did not work. Treurnicht continued to specialise in hit-and-run tactics; Vorster had to learn to live with the smiler with the knife behind his back.

A man of some force of personality, Vorster nonetheless lacked force as a leader. His own personal inclinations were far from liberal, his commitment to white supremacy was complete, but he knew that the Afrikaner could not continue to rule simply by pretending that Verwoerd's political dispensation was final. Yet he wished above all not to split the National Party, which made him prefer apathy to action. His most forceful deeds he kept for radical (and several not-so-radical) dissenters, who were never given cause to doubt that Vorster was a wolf in wolf's clothing. He was most imposing when blustering on party platforms about the necessity for law and order. A not unfamiliar blend of bully and weakling, Vorster was harsh towards those who rejected a system unravelling at the seams, and conciliation itself to those who attempted to keep it together by the continued weaving of fictions about separate freedoms and the special destiny of the Afrikaner. Under his rule the National Party became a battleground for ambitious power-seekers who could scarcely conceal their lust for the fruits of office.

His relish for consensus and the need for party unity explain why Vorster moved in some areas and not at all in others. Most visibly, the changes came in sport, which became more multiracial, although the Government at first continued to insist that it was nothing of the sort, but actually multinational, for the ethnic groups in South Africa were really distinct nations. It meant that at the club, provincial and national levels the different races still had their separate teams, but that they could compete against one another at special 'international' events within the Republic. All Black rugby teams which contained Maoris toured South Africa in 1970 and 1976, although a tour by an England cricket side was cancelled in 1968 because Vorster chose to make an issue of the inclusion of a Cape coloured player who had been forced to go overseas to satisfy his desire to play international sport. No England cricket side visited South Africa again, nor, after 1970, did a representative side from any other country. Still, cricket was primarily the sport of English-speakers: the absence of international tours did not much bother the Afrikaners as long as it did not affect their cherished rugby, which continued to enjoy some semblance of international favour in the form of attenuated tours even into the 1980s.

The sports policy evolved, tortuously, with twists and turns, but by the early 1980s no one subscribed any longer to the myth of multinationalism. By then a coloured rugby player had even represented South Africa at the international level. Sports bodies could decide for themselves how to conduct their affairs; multiracial sport had become too common to excite much attention, but it was too late to prevent the Republic's isolation in international sport, which was virtually complete.

Still, the liberalisation of sport was extensive and relatively painless. It was less so in other areas. Mixed marriages continued to remain illegal, as did 'immorality' between whites and members of other races. Education remained strictly segregated, except for the attendance of limited numbers of African, coloured and Indian children at some of the most select schools of the English-speakers. The continued presence of the Group Areas Act on the statute book ensured that residential areas remained segregated, with no sign that class differences would be permitted to override those of race. Public amenities such as libraries and parks were often desegregated, more frequently and widely in cities like Cape Town and Johannesburg than in country towns or in Nationalist strongholds like Pretoria and Bloemfontein. The best hotels acquired 'international' ratings, which enabled them to dispense with segregation on their premises.

The principle of racial separation had begun to break down in a number of areas, but it was a laborious and patchy affair. It did show that international pressure worked — up to a point. It is inconceivable that sport would have achieved the degree of racial integration it did had international sports bodies not been so adamant about not dealing with apartheid. White South Africans were willing to be pliable about what was after all a relatively minor matter: integrated sport could in no way endanger white rule, whatever the extremists of the Herstigte Nasionale Party chose to believe. If that was the price to be paid for international acceptability in sport, then white South Africans were willing to put their hands in their pockets. When they did, they found that it was already too late. In most sporting activities they found themselves confronted with the new and impossible demand that apartheid itself had to go before contact could be resumed, on the specious grounds that normal sport was impossible in an abnormal society, a criterion which would have ruled out sporting contact between most, if not all, countries of the world. However fraudulent the justification, its effects were enough to inflict some pain on white South Africans. It was not enough to induce them to accept what came to be fashionably known as meaningful or non-cosmetic change, for to them it meant setting out on the road to ultimate black rule, plainly a prospect so awful that it was not even worth considering.

Elsewhere it was not so simple. Areas of constant contact between the races had to uphold the sacrosanct principle of inequality: economic relations meant master-servant relations. Social segregation eroded most readily in the upper-income brackets. More affluent and better educated whites felt relatively few anxieties about admitting members of other races to their exclusive schools or finding them dining at the Carlton Hotel in Johannesburg. If it was to be a matter of class they knew they would have little difficulty remaining where they were: at the top. It would be an unconscionable time before people of colour started crowding into those historically white preserves where high status and high income seemed as inseparable as taxes and civil servants.

Class distinctions would remain weak compared with those of race. Where class did have a tendency to supersede race, it only did so within strict limits. Apartheid involved the separation of the population into rigid racial categories. If they broke down across any wide front, so would the system. This was the ultimate Verwoerdian insight, pursued with unbelievable single-mindedness and ardour. In a world where consistency was all, it followed logically that the presence of Maoris in a New Zealand touring side was only one short step to black rule. It was of course not so simple. The partial breaching of a principle does not lead inevitably to its total abandonment. In the sloppy, inconsistent world of real human beings it is possible to live with contradiction for long periods, even indefinitely, without the compulsion for one principle to triumph over another. Yet it was not difficult to see that in South Africa any widespread break with the supreme principle of racial demarcation would undermine the foundations of the system. Hence the erosion of social apartheid was a tortuous process, one which had to be narrowly contained. It was not because actions have unforeseen consequences that the social engineers tried so hard to maintain the barriers of race. They could foresee the consequences only too well — and did not like what they saw.

Above all, political power remained confined to white, almost completely Afrikaner, hands. As ever, this was the least negotiable aspect of apartheid. Yet it was evident that the theoretical framework bequeathed by Verwoerd contained glaring contradictions, apparent in his lifetime but simply ignored because it suited him. They involved the coloureds and the Indians, accepted by the National Party as permanent parts of the South African population, yet deprived of those political rights which Africans could in theory enjoy in their homelands As regards the coloureds and Indians, the Government of Vorster knew it was a problem and attempted to handle it in a way typical of Nationalist administrations:

it established surrogate institutions for these groups which were completely subject to the dictates of the South African Parliament in Cape Town. In 1968 it had set up the partly-elected Coloured Persons' Representative Council. It established as well an Indian Council, which was wholly appointed. These institutions were no answer to the question of political rights, as the unhappy history of the Coloured Council demonstrated.

In 1976 the Theron Commission, appointed to investigate the position of the coloureds in South African society, trotted out a favourite idea of verligte Nationalists, namely that coloureds be represented directly in Parliament by members of their own race. It proved no more palatable to the Government than before and the suggestion duly went the way of its predecessors. At the same time the relations between the Government and the Coloured Representative Council were proving a case study in how not to co-opt a subject people. Only the previous year the Government had dismissed the Chairman of the Council and leader of the majority Labour Party because of his refusal to accept the Council's budget.

The Government was finding itself more and more in a quandary, all of its own making. The political status quo with respect to the coloureds, and the Indians for that matter, had long been untenable simply in terms of Nationalist ideology itself. The dilemma of the ruling party was that it had to give these groups political rights which it could in some sense portray as non-cosmetic, without at the same time placing at risk Afrikaner control of the country. That was a real possibility if both coloureds and Indians received the franchise on the same basis as the white population, for, with the English-speaking whites, they outnumbered the Afrikaners. Plainly there were limits to reform: the bottom line was continued rule by good Afrikaner Nationalists.

The Government appointed a cabinet committee in August 1976 under the chairmanship of the Minister of Defence, P W Botha, to investigate constitutional amendments which could accommodate the coloureds and Indians. The following year it came up with some strange proposals which attempted to square the circle: there were to be three Parliaments, one for each race group, and there would be an executive President with autocratic powers who in practice would be an Afrikaner Nationalist.

Nothing much came of the proposals at the time, even if they were supposedly part of the Government election platform in 1977. The proposals disappeared from sight as the general election turned into an orgy of xenophobic anti-Americanism, a response to the new Carter administration's elaborately pious condemnations of the evils of apartheid. For John Vorster it was much safer knocking simple-minded and interfering Yankees than making an election issue of political reforms, which, however mild, could only lose many of the right wing votes at large in the electorate. But, amended and modified, the Botha proposals surfaced years later to become the basis of that new South African constitution of 1984 which gave their original propounder autocratic powers so well suited to his bent.

The supreme proviso of continued Afrikaner rule meant that attempts at political reform amounted to finding new junior partners, in addition to the English-speakers, who would give a more credible appearance of legitimacy to the system. Most obviously, there was no room for Africans. They had their homelands; their political future was already cut and dried. In the 'white' areas there would be a place for black town councils and black advisory bodies. That was about as far as it went.

One common theme runs through these proposals. Whether it excluded Africans, or attempted to incorporate coloureds and Indians, Nationalist political thinking found it impossible to go beyond the concept of racial groups as distinct entities, which had to be represented as such. In an obvious sense it suited the Nationalists to make groups the focus of all their policies. Once Africans were excluded from the political system, then the majority group became the whites, of which the Afrikaners constituted a majority. It followed as a matter of simple arithmetic that group representation would ensure indefinite rule by the National Party.

But the Nationalists were running into a new problem during the 1970s. It was becoming increasingly difficult to compartmentalise domestic and foreign policies. By the middle of the decade white-ruled bastions to the north were crumbling and it was becoming apparent that history would not be on their side. In Portugal there had been a coup in April 1974. The new Portuguese administration decided to withdraw from the colonies of Angola and Mozambique, long proclaimed as part of Portugal but now suddenly about to be taken over by black governments highly unsympathetic to apartheid. Vorster had also come round to accepting that the regime of Ian Smith in Rhodesia could not survive, however popular the cause of the colony's recalcitrant white settlers with their 'kith and kin' in South Africa. He now decided to seek *détente* with black Africa. On 23 October 1974 he announced in the South African Senate that 'Southern Africa has come to the crossroads. He went on to express his government's commitment to 'the way of peace, the way of normalising of relations, the way of sound understanding and normal association'.[2]

For a time it seemed as if normality had genuinely arrived to stay. In secret talks with Zambia in December 1974 South Africa agreed to withdraw its paramilitary police from Rhodesia and to put pressure on the usually unyielding Ian Smith to release black nationalist leaders from detention. The talks paved the way for a much-publicised conference on a bridge near the Victoria Falls in August 1975, attended by Smith and the Rhodesian nationalists, as well as by Vorster and the President of Zambia, Kenneth Kaunda. But the conference itself failed. Smith was his intransigent self and refused even to discuss the possibility of black majority rule. For Vorster, however, it was by way of being something of a triumph: he had produced statesmanlike qualities not usually on display in his own country, where repression of African nationalism remained the familiar policy of the day. South Africa gained recognition as a power on the sub-continent which had to be recognised in the pursuit of regional stability, especially if Rhodesia was to achieve majority rule by relatively peaceful means.

It was too good to last for a government which itself rejected the principle of black rule at any time in the future. The end of *détente* came sooner than it need have because South Africa decided to invade Angola in support of its own aspirations to power in that anarchic region.

It was an ill-considered affair from the start and an inglorious mess at the end, the outcome of the particular way in which Vorster chose to lead, or rather not to lead. One commentator on South African foreign policy has summed up the reasons for failure well:

> There is no doubt that the Angolan debacle occurred because of Vorster's inexperience in foreign affairs and his personalised and unsystematic approach to major policy decisions. The invasion was incremental, with no clear objective or end-point. Decisions with far-reaching political consequences were made by military field commanders on the spot. The Department of Foreign Affairs might have provided an accurate assessment of the impact of the invasion in Africa and elsewhere, but it was not consulted. Instead Vorster acted on the advice of his Defence Minister, P W Botha, who believed that South Africa should move into the power vacuum left by the Portuguese and try to influence events to its advantage.[3]

South Africa sent troops into Angola in July 1975, ostensibly to protect two dams in the territory which would provide electricity and water to northern South West Africa. It did not stop there. The Republic began to give military support to the two non-Marxist liberation movements, Unita and the FNLA, as against the MPLA, which was decidedly Marxist and had managed to establish some kind of government in the capital of Luanda. Fighting escalated, with the MPLA responding by bringing in Cuban troops, which amounted to about 3 000 by late November. The South African forces won some and lost some; decisive military ascendancy was denied them.

Worse, there had been a major crossing of the lines along the way. The South African Government had been persuaded that it went into Angola with official American approval to fight the Free World's battle against Communism. Much of this seemed to be wishful thinking. The support of the United States had been more informal than formal, with no ultimate commitment to South African intervention. The Central Intelligence Agency had been the main undercover instigator of action by the South Africans. When the Cubans came in, the CIA pulled out of the enterprise and left its gullible allies to make the best of a rotten business. In December the American Senate prohibited further support to any of the Angolan factions. P W Botha's vision of South Africa as a sub-continental superpower surrounded by weak tributary black states was exposed as no more than megalomaniac delusion. By then the MPLA regime had succeeded in gaining acceptability amongst a growing number of African states.

Worst of all, the South African intervention had brought the counter-intervention of the Cubans, who showed no signs of leaving, a potent possible reinforcement of the South West African People's Organisation (Swapo), which was waging a guerrilla war from Angola against the alien occupiers of the mandated territory. The South African Government found itself without the support it believed it had from those African regimes which might have encouraged the invasion privately. In January South African forces began to withdraw from Angola; by the end of March the last troops had left. It was by all accounts a humiliating setback.

Not only had *détente* been destroyed at a stroke and the habitual enmity between South Africa and black African governments restored, but from 1977 relations with the United States took a distinct turn for the worse as the Democratic administration of Jimmy Carter took office. Simple-minded, uninformed and hypocritical as Democrats traditionally were about South Africa, far too prone to cite the belated granting of civil rights to the American black minority as an example which the benighted apartheid regime would do well to follow, it remains true that Vorster and his colleagues provided the new men in Washington with plenty of ammunition. The South African Government's efforts at conciliation had been mainly for export. At home it seemed obsessed with making a virtue of illiberality at best and brutality at worst. When the Black Consciousness leader, Steve Biko, died in detention after being assaulted by the Security Police in August 1977, anti-apartheid movements abroad received an instant boost. When the Minister of Justice, Jimmy Kruger, told an approving Transvaal congress of the National Party that Biko's death left him cold, no Nationalist politician could complain that his government consisted of injured innocents whose fate it was to be misunderstood by an ignorant world.

The state of South African relations with the United States and other Western countries, also fluctuated with the prospect of an accord over South West Africa, or Namibia, as it was known elsewhere. Vorster had abandoned the idea of carving up the territory into ethnic homelands, as the Odendaal Commission had proposed so egregiously in 1964. After the Turnhalle constitutional conference in the Namibian capital of Windhoek in 1975 it even looked as if the Government had committed itself to eventual independence for the territory under a multiracial alliance. But agreement proved difficult as the United Nations and the South African Government found that they had different agendas for the future of Namibia. It helped to sour relations with the West, already at an ebb since the Soweto uprising.

When the 1977 general election came round the time was ripe for a rousing anti-American campaign. White South Africans showed what they thought of Jimmy Carter and his moralistic prescriptions for their future by returning Vorster to power with 134 seats out of 154, the biggest election victory since 1948.

Gratifying as it undoubtedly was to the Nationalists, no amount of euphoria could conceal an ominous trend. External pressures, more than in the past, were having internal results, seen most dramatically in the psychological boost which the Soweto rebels of 1976 gained from the end of Portuguese rule in Africa and the South African exit from Angola. Security fears began to take a pre-eminent place in the concerns of the rulers of the Republic. The Government managed to persuade itself that the country was the victim of a 'total onslaught' inspired by an aggressive and imperialistic Communist world. As P W Botha put it in 1979, the year after he became Prime Minister: 'The struggle in which Southern Africa is involved is not a struggle between white, black and brown; it is a struggle between ideologies, a spiritual struggle which at times has also become a military one'.[4] A few years before, the head of the South African Defence Force, General Magnus Malan, spoke of an onslaught on all fronts: 'South Africa is today ... involved in total war. The war is not only an area for the soldier. Everyone is involved and has a role to play'.[5]

Apocalyptic thoughts like these had evident uses. They justified calls for a 'total national strategy'. It became even simpler for critics of the Government to cross the ever-thin dividing line laid down by the Nationalists between legitimate criticism and unpatriotic aid and comfort to a ubiquitous and supremely cunning enemy. But the coin had another side. If it was more than a military struggle, if everyone had indeed a role to play, then it became a battle for the hearts and minds of the population. It was a battle which would not be won if the victims of discrimination simply saw it as another subterfuge to maintain white supremacy under a different name. They needed hard evidence that the system was at last moving away from the scarcely concealed efforts to entrench white privilege which had been their own experience of Nationalist rule. From the mid-1970s the Government had to confront an ultimately insoluble problem: how could it ensure the continued dominance of one ethnic group while persuading other ethnic groups to collaborate in doing do? Its attempts to achieve the impossible forced the Government to move away continuously, but haphazardly, from traditional apartheid, while striving to maintain intact such pillars of the system as the Group Areas Act, the Population Registration Act and above all a white-controlled Parliament.

Vorster's slack style of leadership did much to land his government in the Angolan mess. It was to culminate in the greatest scandal in the history of Nationalist rule, Vorster's own resignation as Prime Minister and his forced departure from public life in humiliating circumstances. This was the Information scandal, which, in the words of Kenneth Grundy, 'grew out of a slovenly administrative and decisional style marked by departmental autonomy and debilitating interdepartmental political competition'.[6]

It began in February 1974 when Vorster was persuaded by his Minister of Information, Connie Mulder, that the Government's main problem at home and abroad was bad public relations. If Mulder was right the answer was obvious: an intensive propaganda campaign designed to place the Nationalist regime and its policies in the proper humanitarian light — no matter what the cost to the taxpayer. And that was what happened.

Mulder was a man of consuming ambition. At the time he was only 48 years old and clearly headed for higher things, an impression only confirmed when he became Transvaal leader of the National Party later in 1974. All three Prime Ministers since Malan had come from this province. The Transvaal NP was by far the most powerful of the constituent branches of the National Party.

Conventional wisdom had it that as the Transvaal went, so would the leadership of the Party and the premiership of South Africa. For Connie Mulder a large-scale propaganda effort conducted by his own Department of Information to place apartheid, or separate development as the updated terminology had it, on the global map could only do his chances of reaching the top a power of good.

Mulder was fortunate, he believed, in having at his side a man who was bursting with bright, if expensive, ideas about how to improve the apartheid image. This was his Secretary of Information, Eschel Rhoodie, who had told Mulder in 1972 that he would only accept the job if he could conduct the kind of secret propaganda war he believed was needed most.[7] Not yet 40 years old at the time, Rhoodie came from outside the civil service. He had been appointed at the insistence of Mulder, despite the objection of the Civil Service Commission to the flouting of the seniority principle. He was convinced, especially after years spent in the United States, that it was really a question of marketing:

> I'd learnt from the United States that you had to have a hard sell — that you were competing against 120 other countries all trying to get Uncle Sam's attention. I'd learnt that if you walk into a senator's office you cannot go in there and start talking about the weather and so on. He's far too busy for that. You have to come straight to the point right away.[8]

Mulder and Rhoodie went on a spending spree: thinking big meant acting big. There was a multitude of diverse and often bizarre secret projects with melodramatic code names, controlled by Rhoodie. Loans were made to a film company for the making of pro-South African movies, advertisements appeared in leading world newspapers which made much of the 'double standards' applied to South Africa during a time of Russian expansionism, millions were spent in the attempt to acquire a newspaper in the United States. Above all, there was *The Citizen*. This was a pro-Nationalist English-language newspaper established by the Department of Information with R31-million of public funds advanced through front men. For years it ran at a loss but survived inexplicably until it all became plain at the end.

There were many passengers on the gravy train. Luxury flats

were bought on the sea front of the Cape. There was an expensive, and later well-publicised, holiday trip to the Seychelles by Rhoodie, his entourage and their families. There were substantial advance payments, based on falsified letters, for a publication edited by Rhoodie's sociologist brother. By African standards of corruption it was not much, but by comparison with the past it was plenty.

The taxpayer naturally footed the bill. A simple expedient was found to evade the normal auditing of public expenditure. From the Special Defence Account of the Department of Defence, which was not subject to these monitoring procedures, the substantial amounts needed by Mulder and Rhoodie were transferred to the Bureau for State Security, the intermediary from which the Information Department acquired the money.

The Minister of Defence was P W Botha, who did not like what he was confronted with. He objected to the transfer of funds for which he was publicly accountable to another department for purposes he later claimed he knew nothing about. Nor could he be happy about the way the money was used to advance the career of a man who would be an obvious rival for the premiership. Botha complained to Vorster on at least five separate occasions, to no effect.

Inevitably, stories did the rounds. English-language newspapers were suspicious from the first about the credentials of *The Citizen*. It was difficult to imagine an economically viable pro-Nationalist newspaper appearing in English. *The Citizen* was in fact losing R400 000 a month, with the tab being picked up by the Government. Some opposition journalists had already begun to find evidence of its funding by the Department of Information.

But for the high-flyers of Info the beginning of the end came when Mulder lied about *The Citizen* in the House of Assembly. Earlier in 1978 reports by the Auditor-General and the Parliamentary Select Committee on Public Accounts had been highly critical of the accounting procedures of the Information Department. When the Information Vote came up in Parliament, the Opposition was hot on the trail of Mulder and his associates. On 10 May, hard pressed by the Progressive Federal Party, Mulder stated categorically: 'The Government does not give *The Citizen* funds'. [9]

Vorster knew well that it was a lie. He also knew that the secret propaganda war would soon be public knowledge. The English-language press had picked up the scent and was now in full cry. In June 1978 Vorster ended Mulder's tenure as Minister of Information and transferred him to another portfolio. Eschel Rhoodie was dismissed a month later.

But it was too late for the Info affair simply to blow over. Vorster realised that soon he would have a scandal on his hands. In recent months it seemed as if he had lost his stomach for ruling as other burdens of office accumulated. After Soweto, black unrest never kept far below the surface. In Namibia the prospects of an internationally acceptable settlement were receding. In addition, his health had for some time not been good.

The man who once appeared to have a natural affinity for power took the tempting way out. On 20 September 1978, shortly after he had emerged from a hospital confinement induced by stress, Vorster announced his resignation as Prime Minister. For the country, unfamiliar with the Info story and Vorster's own involvement, it came as a substantial surprise; for most of the white population, which only the previous year had given him such a resounding mandate, Vorster's departure also seemed a significant loss.

Normally Mulder's succession as Prime Minister would have been a formality only. But the Info morass had trapped him and would not let him out. His main rival, P W Botha, now had a fighting chance. As Cape leader of the National Party he could rely on overwhelming support from his own province. He had acquired a formidable ally in the Nationalist leader in the Orange Free State, Alwyn Schlebusch, who had listened to Mulder's denial in Parliament and had not believed a word of it. After Mulder's performance Schlebusch was prepared to inform all and sundry, including Vorster, that the rising star from the Transvaal was no longer in the ascendant, that in fact P W Botha would be the next Prime Minister.

Mulder still believed that he would win. But his last chance disappeared when one of Rhoodie's top front men, the advocate Retief van Rooyen, foreseeing the inevitable and wishing to minimise the damage to himself, decided to line up with the angels by providing them with incomparably valuable information about how Rhoodie had been carrying on. He first told the other man in the race for the premiership, the 46-year old Minister of Foreign Affairs, Pik Botha, who was intent on making a verligte showing, about his pangs of conscience. Together, accompanied by Schlebusch, they went to see P W Botha in Cape Town. Van Rooyen duly delivered: his audience realised that they now had the ammunition to keep Mulder from ever achieving his ambition to be Prime Minister.

Mulder refused to withdraw from the contest, convinced that he could still win, even after Vorster at his last cabinet meeting on 26 September decided to come relatively clean by giving his colleagues a startling account of what the Information Department had been up to.

The National Party caucus met on 28 September in Cape Town to elect its new leader. On the first count no candidate had an absolute majority: P W Botha received 78 votes, Mulder got 72 and Pik Botha 22. The run-off between the two top candidates placed it beyond all doubt. Twenty of Pik Botha's supporters threw their votes to his namesake; Mulder received only two. The caucus chose P W Botha as its new leader and South Africa's next Prime Minister by 98 votes to 74.

The state which Botha was to take into the 1980s differed much from that of 1970. Heribert Adam, the author of the widely cited and praised book, *Modernizing Racial Domination*, which appeared in 1971, was impressed by the adaptive abilities of the white rulers of South Africa. He described them as 'effective technocrats, who are establishing an increasingly unshakeable oligarchy in a society where advanced industrialization in the hands of the few whites coexists with the relative deprivation of the non-whites. If this is to be cemented by a gradual deracialization and economic concessions, South Africa's white elite is capable of achieving this in spite of internal contradictions'.[10] It was, in fact, a 'modernizing oligarchy'. Few commentators would have been willing to endorse these words when Vorster relinquished office. The oligarchy had been decidedly shaken by the events of the decade, especially by the resurgence of black turbulence on an even larger scale than before. At the same time the world outside was encroaching, increasingly insistent that apartheid was not just the domestic affair of white South Africans. The oligarchy's handling of reform had been haphazard and patchy, most complete in the field of industrial relations, hardly at all in that of politics. P W Botha's test would be how he would handle the new-found self-confidence conferred on urban black insiders by economic advance. South Africa was proving no exception to the established generalisation that economic change must have political consequences.

CHAPTER SIXTEEN

Unfabian Strategies

When he stood on the steps of Parliament on 28 September 1978 as the new leader of the National Party and Prime Minister-elect of South Africa, P W Botha promised clean government. He promised several other things too, but they were the standard assurances expected of any Nationalist leader: the improvement of race relations, the promotion of economic development and maintenance of law and order. His own record as a politician could leave no doubt about Botha's absolute dedication to at least the last of these. But disclosures about the Information disaster, then still in their early stages, had revealed many unsavoury things done by political and bureaucratic careerists, ostensibly in the interests of the public and certainly financed by the public. For Botha the ways of duty and self-interest coincided: the public interest demanded both the cleaning up of the mess and the prevention of anything like it in the future; at the same time his main rival for the premiership, Connie Mulder, still a power in the party, could only suffer damaging blows to his prestige and influence. Clean government had to be right at the top of the new Prime Minister's agenda.

The Information scandal was not the inevitable outcome of the South African system of government, nor was it an inherent feature of the Nationalist way of rule. But it was a logical outcome of both, especially the second. From the Mother of Parliaments South Africa had in 1910 inherited the Westminster style of government. As the British themselves discovered only later with some surprise and dismay, it was a system in which power becomes concentrated in the hands of the man, or woman, at the top. The party with a majority in Parliament rules the roost and the top rooster is the Prime Minister. Those with a relish for authority would take to it as naturally as academics to jargon. When the form of government is unitary rather than federal and the constitution can be amended easily, like that of South Africa, possibilities of abuse must accumulate, subject ultimately only to the discipline of the ballot-box, the threat of a rival crowd of seekers of power and patronage taking office and the freedom of the press. In South Africa a change of government became less likely with each passing year of Nationalist rule, even if the United Party continued to delude itself till after 1970 that such a thing was possible. The restraints on politicians with a naturally authoritarian bent disappeared as Nationalist rule became entrenched, part of the nature of South African things. The Afrikaners were in any event happy to give the benefit of most doubts to 'their' government, one which had with such persistent drive advanced the cause of South Africa's particular people.

So it had become not too difficult for panting lusters after power like Mulder, flashy and ego-tripping technocrats like Rhoodie and a host of more mundane featherers of their own nests to get away for so long with the squandering of public money. All they needed was the assent, which turned into the complicity, of the ostensible chief, Vorster, who became the victim of that leadership style which was at first so widely praised as the breath of fresh air the country needed after Verwoerd. As one observer put it, 'Vorster's rule, in retrospect, was an organizational and administrative nightmare in more ways than one'.[1]

If there was one thing P W Botha would do, it was not to let things slip out of control the way Vorster had done. It was not for nothing that in his youthful days before 1948 as National Party organiser he had gained a reputation as an organiser of formidable talents. He may have lacked charm, bonhomie and what has become widely and loosely known as charisma, but his organisational skills became sharpened and polished over more than a decade as Minister of Defence. He would lay down clear lines of authority, reorganise the cabinet, establish co-ordination between departments as an everyday event, and centralise the making of decisions — for Botha thrived on the display and exercise of power.

But first he had to establish his authority in the National Party. Botha, as a man from the Cape, had become Prime Minister by default. The god from the machine which put paid to Mulder's chances, the Information scandal, fortunately lingered a while longer, long enough to destroy all hopes the much younger Mulder may have had of rebuilding his fortunes as a Nationalist. The former 'crown prince' to Vorster would not be around as a focus of opposition to any reforms Botha might choose to initiate. There was also John Vorster himself, kicked upstairs to become State President and in principle above politics, which suited Botha very well; it meant that no disgruntled ex-Prime Minister would be coming out of retirement to complain about 'liberalistic' innovations. In the end though, Vorster still had immense prestige in the National Party and amongst a white public unaware of the extent of the Info affair. His disapproving presence in the background would do the cause of fairly radical reform, by Nationalist lights, no good at all. If the scandal managed to embrace the former strong man the new ruler would only weep crocodile tears.

In November Botha appointed a three-man commission to investigate the 'irregularities' in the defunct Information Department. Its chairman was Rudolf Erasmus, a Supreme Court judge from the Orange Free State and former legal adviser to the National Party in that province. The other two members were career civil servants, one of whom the Botha Government later elevated to the Supreme Court in the Cape.

Only a few days before, Botha had had an abrasive confrontation with another judge, Anton Mostert, who had been appointed by Vorster in May 1978 as a one-man commissioner to investigate allegations of exchange control contraventions. Late in September Mostert discovered many contraventions committed by the Department of Information, which only confirmed what members of the Nationalist caucus were just discovering themselves. When a month later Mostert declared his intention of making public what he had learnt, Botha attempted to dissuade him on the grounds that the apparently guilty ones should have an opportunity to present their case. What he really meant was that the kind of information Mostert had was an excellent weapon for doing a hatchet-job on a political opponent, but that what the public did not know it could not whinge about. Mostert refused, even after Botha warned him that state law advisors regarded what he proposed to do as illegal. He walked out and released his evidence, which was at once taken up by the press all over the country in spite of an official attempt to prevent publication as it supposedly contravened the Commissions Act.

Shortly afterwards Botha relieved Mostert of his commission when the judge announced that he would continue to investigate exchange control irregularities. Apparently his activities would obstruct those of the Erasmus Commission. Botha had ensured, at least for a while, that more uncomfortable information would not go out into the wider world.

He could have no cause to complain about what the new commission came up with. There were two reports, published in December 1978 and May 1979. The first one enabled Botha to get rid of Connie Mulder. It found that Mulder 'had been incompetent in his administration of the department, had acted irregularly in a number of deals and had exercised improper pressure on others to secure favourable results for himself'.[2] It only confirmed what investigative journalists from the *Sunday Express* and the *Rand Daily Mail*, and Judge Mostert himself had already uncovered, but it had the authority of an officially approved commission. After his defeat in the Nationalist caucus Mulder had thought that life could go on for him as cabinet minister and Transvaal leader of the party. He soon found out how wrong he was: in November he was compelled to resign both positions. He discovered that his continued presence as Member of Parliament was 'not in the best interests' of himself, the Party or South Africa, as P W Botha told him in writing.[3] He resigned in January, most reluctantly, but his final humiliation came in April when he was expelled from the Transvaal National Party by its new leader, Andries Treurnicht.

The Erasmus Commission's first report had found that Vorster's integrity was 'unblemished'. The supplementary report of 29 May 1979 was big enough to admit its mistake. It found that Vorster actually did have his share in the joint villainy: he did not reveal irregularities, he kept them from the cabinet and did nothing about them for a long time.[4] The additional evidence on which the Commission based its revised conclusion was not compelling, but for

Botha it was sufficient. He demanded Vorster's immediate resignation as State President, which the victim duly submitted on 4 June 1979. Vorster retired to the Eastern Cape, a bitter and aggrieved man, increasingly prone to public statements which encouraged extreme right wing sentiment. He died in September 1983 at the age of 67, hating P W Botha to the end.

The findings of the Erasmus Commission had enabled the new leadership to emerge from the scandal with an image which was relatively untarnished. The bad guys were Mulder, Rhoodie, General Hendrik van den Bergh, head of the Bureau for State Security and a close Vorster confidant, through whom Info funds were channelled, and, eventually, Vorster himself. They were no longer around. The good guys were P W Botha, Schlebusch, Pik Botha and all the other members of the cabinet, otherwise clearly they would not have been there.

The evidence suggests that the distinction required some sleight of hand. The most striking illustration was the case of Owen Horwood, the Minister of Finance. A former academic economist of moderate qualifications and abilities, Horwood had risen to become Principal of the University of Natal, from which position he had negotiated for himself a senatorship in the National Party, which needed an English-speaking showpiece. This was Horwood's great advantage when the scandal was revealed: he was an English-speaker from Natal where he was also the leader of the National Party. Horwood's continued presence in the cabinet was necessary as it personified the Government's commitment to 'national unity'. The trouble was that he had hardly distinguished himself in the Info drama. In particular, he could not get away from the fact that as Minister of Finance he had once initialled a schedule of payments totalling nearly R15-million for secret Info projects. Horwood eventually admitted in Parliament that he had signed the schedule at the foot of the page, after covering the contents with a piece of paper so that he need not see the contents. In spite of what can most charitably be described as monumental incompetence, the Erasmus Commission exonerated Horwood, nor did Botha find it necessary to dismiss him from his cabinet, however richly he deserved such a reward.

It is small wonder that Hendrik van den Bergh, the former boss of BOSS, described the commission as a 'farce'. Although technically in contempt of the commission, he never had his day in court to prove that he knew what he was talking about. The Attorney-General of the Transvaal refused to prosecute Van den Bergh as it was 'not in the national interest'; 'not in the interest of the National Party' was a widely held and plausible gloss on his words.

It scarcely mattered how great the farce was. Perhaps it did nothing to dispel vast and general cynicism about standards of public morality. What was important, however, was that the new administration of P W Botha had minimised the possible damage to itself. It could get on with what Botha himself had come to recognise as the urgent, overdue business of reform.

As long ago as the 1960s, while still a member of Verwoerd's cabinet, Botha liked to suggest that he had enlightened attitudes. 'I talk to the right so that I can act to the left' *(Ek praat regs sodat ek links kan doen)*, he used to say, in private.[5] In those days, for he was at first Minister of Coloured Affairs, it was the coloured community which must have benefited from Botha's early verligtheid, in the form of spending on education and social welfare. After that Botha had revelled in his dozen years as Minister of Defence. His organisational flair and technocratic bent found their expression in a modernised army and sophisticated equipment. But he had also made a point of introducing the principles of equality of pay and opportunity in the defence force, regardless of race. As Defence Minister, Botha had pioneered the notion of the total onslaught on South Africa orchestrated by the Soviet imperialists. Whatever its limitations as a world-view, it made for a willingness to disregard racial differences: South Africans of all colours were the victims of this godless assault led by the South African Communist Party and the ANC; all had to stand together in repelling it.

If Botha was keen on a strong if limited dose of reform, he knew that some clearing of the decks was necessary. First, there was the bureaucracy. Over the previous three decades it had become a massive instrument of Afrikaner upliftment, overstaffed, committed to the enforcement of apartheid regulations, a major absorber of resources which could have been employed more productively elsewhere. In principle it was easy to identify the remedy: eliminate duplication, provide incentives for early retirement, actually dismiss the most obtrusive deadwood, even get rid of some of the apartheid measures which required enforcement. In practice it was not so easy to apply. Vested interests have a natural resilience, based on the prospect of the unfavourable alternatives that await them if their perks and privileges go. P W Botha had limited success only in achieving a leaner bureaucracy, even if he did reduce the 39 departments of the public service to 22. As his reform programme unfolded, the civil servants actually made a come-back as parallel bureacracies emerged to staff the new tricameral Parliament.

Where this organisation man bypassed the bureaucracy most successfully was in his streamlining of decision-making. He had inherited twenty-odd cabinet committees from Vorster, but some of them existed only on paper, others had vague functions and met hardly at all. Botha reduced them all to five major cabinet committees. He gave them clear assignments, ensured that they met periodically, and co-ordinated and regularised their procedures. Over time, however, this early simplicity was to become recomplicated: lines of communication became tangled as authorities resumed their temporarily interrupted growth and red tape flourished once more.

Most important, Botha established the National Security Management System (NSMS). Originally designed to cut down on ubiquitous red tape, the NSMS became a parallel system of government, an alternative to Parliament and the cabinet. At the top was the State Security Council (SSC). It had a permanent secretariat, met twice a week and included key members of the cabinet, the military and the police. The SSC was to become virtually the *de facto* government of the country. At the base of the new system was a network of about 500 Joint Management Centres (JMCs). They consisted of both security and civil administrators and were designed to smell out local grievances and disturbances. The detailed information the JMCs provided was supposed to lay the foundation for preemptive and remedial action by the relevant branches of the civil service. In practice it was not so simple: the JMCs could determine outcomes by their choice of the information they saw as important. In short, huge areas of decision-making in South Africa under P W Botha were only in principle subject to the scrutiny of Parliament and sometimes it did not even go so far.

One striking but unsurprising feature of this revamped system of decision-making was the increased importance of Botha's beloved military. It served not only in key positions of the NSMS, but came to provide the intelligence on which Botha most relied in his handling of domestic events and his dealings with neighbouring states. As always when the military plays an important role in political decision-making, there was the obvious question which persisted as events unfolded: how sound is the judgement of men trained to accept commands without question, to go for targets unerringly and who are not required to consider the political niceties for which their civilian colleagues have a sharper sensitivity?

P W Botha's handling of the bureaucracy showed one thing: important decisions would need his approval. He himself would chart the course ahead. Neither was he prepared to endure the obstruction of bureaucratic foot-draggers nor heed the finical complaints of opposition politicians that crucial choices about the country's future were being made behind the back of Parliament. If South Africa was heading for reform it would be authoritarian reform, in keeping with the temperament of a man who had always believed in centralising the most crucial decisions in his own hands.

Botha's treatment of the National Party was on a par with his approach to the bureaucracy. Here too he reduced the ability of Party regulars and stalwarts to delay and resist as they complained that recent changes from above were un-Nationalist and untraditional. Yet excessive high-handedness carried its own risk. The National Party was bursting at the seams with conservatives who would not take kindly to abrupt deviations from the ways of the past. There was the new leader of the Party in the Transvaal, Andries Treurnicht, a committed right-winger and a man upon whom it was not safe to turn one's back. For years the Opposition and its press had been waiting for the Nats to split, in fact it had been one of their favourite pastimes since 1948. It had happened only once before, in 1969, and then the damage had been kept to a minimum. But the price of avoiding a major split had been inertia, the inability of the leadership to take major political initiatives, even had it wished to do so, which under Vorster was debatable. If Botha did wish to revive the virtually forgotten 1977 constitutional proposals he would have to watch his step in the minefield of provincialism and grass roots conservatism that represented the political attitudes of all-too-many ordinary Nationalists in the street.

Botha moved quickly and unsentimentally to allay provincial resentment by ensuring that Vorster's successor as State President would be another man from the north, Marais Viljoen. It cost him the lasting enmity of his fellow-minister and old comrade-in-arms, Louwrens Muller, who had thought with some reason that the job was his for the asking — until Botha realised that two men from the Cape in the two top positions would never do. The parting of the ways between Botha and his friend was bitter, but the Prime Minister never let on that it made him lie awake at night.

For Botha it was essential not to alienate the Transvaal, the main breeding-ground of verkrampte sentiment. Andries Treurnicht had always been quick, in his circumspect manner, to suggest that the old ways remained the best and that change would destroy the national soul of the Afrikaner. But Treurnicht was not a man for open confrontation, especially with someone who relished it like Botha, which had a dampening effect on some of the more ardent partisans of immobility in his province.

If Botha could not always impose his authority on the National Party, and the election of Treurnicht as Transvaal leader suggested just that, then he could bypass it, as he was doing with the bureaucracy, and reduce it at worst to a harmless complainer about breakneck changes. Here he could also attempt to insulate himself as far as possible from pressures he did not like.

From the earliest days he drew a distinction between *policy* and *principle*. As Botha explained to the Natal National Party Congress in August 1979, the first he addressed as party leader, it was for the congresses to decide on principles; it was for the Government to implement them as policies. It sounded so simple there had to be a catch. There was. The interpretation of how policy should be carried out by a supposedly dutiful government could be so broad as to amount to the introduction of new policy. For instance, the twelve-point plan for a 'total national strategy' which Botha announced in the Natal Congress contained as one of its points, 'the recognition of economic interdependence and the proper co-ordination of labour resources',[6] an unexceptionable platitude on the face of it, but which could be interpreted as the green light for the abandonment of the last scrap of protection for white workers — or the removal of the pass laws for that matter. By a process of subterfuge and sleight of hand, harsher critics would have said deceit, devoted Nationalists of the old school could wake up one morning to the kind of 'integrated' South Africa they had always believed their party repudiated.

There were other ways in which P W Botha gave himself room to manoeuvre. He had been operating the party machine virtually since reaching the age of consent. Contentious resolutions had a habit of not making it on to the agendas of Nationalist congresses. Dissent and discontent about what many old-timers saw as the headlong pace of reform did not rise to the surface; unity and goodwill apparently never had it so good. Congresses of the National Party tended to be sycophantic affairs, with the wisdom of the leadership at the receiving end of moving tributes.

Nor could the total onslaught be forgotten. The survival of the white population was at stake, it had to 'adapt or die', as Botha announced memorably in 1979. It placed a premium on the strength derived from unity. But it also tended to make foreign policy a casualty of Botha's drive to establish his authority at home. Scaremongering about threats engineered from abroad could only encourage white fear and suspicion of a world which did not understand South Africa's unique problems. At first Botha was little concerned about such heightened mistrust of foreigners, for he himself had developed a strong distrust as Defence Minister of what other countries, whether Western or Communist, intended towards the Republic.

Botha gathered power steadily into his hands during those early years as Prime Minister. It happened gradually but surely as he bypassed the entrenched positions of apartheid bureaucrats and interpreted established Nationalist policy flexibly. It was not for the sheer love of power that he did so, although he surely loved it sincerely. Botha was a man with a mission, for he knew that South Africa could not continue to mark time as it had under the late Vorster. White South Africans truly had to adapt if they wished to survive in a country where with each passing day the master plan of

Verwoerd was resembling more and more the fantasy of a mad professor. To a large degree, Botha wanted power because he knew reform was unavoidable and had no doubt that he was the man who could best guide it in the interests of white survival.

His twelve-point plan for a total national strategy placed before the Natal National Party Congress in August 1979 indicated what he felt needed reforming at the beginning of his time of power.[7] It was a typical Nationalist blend of belated groping towards genuine if limited reforms and continued refusal to face up to the most obvious shortcomings of apartheid, or 'good neighbourliness', which Botha had begun to insist was a more accurate description. As always, the group principle was uppermost. The total strategy had to recognise 'the existence of numerous nations *(veelvolkigheid)* and of minorities' in the Republic: 'They cannot be wished away'. Most radically, although Botha and his fellow-reformers spent many hours denying that it was radical at all, he proposed 'the sharing *(verdeling)* of power' between whites, coloureds and Indians 'in a system of consultation and co-responsibility where common interests are concerned'. Most conspicuously, there was no portion for blacks when power was being shared. Botha expected Africans to continue down the dead-end Verwoerd had devised for them twenty years before: 'The creation of constitutional structures for the black peoples *(volkere)* to make possible the largest possible degree of self-government in states which are consolidated as far as is practically possible.'

Power-sharing had no bearing on the principle of segregation; 'own schools and communities' were still seen as 'fundamental for happy social conditions. It is not discrimination; it is the recognition of the rights of others'. To dispel any lingering doubts Botha repeated a familiar refrain: 'I support the removal of wounding, unnecessary discriminatory measures, but I am not in favour of forced integration and that the right of self-determination of my own people should be threatened'.

A feature of the twelve-point plan was its support for the 'maintenance of free enterprise as basis for economic and financial policy. It also presupposes the efficient training and use of labour'. Nationalist leaders had not always been so ringing in their endorsement of capitalism; it was the beginning of a honeymoon between Nationalist politicians and businessmen which was to flounder on the rocks of incompatibility.

For the rest the plan contained what could have been expected from a man of P W Botha's background. His disillusionment with a West which had abandoned South Africa in Angola was reflected in his endorsement of a policy of neutrality between the superpowers. Nor would any of this be possible without law, order and efficient organisation: 'The maintenance of effective decision-making by the state, which depends on a strong army and police force to guarantee orderly government, as well as clean administration. Clean administration is essential at all levels.'

The twelve-point plan impressed as much by what it did not say as by what it did. It had bound the Government to power-sharing, previously denounced by its spokesmen with intemperate exuberance as a liberalistic Prog notion, sure-fire proof that its supporters were enemies of the white man's future in South Africa, as the tired phraseology went. From then on there would be endless semantic quibbling as Botha and his colleagues explained that they believed in 'healthy' power-sharing as against the 'unhealthy' variety of the Progressive Federal Party. It did not satisfy the Nationalist right wing, which rejected any kind of power-sharing automatically. Nor did it satisfy the Government's liberal critics, who pointed to the main and perfectly obvious defect of the plan, which was that power-sharing did not include Africans.

The leadership of the National Party had arrived tortuously at accepting that political power outside the homelands was not the exclusive preserve of white South Africans. But at most it would involve giving crumbs from the table to the minority groups, the coloureds and the Indians, which it wished to co-opt as allies against the 'total onslaught'. With only a little ingenuity, continued Afrikaner rule would be preserved. The more things changed, the more they would remain the same. Yet it would only be possible if Africans were kept out. Once they were included in the structures of power-sharing it seemed obvious that majority rule could not be far behind, a prospect that not even the most verligte Nationalist could contemplate. But it was becoming increasingly clear that the homelands were no serious answer to the question of political rights for blacks. They continued to be economically backward labour reservoirs for the 'white' areas, regions of population congestion where additional jobs were mainly created by increasing the number of bureaucrats, itself only made possible by the largess provided by a South African Government still intent on showing that life continued in the idea of Bantustans. From this dilemma of being damned if it did and being damned if it didn't, the Government could not escape. It preferred to pretend that there was no dilemma at all and that the defunct policies of Verwoerd were actually alive and well and the only hope for the future.

It was not easy to see what the Government of P W Botha could have done, short of accepting the unthinkable, namely, the principle of majority rule. Had it done so, in however qualified a manner and however distant into the future, it could not have survived. The Afrikaners would tolerate much from their rulers — as long as they saw them as theirs. But they would have rejected any government willing to capitulate, abdicate, surrender or sell out, as the terminology went, by accepting that blacks would one day have political power over whites in a common South Africa. As it was, power-sharing with coloureds and Indians was in itself a prospect awful enough for the right wing in the National Party. From now on, a public parting of the ways between Nationalists ceased to be just a fantasy of the Opposition imagination. Divisions within the Party ran deep, whatever the official facade of unity. Right wing sentiment was particularly strong in the strongest branch of the National Party, that of the Transvaal. It was there that Andries Treurnicht was the leader, the embodiment of conservative hopes and unremitting sower of suspicion against the official line. If the right wing seceded, with the Transvaal Party under its control, then even the limited reforms of P W Botha would have failed before they had a chance. He would have been correct had he concluded that the reformer's lot was not a happy one.

Botha developed a style of reform which had its own contradictions. His predecessor, Vorster, had done little to prepare the white voters for the future into which they were heading. 'Sufficient unto the day is the evil thereof' seemed to be his motto. He had been most flexible when it came to multiracial sport, hardly an issue to shake the volk to its foundations. There had been increased desegregation of public amenities. Most important had been the changes in the labour market, but they came under pressure, the result of strike waves, Soweto, and, above all, the government's aversion to making economic growth the captive of the limited amount of skilled labour the white population could supply. Politically there had been talk of a break with a supposedly inappropriate Westminster system, but nothing had come of that, or of anything else. Whatever reforms did come were presented as in line with existing policy; officially there were no breaks with the past. Change was only possible if it could be presented as no change. Botha's way was different. He believed that the whites, and his own Afrikaner constituency in particular, had to be prepared for the new. They had to be shaken into realising that they had to adapt or die. He and reformist colleagues like the Minister of Foreign Affairs, Pik Botha, and the Minister of Manpower, Fanie Botha, were strong on the rhetoric of reform; compared with Vorster they were impressively strong on doing something about it. But they aroused both expectations they could not satisfy and antagonisms they would have preferred to do without.

It was the labour reforms of the Botha Government that were most successful. In 1979 it had adopted the main recommendations of the Wiehahn report. When the Industrial Conciliation Amendment Act came into operation on 1 October later that year, African trade unions could acquire official recognition and engage independently in collective bargaining with employers. Earlier in 1979, 6 500 white miners had gone on a wildcat strike, ostensibly in sympathy with a strike on a copper mine in the northern Cape where job reservation had been at issue. In fact it was a protest against Wiehahn's new-fangled principles of non-discrimination. In spite of the call by the executive of the right wing Mine Workers' Union for an all-out strike and for intervention by the Government it was a failure. The Government refused to intervene, true to its new-found principle that these matters were best left to workers and their employers to resolve between themselves. The white miners went back to work, having suffered financial losses they had not bargained for. P W Botha had shown that he would not be deflected by threats from right wing workers who rejected the new dispensation. They had learnt a costly lesson and would not be so foolish again — but when the time came they would also abandon the National Party in droves.

The Government did not perform too impressively in the by-elections of 1979 and 1980. While it drew the support of changeable English-speakers from the Progressive Federal Party on the left, it lost votes to the Herstigte Nasionale Party on the far right. In a number of Transvaal constituencies the HNP, taking its stand on the Government's supposed favouring of blacks at the expense of whites, had succeeded in reducing the Nationalist majorities substantially, often by more than half, even if it was more the result of voter stay-aways than of any populist appeal of the Herstigtes. Here was real cause for anxiety: a right wing party with a more respectable image than the somewhat shabby HNP was bound to attract grass root Nationalist voters.

In 1981 the Harvard political scientist, Samuel Huntington, delivered an address to the Political Science Association in Johannesburg in which he attempted to outline a strategy for reform that the South African Government could follow profitably if it really was serious about the whole business.[8] Huntington gained some fame, or notoriety, in South Africa for his argument that a reformer should be a master of deception:

> The politics of reform is basically a tripartite process with the reform leader fighting a two front war against both stand patters and revolutionaries while at the same time attempting to divide and confuse his enemies. The increasing strength and activities of the HNP, Afrikaner Weerstandsbeweging, and other groups opposed to change, on the one hand, and of the PFP and black groups, on the other, would appear to place the South African government in a classic reform position. That does not, of course, mean that it is necessarily a reform government. It means simply that the opportunity for reform exists. Whether efforts are made to utilize that opportunity only history can tell for sure because it is of the essence of the reformer that he must employ ambiguity, concealment, and deception concerning his goals.

Huntington also argued, in words that must have been congenial to P W Botha and his lieutenants, that 'narrowing the scope of political participation may be indispensable to eventually broadening that participation'. It was essentially a recipe for reform from above and was to have some influence with the constitutional planners who were about to come into their heyday.

Five years later, Huntington returned to South Africa and attempted to explain why the Government had not learnt the lessons of reform from other parts of the world, so conveniently set out in his address. He found that it had gone about it in just about all the wrong ways. Reformers should not go around raising expectations and then do little to satisfy them. That was what the South African Government had been doing, 'raising expectations and delivering much less than it seemed to promise'. Huntington had also argued that a reform government should follow what he called a Fabian strategy whereby it 'deals with one issue at a time, moving slowly from one to another'. At the same time, 'in order to accomplish individual reforms, it was usually best to follow *blitzkrieg* tactics. Announce a reform, move as fast as possible to put it into law, rush to implement it before the opposition can mobilise'. Already in 1981 Huntington had identified that as one of the defects of the Botha style of reform: lots of expectations had been raised by the heady talk of apartheid being out of date, but in truth it was still around in many obvious ways. At the same time the white right wing took it all in deadly earnest and had been given plenty of time to mobilise.

What seems odd is that the Government remained stuck in its erroneous strategies five years after they had been identified by a man whose analysis had apparently so impressed the would-be reformers. In 1986 the Minister of Defence, Magnus Malan, told Huntington: 'Because of the nature of our governmental system, we just cannot operate very quickly'. South Africa had a culture of commissions: big issues first had to be scrutinised at length, facts had to be found, before anything could be done. In Huntington's words: 'It thus seems to take several years after something is announced as a goal of the government before it can be put into operation ... There seems to be something about the political processes in South Africa that makes it very, very difficult to push legislative changes through quickly'.

Somewhat unsatisfactorily, Huntington did not attempt to

identify this 'something'. But he made a key point, perhaps the most important, for the success of reform anywhere, which would help to account for the slow pace of change: 'a reform government has to change its constituency. It will start off with one constituency, but if the process of change is going to go ahead, it will have to shift that constituency'. In South Africa that hardly happened, except when Botha got rid of his own right wing in 1982. But five years later Huntington did not find any really significant broadening of the government's constituency by bringing in new groups to support it:

> In 1981 there were a whole series of groups which formed potential elements of a reform coalition; moderate black groups, the English and Afrikaner business establishments; some elements in the civil service; middle class whites as well as the coloured and Asian communities. The government has not built a reform coalition from these groups.[9]

Superficially, this is not correct. Botha's willingness to abandon the extreme right made the National Party seem worthier of support to an increasing number of English-speakers, as the general election of 1987 was to show. Botha had done what none of his predecessors had dreamt of doing. He had been prepared to leave behind much of his traditional support and reach out instead to a larger white constituency, even if it meant depending more on the votes of English-speakers, who had been unreliable Nationalist supporters in the past. Yet it was not such a gamble after all. For conservative English-speakers who thought the Progressive Federal Party too liberal the Nationalists were the only alternative, all the more as the official rhetoric about reform made it seem as if the Government was preempting the middle ground of South African politics. The National Party gained new supporters after the defection of the right, but they were happy enough with the Government's programme of reform based on the premise of continued white rule. It did not in fact add up to a substantial widening of a reform coalition.

P W Botha had no intention of ditching the National Party in his pursuit of reform. He had been a professional Nationalist his life long, from his early days as party organiser. His ties were not just the powerful ones of a shared and intimate past. He had a goal, to make South Africa safe for continued Nationalist rule in the future. His vision of a new South Africa was one where the Afrikaner would remain substantially in charge, with the English-speakers, the coloureds and the Indians getting a look-in as consenting, if perhaps reluctant, partners. Africans did not feature at all. Their political destinies lay elsewhere.

Botha made the National Party his creature, but he was also a creature of the party. He could not move beyond it. In his strategy he had to take the party with him. He might abandon part of the constituency which had been so essential to Nationalist rule in the past, but finding new constituencies was quite another matter. For a time he appeared to be reaching out to the business community: in November 1979 Botha had a much publicised meeting with the leading businessmen of the Republic at the Carlton Centre in Johannesburg. The tycoons were immensely flattered that a Nationalist leader should have seemed so eager to listen to them or talk to them, which is what it was mainly about. But Botha valued capitalism for its ability to produce the goods; when businessmen later began to criticise him in public for not moving faster on reform, he at once turned resentful and abusive.

In truth P W Botha had a South Africa in mind that would not be so very different from the one he had known before 1978. He was prepared to reform within those limits, but not beyond. His understanding of reform was not that of his liberal critics. For him it meant a fixed quantity: once it had been attained reform would be complete and the Afrikaners could get back to running the country without hindrance. The last thing he understood by reform was a continuous process where there were no ultimate solutions but simply a moving-on from one fallible and incomplete answer to the next.

CHAPTER SEVENTEEN

Treurnicht Makes it Final

When the Nationalists split for the second time in 1982, perhaps the most surprised man of them all was the leader of the breakaway, Dr Andries Treurnicht, himself. For years he had been the white supremacist hope of the many hardliners in the National Party: the former Dutch Reformed minister would restore the old-time religion of apartheid as it was supposed to have been practised under Verwoerd, before his unworthy successors began to tamper with the true faith in a futile attempt to appease world opinion and, worse, misguided verligtes at home. But for years too, Treurnicht had practised brinkmanship as if to the manner born, never quite pushing ideological differences to their final conclusion.

About his dyed-in-the-wool conservatism there could be no doubt. He became noted as the conservative editor of *Die Kerkbode*, the mouthpiece of that very conservative institution, the Dutch Reformed Church. In 1967 Treurnicht became the first editor of the Pretoria newspaper, *Hoofstad*, and so acquired a wider audience for his message that separation between the races was a true Christian imperative and represented no less than the will of God.

When Albert Hertzog and Jaap Marais left the National Party in 1969, Treurnicht did not keep them company, despite his evident ideological affinity with the dissenters. For a while he sat on the fence, but soon decided that it was a far, far better thing to remain within the party and to capture it from within, than to rough it out in the political wilderness with Hertzog and Marais; in 1971 he entered Parliament as a Nationalist MP. Given the strength of right wing sentiment within the Party it was a sound decision. The pathetic electoral performance of the HNP after 1969 could only have confirmed Treurnicht in his conviction that what he had done was for the greater good of the volk and himself.

But he had been testing the waters for a long time. He was prone to public statements which suggested that he was not at one with the reformist trend, such as it was, within the National Party. Artful use, however, of the Afrikaans language, of which he had an excellent command, made it difficult for his several enemies to pin him down as a troublemaker who would not toe the party line. As P W Botha was later to describe Treurnicht's activities to a friend, from his own unique perspective: 'He is a verbal master; he can make big and attractive words resound, but when it is all over and one analyses them, he has either actually said nothing or taken a few jabs at changes which we believe essential for survival of the white man in South Africa'.[1]

Vorster tried to bring the maverick within the fold by giving Treurnicht office as a deputy minister. It was an old ploy and for a time it seemed to work. Treurnicht now, it seemed, went along with policies which a genuine true-blue conservative might have been expected to spurn with disdain.

When, still a mere deputy minister, he defeated the very senior member of the cabinet, Fanie Botha, to become leader of the Transvaal National Party, his future rise to the top appeared irresistible. P W Botha had no choice but to make Treurnicht a full member of the cabinet, in June 1979. He then emerged as the most likely successor to Botha. As Transvaal leader he inevitably had to be taken seriously. As a noted conservative he represented powerful grass-roots sentiments that apartheid was something to be preserved till the crack of doom.

At once, after becoming a minister, Treurnicht showed his determination to keep the Party on the far-right track, even if it meant confronting one of his established colleagues in public. Piet Koornhof, the Minister for Co-operation and Development, had apparently just said at Palm Springs in the United States, that apartheid was dead, a statement of which the Government was to be reminded with varying degrees of derision in later years.

Treurnicht did not like what he had read in the local press, and did not hesitate to say so. Public repudiation of one Nationalist minister by another was virtually unheard of; from a newcomer it was sheer presumption.

It was all a misunderstanding, or so it was presented. Koornhof had not actually announced the demise of apartheid. Even from a South African propagandist abroad, trying to put the best construction on the unacceptable, that would have been too blatant a venture into fantasy. What he said was that 'apartheid as it has been heard of in America has been dying in South Africa'.[2] That at least had a measure of plausibility, as arguably there was little correspondence between the actual application of apartheid, however unpleasant, and the typical American stereotype of it as a case study of the theory and practice of hell.

Plainly, P W Botha had to assert his authority. He pointed out that Koornhof was in fact a misunderstood man. Moreover, he spoke harsh words to his new minister in private.

But Treurnicht had the bit between his teeth. For him it was only a beginning, and a situation well suited to his special talents. From now on he maintained a tricky balance between outward loyalty to the current party line and backroom stirring of discontent at what verkramptes saw as departures from high principle.

Treurnicht's next major stirring of the pot came over sport, so central to the lives of white South Africans. The Craven week was an annual event at which the best school rugby teams played one another. But Craven week in 1980 was to be different, for one of the 24 teams would consist of coloured schoolboys.

At a public meeting, in Johannesburg in March, Treurnicht had been asked about the alien presence in the tournament. Did he approve? He did not. He made it plain that a coloured team in what had until then been an all-white affair was totally unwelcome.

P W Botha learned about it the next day in the press, and was outraged. Treurnicht's statement was guaranteed to sharpen the already considerable hostility of coloureds to their white rulers. Perhaps worse, in a country where Afrikaner addiction to rugby is obsessive, it could sabotage the long-awaited tour of the Republic by a British Lions team.

So Botha departed from his usual rule of not hanging dirty Nationalist washing in public. He issued a forceful statement which reaffirmed the Government policy of non-interference in the decisions of sports bodies. Botha went further. He accused Treurnicht, although he carefully did not mention him by name, of treating coloureds as if they were 'lepers'.[3]

When Treurnicht returned for the parliamentary session to Cape Town from the Transvaal, he found the choleric Botha in his most abrasive mood. They met on 10 March. Botha insisted that Treurnicht accept party policy or resign. When Treurnicht left Botha's office he was visibly upset — but he did not resign. He even issued a short statement appealing to all Nationalists to help the party carry out its policy for the good of all in South Africa. Botha in turn suddenly discovered that there were actually no differences between himself and the Transvaal leadership.

The cracks had been covered up — at least for a while. Breaking ranks, splitting the party, had always been a cardinal sin, akin to treason to the volk. Botha himself had been a life-long faithful party man, always willing to go along, even if on occasion reluctantly (by his own admission), with measures which promoted nothing but obscurantism and intolerance. Resignation in his book was a last resort — when fundamental principle was at stake. Somehow the conscience of P W Botha had never been tortured in that way. Botha, in short, always a loyal Nationalist, expected Treurnicht to follow the party line, however unpalatable he may have found it, especially as the new leader only saw his policies as adaptations to changing circumstances, but never as a break with separate development. Whether he actually believed that Treurnicht would conform is another matter.

In truth, Treurnicht's interest dictated that he sit tight and remain in the National Party. He could reasonably expect to succeed Botha as Nationalist leader and head of the Government. He was five years younger and there was nothing wrong with his health. He appeared to have arrived on a good wicket, conniving with the wild men of the right in their portrayal of Botha as the seller-out of white South Africa, but continuing to stroll the corridors of power as a member of Botha's cabinet and the powerful leader of the National Party in the Transvaal, as well as of the Broederbond, the secret organisation devoted to putting the right Afrikaners in the right places. It is difficult to imagine that the final split did not come because someone on the far-right had blundered.

The parting of the ways came over 'power-sharing'. After previously spending so much time and energy denouncing it as an alien Prog notion, Nationalists in the early 1980s had to start getting used to the idea that this was now official party policy. White supremacy could no longer be justified by the simple mouthing of clichés about separate freedoms. Huge sections of the South African population could not even theoretically be incorporated within the ideology formalised by Verwoerd. For them more sophisticated means of white domination had to be found in a world which was proving surprisingly unreceptive to the message that apartheid was actually no more than good neighbourliness.

What it amounted to was refurbishing the largely forgotten proposals of the constitutional commission of 1976, chaired by P W Botha himself, then still Minister of Defence. There were to be three parliaments, for the whites, the coloureds and the Indians, each with its own cabinet, which would deal with relevant 'group' affairs. Legislation affecting all three groups would be initiated by a council, in which the whites would have an overall majority, consisting of the members of all three cabinets. For the blacks there was nothing. They had after all their own separate areas where they could realise themselves.

The Botha proposals were, in short, a somewhat unsubtle facade for continued white supremacy. The Official Opposition rejected them, naturally, but this was not so important. Coloured and Indian 'leaders' also rejected them, which was important, for without their support the window-dressing would not work. For the time being then, the proposals were shelved. Yet the notion of 'power-sharing', as interpreted by the ruling party, refused to die. In 1979 another constitutional commission was appointed, under the chairmanship of Alwyn Schlebusch, leader of the Nationalists in the Free State. Out of the deliberations of this body, in January 1981, came the President's Council, which replaced the Senate. It was a deliberative body, consisting of sixty appointees, fifteen of them coloureds and Asians. Its immediate brief was to investigate a new constitutional system for South Africa. Its ongoing excuse for existence was to be its weighty deliberations on issues involving economics, the sciences, race relations and so forth.

In part the President's Council was simply a substitute for the unlamented Senate. It provided sheltered and comfortable employment for many party hacks who otherwise would have had no claim to support by the taxpayer. But the Council did not possess even the nominal legislative power of the Senate; it could only make recommendations on matters which had been referred to it. If this was power-sharing the future could truly hold no terrors for white South Africans.

Yet the President's Council had a symbolic significance which was at once appreciated, both by white supremacist last-ditchers and by leaders of the two subject groups which the Government was hoping to co-opt. For the first time under Nationalist rule it was possible for whites, coloureds and Asians to talk about their future, in an official body of the state, on the unquestioned assumption that it was indeed a common future. Given the exclusion of the black majority and given the toothlessness of the Council itself, it could rightly be objected that it came to little, that it was a mere grudging admission of what Official Oppositions, including the highly conservative United Party, had been saying those many years. But it was also true that while it might only have been one small step for South Africa it was one giant leap for the National Party. The President's Council amounted to an intellectual break with that obsessive drawing of dividing lines which had been the main theme of Nationalist rule since 1948.

Naturally nothing was further from the Government's mind than the abandonment of white rule, but all at once it was forced back to the drawing-board. If coloureds and Asians could be taken into the councils of state, it could be asked legitimately, and it was, where separation began and where it ended.

For the Government the best thing which came out of the Council was that coloureds and Indians were now prepared to listen to proposals which did not differ substantially from those they had found so unappealing only a few years before. The actual involvement of coloureds and Indians in high-level discussions with whites partly explains the change. Nor is appreciation of the fruits of office a white monopoly. The substantial perks and privileges which co-optation into the new system would bring could only have had their expected effect on those who claimed to be leaders of the coloureds and Indians.

So power-sharing came into fashion. But the Government had to do some fancy footwork. Its new policies had to be distinguished sharply from the power-sharing which the Official Opposition, the Progressive Federal Party, had been proclaiming as its own policy. Government spokesmen now had a problem: how do you proclaim the wonders of power-sharing without being accused by verkrampte fellow-Nationalists, of whom there were many, of being mere diluted Progs who were paving the way for black domination?

There was, it seemed, a difference. Power-sharing could be 'healthy' or it could be 'unhealthy', as P W Botha explained. The Nationalist variety accepted the reality of group differences and the right of each racial group to decide its own destiny in matters which concerned itself. It was the unhealthy Prog variety which would end in disaster, ignoring as it supposedly did the importance of group distinctions and the white man's right to self-determination. The message was obvious: Nationalist power-sharers were not in fact closet liberals, as was indeed clear to all, except to Treurnicht and his fellow verkramptes.

After the Craven week crisis, an uneasy peace descended on the National Party. Treurnicht and his following in the Transvaal continued to flourish in back rooms. The leader himself went on addressing meetings, both open and closed, of the Party faithful, while his supporters entrenched themselves conspicuously in influential positions as chairmen of Nationalist MP study groups.

But all their right wing fervour could not prevent the emergence of a new, more moderate grouping of MPs in the Transvaal Party. For them the activities of Treurnicht and his disciples came close to the especially heinous Nationalist sin of splitting the Party. The group began to take shape after Craven week, disillusioned by the patent willingness of so many hardliners in their province to incur fraternal bloodletting 'over so small a thing'. The rise of the loyalists was something the verkramptes did not reckon with, to their cost.

This was perhaps understandable, for in the meantime the right wing continued to flourish, as the general election on 29 April 1981 brought home with striking effect. The far-right Herstigte Nasionale Party won 200 000 votes, little less than that of the Official Opposition, the Progressive Federal Party. It did not gain a seat, but in 19 constituencies it averaged more than 3 000 votes, mostly in the Transvaal. The Nationalists retained their two-thirds majority in Parliament, but in general constituency majorities had come down sharply. However, although the Government had lost seats in the Cape and Natal, the Transvaal had held firm, yielding no seats to an opposition party. For Treurnicht and his following the result had been truly gratifying, enhancing the prestige of the Transvaal National Party and confirming them in their conviction that the way to go in politics was to the right.

Even so, it was more than a straw in the wind when the Treurnicht group did not perform as well as it expected in electing nominated MPs and party whips at the beginning of the short parliamentary session in July 1981. The loyalists did surprisingly well and they defeated Treurnicht candidates in doing so.

The Treurnicht supporters were not deterred. They cultivated the new Transvaal MPs who came to Parliament after the April election. They continued with their plans to get rid of 'liberalists' on the Transvaal executive, especially the senior deputy chairman and Minister of Manpower, Fanie Botha, much detested for policies which were supposedly destroying 'the white man's right to self-determination on the labour front'. The year ended with the struggle for control of the Transvaal unresolved. The loyalists were stronger than they had been twelve months before, but the right wing was still convinced that it could win any showdown and so take over the most powerful of the four constituent parties of the National Party.

Further, some of Treurnicht's more excitable followers were eager for a showdown. They resented snide remarks by Herstigtes about 'Andries Wit Handjies' (Andries Little White Hands) and their leader's hit-and-run tactics, a proven technique which he showed no sign of abandoning for more and bloodier confrontation. After all, life as a minister had its attractions. Treurnicht indeed was not noted for pushing hard right wing lines at meetings of the cabinet, of which he was 'rather a taciturn member', according to the possibly partisan testimony of P W Botha himself.[4]

Casting doubt on party policy to *die volk daarbuite* (the nation outside) and waiting for the succession to fall into his lap seemed more suited to Treurnicht's particular talents. Unluckily for him, he made a mistake from which his enemies and, perhaps even more, his own hot-heads did not allow him to recover.

The great newspaper editor, J L Garvin, liked to say, 'Destiny always comes to one sideways'. So it was with Andries Treurnicht. Destiny sidled up to him and took him unawares. He had hardly recovered from his surprise when he and his band found themselves out in the political wilderness.

It all began with an editorial which appeared in February 1982 in the Nationalist propaganda journal, *Nat 80's*. The editor, Jan Grobler, made statements which were by then the common coin of those who preached 'healthy-power-sharing'.[5] South Africa, Grobler stated, was one country which could only have one government. As whites, coloureds and Indians inhabited a common geographical region, albeit in separate geographical areas, it was essential that these groups should all participate in its decision-making processes.

To non-South Africans these remarks would have been platitudinous, devastating in their obviousness, and equally devastating in the continued refusal of even verligte Nationalists to face up to the problem of political rights for the black majority of South Africans. That they should have offended because of their dangerous radicalism would seem past belief, but offend they did.

Treurnicht decided that heady thoughts such as these could not just be ignored. In a letter to Grobler he requested him to qualify his statements in the next issue, as the idea of a single mixed government, with coloured and Indian ministers who had authority over whites, was 'totally unacceptable'.[6] From then on there was no turning back, whatever Treurnicht's intentions may have been. Perhaps he simply wanted to evade future accusations of accepting by omission arguments which had become the common coin of verligtheid, perhaps he merely aimed at storing up ammunition for the President's Council's report-back on power-sharing. His record makes it totally unlikely that he was seeking a pretext for a final split. But the force of events burst asunder the framework of provocation and retreat, of hitting and running, that 'Andries Wit

Handjies' had so carefully constructed for himself.

In his reply the editor of *Nat 80's* politely but firmly refused to retract, or even qualify. He was only reaffirming, he said, what had been Nationalist policy since the constitutional proposals of 1977. Today the whole incident looks like a concerted effort to flush out a shy creature which hated the light of day. It is possible that the original article in *Nat 80's* was not designed to force the issue. Grobler told two Nationalist journalists, who wrote an inside though highly partisan account of the drama, that he was surprised by the reaction.[7] And the journalists do not say in so many words that the confrontation was engineered. Yet a careful reading of their account suggests that Grobler was being disingenuous and that some comprehensive engineering had in fact been taking place.

The news that Treurnicht was at it again soon became common knowledge amongst Nationalist politicans and journalists. For a while nothing much happened. Speculation grew about just how the latest Treurnicht crisis was going to be resolved. The stage of fermentation was finally over when the three newspapers of Nasionale Pers, *Die Burger, Beeld* and *Rapport*, all committed supporters of the Prime Minister, made public Treurnicht's dissent, which they presented in dramatic terms as a questioning of the essence of party policy. This was after Alf Ries of *Die Burger* had gained P W Botha's own assurance that the Grobler article contained nothing but sound Nationalist doctrine. The evidence suggests, in short, that these newspapers, long hostile to Treurnicht's way of thinking and doing, had decided once and for all that the great back-room artiste should be made to commit himself in public on the Party line and power-sharing. It is of course unthinkable that they should have done so without P W Botha's encouragement. In brief, Treurnicht had been set up.

Events now gained momentum. The Nasionale Pers stories appeared on 20 and 21 February. When *Die Burger* quoted Treurnicht on Monday, 22 February, as casting doubt yet again on the ideological soundness of the *Nat 80's* editorial, which, it revealed, had been cleared before publication by Piet Koornhof, chairman of the National Party's Federal Information Service, P W Botha moved in for the final flushing-out. A special cabinet meeting took place the same day. Afterwards, agreement apparently having been reached, Botha issued a statement in which he endorsed 'power-sharing' explicitly, interpreted by him as 'co-responsibility' rather than as acceptance of a unitary state on PFP lines.

Semantic quibbling over 'power-sharing' aside, Botha had plainly given the lie to Treurnicht, who, perhaps surprisingly, but true to form, preferred to lie low for the moment.

An ordinary cabinet meeting took place the next day, but once more there were no public announcements. It seemed that differences had been resolved, at least temporarily, even if precariously. A caucus meeting was due on 24 February; after the two cabinet meetings it was possible that Botha did not expect an irrevocable split over power-sharing, however keen he may have been to bring the notorious fox into the open. As a Party loyalist, he quite likely believed that considerations of Nationalist unity would prevail in the end, especially as Treurnicht had maintained so low a profile at cabinet meetings. Bringing him into line would have been a victory in itself. Botha advanced the time of the caucus meeting so that he could leave for Namibia later that day for important discussions, which hardly suggests that he anticipated a split in the party.

The caucus was to resume a debate from the previous week over the international position of South Africa and its relation to domestic affairs. Treurnicht was one of the first to speak. He did not mince his words. Obviously prepared, he made a long and scathing attack on power-sharing, which he described as no more than Prog policy. He was followed by two of his most ardent supporters, Daan and Willie van der Merwe. After they had spoken there was no going back for the enemies of power-sharing. Both Van der Merwes made it plain that they utterly rejected the idea, even if they had to leave the National Party.

In the loaded atmosphere, P W Botha's own speech made no attempt to bridge gaping chasms. By now he had lost his temper, at the best of times no easy thing for him to control. His onslaught on the dissenters was vehement, expressing both his disgust with fellow-Nationalists prepared to break the Party, and his own willingness now to push the conflict to the limit. When Fanie Botha proposed a motion of unqualified support for the Prime Minister and his policies, a hundred MPs voted in favour, but twenty-two rejected it, twenty of them from the Transvaal. After more than three hours of acrimonious debate, the National Party had undergone its most serious split since 1948.

Only a minority of the 67 Transvaal MPs had broken ranks, but the Treurnicht supporters were optimistic, even exhilarated. They believed they had plenty of support among provincial councillors and constituency chairmen in the Transvaal. They had no doubt that they could muster a majority on the provincial head committee of 230, consisting of all Transvaal Members of Parliament and the Provincial Council, as well as representatives from the 76 constituencies and a number of co-opted members. If successful, the pay-offs would be immense. The National Party was a federation of highly autonomous provincial parties; control of the Transvaal would have meant that Treurnicht and his supporters could drive their opponents from the Party. The organisation of the Party and its large financial resources would fall into their hospitable laps.

Treurnicht, as Transvaal leader, called a meeting of the provincial head committee for 27 February, only three days after the split in the caucus. He did not consult his three deputy chairmen, Fanie Botha, F W de Klerk and Hendrik Schoeman, fellow-members of the cabinet but Botha loyalists to a man. De Klerk, who had to read the newspapers to find out about the meeting, later described it as 'premeditated confrontation, a planned strategy to hijack the National Party of the Transvaal'.[8]

So it was. But even before the meeting the *Financial Mail* reported that Botha followers discounted the chances of a Treurnicht victory, claiming that his support lacked depth and quality.[9] Even so, the loyalists canvassed the members of the head committee intensively. They estimated the day before the meeting that 134 would support the Prime Minister and 90 would back Treurnicht.

In the meantime Botha had decided, after discussions with his lieutenants in the Transvaal, to go to Pretoria instead of Cape Town upon leaving Windhoek. The idea was that Botha would attend the meeting of the head committee — if invited. It was a calculated risk. It could yield huge gains, or backfire disastrously.

The meeting lasted six hours. All the old issues were trotted out and given a beating; nothing new was said. When Hendrik Schoeman's nominee for an independent chairman was accepted at the start by 126 votes to 86 it appeared that the estimate by the loyalist leaders in the Transvaal of their support on the head committee was close to the mark. But what was probably decisive in pushing up their majority was the intervention of P W Botha himself. The announcement by Schoeman of Botha's presence in Pretoria was a disagreeable surprise to Treurnicht and his supporters, but they could not refuse to join in inviting the supreme leader of the National Party to attend the meeting.

Botha did so without fail, and spoke about party loyalty, about his own failure to agree with everything done by previous Prime Ministers, and about his willingness nonetheless to accept decisions once they had been taken. He reproached Treurnicht for never discussing any of his objections to the *Nat 80's* article with himself as Prime Minister. He criticised him for not disclosing his intention of raising his objections in the parliamentary caucus. It was a fine blend of an appeal to ingrained party loyalties and a hatchet-job on his long-standing enemy-in-chief. Botha was applauded when he sat down. The debate was to continue for some hours still, but the battle had effectively been won and lost.

Finally, the head committee voted on a motion proposed by F W de Klerk which expressed full support for the Prime Minister and his interpretation of party policy. One hundred and forty-one voted for it, 33 against. The right wing attempt to hijack the National Party in the Transvaal had failed.

Seventeen Members of Parliament eventually left the Party. Some of the original dissidents later decided to accept the Botha doctrine, partly perhaps out of genuine conviction, and partly no doubt because they knew it would be cold out there in the political wilderness.

On 20 March 1982, Treurnicht and his hard core formed the Conservative Party in Pretoria, amidst scenes of intense emotionalism and protestations of eternal commitment to the highest ideals of the volk. Treurnicht was succeeded as Transvaal leader of the National Party by the rising star, F W de Klerk. As for P W Botha, it was probably his finest hour. For once, he had managed to restrain his temper. His sense of timing, his sure touch, had turned what seemed a deeply unenviable situation into an unqualified triumph. But it was also the beginning of that unchecked autocratic sway over the National Party and the Government which was to yield bitter fruit for both Botha and South Africa in later years.

Crises are useful for students of the past. They represent the sudden crystallisation of latent possibilities and the joining of currents which have been flowing smoothly and separately. At least for a while there appears to be a break in the continuity of history. Understanding the 'true' significance of a crisis such as the Treurnicht defection helps us to a better grasp of the times.

A common interpretation of the Nationalist split is that it bore witness to the declining hold of ethnic ties on your average Afrikaner. Originally a close-knit ethnic community, the Afrikaners, the argument goes, have found themselves increasingly set apart from one another by the class divisions which economic change has introduced and intensified in their midst. More and more, Afrikaners have had their political views shaped by their class position and less by their ethnic identity. Economic development has softened the racial attitudes of the better-off, less economically threatened Afrikaners, while farmers and blue-collar workers have taken refuge in a more accentuated verkramptheid.

In a quite general sense, the argument contains some truth, but is not particularly illuminating. A changing class structure shaped by economic growth is a familiar historic animal, especially obtrusive since the arrival of what the textbooks still call the Industrial Revolution. The evidence of the last few centuries suggests that industrialisation is a genuine solvent, eroding traditional social structures and replacing them with class-based forms of stratification more compatible with economic development. There is no reason to think that Afrikaners, any more than other groups, are immune to the so-called logic of industrialism and the pressures it brings.

Yet the argument has been pushed much further, to the extent that the whole of the past is seen as a mere prelude to the era of class struggle which must accompany capitalist development. So for those who are eager to see South African history as only another illustration of the immense truths perceived by Karl Marx,

Afrikaner nationalism becomes essentially a class, rather than an ethnic, phenomenon.

It was a class alliance, in this perspective, which won power in 1948, 'a coalition dominated by the Afrikaner petite bourgeoisie, a handful of Afrikaner finance capitalists, and the Cape agricultural bourgeoisie, drawing votes from farmers, lower state officials, and the Afrikaans-speaking majority of the white working class'.[10] That was the original alliance, but by the late 1970s there was 'a new balance of class forces within Afrikanerdom', created by 'the racially exclusive regime of accumulation called apartheid'. Business interests had by now become dominant in the National Party. So the 1982 split suddenly becomes fraught with a deep class significance; P W Botha and Andries Treurnicht now emerge as warriors of the class struggle.

Botha faithfully represented the desires and interests of Afrikaner business, increasingly disaffected with the practices of 'petty apartheid'. Treurnicht embodied the fears and anxieties of Afrikaner workers and a once powerful but now embattled petty bourgeoisie. Previously, the accumulation of Afrikaner capital took place within an ethnic alliance based on the principle of Afrikaner unity. By the late 1970s it had become the interest of Afrikaner capitalists to ditch their former ethnic allies and to embrace instead their fellow-capitalists of the English-speaking variety.[11] As another writer of this persuasion put it: 'By the 1980s ... *volkseenheid* had become an obstacle both to the accumulation of capital by Afrikaner 'Hoggenheimers' and to the policies of the dominant faction in the NP itself. It was sacrificed on the altar of 'Total Strategy' and the unity of the capitalist class'.[12]

As usual, this kind of argument says both too much and too little. It says too much in reducing complex historical processes to the class struggle and the imperatives of accumulation, whether it is in the interests of a thrusting petty bourgeoisie or of a business class preoccupied with arriving. It also says too little, for the link between the conclusions and the facts on which they are supposedly based is often quite tenuous, suggesting the pervasive presence of a powerful will to believe.

A more sophisticated story would acknowledge the lesser role of Afrikaner ethnicity, but would point out that it became evident at least as early as 1958, after Verwoerd had become Prime Minister and shortly after the Nationalists had gained an electoral victory which suggested that for the first time a majority of the white population supported the Government. In an increasingly race-conscious world Afrikaner survival could not separate itself from white South African survival. Where Afrikaners accounted for 60 per cent of the white population, white domination still had to come down to Afrikaner domination. English-speaking whites were no less committed to white rule than were Afrikaners, however much they might claim to reject the less gentlemanly aspects of apartheid. If the continuation of their privileges meant finding redeeming features in their Nationalist rulers, then they were willing to do so. Over the years, and especially after the coming of the Republic in 1961, English-speaking white South Africans voted for the Nationalist Government in growing numbers. At first their support came in a trickle, but during the 1977 general election it turned into a veritable flood.

For the English-speakers it was an attractive deal. As junior partners in the white ethnic alliance they had endured periodic outbursts of Afrikaner chauvinism, as with the Oudtshoorn by-election of 1972 when the Nationalists were determined to show that the 1970 general election result had only been a temporary setback. But their privileges were guaranteed as long as the alliance held. Nationalist leaders became more conciliatory towards English-speakers, more diplomatic in the way in which they handled their sensitivities. English-speaking businessmen were no longer treated as enemies of the Afrikaner people, they ceased to be personified by the sinister caricature of Hoggenheimer.

Yet all this was simply about the most efficient methods of ensuring continued Afrikaner rule. 'Power-sharing' as understood by the Nationalists never meant anything else. It makes little sense to see the Nationalist split in terms of the newly-established dominance of business interests in the party and the need for unity of the capitalist class. If this was so it is odd that it was precisely during the 1980s that businessmen were increasingly outspoken in criticising the Government. The Nationalists could have been expected to have been more obliging in tailoring their policies to the needs of capitalists.

The truth seems to have been more straightforward. The Government was committed to continued white supremacy. 'Power-sharing' was its way of doing so in a world where old-fashioned *baasskap* was just no longer feasible. The Government did respond to capitalist interests, having come to realise the benefits of economic growth, but, as the protests of businessmen in the 1980s showed, it was always willing to flout these interests if they thought them incompatible with continued white rule. So the Nationalists went their separate ways in 1982, not because they quarrelled over the need for the white man to remain on top, but because many of them had no doubt that this was the one thing that power-sharing could never achieve.

CHAPTER EIGHTEEN

A New Constitution

The right wing of the National Party departed in February 1982 because it rejected 'power-sharing' – or so it claimed. Had the conservatives been content to stick around in the Party a bit longer they might have regretted an unseemly haste. The constitutional proposals the National Party produced later that year showed how little power it was willing to share.

In May 1982 the President's Council presented the report of its Constitutional Committee on constitutional reform. As the Government appointees on the Council included a smattering of coloureds and Indians, it had at least the semblance of a multiracial advisory body. There was, however, no doubt where the power, if that be the word, resided in the President's Council: most of its members had a record of devoted service to the National Party.

One of them was the chairman of the Council's Constitutional Committee, Denis Worrall, although his service record was of fairly recent memory. A former academic, with a training in political science, Worrall was one of the few English-speakers in the National Party, well aware of his scarcity value in that Afrikaner-dominated organisation. Worrall had an ambition he scarcely disdained to conceal, and was a loyal, if relatively new, Nationalist to boot: he could be relied upon to turn up with constitutional proposals which would be acceptable to the man who had reduced the National Party to subservience, P W Botha. He did, but in the end it was not enough to make him a winner in the struggle within the Party for power and preferment.

It was a measure of the National Party's determination to keep power to itself that the Constitutional Committee, in spite of containing several trained political scientists, could only bring forth proposals which had already been identified as intellectually and politically bankrupt. The previous year Worrall had referred, in a paper read to the Political Science Association of South Africa, to 'the extent to which consociational democratic theory rules the theoretical roost in political science in this country'.[1] It was upon this fashionable theory of consociation that the Constitutional Committee relied to give a veneer of academic sophistication and intellectual respectability to its proposals. That it did not even come close to doing so suggests that there are limits to the degree to which academic hypotheses can be called up for political ends.

The most prominent exponent of 'consociational democracy' was the Dutch political scientist, Arend Lijphart, who had derived from his own plural society a theory of the conditions for democracy in plural societies everywhere. The South African Government should have found the theory of consociation appealing: its starting-point was the acceptance of cultural diversity in ethnically divided societies. But it came with hitches which did not make it tailor-made for the Afrikaner-ruled South Africa the National Party was trying to preserve.

Consociation involved a coalition representing all the population groups in a country, each of which had a 'mutual veto' on government policy. It meant proportionality, both with respect to political representation and the distribution of office. Groups would have high levels of internal autonomy.[2]

As Samuel Huntington has argued, this was not consociational democracy, but consociational oligarchy.[3] It implied high degrees of trust between the leaders of the groups. It assumed that they could deliver the support of their followers. 'In essence it is an elite conspiracy to restrain political competition within and among communal groups ... Consociational arrangements tend to break down when increasing social mobilization undermines the authority of the leaders who negotiated the arrangements and new, younger leaders appear with more explicitly ethnic appeals'.

The preconditions for consociational institutions, flawed as they were in their oligarchic essence, hardly existed in South Africa, for reasons which Huntington made clear, as consociation 'implies autonomous communities with élites who can recognize the élites of the other communities as equals and who can occupy reasonably secure positions in established communal stratification systems'.

However, not only was the Republic no promising hunting-ground for consociationists, but the proposals were never seriously intended to adapt South African realities to professed theory. It became evident from the start where the Constitutional Committee was heading when it stated that 'a single political system in South Africa which includes blacks on an unqualified majoritarian or consociational basis could not function as a successful democracy in current or foreseeable circumstances'.[4] Africans would continue on their current road of independent homelands, to be linked to the rest of South Africa in a confederal framework. Once the principle of black exclusion had been established it was plain sailing, or so it must have seemed to Denis Worrall in his pursuit of the favour of his awe-inspiring leader.

The Committee recommended consociational room at the top for the coloureds and Indians, who would be represented in their own distinct ethnic chambers in a tricameral legislature. But the most important feature of the proposed new constitution was not the multiracial legislature. The Committee favoured an executive President with powers subject to scarcely any checks and balances. He would be elected for seven years by an electoral college of the legislature consisting of representatives chosen by the majority party in each chamber in the ratio of 50 whites, 25 coloureds and 13 Indians. As the whites had an overall majority and they would all come from the party in control of the white chamber, there was never the least danger that the executive President would not be an Afrikaner Nationalist. The proposals of the Constitutional Committee were in fact tailor-made for P W Botha.

In his book, *The Last White Parliament*, Frederik Van Zyl Slabbert, the leader of the Progressive Federal Party at the time and one of the most articulate critics of the constitutional manoeuvrings of the Nationalists, described the report of the Constitutional Committee as 'an embarrassment and an insult to anyone's intelligence. Apart from using some pseudo-consociational claptrap to justify black exclusion from the same constitution as whites, coloureds and Asians, it recommended virtually *carte blanche* powers to an executive President to create his own constitution for coloureds, Asians and whites'.[5] Slabbert attributes the half-baked nature of the report to Worrall's fear that the Committee on Economic Affairs of the President's Council would complete its own report first and deny him valuable publicity. Worrall did eventually manage to make it first past the post, but his rush into print did little to advance his upward mobility in the ruling party. He came up against a more seasoned campaigner in the person of Chris Heunis, Minister of Internal Affairs.

Heunis was a man from the Cape and a long-time confidant and comrade-in-arms of P W Botha, whom he had hopes of succeeding. He too would do all he could to produce constitutional bright ideas (or polish up old ones) which would gratify Botha. Heunis and Worrall clashed repeatedly, as ambitious men will who crowd one another's space. In the end Heunis won, although his amendments of Worrall's proposals arguably were no improvement and only made a bigger mockery of the consociational pretensions which were the new clothes worn by the emperor named Reform.

Worrall's mistake was in not properly acknowledging the role of the National Party. The executive President in his scheme would still depend on the Party for his election, but after that he would be on his own. He would appoint a premier and a cabinet of his choice, none of which would belong to any of the three chambers of Parliament. One commentator impressed by Worrall's 'cosmopolitan background' has described the proposal as reflecting his belief, and the Constitutional Committee's, that it was 'vital in order to establish a presidency with sufficient flexibility to embark on substantive reform without having to be narrowly bound to party prescription. A supra-national, supra-party presidency was essential to generate popular support in a divided society'.[6]

Botha, however, was the victim of ignobler impulses and more sectional concerns. He 'wanted both the benefit of a strong executive presidency *and* that of being the boss of the majority party in the most powerful component of the legislature. Botha had the National Party licked neatly into shape. He intended to keep that position by remaining a 'hands-on' party leader while enjoying the benefits of an executive presidency subject to few constitutional checks and balances and hardly any political ones at all, so long as he retained control of the majority party in the white component of the legislature'.[7] Botha also knew how to get there. Heunis, the loyal enforcer, would see to it that the chief would get what he wanted.

In short, so runs the argument, if the President was going to be a near-dictator anyway, then a non-partisan near-dictator would have been rather better than one constrained within the limits of Nationalist sectarianism. The only choice was between which variety of authoritarian reform P W Botha would opt for. Unfortunately, he succumbed to his own inadequacies. Botha became a professional organiser for the National Party in 1936 at the age of twenty. He had spent his whole career in the party; without it he could not conceive of a political future for himself or for South Africa. In spite of early difficulties in imposing his personality on the National Party, after the exit of the right wing in February 1982 Botha well and truly established his authority. Yet, even if he did reduce it to subservience to his domineering will, Botha would not set out on the road to reform without the party that had shaped his political being. It may have become a poor thing, but it was his own. By choosing to be an executive President who would also be an unashamed Nationalist partisan, he forfeited the chance of basing reform on a wider constituency than that commanded by his own party.

It is a persuasive argument, but it has its flaws, the most serious of which is that it ignores the fact that the whole purpose of the Constitutional Committee's report was to provide a camouflage for continued Nationalist rule. A free-floating executive Presidency above the constraints of party prescription was a figment of the imagination, at odds with the ultimate unwillingness of the National Party to do anything about power-sharing except talk about it. A document which could exclude blacks explicitly from its 'consociational' proposals had no business devising clever plans for a supposedly non-partisan executive President who could bring together a divided society. Finding a wider constituency was no doubt a long-overdue item on the agenda of the Nationalist Government, but the Worrall report could be no help in the search.

Heunis proceeded to amend the report closer to that which his exacting master demanded. It was simple. He hauled out the virtually forgotten and much ridiculed 1977 constitutional proposals, supposedly endorsed by the electorate in the 'America, no!' general election of that year, and began to prepare them for heavy duty.

The main difference was that five years before the proposals were for three racially segregated Parliaments, while there was now to be one Parliament, containing three racially segregated chambers. This was in line with the report of the Constitutional Committee. What was not in line was the executive placed squarely in the legislature. The Committee had recommended that the President appoint a premier and a cabinet from outside the legislature, beholden to him rather than to the political party. Under the Heunis dispensation there would be no premier (perhaps because he knew that two men from the Cape could not at the same time occupy the highest political positions in the land) and members of the cabinet could belong to the legislature, even if it was not essential. Predictably, however, ministers were to come mainly from the tricameral Parliament and, as it turned out, except at first for the majority leaders in the coloured and Indian chambers, they were exclusively members of the National Party. P W Botha at least would make no phoney claims about the non-partisan nature of his rule.

The carefully contrived procedures for electing the State President only confirmed that he would be a party chieftain first and above all. They came straight from the report of the Constitutional Committee, which provided for his election by representatives of the majority parties of the three chambers in the ratio of 50 white to 25 coloured to 13 Indian. As long as the Nationalists controlled the white chamber, the House of Assembly, and there was no prospect that they would not, they could sleep peacefully at night, secure in the knowledge that the supreme autocrat was one of their own.

Heunis did not abandon what Van Zyl Slabbert called the 'pseudo-consociational claptrap' of the Constitutional Committee's report. It found its main expression in the distinction between 'own' affairs and 'general' affairs. This was based on the notion of 'segmental autonomy', so dear to the consociationists. The distinction was invidious, assuming as it did that there were such separate things as white, coloured and Indian housing, education, welfare and so on. But it had to be made, for otherwise there would have been no point to the tricameral system. Once made, it would further entrench segregation as the only South African way of life. As for 'general' affairs, few could doubt that under the reformed dispensation members of the National Party would continue to see themselves and their leader as the best judges of their own interests and those of all other South Africans.

There was an obvious difficulty, or so it seemed: what would happen if the three chambers fell out with one another, or any of them with the President? In the era of segmental autonomy there could be no question of the white chamber or the President doing anything so crude as to coerce the coloured or Indian chambers. But it was really no difficulty. There was the President's Council, which would arbitrate disputes of this kind. As before, it would consist of nominated members, most of them Nationalists. There would be no awards for correctly predicting the outcome of any differences the Council was asked to settle.

The Nationalist caucus adopted the revised proposals at a special meeting on 5 June in Cape Town. The next month the federal congress of the National Party met in Bloemfontein to approve the proposals, or 'guidelines' as they were called. They were passed with scarcely a hitch, with only one intrepid, or foolhardy, dissenter amongst the more than 1 000 delegates who publicly expressed their enthusiasm for the statesmanship which was so surely taking them into the brave new South Africa of power-sharing. As for Denis Worrall, the official seal was placed on his defeat by the old pro, Chris Heunis, when he resigned from the President's Council to take up an appointment as South African Ambassador in Australia.

Outside the National Party the acclaim was less overwhelming. The newly-formed Conservative Party naturally wanted no part of dangerous schemes which would take the country straight to black rule and certain ruin. To the left of the Government the critics were more or less unanimous: the constitutional proposals were deeply flawed and no answer to the question of how South Africans of all races were to live together. But there the critics parted. Some rejected the proposals out of hand as the merest sleight of hand behind which Nationalist rule would be entrenched as deeply as ever: old wine in new bottles indeed. There were others who did not think much of the proposals either, but claimed they were at least 'a step in the right direction'. This was a fatally attractive argument, or rather slogan, for its intellectual content was limited. However inadequate as an exercise in logic, it was to persuade many supporters of the Progressive Federal Party that just this once they would be doing the correct thing by backing the Government.

The 'step in the right direction' devotees were impressed that for the first time in the history of South Africa people of colour would be able to take their place in Parliament. They admitted that as long as blacks were excluded a new constitution could not hope to offer a serious solution to the problem of how South Africans of all complexions were to get on with one another. However, they chose to believe that the arrival of coloureds and Indians in Parliament would be a harbinger. Once they were there, could it be doubted that Africans were not far behind? Then also there were the vociferous right-wingers in the Conservative Party and the Herstigte Nasionale Party. Their vehemence in denouncing what the Government was about suggested that its constitutional proposals could not be all bad. The Nationalists had to be coaxed into further travels down the road of reform, not discouraged by outright rejection. Arguments like these did the rounds amongst mildly left-of-centre voters who were doing their best to believe that 'real' change had at last come to stay.

The Progressive Federal Party found itself in a quandary. There was no way in which it could support the latest attempts to make South Africa safe for Nationalist rule, mere variations on the 1977 proposals which the PFP had then found so absurd. After all, nothing much had changed, except for the conversion of the three separate Parliaments into one tricameral Parliament. The proposals still entrenched ethnicity, the executive President would virtually possess the keys to heaven and hell, and the exclusion of blacks was in itself sufficient to damn the whole enterprise. As an exercise in the sophisticated type of oligarchic rule known as 'consociationism', the Worrall-Heunis hotchpotch failed badly. But the PFP could be in no doubt that the political mileage to be made out of rejection was insignificant. A survey of white political attitudes undertaken in May by Lawrence Schlemmer of the University of Natal showed that a clear policy of reform, or at least what appeared to be so, would bring distinct gains to the Nationalists, mainly at the expense of the PFP.[8] The Official Opposition was running the risk of alienating impressive chunks of its essentially urban, English-speaking constituency.

That was how the Nationalists figured it. In the months to come they would emphasise, when angling for English-speaking support, that here was only a first instalment, that reform would broaden out into an irresistible process that would eventually include blacks. To Opposition supporters who believed in 'reform' of some kind, 'power-sharing' of a sort, without actual black majority rule, it was all beguiling. Many found an additional reason: a 'No' vote could only play into the hands of the Conservative Party.

The Government had its 'guidelines' approved with acclamation by party congresses, but for once such a response was not the green light to press on regardless. Reform from above, if there had to be any at all, may have suited both the temperament of P W Botha and authoritarian habits ingrained after many years of Nationalist rule, but it was not possible to ignore completely the groups which were to be co-opted, the coloureds and the Indians. Of these it was the coloureds, accounting for ten per cent of the South African population, as against the three per cent of the Indians, who would be decisive. If they, or rather remotely credible representatives of theirs, could be persuaded to experiment with the new system then the Government would have the reason it needed to change the constitution.

It found its coloured allies, mainly due to the efforts of the indefatigable Chris Heunis, who in July had become Minister of Constitutional Development. (His successor as Minister of Internal Affairs was the recently chosen Transvaal leader of the National Party, F W de Klerk.) The Labour Party had been the Opposition on the Coloured Representative Council when it first met in 1969, but only because the Government chose to undo the victory of Labour in the coloured elections by appointing enough pro-Government hacks to put the losers into office. It did not last. In 1975 the Labour Party won comfortably and took over. Its purpose was to prove that the CRC was unworkable. It succeeded. A year later the Government dismissed the Chairman of the Council because of his party's failure to pass the budget. The Council became moribund; in 1980 it was dissolved by the Government after the Labour Party passed a motion to boycott its activities. These were the apparent hard-liners whom Heunis managed to win over to the notion that the constitutional proposals of 1982 were worth a try. It was all the more surprising as the Labour Party, after much dissension, had years before decided to reject the 1977 constitutional proposals, not after all so different from those in which it now discerned some merits.

The leader of the Labour Party was the Reverend Allan Hendrickse, a man with anti-apartheid credentials of his own. In the fateful year of 1976 he had been detained for two months. Hendrickse had led the resistance within the Labour Party to the 1977 constitutional proposals; when his views prevailed he became the leader of the party. It was under his leadership that the Labour Party refused to participate in the President's Council of 1981. Hendrickse had special cause for his resentment of apartheid. Under the Group Areas Act his family had years before been thrown out of their home in Uitenhage in the Eastern Cape. The memory still rankled.

Chris Heunis decided that winning over the Labour Party was not a totally lost cause. With endless patience he 'consulted' with potential allies who had every reason to be suspicious of a government which thirty-odd years before had spared few scruples to remove the coloured voters from the common roll. Heunis told them the familiar story that the new constitution would only be a beginning, that in the natural course of events further reforms would follow. He made no binding commitments. What counted was the fresh start: one improvement would follow another.

Heunis clearly had formidable powers of persuasion. At its 1983 congress in Zululand the Labour Party decided, after much debate, to participate in the new constitutional order — without preconditions. In the end it was not a contest: of the 300 delegates only nine voted against participation. The justifications for the decision were to become popular amongst coloureds and Indians who went for co-option. Participation would force the pace of change, the boycott strategy did not properly distinguish between those who wished to collaborate with the Government and those daring spirits who wanted to exploit official platforms for advancing the cause of liberation and democracy, and so forth.[9] The Prime Minister's willingness to break with his right wing the previous year must also have conveyed a message. The leadership of the Labour Party had evidently decided to accept P W Botha's embrace; the rationales were made to order. The decision came after an address to the congress by the Chief Minister of KwaZulu, Mangosuthu Buthelezi, who was also chairman of the South African Black Alliance, of which the Labour Party was a member. Ironically, the main burden of the speech by the guest of honour had been an appeal to the Party to reject the constitutional proposals as their acceptance would endanger black (that is non-white) unity.

The decision by the Labour Party seems to have been the tie-breaker. After that the Government knew that it could go ahead with proposals it had been dithering about, so widespread had been the scepticism about their workability. No credible Indian political organisation had yet stuck its neck out, nor was any to do so until the whites had finally committed themselves. The announcement of Hendrickse and his followers that they would fight apartheid from within the heart of the legislature was enough. P W Botha now had only the white political parties to cope with. He handled them like the professional politician that he was.

There was the Conservative Party. Nothing the Government could say or do would reconcile the right wing to the constitutional proposals. Possibly the conservatives did believe their own propaganda that the tricameral Parliament would only soften up the country for black rule. Treurnicht had been going around saying that the three Parliaments of the 1977 proposals did not involve power-sharing; it was the single Parliament with its three chambers that was decisive. He was compelled to adopt this line only because he had endorsed those early proposals as a deputy minister under Vorster. Detached observers might have found such talk no more than nit-picking: neither in 1977 nor in 1982 did the National Party exhibit the remotest intention of producing a constitution that would diminish its monopoly over power. However, what the right wing most detested about this new Parliament with its three chambers was its inclusiveness. In his political autobiography Van Zyl Slabbert has put it particularly well:

> This new Constitution co-opted people who were not white *into* the centre of political power, although still in segregated structures. It was a shift from *exclude*-divide-and-rule to *include*-divide-and-rule. This inclusion, rather than any clearly definable power-sharing, 'healthy' or otherwise, was what Treurnicht and company found so objectionable. And understandably so, because co-optive domination into the power centre was a shift away from NP orthodoxy.[10]

The right wing was irreconcilable, but P W Botha knew that he could pick up plenty of support from traditionally Opposition voters who believed in a vague kind of reform that would not endanger white rule. If they had reservations about the encompassing powers the State President would acquire, if some few were concerned about the exclusion of Africans, they would still swallow what was dished up to them because of that step in the right direction and because they did not want to be on the same side as the troglodytes of the right.

On 5 May 1983 Chris Heunis introduced the Republic of South Africa Constitution Bill in Parliament. In July a parliamentary select committee considered evidence on the Bill, which was then debated in August. The Conservative Party and the Progressive Federal Party repeated their by then familiar criticisms and the debate followed a predictable course, except perhaps for the fact that the Government became tired of the lengthy talk about so foregone a conclusion and guillotined further discussion at the end of August. The old-style ceremonial State President assented to the Republic of South Africa Constitution Act on 22 September.

Early in his administration P W Botha had committed himself to a referendum for whites on the introduction of a new constitution. On 24 August he announced that it would be held on 2 November 1983. The voters would have to answer Yes or No to the simple question whether they favoured the implementation of the Republic of South Africa Constitution Act as approved by Parliament. Simple it was, but ambiguous as well. There would be no way of knowing from the actual ballots themselves whether those who rejected the new constitution did so for right reasons or left reasons, whether they wished to keep coloureds and Indians out, or bring blacks in. It was hardly an accident. When Van Zyl Slabbert pointed out in Parliament that the clarity of the question could be improved, the 'Prime Minister smiled and licked his lips in that familiar way of his. I could see he knew I was in for a beating. It was the kind of political contest he relished'.[11]

The referendum campaign was marked by the Government's slick and unscrupulous use of the media. It placed huge advertisements in the Sunday papers about the era of racial co-operation and goodwill awaiting all South Africans under the new constitution. The South African Broadcasting Corporation had for many years, in violation of its charter as a public corporation, been a servile endorser of any policy the Government saw fit to pursue. It now plumbed still lower depths as it twisted the news in the Government interest and with no apparent shame made itself a tool of the propaganda purposes of the National Party.

The Afrikaans press naturally supported the constitution. What was surprising were the divisions within the Opposition press. Most were hostile, but some of the leading publications, notably the *Sunday Times* and the *Financial Mail*, came out with their reluctant support, for the familiar reasons that it was 'a flawed document but an improvement', and so forth.

Perhaps most astonishing was the response of the business community. It supported a Yes vote overwhelmingly for reasons which suggested that when the will to believe is strong enough, no arguments to the contrary will have the least effect. A group of businessmen set up a 'Reform Fund' which was supported by some of the country's most prominent capitalists, as well as professional people and academics. A typical rationalisation was that of the chairman of the Anglo American Corporation, Gavin Relly, who believed that 'acceptance of the government's reform proposals would be acknowledged as a minor positive movement along the road to open-mindedness'.[12] The Transvaal Chamber of Industries made its own contribution to open-mindedness by asserting that its call for a Yes vote was made in the belief that political rights for blacks would be the next step,[13] despite the Government's repeated insistence that the political future of Africans was not negotiable within a common parliament. Van Zyl Slabbert tells the classic story of the 'extremely influential businessman' who, when asked by Slabbert whether he had actually read the constitution, turned 'puce with irritation' and replied: 'I haven't read it, and have no intention of reading it. It's your problem to explain to me why I should not support it'.[14] Amongst the entrepreneurs there were the exceptions who could not bring themselves to support so illiberal a constitution; the most conspicuous was Relly's predecessor as Anglo chairman, the famous Harry Oppenheimer. Yet they were a minority. As far as businessmen were concerned, it was truly a time to send in the clowns.

The only question of any interest in the referendum campaign was how large the Yes vote would be. There could be little doubt that most of the naysayers would be conservatives. Earlier in the year the Conservative Party had mustered an impressive turn-out in two by-elections in the border regions of the Northern Transvaal. They were the result of a foolish challenge by the Minister of Manpower, Fanie Botha, to Andries Treurnicht and his fellow-Conservative, Tom Langley, to resign their constituencies, upon which he would resign his. They called his bluff and did resign. Treurnicht retained his seat with the greatest of ease. Botha, who was opposed by Langley, retained his as well, but only with extreme difficulty. If the by-elections demonstrated one thing it was that the famed Afrikaner unity had gone irrevocably. P W Botha could count on many of his fellow-Afrikaners to come out against his plans for reform. But there were still the English-speakers, many of them increasingly pro-Nationalist or PFP supporters who thought their party had this time got hold of the wrong end of the stick. The Nationalist marketing campaign set them in its sights, and was right on target.

On 2 November, 76 per cent of the electorate voted. The Yes vote came to 66 per cent of the total. More than half the PFP supporters appeared to have voted in favour. Only 10 per cent of the No voters came from the PFP.[15] What the Government had lost on the swings it had more than gained on the roundabouts – or so it seemed. P W Botha had every cause for gratification. He had gained an overwhelming mandate for a constitution which was designed to alter the South African power structure as little as possible – except that it would give him as executive President far wider powers than any Nationalist leader had ever had. What he and his euphoric supporters did not reckon on was the backlash. Botha thought that he could handle any backlash from the right wing. But what neither he nor his colleagues anticipated was the outrage of blacks who interpreted the new constitution as a definitive attempt to exclude them from a common South African society and relegate them to permanent second-class citizenship, or even to none at all. In a way the decks had been cleared. For this reason alone 1983 was a watershed in South African history.

CHAPTER NINETEEN

States of Emergency

For a time after the referendum of November 1983 everything seemed to be going just P W Botha's way. The reactionaries who had voted No came across as relics of a past which had been left behind decisively by a large majority of white South Africans. The left-of-centre types who had voted No could be dismissed patronisingly as doctrinaire liberals or worse, oblivious of the well-known fact that politics is the art of the possible; in their own way, the story went, they were as obsolete as Treurnicht, Jaap Marais and their crowd.

Abroad, amongst the Western countries which could still be counted as South Africa's friends, the result of the referendum had made some impression, perhaps in part the result of that will to believe which had been so evident recently in the support for the constitution by traditional PFP voters. The United States and British Governments took much the same line as the PFP hopefuls: the constitution may have been pretty inadequate in itself but stepping in the right direction was what counted. In a typical bromide, the British Foreign Secretary, Geoffrey Howe, expressed his hope that the result would facilitate progress towards constitutional arrangements 'acceptable to the people of South Africa as a whole'[1]; encouragement by a dead sheep was presumably better than none at all. It appeared as if South African whites were not totally beyond redemption, still capable of making choices that would save themselves and other South Africans.

Even those who had publicly opposed the new constitution in South Africa felt compelled to say kind things about it when abroad. In October 1984 Harry Oppenheimer told the Foreign Policy Association in New York, 'It is quite wrong to think of the new constitution as a sham, or as a device to entrench apartheid in a new form, even though the division of parliament into separate racially constituted chambers is a clumsy device which reflects the prejudices of the past'.[2]

P W Botha managed to pick up extra kudos in the West with a sub-continental breakthrough. This was the Nkomati Accord of March 1984. The Marxist regime of Samora Machel in Mozambique had for nine years been in heaps of trouble, partly the result of drought and its own economic incompetence, and partly the result of a guerrilla campaign of sabotage subsidised by the South African Government, which had both openly and covertly been 'destabilising' its more troublesome neighbours to discourage them from providing shelter to anti-apartheid 'liberation' movements. The Government of Mozambique had in fact been doing just that for ANC guerrillas, also known as 'terrorists' or 'freedom fighters' according to political taste. From Mozambique it had been relatively easy for ANC insurgents to cross over into Swaziland; once there operatives would issue them with instructions and stockpiled arms for use in South Africa itself.

By March 1984 the economy of Mozambique was on the verge of collapse as the South African-supported dissidents, who called themselves the Mozambique National Resistance, or Renamo (from the Portuguese acronym), had succeeded in removing substantial parts of the country from the writ of the official government. Samora Machel had little choice but to get South Africa to call off its running dogs, or at least to stop subsidising them. He requested United States intermediation, a disagreeable enough decision in itself. The Americans were working on their image in the region and were happy to oblige: on 16 March Machel found himself signing a mutual non-aggression pact with the detestable apartheid regime. Under the Nkomati Accord neither government would allow its territory to be used as a base for aggression against the other; there would be no more sanctuary and support for groups or individuals planning acts of violence against its neighbour. The ANC took it bitterly at first but later attempted unconvincingly to minimise the pain. The truth was that the liberation of the oppressed South African masses would now have to wait a while longer. But old habits die hard. Nkomati did not signal an end to destabilisation. Renamo continued to receive supplies from South Africa, although the top leadership's complicity is not clear. At the very least, there were elements in the military which did not consider themselves bound by the agreement and still believed that a more sympathetic regime than that of Samora Machel could be installed in Mozambique. The first iron fist was to show itself in other ways. In January 1986 the South African Government blockaded the land-locked Lesotho in a successful attempt to induce its government to restrict ANC activists. In May that year South African planes raided the capitals of Botswana, Zimbabwe and Zambia.

In the meantime, however, coming after the decision for 'reform' in the referendum four months before, Nkomati helped further to clean up the image of the South African Government. For a while its relations with Western countries appeared to be heading for a thaw. In Britain and the United States there were conservative administrations which saw no merit in the confrontational styles of their Labour and Democratic predecessors as a means of dismantling apartheid. The Reagan administration was experimenting with 'constructive engagement', a term coined by its Assistant Secretary of State for African Affairs, Chester Crocker; it amounted to an acceptance that there was a powerful reformist current within the South African Government, which would gather strength if encouraged by sympathetic Americans.

In June 1984, P W Botha went on a tour of Western Europe. The climate was as ripe as it had ever been for such a trip by a Nationalist head of government. Afterwards Botha saw it as a success, as did the general run of white South Africans, but the truth was that his reception by the leaders of other countries was not universally warm (in France the Government ignored his visit completely). Instead of telling Botha what a splendid job he was making of reform, European politicians, under pressure from anti-apartheid lobbies and the Third World, were more likely to ask when he was going to do something serious about political rights for blacks. It must have been disappointing for a man who had travelled some distance from an unyielding pro-apartheid past and had been prepared to do the unthinkable for a Nationalist leader, namely, split the Afrikaners. The message was clear: even at the best of times Western goodwill towards South Africa would depend on continued performance, in fact on the abandonment of white supremacy, as yet undreamt of by any Nationalist leader.

The signs of future trouble were already there. One was reflected in the Government's decision not to have coloured and Indian referendums on the introduction of a new constitution. Word had come back from those coloured and Indian politicians who were about to give the system a chance that their communities would not be so happy to be co-opted. They would pounce on a referendum as an opportunity to express their rejection of apartheid. Of course, the Government would provide them with no such godsend. The coloureds and the Indians would simply have to accept that the whites had also decided on their behalf the previous November. The Government may have believed, or hoped, that once the new constitution had demonstrated its virtues these communities would come to realise their mistake. For the time being, however, not even the most ardent fan of the constitution could claim that it had legitimacy amongst those who were supposed to benefit most from all this broadening-out of democracy.

The previous year there had been a more ominous development. The Government's intention of introducing a constitution which would exclude blacks reactivated the strategy of boycott. It was hardly new in South African history. Most spectacularly, there had been the PAC campaign against the pass laws in 1960 which ended in the massacre of Sharpeville. But the strategy, which took such forms as stayaways from work and the successful boycott of the South African Indian Council elections in November 1981, had never before been applied consistently on a country-wide basis. The formation of the United Democratic Front (UDF) ensured that boycott would become a central feature of the strategy of the extra-parliamentary resistance to apartheid. As Allan Boesak, a minister in the coloured branch of the Dutch Reformed Church, recently elected President of the World Alliance of Reformed Churches and a driving force in the creation of the UDF, announced, 'the politics of refusal needs a united front'.[3]

The UDF would take its stand on refusal. It would refuse to

regard the new system of black township councils as anything but an attempt to fob off blacks with a wretched apology for genuine political rights. Most of all, the UDF would refuse to give any legitimacy to the new constitutional dispensation.

The new anti-apartheid resistance movement was launched nationally on 20 August 1983, when 1 000 delegates representing close on 600 associations met at Mitchell's Plain near Cape Town. The UDF was not a political party but an umbrella organisation, linking together a disparate collection of trade unions, women's and youth organisations, civic associations, religious bodies and even sports clubs, more than 600 in all. The UDF was united not so much by what it stood for, apart from such unexceptionable items as 'a united democratic South Africa', as by what it rejected, which was P W Botha's vision of a streamlined oligarchic Republic under permanent Nationalist rule. The continuities between the UDF and the banned ANC were clear, however, as members of the Government were to repeat with monotonous insistence over the next few years. The UDF subscribed to that ambiguous, indeed muddled document, the Freedom Charter; the very existence of the UDF testified to the continued vitality of the ANC strategy of 'a broad alliance of class forces'.

The UDF grew rapidly, particularly in the highly politicised Eastern Cape and in the industrial centres of the Transvaal. It was weaker in the Western Cape and in Natal, where it faced strong rivals. As an amorphous collection of bodies representing a host of trends and opinions, the UDF had both the strengths and weaknesses of its structure. The absence of a centralised leadership made it less vulnerable to the familiar Nationalist technique of banning and imprisoning those at the top. Going for the head did not work so well when it had no noticeable effect on the body. But the width of the coalition also made the UDF a cumbersome body, subject to internal policy conflicts and difficult to mobilise on specific issues. Yet there was no doubt that the UDF became a power in the land and a thorn in the side of the Government. It was an early symptom of the rejection inspired by a constitution which was itself based on the rejection of blacks.

The UDF was not the only umbrella body. In June 1983 the National Forum was formed. It represented about 100 organisations and also called for a common black front against the constitutional proposals of the Government. But it represented a different strain in African nationalism. While the UDF was in a direct line of descent from the ANC, the National Forum stood for black consciousness and Africanism. Since the founding of the PAC in 1959 Africanism had discovered socialism. Like the South African Communist Party of 1922 with its slogan, 'Workers of the World, Fight and Unite for a White South Africa', the new Africanists wanted to have both their black exclusiveness and their class struggle. The main affiliate was the Azanian People's Organisation (AZAPO), which insisted on keeping whites out as they were incapable of identifying with the class interests of the suffering black workers, the 'driving force of the struggle'. The National Forum was strong on rhetoric, but never achieved the same mass base as the UDF. It was significant rather as one sign of the times: black resistance would reassert itself, and it would take diverse forms.

The new constitution called into being the UDF and the National Forum, but in a wider sense they were the outcome of a renewed mood of black self-assertion. The previous crises of the South African state had shown a cyclical pattern. After Sharpeville repression by the Government had been so effective and ferocious that for the remainder of the 1960s black protest was largely dormant. But it re-emerged at the beginning of the next decade and led straight to the still greater upheaval of Soweto. After 1976 official repression once more came into its own. The Black Consciousness movement was crippled. The banned ANC talked impressively of armed struggle, but its attempts to launch military operations in the Republic were pitiful in their ineffectiveness. Yet, slowly but unmistakeably, black protest surfaced again, but with a difference, for it took place across a far wider front than before. Soweto in 1976 had mainly been the outcome of student discontent; in the early 1980s black activism embraced a broader spectrum of the population, as the composition of the UDF was to show. It was reflected before 1983 in the development of the 'Charterist' movement, which professed to find in the Freedom Charter the outlines of a state which would embody both political and economic democracy. There were the post-Wiehahn black trade unions, gradually testing the waters before deciding how they would cope with the new industrial relations system which had suddenly arisen before them. In the absence of political rights for blacks it was virtually inevitable that they would not be simple 'economistic' organisations confining themselves to gaining more bread and butter for their members. In so far as they did pursue and achieve higher real wages it was bound to be at the expense of Africans who would have been willing to accept employment at lower rates of pay. Here was one of the legacies of neo-apartheid: the distinction between insiders and outsiders. It gave bargaining power to those who found themselves inside and made those outside more susceptible to unemployment. When recession apparently arrived to stay in the 1980s, economic polarisation amongst Africans increased: income inequalities between urban and rural blacks widened. The new black resistance would not have been possible without neo-apartheid.

Since 1970 the rate of economic growth in South Africa had been falling steadily. Until then the Republic's growth performance had compared well with those of similar industrialising countries elsewhere. Even in the first half of the 1970s the economy did well enough: gross domestic product increased at an average annual rate of four per cent. After that it became the captive of drought, political unrest, a falling gold price and the state of the world economy, which after 1979 took a turn for the worse following increases in the price of oil. Between 1975 and 1980, the average growth rate was less than three per cent; in the next five years it just exceeded one per cent.[4] Between 1979 and 1981 there had been a boom, mainly due to a remarkable rise in the gold price. But gold went down as abruptly as it had risen, domestic inflation continued to exceed an annual rate of ten per cent as a result of accommodating monetary policies and by mid-1984 the exchange rate was falling fast.

The conduct of economic policy in the first years of the 1980s indicated the confidence in the country's political future still prevalent at the top. In February 1982 the Reserve Bank lifted exchange controls on non-residents and abolished the dual exchange rate which had only allowed foreign investors to repatriate their funds at a discount. In 1984 the economy went through a consumer-led boom, partly the effect of a brief resurgence in the gold price between mid-1982 and early 1983 and the premature reflation of the economy by the authorities. Imports increased rapidly and the balance of payments deteriorated. One result of the mini-boom was that real output grew by 4,5 per cent during 1984. It was clear at the time that such a rate could not be sustained, the danger signs were there, but no one quite anticipated the storm to come.

The new tricameral Parliament first met in an extraordinary session in September 1984. In August there had been elections for the coloured House of Representatives and the Indian House of Delegates. They were an object lesson in how boycotts could deprive the new multiracial deal of legitimacy. In the coloured elections the Labour Party of Allan Hendrickse won all but three of the 84 seats contested. But there was scant room for euphoria. Only 32 per cent of registered coloured voters went to the ballot-box; the turnout was lower than in the 1969 and 1975 elections for the Coloured Representative Council. The Indian results were even less encouraging. The elections themselves were closely contested and were won by the National People's Party with 23 seats to the 18 of Solidarity. The trouble was that hardly anyone bothered to vote: a mere 20 per cent of registered voters made it to the polls. In both cases it came to an even lower percentage of those actually eligible to vote.

The Government was disappointed and blamed it on intimidation, inexperience, and lack of information on electoral procedures. Nothing could disguise the fact that coloured and Indian voters could hardly care less about the system which was supposed to bring them so much. The leader of the Progressive Federal Party at the time, Van Zyl Slabbert, later wrote that he did not regard the low polls as 'entirely a reflection of the support for the United Democratic Front, but it certainly could claim the propaganda victory; whereas those who were elected were on the defensive and laboured under credibility crises right from the outset. They certainly did not look like warriors who were going to dismantle apartheid from the inside, and who had the complete confidence of their respective communities'.[5]

The new Parliament met in September for only a few days. P W Botha became executive President after he had been unanimously elected by the electoral college in which only the majority parties of the three Houses were represented; the National Party had an unassailable overall majority. After a short debate in the white House of Assembly on the state of the economy, the tricameral Parliament adjourned until January 1985 for its first full session. By then South Africa had entered the deepest crisis of its history.

It began with rent increases. In August 1983 a new system of local government for Africans came into existence. Town councils with specific powers of their own replaced the community councils which only possessed powers delegated to them; it was part of the Government's plan to upgrade the conditions of urban life for African insiders without having to give them representation in the central Parliament. At its founding meeting the UDF rejected the whole scheme as a poor surrogate for real political rights. When the elections to the councils took place in November and December the overall percentage poll was barely 20 per cent, compared with the 30 per cent for the community councils in 1978. No doubt there was plenty of intimidation by 'agitators', as the Government was always quick to allege when black support of its policies was not forthcoming. It remained implausible that the wretched turnout was the result of strong-arm methods rather than of genuine black rejection of what was seen as another apartheid institution. The town councils enjoyed as little legitimacy as the coloured and Indian Houses of the new Parliament.

They also differed in at least one important respect from their white counterparts. They did not have comparable sources of revenue. House rentals would still go to the administration boards which previously had performed most of the functions now taken over by the town councils. But the councils were expected to be self-sufficient, which left them with little choice. A year after their creation the town councils in the Vaal Triangle south of Johannesburg increased their service charges.

Appropriately enough, it was in the East Rand township of Sharpeville that the trouble began. A crowd gathered outside the house of the Deputy Mayor of nearby Lekoa on 3 September 1984. His town council had just raised their rents and the protesters held him responsible. The police were there originally, but left after they dispersed the crowd – which came back. The protesters proceeded to murder the unfortunate town councillor in circumstances which were to become shockingly familiar over the next two years: according to the court record of the trial of the six people later convicted of murder, they were accomplices in pouring petrol over him and burning him alive.

After that the unrest and violence spread. There were more protests. On the same day an estimated 60 per cent of workers and school children in the Vaal Triangle stayed at home. Twenty-six people lost their lives.[6] Other regions became caught up in the violence. It went to the East Rand and then to the Eastern Cape. It reached the Western Cape, Durban and Pretoria. Thousands were arrested and detained. In Operation Palmiet in October the army entered three black townships on the East Rand *en masse* to reinforce the police. In 1985 troops numbering 35 000 were to find themselves 'restoring law and order' to the townships as the Government turned to straightforward repression.

The initial outbreaks of protest and violence were spontaneous. Many of their later expressions bordered on the anarchic as protesters abandoned all restraint and indulged themselves in orgies of brutality and destruction of property. But there was also method in what seemed to be madness as self-styled 'revolutionaries' dedicated themselves to ending the local council system and making the townships 'ungovernable'.

It was then that the 'comrades' came into their own. These were youths, brutalised after years of family dislocation and the violence endemic in township existence, who believed that the revolution was at hand and that they were the chosen ones who would end white rule. They frequently dominated the street committees which enforced rent, consumer and school boycotts. The 'comrades' made black-on-black violence an everyday occurrence. They set up 'people's courts' to try informers and black policemen and councillors, 'collaborators' all. Under the rule of the 'comrades' enforcement by atrocity became commonplace: victims of the 'necklace' were murdered by having a rubber tyre placed around their necks, which was then filled with petrol and set alight. Black councillors resigned in droves.

The Government blamed much of the 'unrest' on the UDF, which it claimed was acting as a front for the ANC. It did not admit that the UDF was expressing popular grievances; rather, it was through intimidation that the Front brought out the masses. The deep involvement of the UDF and its affiliates in the events of the time was undeniable, but there the validity of the official interpretation ends. On 5 and 6 November the UDF, in collaboration with student groups and, significantly, the Federation of South African Trade Unions (FOSATU) organised a stayaway in the Pretoria-Witwatersrand-Vereeniging (PWV) area which brought business to a virtual stop. It was a response to Operation Palmiet and 300 000 to 500 000 workers did not go to work. Intimidation there may have been, but the widespread participation suggests that its roots in popular grievances went deep. The UDF was not masterminding events. Instead it was riding a wave which it hoped would overwhelm the apartheid regime. When the Government announced a state of emergency in July 1985 and proceeded to arrest a legion of UDF officials and activists, the wave swept on, regardless of so puny an attempt to hurl it back.

Even less did the ANC guide the violent events which began in September 1984. It had for years been talking about the armed struggle, but little had come of it. Between 1976 and 1986 the frequency of bombings, raids and political assassinations by the ANC rose more than 60 times. However, as one sympathetic commentator has written: 'Umkhonto we Sizwe had demonstrated an unmistakable ability to strike at the economy's weak spots, but only infrequently and with inconsistent success.' The truth was that 'the ANC's war, even as it expanded, remained low in intensity'.[7] In May 1983 the ANC had succeeded in exploding a car bomb near Air Force headquarters in Pretoria; nineteen died, mostly civilians, and 217 were injured. It was a spectacular act of terrorism, but also an isolated event. There was little sign that it shook the morale of the Government or of the white population. After Nkomati the ANC found it still more difficult to establish bases in states neighbouring South Africa: sympathy for the cause of liberation would not overrule fear of a reprisal like that which followed the Pretoria explosion, when the Government attacked alleged ANC bases near the Mozambican capital of Maputo.

Yet the ANC benefited hugely from the turbulence. Since 1960 it had been cut off from mass mobilisation, but had retained considerable support in the black community. The Government portrayal of the events as orchestrated by the ANC and its Communist allies now did wonders for their prestige in the townships. The truth, however, was that the ANC had no control over the actions of the 'comrades' but made a pretence of being in charge, even to the extent of making light of the use of the 'necklace' as one of those unfortunate things which happen during times of war. Both the Red Flag and the flag of the ANC featured prominently at public gatherings. The ANC came to symbolise black resistance, however small its own contribution was to making the townships ungovernable.

The violence took the Government by surprise. In its self-confident mood after the referendum of November 1983 it had not banned the UDF, in spite of the undisguised ANC sympathies and boycott strategy of that disparate organisation. Nor would it have been good international public relations to be too hard on the UDF, particularly as the Government was basking in rare overseas praise for being so enterprising about reform. For a time it seemed as if the new constitution would ring in the new tolerance. The trouble was that the radical opposition, both right and left, was liable to mistake goodwill for weakness. And it did.

There was of course nothing to be done about the white ultra-right. The Conservative Party, the Herstigte Nasionale Party and the Afrikaner Weerstandsbeweging (Afrikaner Resistance Movement), a neo-fascist military-type outfit which rejected parliamentary politics, knew that all the upheaval which had suddenly descended on the country was the result of P W Botha's betrayal of the Afrikaner's right to rule his own country. It could not have happened under Dr Verwoerd, who knew how to keep order.

The invective and vituperation from the right meant that, for this reason alone, the Government would soon reach the limits of its new-found tolerance of left wing dissent. But for P W Botha acting tough and being tough was what came naturally. He was not the man who would let the country go to rack and ruin because of a total onslaught by left wing radicals, domestic and foreign, on order and stability, which after all were the preconditions for reform.

At first Botha's response was uncharacteristically restrained. One way in which the crisis differed from those of 1960 and 1976 was in the real possibility of concerted international action against South Africa. Businessmen were becoming increasingly agitated over the threat of sanctions. Even in the United States the Reagan administration, never before much concerned with the awfulness of apartheid, but now under pressure from sanctioneers in Congress, felt compelled to say a few critical words about the forced removal of blacks from their communities and about detention without trial. More confirmation of global involvement in the fate of South Africa came in November 1984 when the Bishop of Johannesburg, Desmond Tutu, was awarded the Nobel Prize for Peace. Of all the Nobel Prizes the one for peace has been the least worth taking seriously and the most unrelated to recognisable achievement: Malcolm Muggeridge once observed that most of its recipients had been buffoons. Compared with some of his predecessors Tutu was perhaps not an unworthy choice. Whatever the merits of the decision, the award to an exceedingly vocal black South African, an enthusiastic sanctioneer himself once he realised that the Nationalist Government would not act against so high-profile an activist against apartheid, conveyed an unmistakable message to all the whites of the Republic.

In January 1985 P W Botha opened the first full session of the tricameral Parliament and spoke of further reforms: a non-statutory forum for blacks where they could discuss constitutional issues with the Government, possible freehold rights for Africans in urban areas and return of citizenship to blacks who had lost it when their homelands were declared independent, less rigid enforcement of influx control and the removal of blacks from 'white' areas. It earned him praise in the West and from white liberals in South Africa. There was none at all where it counted most: from the militant black organisations which had committed themselves to a strategy of boycott. They had their own knee-jerk reactions. A spokesman for the UDF repeated the well-known proposition that 'only a constitution based on the will and full participation of all South Africans can be the basis for lasting peace'. AZAPO demanded the 'repossession of the land'. Even Mangosuthu Buthelezi of KwaZulu and leader of Inkatha, the Zulu ethnic movement, long at odds with the boycotters over his willingness to turn apartheid institutions to his own purpose, declared that participation in the non-statutory forum would be 'like co-operating in our own political suicide'.[8]

The violence showed no sign of subsiding. From January 1985 it began to spread from the metropolitan areas to the countryside, stretching the ability of the security forces to handle the situation. Black-on-black violence became increasingly prevalent as the 'comrades' made the necklace the latest addition to the South African way of life. Much later, from June 1986 onwards, a new trend would emerge as black township vigilantes, representing an older generation and often instigated by the security forces, turned on the youthful torturers and subjected them to a campaign of counter-terror. As resistance grew the South African police, never noted for its squeamish ways when it came to suppressing black dissent, turned more unpleasant. On 21 March, the 25th anniversary of the Sharpeville massacre, the police killed twenty protesters at the Langa township at Uitenhage in the Eastern Cape. Between 1 September 1984 and 24 January 1986 the security forces killed 628 persons in unrest-related incidents and wounded 2 229.[9] Political funerals became a focal point of resistance: huge crowds gathered for the burials of victims of the security forces. These gatherings led to more violence and more deaths; political funerals acquired an in-built capacity for self-generation. Nor were participants in the tricameral Parliament exempt, as members of the coloured House of Representatives discovered when they were at the receiving end of grenade attacks by a group which called itself the 'SA Suicide Squad'.

On 21 July 1985 P W Botha declared a state of emergency in 36 magisterial districts in which rioting had continued for nine months. Most of them were in the Eastern Cape and the PWV region of the Transvaal. More than 1 200 activists were detained. From then on there would be restrictions on the freedom and ease with which funerals could be transformed into occasions for anti-Government demonstrations. The security forces could arrest without a warrant and at any time search any person, premises or vehicle.

The state of emergency had been a long time coming, inordinately so by the record of times past. The Government had been over-confident of its control of the internal situation. It never dreamt that the resentment by blacks of a constitution which was designed to exclude them in perpetuity could be so intense. For years members of the Government were kept in thrall by the 'agitator' theory of black unrest, which held that Africans were basically happy souls, by no means averse to the separate freedoms the Nationalists had designed for them – until they were worked upon by left wing troublemakers. It was difficult to admit so massive a miscalculation. There were also the countries of the West to think about, several of which had been appreciative of recent forward trends in South Africa. Excessive firmness in dealing with local dissent could bring back the bad old days of misunderstanding and distrust. Pressures for sanctions would inevitably rise, foreign firms and banks would face renewed demands to get out of South Africa.

Yet the state of emergency could not be delayed for ever. The radical opposition had made miscalculations of its own. The Government's reluctance to react with quite the heavy hand of before led to elementary errors, based on the premature conclusion that finally the white supremacists were on the run. The unrest and violence seen on television screens over the world created the unmistakable impression that at last the South African Revolution was at hand. In June 1985 Radio Freedom of the ANC summarised the latest state of wishful thinking on the left: 'The upsurges that are taking place in our towns, civic organisations, Asian communities, are acting in unison as one sort of broad formation which at the time is organised under the United Democratic Front. There can be no doubt these uprisings have shaken the very roots of the white minority domination in our country.'[10]

At first the state of emergency and the many arrests hardly affected the intensity of civil resistance. The theory that the UDF was behind it all was refuted when the uprising continued, apparently oblivious of the removal of so large a number of the supposed masterminds behind it. On 26 October the emergency regulations were extended to another eight magisterial districts in and around Cape Town. It took time, but it worked. Security forces which are prepared to be sufficiently ruthless can usually go far in achieving their immediate ends. By March 1986 they had succeeded in imposing a precarious peace. Violent mass action seemed at last to be part of history. On 7 March the Government lifted the emergency in all the districts where it had applied.

Whatever the state of emergency was to achieve, it had to come at a price. The most obvious and immediate cost was economic. During the euphoria of the early 1980s South African borrowers, private and public, had thought nothing of incurring foreign debt, of which a large proportion was short-term: the current account of the balance of payments was now in deficit, domestic interest rates were rising, those overseas were falling. By July 1985 the Republic had a short-term debt of $14-billion, nearly 60 per cent of its total foreign debt. Its foreign exchange and gold reserves and its trade surplus for 1985 were not enough to cover it. Nor was the economy in good shape. Inflation was high, profits and dividends were down. In 1984 the rand depreciated by more than 40 per cent against the American dollar.

For economic reasons alone foreign capital could have been expected to look for more hospitable shores. The declaration of the state of emergency now provided one extra incentive for overseas lenders to take their short-term loans and leave. That was just what the Chase Manhattan Bank in New York decided to do at the end of July when it refused to renew its short-term credits to South African borrowers. It would also freeze all unused lines of credit. Chase Manhattan later claimed that its decision was based on economic considerations, which only made sense. The chairman of the bank, Willard Butcher, ingenuously told Gerhard de Kock, Governor of the South African Reserve Bank, that it was part of the routine monthly revision of credit risks around the world. [11] But clearly political concerns concentrated Butcher's mind. He was after all the head of a world-wide enterprise and South Africa accounted for less than half a per cent of its total assets of $87-billion. Chase Manhattan's decision was widely and correctly seen as an ultimate expression of no-confidence in the South African economy. Other American banks trampled over one another in their frenzy to get their money out in time. During August they withdrew a tenth of their loans to South Africa, totalling about $400-million.[12]

It was against this background of accelerating economic decline and global hostility that P W Botha crossed a self-admitted

Rubicon and made a sorry mess of it. Botha was due to address the Natal congress of the National Party on 15 August 1985. Word had got around to the wide world that great things were in the making. The Minister of Foreign Affairs, Pik Botha, had been in Europe, raising expectations about the major reforms his master would announce. The Nationalist press had been assiduous in encouraging hopes about daring initiatives. There was speculation that at last Nelson Mandela would be released, that the Government would enter into 'real' negotiations about the country's future and that genuine power-sharing would begin. No one who knew anything about Botha's past and that of Nationalist rule could have given much credence to rumours such as these. Some of the better-informed or more pessimistic believed that the most likely outcome of such exaggerated expectations from so unpromising an event would be a sharp fall in the rand. They were right.

The plain truth was that Botha blew it. No South African leader had ever had so large an audience, for his address to the Natal congress of his party had become a global media event. In front of millions of television viewers Botha chose to deliver the kind of defiant xenophobic speech guaranteed to stir the locals, and equally guaranteed to make foreigners wonder what was happening in South Africa if boors like these were in charge.

Botha began promisingly enough when he repeated his reformist resolve: 'My Government and I are determined to continue with our reform programme ... I believe that we are today crossing the Rubicon. There can be no turning back'. But he soon switched to what he found more congenial: telling off interfering foreigners and drawing the lines beyond which reform would not go. He harped on one of his favourite themes, that South Africa was a country of minorities: 'We are not prepared to accept the antiquated, simplistic and racist approach that South Africa consists of a white minority and a black majority'. Nor was he prepared 'to lead white South Africans and other minority groups on a road to abdication and suicide.'[13]

Botha made none of the spectacular announcements his Foreign Minister had led credulous foreigners to expect. He made it clear once more that blacks would not participate in the same political system as other South Africans; no one could in truth complain that he had ever, at any time, given a different impression. It was a bombastic, posturing performance in which Botha outdid himself in shaking his notorious finger at critics of his way of doing things. The Rubicon effort went down well with rank-and-file Nationalists, who had long been weary of know-alls from abroad telling them that one man one vote was the only and obvious answer to the political problems of South Africa. International financial markets did not respond so appreciatively. The following day the rand fell even lower against the US dollar, from 44,5 cents to 38,5. By 28 August it had gone down to below 35 cents. The capital flight continued, share prices fell, and the Johannesburg Stock Exchange closed for three days. The Government reintroduced a dual exchange rate and imposed a four-month moratorium on the repayment of some kinds of foreign debt. It was a memorable lesson in how not to cross a river.

After the first state of emergency and the Rubicon speech, the affairs of South Africa became irresistibly, unprecedentally, the concern of the rest of the world, which watched the daily scenes of carnage crossing its television screens and grew convinced that here was another Lebanon in the making. The pressures on Western governments to impose sanctions against South Africa became so intense that even the most reluctant felt compelled to make some token gestures, always far short of what the extreme sanctioneers were demanding. Apartheid became the great moral issue of the time, uniquely evil, the epitome of man's inhumanity to man. Not surprisingly, all this international outrage resulted in a veritable orgy of hypocrisy, self-righteousness and opportunism.

The growing demand for sanctions against South Africa had, in one sense, a simple cause. It was a response to the felt need that the repressiveness of the apartheid regime, so effectively publicised by the international media, could not simply be allowed to pass noticed but unchecked. Standing by in horror was not enough; something had to be done, most obviously by hitting the apartheid regime where it hurt. South Africa had a small open economy, heavily involved with the rest of the world through trade and investment. It seemed fairly obvious that if the economy could be crippled then the capacity of the Government to continue with its racist policies would suffer. Official sanctions were necessary to supplement the 'private' sanctions imposed by Chase Manhattan and other American banks after the declaration of the state of emergency. Moreover, businessmen, in the radical lexicon, prime beneficiaries from and accomplices in apartheid, would impel the Government to change its ways. This was the simplest rationale for sanctions. Inevitably, other reasons, less overt but perhaps more compelling, also entered into the demand for tough action. There was a country like Australia, one of the foremost in its expression of moral outrage. But it was also a leading exporter of coal, as was South Africa: the elimination of a formidable competitor would do the Australian economy no harm. Then there were the anti-apartheid organisations which had acquired a vested interest in combating the devil: plenty of publicity and high returns could go to those which best packaged moral indignation.

Yet the record of the past did not suggest that when sanctions were applied they were especially effective. There were difficulties in collective action: persuading countries with disparate interests to combine against the chosen victim did not come easily. The prospect of profits would always be a lure for individual sanctions-busters, indifferent to the wider moral issues. And what the outcome of sanctions would be was guesswork. Perhaps they would cause the apartheid regime to realise its own folly. But perhaps they would result in a right wing backlash and an intensification of racist oppression. It was of course possible to justify such a result: things had to get worse before they got better; eventually black suffering would lead to a vast upsurge of the people, major Western countries would be forced to intervene, and the hated regime would go.

One conclusion seems fairly obvious. The most ardent supporters of sanctions had little idea of the effects they would have. They had their good intentions and their determination to 'do something'. Feeling good, bearing witness, these things were important. The American economist and Nobel Prize winner, George Stigler, wrote aptly of those colleges in the United States which wished to unburden themselves of their investments in companies dealing in South Africa: 'There are at least 1 000 pages of appeal to racial justice for each paragraph of analysis as to whether disinvestment would affect the amount of foreign investment in

South Africa, and, if it did, whether the condition of blacks in South Africa would be improved or injured'.[14] Such people were not especially interested in how ordinary impoverished Africans in the street felt about being without jobs in a broken-down economy. A man like Desmond Tutu had after all assured them that blacks would be willing to suffer for the cause. But, as Alan Paton wrote in May 1985 about Africans who supported disinvestment by foreign firms: 'Most of these black South Africans will not be the ones to suffer hunger and thirst. Many of them are sophisticated, highly educated, safely placed. I also know sophisticated and highly educated black men and women who will have nothing to do with disinvestment. I choose to associate myself with them'.[15]

There was a decisive reason why the campaign for sanctions and disinvestment could only be wasted effort – if indeed it was apartheid which was supposed to be destroyed. The campaign was aimed at dismantling the South African economy, yet if there had been one enemy of apartheid over the years and which had put an end to the Verwoerdian pipe-dream, it was economic growth. To repeat the words of that other Nobel Prize winning economist, Arthur Lewis, 'the most effective destroyer of discrimination is fast economic growth'. It was the expansion of the economy which had ended nearly all legalised job reservation, had allowed increasing numbers of Africans to become skilled and semi-skilled workers, and had brought them the bargaining power that was on display by trade unions that could not be ignored. Of this the sanctions campaigners knew nothing, or preferred not to. The erosion of apartheid was mainly the result of trends operating within South African society. The world outside could have hastened those trends, but, with the conspicuous exception of the British Prime Minister, Margaret Thatcher, who had the astonishing merit of discerning the obvious and was rewarded with vulgar abuse from most of her Commonwealth colleagues, it did its best to reverse them. Of the official variety of sanctions, it was the arms embargo which was most effective. Denied the most up-to-date military equipment, South African forces began to experience tougher times on the sub-continent, as their failure to take the Angolan stronghold of Cuito Cuanavale in 1988 showed.

However, it was unofficial sanctions which were most effective, and they came mostly at the beginning. The capital flight induced by Chase Manhattan's 'routine revision of country risk' had devastating consequences. The Government managed to secure a rescheduling of debt repayments, on terms favourable to itself. The banks would extend their loans for another year, to the end of March 1987. They would also receive token repayments of the principal. Given the alternative of default, the banks had little choice but to ignore the urgings of the anti-apartheid lobbies and to accept. Yet from then on the Republic's economic growth would be a captive to debt repayments, to the need for a substantial surplus on the balance of payments. Also, the rand had virtually collapsed and investors abroad would find many other economies worthier of their confidence.

Favourable terms do not come without cost, especially in the world of anti-apartheid. The Government had to reassure the frustrated creditors that important reforms were just round the corner. At the end of January 1986 P W Botha announced that influx control would be abolished, freehold rights extended to Africans in the 'white' areas and South African citizenship restored to those who had been deprived of it with the independence of their homelands. It was a different Botha from the one responsible for the public relations disaster of 15 August the previous year. Had he spoken differently at the time, it is probable that the country and the economy would have been in better shape at the beginning of 1986. It is true that influx control had already collapsed under the weight of blacks fleeing impoverished rural areas which could not sustain them, but this was an official abandonment of what had been regarded as one of the keystones of apartheid. It could not be shrugged off easily as 'cosmetic'. Yet Botha had missed his chance. The announcements, which had been in the pipe-line for some time, looked as if they were grudging concessions to pressure. To his radical opponents only one response made sense: increase the pressure. Negotiation and compromise amounted to laughable attempts to modernise a system which needed eradication. World uproar over events in South Africa raised expectations that the Nationalist Government would have to crack eventually. The pain simply had to be severe enough.

P W Botha was so charmless an individual, so singularly unlovable in his authoritarianism, vindictiveness and intolerance, that it is difficult to be objective about his performance as a reformer. Yet the effort must be made. An essential precondition for his type of reform was a willingness to break with his Afrikaner constituency. During his time of power, Afrikaner unity ceased to exist because Botha brought or accepted changes which many of his own people rejected. Most important was the new dispensation in the field of labour, the acceptance of blacks as participants, however uncomfortable, in a transformed system of industrial relations. The new constitution was naturally quite inadequate as an answer to the question of how political power should be exercised in a reformed South Africa. Its basic flaw was obvious: it excluded Africans, who resented it bitterly, and included coloureds and Indians on a purely ethnic basis. But even the tricameral Parliament had redeeming features. Decision-making at the centre was, in principle if not in practice, no longer an exclusively white preserve. It provided the opportunity of getting rid of some of the most offensive, if not most important, apartheid laws: the Mixed Marriages Act and Section 16 of the Immorality Act were scrapped in the first full session of the new Parliament. That too came in for abuse by the ultra-right as a betrayal of white civilisation. Botha continued the trend of spending more on black education. Unfortunately it came at a time of slow growth and school boycotts – as the slogan went: Liberation Now, Education Later. Thousands of undereducated young Africans came onto the labour market every year and found that the future held even less than before.

In September 1983 P W Botha told a congress of accountants, 'My experience is that the reformer is never very popular till after his death'.[16] In those days he was still riding relatively high; the real Time of Troubles would only start a year later. If Botha's later experiences deepened a powerful sense of grievance it is easy to understand, and perhaps even to sympathise. For a Nationalist leader he had come a longer way than any of his predecessors. Much of what he had done was an adaptation to circumstance, which could not be forever delayed. Yet his predecessor, Vorster, had in his later years made of inertia a way of life. Botha at least realised that there was adapting or dying to be done, and acted on his conviction, willing, as ever, to make enemies. When friends had to be made he was less adept.

Yet his limitations as a reformer are glaring and have often been dwelt upon, with varying degrees of relish. He saw South Africa as a country of minorities, of distinct ethnic groups, each with its own culture and sense of identity which set it apart from others. It was a convenient belief and full of its own inconsistencies. If the country was full of separate black 'nations', why were the whites supposed to be one nation? There was at least as good a case for the separate development of the Afrikaners and the English-speakers. But the drift of the contention was clear: improvement would have to be on an ethnic basis. Group areas and separate education would in his book be abiding features of a reformed South Africa. Botha was willing to condemn discrimination but not segregation. For him they were utterly different things, a distinction his critics found exceedingly difficult to grasp. Botha was in fact committed to the doctrine of 'separate but equal', condemned long before by the United States Supreme Court as involving inherent inequality. Ironically, the early Nationalist Government of Malan had attempted to justify separate amenities for the races as long they were equal, but had then abandoned even this bit of special pleading when it found its argument being taken seriously. So for Botha this was an advance over a frankly discriminatory past. But in that day and age it was no more than a quaint survival from what seemed prehistory.

In his famous address of 1981, Samuel Huntington had emphasised that a reform government should above all be committed to 'a political process not to a political system. The goal for the reformers is to keep that process alive, not to realise a particular type of polity ... This strategy not only keeps the options of the government open, it also strengthens the reform process by avoiding divisive and damaging debates among reformers.'[17] What seems to have impressed members of the Government most about Huntington's argument was his notion of 'reform by stealth', that a reformer should hide his goals so as to keep his opponents to the right and the left off balance. The Government was never much good at implementing Huntington's suggestion that reforms should be introduced fast. Usually there was much preliminary talk and belated action which did not come up to expectations. Above all, it missed the point about commitment to a process and not to a system. Reform by stealth was only possible if there was genuine ignorance about a government's goals; Huntington cited recent Brazilian experience under military reformers as especially relevant. Yet there was no mystery about what the South African Government wanted. The exclusion of blacks and the carefully loaded electoral college which chose the executive State President could leave no one in any doubt: it was permanent Nationalist rule over most of South Africa. P W Botha's failure was inherent in his beginnings as a reformer. He was committed to a system and not to a process.

Huntington returned to South Africa in 1986. He found a marked change since he had been there five years before, one which no longer made a policy of unilateral reform from above feasible. The most important change was 'the high degree of politicisation' throughout South African society, of individuals, groups and issues. Related to this was the Government's decreased authority: 'It seems to me that the Government is much weaker, by and large, than it was in 1981. It does not command the authority, respect and legitimacy of major groups in South African society. There is an alienation from the government which, if it existed in 1981, was certainly at a much lower level in terms of overt manifestation'.[18]

There was another feature of Botha's rule which Huntington found inimical to reform and which had indeed been evident right from the start. He did not bother much about finding new constituencies. He broke with the ultra-right, which at once made the National Party more attractive to conservative English-speakers. It was quite enough to keep the Government in power. Other bases of support Botha hardly bothered about. Given the ethnic foundation of the tricameral Parliament, Botha had no need to rely on the coloured and Indian representatives, who in any event enjoyed little legitimacy in their own communities. All he needed was that Nationalist majority in the House of Assembly. For a time it seemed as if he might be more receptive to the views and interests of businessmen than Vorster had been, but when they became critical of the slow pace of reform the capitalists soon discovered how little influence they really had.

There was one constituency Botha did take seriously, but that was because it went with his style, temperament and background. As the turmoil increased Botha showed himself more prone to listen to the security establishment, especially the military. He had spent a dozen years as Minister of Defence and trusted those trained to ensure the security of white rule. The military's simple perception of what the struggle was all about sat on Botha like a tailor-made suit. He had no problems in seeing the turbulence around him as the result of a Communist-orchestrated take-over bid for mineral-rich South Africa.

In May 1986 Botha provided definitive proof that he would no longer walk that extra mile to conciliate the outside world. In October of the previous year the Commonwealth Conference in the Bahamas decided to send a so-called Eminent Persons Group (EPG) in an attempt to negotiate a settlement within South Africa. The Group had two co-chairmen: one was an ex-military ruler of Nigeria, the other was a former Australian Prime Minister who had lost office in 1983 and was now making a comeback as an international statesman. Botha accepted its presence reluctantly, after persuasion from Margaret Thatcher. Despite its unpromising origins the EPG did surprisingly well at first.

Between February and May 1986 the EPG made several visits to the Republic. It met P W Botha, Nelson Mandela in prison, and the President of the ANC, Oliver Tambo, in Zambia. The Group came up with proposals which looked as if they might be acceptable to all parties: the release of Mandela and the unbanning of the ANC and PAC in return for the suspension of the 'armed struggle'. P W Botha now found himself facing a prospect he had not really bargained for: actually sitting down at the same negotiating table as 'terrorists' and 'Communists' hell-bent on ending white rule. He had in any event been getting tired of the self-righteous foreigners who kept arriving in South Africa to lecture him on the wonders of majority rule.

Botha took a decision that had been in the making for some time: there would be no more appeasement of the outside world. He would restore order in the Republic no matter what the price and irrespective of how outraged foreigners managed to be. On the morning of 19 May, while the EPG was in the country, South African planes bombed alleged ANC targets in the neighbouring countries of Mozambique, Zambia and Zimbabwe. No message could have been clearer. The EPG initiative came to an end.

It was Botha's decision, although he took it with the wholehearted endorsement of the security chiefs. When the first state of emergency was lifted in March 1986 the military had been opposed strongly. Partly it was an attempt to show goodwill towards the EPG; there were also businessmen who kept worrying about escalating demands for sanctions. So recently had a concern for foreign opinion borne upon the mind of P W Botha. But the suspension of the emergency did not bring peace. Civil revolt continued. There was also the prospect of massive demonstration and violence on 16 June, the tenth anniversary of the Soweto riots. This time Botha took the advice of the defence chiefs. On 12 June he declared a national state of emergency, giving more or less *carte blanche* to the security forces to detain anyone they pleased and placing sweeping restrictions on the media in their coverage of what the military and the police chose to do. Even traffic police now had the power of summary arrest. Propagation of boycotts became illegal.

Arguably the case for so drastic an enterprise was no better than it had been when the first partial state of emergency was lifted. The violence was not so conspicuously worse, and the security forces had pretty wide powers anyway to deal with riotous radicals. But the mood had changed. P W Botha would do no more to persuade a disbelieving world that fundamental changes were happening in South Africa. Law and order was an essential precondition for reform. He would restore it no matter what it took. If it meant still more ritual outrage from the United Nations, with its majority of authoritarian regimes, and the Republic's supposed friends in the West, so be it.

The shock and dismay of the foreigners were indeed a wonder to behold. In London the South African horror show virtually crowded all else off the front pages of the newspapers. Television coverage began early in the day and continued: to all appearances the land of apartheid was ending in fire. South Africans who were there when the state of emergency was announced (as this writer was) were entitled to ask themselves whether it would be safe to return to the country they had left only a short time before. It seemed inconceivable that in a few brief weeks it could have disintegrated so utterly.

At home little of this came through. Censorship was harsh. Newspapers could only publish reports on the unrest which had been passed by the suddenly far more powerful police. South African television, traditionally servile to the National Party and its interests, now surpassed itself. The blandness of its 'news' could only have made many, perhaps most, white South Africans wonder what all the foreign hysteria was about, which of course was the intention.

Unsurprisingly, the new measures worked. Detentions rose to above 20 000 in the year after the announcement of the state of emergency. So many UDF leaders were removed from circulation that even that multi-headed body had to admit being wounded. But the death toll went down conspicuously: 339 people were killed between 1 January 1986 and 11 June 1986, but from June 1986 to April 1987, a period twice as long, the number dropped to 145. The level of street violence fell even more sharply.[19]

The absence of the television cameras of the international media from the townships deprived would-be revolutionaries of the opportunity of display on a world stage. Radical anticipations of the impending collapse of the racist regime subsided quickly.

P W Botha achieved his overriding purpose, but at the cost of a state of emergency which it seemed would be renewed every year. During such times security establishments are bound to assert themselves. A marked feature of the states of emergency had been the role of the Defence Force, which had more than just supplemented the activities of the police. In South Africa it had the additional advantage of having the ear of an exceptionally sympathetic President. There were suggestions that South Africa was liable to become a military autocracy now that repression had taken precedence over reform. But that would have been to mistake what was happening in South Africa. P W Botha loved the military, but he was not its prisoner, as he did not appear to be the prisoner of any other interest group. A more convincing portrayal by critics was that he converted his office into an 'imperial Presidency';[20] it seemed to be inherent in the autocratic powers which went with the job. But appearances are sometimes deceptive. Botha could not place himself above all vested interests. In particular, there was the National Party, which had made him and through which he had risen. Botha had gradually reduced it to embarrassing subservience. He could do with it more or less as he pleased – but he could not do without it. The belief of the imperial President that he could cut himself loose from his party was to be his fatal error.

CHAPTER TWENTY

One Step Forward, Two Steps Back

The national state of emergency of June 1986 embodied a mood of defiance in the South African Government which seemed irreversible, at least as long as P W Botha was in charge. He had plainly reached the end of his tether when it came to carping foreigners and restless Natives at home. Officially reform was still on the agenda, but no one could now question that 'real change' was further away than ever.

Abroad the sanctions frenzy continued without pause. After the failure of the EPG, members of the Commonwealth imposed additional restrictions on economic ties with South Africa. Once again Margaret Thatcher was the lone maverick, but even she consented, under extreme pressure, to a voluntary ban on new investment in the Republic. In the middle of September the Foreign Ministers of the European Economic Community also agreed to ban new investment, as well as imports of iron, steel and gold coins from South Africa. Neither the EEC, however, nor Japan, imposed a ban on the import of South African coal, which would have inflicted definite pain on the supposed target. If South African businessmen felt inclined to dismiss sanctions as a paper tiger it would have been difficult to accuse them of complacency.

The measures were not especially harsh. They were rather token gestures than anything else, as the more rabid sanctioneers like Robert Mugabe of Zimbabwe and Kenneth Kaunda of Zambia were swift to point out. The vituperation of these men would have been more persuasive had they themselves been willing to break off economic contact with the evil regime to the south. But they recognised what the consequences would be for their own economies if they took their invective seriously. Zimbabwe and Zambia continued to have close economic links with South Africa, while demanding that other countries break off theirs. Such behaviour was not unique: high moral posturing and a personal unwillingness to make notable sacrifices were among the most overt features of the sanctions campaign against the land of apartheid.

The drive for sanctions became most intense in the United States. The American diplomatic historian, George Kennan, commented in 1951 on 'the erratic and subjective nature of public reaction to foreign-policy questions ... I think the record indicates that in the short term our public opinion, or what passes for our public opinion in the thinking of official Washington, can be easily led astray into areas of emotionalism and subjectivity which make it a poor and inadequate guide for national action'.[1] Little had changed over the years. Well-intentioned Americans wished to feel that they were doing something tangible about apartheid. At the same time the Democrats could scarcely conceal their urge to score points off the Reagan administration. In October 1986 it all culminated in the Comprehensive Anti-Apartheid Act, passed by Congress over the Presidential veto. From then on there would be no new US investment in South Africa. Loans to the South African Government were banned, as were exports of crude oil and computers to the Republic. Direct air links between the two countries ceased to exist. The United States would no longer import coal, uranium, steel, agricultural products and textiles from South Africa.

Congress was not however willing to deprive Americans of 'strategic minerals' from South Africa, for which there were no ready substitutes. Chrome and vanadium from the Republic would continue to enter the United States.

By the end of 1986 the sanctions campaign had become one of the great and fashionable moral causes of the time. If the sanctioneers believed their own inflated rhetoric, they had no doubt that opposition to disinvestment and trade bans differed little from an enthusiasm for genocide and indeed reflected an irredeemable racism. Inevitably, the sanctions lobbies and pressure groups proliferated: power, prestige and substantial material reward awaited those who best knew how to keep the sanctions fires burning.

In spite of the sound and the fury, it is doubtful that official sanctions did much to harm apartheid. They were supposed to hit white South Africans where they felt it most: in their pockets. However, about 60 per cent of South Africa's exports consisted of precious minerals and metals which were virtually impossible to sanction. In particular, there was gold, a fungible metal which accounted for more than 40 per cent of the Republic's export earnings and was assured of a world market.

Nor was it at all likely that sanctions could eliminate the remaining 40 per cent of South African exports. How the Republic's coal and agricultural products would sell abroad would depend on the state of international markets. If these were glutted the South African article would have to go at larger discounts than would otherwise have been necessary. The truth remained that, short of a blockade of the Republic, its products were always liable to sell abroad at a price. Sanctions could be a nuisance. They could cause lower profits for particular South African producers. But they were an implausible instrument for securing the country's economic collapse.

The truth remained that the most damaging sanctions were unofficial and were imposed during the debt crisis of 1985, when foreign bankers called in their short-term loans and refused to extend new credit to South African borrowers. It was only afterwards that many countries imposed official restrictions on lending and investment to South Africa. The Republic's rate of growth would from now on be restricted by the need to export capital to repay its debt. Impaired confidence about the future would only deepen the reluctance of South African businessmen to invest, a trend already evident since 1981. Capital inflows from abroad which had in the past helped to oil the wheels of growth would no longer be there. The pinpricks of the later sanctions campaign could not compare with body-blows such as these.

If apartheid was being dismantled it was largely because of developments in South Africa itself. They had been happening long before and came mainly from the steady growth of an integrated economy. They had made a mockery of the dreams of Verwoerd, his apartheid bureaucracy and those Nationalist journalists and academics who had for years done their considerable best, against all the evidence, to convince themselves and everybody else that fantasy was realisable fact and that the massive attempt to restructure society could sow anything but the seeds of rancour and division. When growth was rapid the pressures on apartheid grew. Not least, white workers became more receptive to black economic advance. When growth slowed down the pressures on apartheid diminished and the demand for protection by white workers increased. During the 1980s the South African economy fared conspicuously worse than it did in the previous decades, but by then the irreparable damage to apartheid had already been done.

The poor economic performance had several causes. There was the gold price, which was generally weak after 1981. The monetary authorities attempted to maintain the rand earnings of exporters by keeping the exchange rate down, but at the price of a persistently high rate of inflation. From 1984 political instability came increasingly into its own as an independent cause of economic stagnation. It was a poor climate for profits and the indulgence of capitalist animal spirits. Yet South Africa badly needed the enlargement of resources which only growth could bring. It would put further pressures on apartheid, not least because of the increasing numbers of Africans doing skilled work. Higher incomes would widen the area of choice available to those who gained, and enhance their feelings of security. Reform, in short, needed growth.

Yet during the 1980s it seemed as if the South African economy was heading for indefinite stagnation and that kind of backwardness which would place the country beyond any kind of political solution. The many groups of a fragmented society would find themselves locked in an increasingly acrimonious struggle for the resources the economy was turning out so grudgingly. A supercilious British Labour politician who visited South Africa during these desperate years described it as a banana republic. He was wrong, of course. The country was not there yet, but it was a sign of the times. Even in their wilder moments, South Africa's worst critics had never before thought of comparing it with the more benighted parts of Latin America.

Another sign of the times was the disconcerting progress of the far right. Naturally many of the lower-income Afrikaners who had previously voted Nationalist would turn their backs on a party which had recently been so ineffective in protecting them against black competition and the erosion of their living standards. In the 1981 general election the Herstigte Nasionale Party had done unexpectedly well by attracting fourteen per cent of the vote, compared with its miserable three per cent of 1977. It was all the more impressive, or disturbing, as the HNP had a somewhat disreputable image, appealing, as it always had, to the racial fears and animosities of the least educated Afrikaners. The threat from the right acquired still larger dimensions when the Conservative Party arrived in 1982. It had upper-middle class leaders who kept their seats in the House of Assembly after they left the Nationalists. They looked infinitely more respectable than the crowd running the HNP. Suddenly the appeal of ultra-conservative policies widened.

By-election results showed how wide the attraction had become. There were remarkable swings to the right in formerly safe Nationalist seats. At the end of 1984 the Conservative Party reduced the Nationalist majority in the East Rand constituency of Primrose to 748; it represented a swing of more than twenty per cent. In October 1985 there were huge swings to the far right in the farming constituencies of Vryburg and Bethlehem in the Orange Free State. In Sasolburg in the same province, where the Conservatives decided not to stand in a show of right-wing unity, a swing of more than seventeen per cent gave the HNP its first and probably last parliamentary seat. Even in the English-speaking Durban constituency of Port Natal the CP did well and gained more than 1900 votes.[2]

The far right did not limit itself to parliamentary strategies. Frustration with a political process which was apparently depriving Afrikaners of their birthright resulted in the growth of a host of organisations which had other strategies in mind. By far the most spectacular was the Afrikaner Weerstandsbeweging (AWB). Established as early as 1973 the AWB only became a mass-based movement in the 1980s. Led by a talented demagogue, Eugene Terre'Blanche, the AWB spurned tame constitutional ways, although after the 1987 general election it was happy enough to endorse the Conservative Party's own concentration on the parliamentary route. But the AWB was more at home in its drive to gain grass-oots support among the volk as a basis for the eventual Afrikaner-ruled one-party state it wished to establish in the Orange Free State, the Transvaal and Northern Natal, all scenes of Boer republics at some time or other during the nineteenth century. The signed-up membership of the AWB in the mid-1980s was relatively small, estimated at between only 5 000 and 9 000,[3] but the large enthusiastic audiences at its meetings suggested that plenty of Afrikaners were only too susceptible to the rabble-rousing at which Terre'Blanche was a supreme master.

The right wing current was running strong when the national state of emergency was proclaimed in 1986. Yet it hardly came across as irresistible. The findings of an opinion poll published in February 1986 suggested that the far right would have difficulties in forging the kind of ethnic alliance cutting across class lines which had for so long been the basis of Nationalist power. Only ten per cent of HNP/CP support came from upper-middle income groups, compared with twenty per cent for the Nationalists. Forty-nine per cent of support for the far right came from middle income households and 41 per cent from lower middle and lower income groups. The comparable figures for the National Party were 45 and 35 per cent.[4]

For the Nationalists the findings could only be a comfort. The Conservative Party had the makings of an inordinate nuisance, but on current form it was far from power. Unlike the HNP, the CP neither excluded English-speakers, Jews and atheists, nor would it proclaim Afrikaans as the sole official language, but it was quite plainly a party which concerned itself mainly with mobilising Afrikaners. If it could not reach out to the best educated and more affluent members of its chosen constituency it could forget about ever being able to turn back the clock.

The findings also showed that the National Party had not moved so far away from its original bases of support as neo-Marxist writers liked to argue. As one of them has put it: 'As a party of the bourgeoisie, the NP developed an ideology presenting its class interests as "general interests", while still trying to retain the image of an Afrikaner ethnic party. However, the party's new line was increasingly incompatible with the NP's traditional alliance of Afrikaners of all classes, bound by rigid racism and exclusive access to the state'.[5] What is true is that the Nationalist line had changed. What is only partially true is that it was incompatible with the 'traditional alliance' which sustained the Nationalist Government. Afrikaners were defecting in large numbers during the 1980s, but the National Party continued to have sizeable support from Afrikaners of all classes.

The opinion poll of February 1986 indicated, and it was to be confirmed by the result of the general election of 1987, that the National Party retained a solid core of white worker support. Nor was it evident from the rapidly deteriorating relationship between the Government and businessmen during the 1980s that the Nationalists were 'a party of the bourgeoisie'. After P W Botha became Prime Minister he had some much-publicised conferences with South African businessman, who were substantially flattered by such unwonted attentions. But they misunderstood their man. Botha was a technocrat, interested in what the private sector could do to promote economic development, which he saw as crucial to successful reform from above. He had no intention of allowing businessmen to dictate policy to him. The entrepreneurs were disillusioned speedily. The new leader made no special effort to pursue ends 'functional to capital', as the modish jargon used to have it. Some Government policies like the abolition of the pass laws were undoubtedly in the interests of businessmen. Yet there is no evidence that influx control went because capitalists wished it so. For one, it had long been ineffective; in official circles it had been seen as such. But it was only after prolonged deliberation and investigation over several years that the Government decided to scrap the execrated system. It suited capitalists, but it also suited the Government for reasons of its own.

One commentator has generalised the episode:

> The pattern of events which led to the repeal of the influx control laws would suggest that the government can be responsive to private sector influence, but only where such influence is in agreement with expert opinion, where there is substantial acceptance of the reform measure within the gov-

ernment's support groups, *and* after its own inquiries have provided evidence and a rationale for the reform.[6]

There is one theme which runs right through the whole history of Nationalist rule. It has been the Government's considerable independence *vis-à-vis* specific interest groups. After it came to power the National Party naturally did its very best to satisfy the crucial members of the Afrikaner ethnic alliance, namely the workers and the farmers. Appropriate labour policies came into place: job reservation and stricter control over the movement of black workers. Yet the National Party represented more than just particular interests. As long as its ethnic constituency saw the Government as holding Afrikaner domination dear to its heart, it had much latitude in decisions on the ground. In the decisive decade of the 1970s the scarcely disguised acceptance of a permanent black presence in the urban areas meant breaking with a basic feature of Verwoerdian ideology. Official Nationalist theory had long held, as an axiom, that this presence could only prepare the way for the demise of white rule, and indeed of the white man. White workers were becoming increasingly alienated by new labour policies which they were sure left them deprived of protection in the marketplace. Yet in 1977 the Government gained its greatest victory ever in a general election, receiving an estimated 85 per cent of the Afrikaner vote, as well as 33 per cent of the ballots of English-speakers. Circumstances surrounded that election which especially favoured the Government: the blatant exploitation of anti-American sentiment turned out to be highly rewarding. Still, the message was clear: the National Party was seen by its supporters, whatever their specific grievances, as the representative of a more general Afrikaner and, increasingly, a white interest. In so far as this was true, it was free to pursue policies which were not tailored to the needs of particular groups, whether capital or labour.

There were of course divisions amongst Afrikaners. Many had come to doubt the commitment of the Government to either their own interests or to those of the Afrikaner people as a whole. It was reflected in the relatively low poll of 65 per cent in 1977, as well as in the declining proportion of voters who turned out to support the Nationalists: 44 per cent in 1966, but 42 per cent in 1977. In 1981 it was down to 37 per cent.[7] After the strong electoral performance of the Herstigte Nasionale Party in 1981, it seemed that all Nationalist conservatives were waiting for was a right wing party which did not appeal primarily to the down-and-outs, the losers, within white society. The next year it did arrive and made immediate progress amongst disaffected Afrikaners.

But there was another trend which only reinforced the National Party's independence of particular vested interests. Over the years English-speakers had gradually been voting Nationalist. When Verwoerd became Prime Minister he had made the first move to widen the ethnic appeal of the National Party: now that Afrikaner unity had been so substantially achieved white unity became the catchword. English-speaking support was muted at first; it was not easy to start voting suddenly for a party which had for so long been an unashamed partisan of Afrikaner interests. But the support came, both slowly and erratically, for the English-speakers were nothing if not capricious. A third of their vote may have gone to the Nationalists in 1977 but four years later it was down to 28 per cent.[8] But even that was a significant turn-out for a party which had once made a particular merit of wearing its Afrikaner heart on its sleeve. What was more, it only made sense to expect more English-speakers to vote Nationalist as the party moved further to the centre after getting rid of its extreme right. The opportunity of the English-speakers to empathise with the 'new' National Party came soon. In 1983 they deserted the PFP *en masse* to vote for the Government's new constitution. As the result of the next election was to show, for many it was more than just a temporary abandonment of low-key liberalism.

The ability of the Nationalists to take over the middle ground, to persuade numerous English-speakers that they could have their reform and their continued white privilege in one attractive package, made of them the white party *par excellence*, with a broad cross-section of support from both the white language groups. It was more than the Progressive Federal Party and the Conservative Party could claim for themselves. As long as the Nationalists were perceived as pursuing white survival, they, or at this time, P W Botha, had a pretty free hand. It made them less beholden to specific vested interests, which they could disregard at little risk to themselves, or even treat with disdain. They could also look forward to a general election with some confidence. Even if for the sake of 'reform' they forfeited some traditional sources of Afrikaner support, they knew that they would still have little difficulty in being returned with a large overall majority at the polls.

Under the previous constitution a general election was due not later than in 1986. But since then the new dispensation had arrived. As the tricameral Parliament first met in 1984, an election for all three houses was due in 1989. The Conservative Party naturally was opposed. It was straining at the bit to test the right wing waters. After the passing of the original expiry date in 1986 the Conservatives had a splendid time abusing the Government for not having a mandate to govern.

Perhaps some of the complaints reached a sensitive spot. In any event, the Government could expect to benefit from the mood of the white population, which was hardening as foreigners looked for ways to cripple the South African economy. In his televised New Year's message for 1987 P W Botha announced an election for the white electorate. Later in January he set the date for 6 May. White South Africans could prepare themselves for the longest and dirtiest election campaign within memory.

At first it seemed as if the Government might have a hard time of it. There was the alliance between the Progressive Federal Party and the New Republic Party, the rump of the United Party which had finally expired in 1977. In 1981 the Nationalists had won some seats because of a split Opposition vote. This time round it looked as if Nationalist candidates would not slip so easily into Parliament. There were also indications that Nationalists were falling out amongst themselves over the slow pace of reform. In January the extreme verligte MP for the Transvaal constituency of Randburg, Wynand Malan, had resigned from the National Party for just that reason. He was joined in his disillusionment by the former constitutional planner, Denis Worrall, who had resigned as South African Ambassador in London, where he had performed impressively, to hurry back to the Republic as a vehement critic of his former comrades.

Until the end of March it did appear, according to opinion polls, that the Nationalists would lose out substantially to the alliance, while the far right did not seem to be shaping at all.⁹ The Government realised it had been running the wrong kind of campaign. The declared purpose of the election had been to discover how the voters felt about continued reform. The Nationalists at first made the mistake of attempting to discuss the issues seriously, as well as defending their many failures. On both counts they were made to look foolish. They changed their tactics. The Nationalists now took to smearing the PFP as being soft on security and a putative bedfellow of the ANC and its Communist sidekicks.

It was a time-honoured tactic and as effective as ever. Security crowded out reform. Nationalist control of the South African Broadcasting Corporation proved an immense advantage. Every evening befuddled viewers had to watch supposed news broadcasts which looked as if they had been prepared by the professional propagandists of the ruling party. It was crude and shameless and it worked. White fears and anxieties received a further boost when the Government discovered an ANC 'plot' to disrupt the election by violent means. To drive the point home truly many uniformed members of the security forces were to be seen safeguarding the democratic process at polling stations on election day.

For the PFP/NRP alliance the results were a most unpleasant surprise. The PFP went into the election with 25 seats and came out with 19; the already miniscule NRP was virtually wiped out and retained one seat of the five it had before the election. Wynand Malan kept his seat as an independent and Denis Worrall inflicted on his old enemy, Chris Heunis, a vast humiliation by limiting him to a victory of a mere 39 votes in his own constituency of Helderberg. It was the far right that had the most reason for joy. The CP had 17 seats before the election and the HNP one. After 6 May the Conservatives found themselves as the only representatives of the extreme right with 22 seats. They were now also the Official Opposition.

The Government still had a sizeable majority. It had, in fact, increased its number of seats from 116 to 123. But that was misleading. The Nationalist share of the vote had dropped from 56 per cent in 1981 to 52,5 per cent. The far right increased its share from 14 to 30 per cent. Inevitably, it seemed, the focus of South African politics would shift to the right as the Government did its best to refute the allegations of the new Official Opposition that its liberal policies could only, and soon, end in black majority rule.

The advent of the extreme right could do reform no good, but then it had hardly been going at a cracking pace. Well before the 1987 election security needs had replaced reform at the top of the Government's agenda. In June P W Botha renewed the state of emergency as a matter of course. There had never been a prospect of anything else. Now the CP would place the Government further on the defensive about the reforms it had already introduced; the Nationalists would become still warier about future changes which could be portrayed as a betrayal of the white man's right to have and to hold the country for which his ancestors had fought and died. But the trend was already there. The outcome of the election would only reinforce it.

Yet the election showed clearly that the Government had plenty of margin for reform – if it were interested. It was not, or at least P W Botha had lost interest in reform. There was evidence that the far right was flourishing in certain regions and amongst certain groups, but that it would have problems if it wished to build a wider anti-reform coalition. The Conservative Party had done well in the rural areas of the Transvaal, where it won 16 of its 22 seats. It had also picked up plenty of votes in the Orange Free State countryside, without winning a seat. The other six Conservative seats came from the highly urbanised Pretoria-Witwatersrand-Vereeniging area. However, five of the constituencies were on the periphery of the PWV region. The far right only gained limited support amongst inner-city voters. Small farmers, blue-collar workers and mineworkers made up the core of the CP's urban constituency. In the Cape and Natal the far right did relatively poorly, in spite of the large numbers of Afrikaners in the former province.

The outcome of the election confirmed the findings of the opinion poll of the previous year. The far right did not have broad enough support amongst Afrikaners of all income groups, especially upper-middle income Afrikaners, to be able to construct an ethnic alliance capable of winning an election. That is what the National Party did do in 1948. Much of the CP's urban support came from blue-collar workers, no longer the power in the land they were in 1948, a declining class, made increasingly obsolete by decades of white economic advance. In short, while the CP could confidently expect to win more seats in any future election, especially if the Government continued its slow retreat from landmarks of the past, the chances of a national triumph for the ultra-right were remote.

Further reforms, like the scrapping of the Group Areas Act, would have alienated more traditional Nationalist voters, but their defection would at worst have brought discomfort to the Government. There was the certainty that, as the Government moved closer to the centre, more PFP supporters would have defected to the governing party. They already had a foretaste of voting in their masses for a Nationalist cause in the referendum of 1983 and evidently found it smooth enough on the palate. In the 1987 election the Nationalists still attracted a majority of Afrikaans voters, but it was a mere 55 per cent, compared with the 63 per cent of six years before. The English-speakers, however, more than compensated for their temporary desertion of the Government in 1981, when only 28 per cent of those who voted supported the Nationalists. In 1987 it rose to 47 per cent.[10] The National Party had ceased to be a party rooted in Afrikaner nationalism. It now represented a more general white interest, based on a widely-held view that reform was all very well, but only within the overriding limits of continued white control.

The ultimate constraint on continued reform was the State President himself. P W Botha had travelled a long way since the uninhibited Nationalist racism, in which he had shared fully, of the early apartheid days. He had the courage, which Vorster never had, to discard the fetish of Afrikaner nationalist unity for the sake of his vision, however flawed, of a reformed South Africa. But the credit he received for rising above his past so demonstratively had been diminishing steadily in recent years. The announcement of the national state of emergency in 1986 marked the *de facto* end of his period as reformer. It was not simply that he had endured enough criticism and insults from critics at home and abroad. The truth was that if ever there had been a time for Botha's kind of reform – imposed from above, committed to a system and unyieldingly based on the principle of separate racial groups – it had also gone. Botha may have taken over the National Party and reduced it to subservience. There is little doubt that if he wished to break out of the strait-jacket of the existing way of reform he could have taken the party with him. But to P W Botha such a change of course was unthinkable. He had quite simply exhausted his potential for reform.

Above all, there was the question of black political representation, which the tricameral Parliament did not even begin to answer. Botha gradually came to accept that the policy of ethnic homelands for Africans had its shortcomings. He did not accept that more than a few adjustments were needed to take account of the existence of the millions of urban blacks who found the notion of their very own homelands bizarre and objectionable. One of the first adjustments Botha did propose was that Africans in cities should be represented through their 'national states': it was fully in accord with the Verwoerdian doctrine that Africans were tribal animals defined by ethnicity. But none of the intended beneficiaries appeared to be interested; the proposal got nowhere. It epitomised the record of the Botha Government on black political rights. One expedient followed another, but all had a common feature: the homelands policy was a given, majority rule in a single state was ruled out in any form. It could be no surprise that for more than a decade the National Party made no progress on the issue of black political rights in central government. Most of the time it played around with the notion of some kind of council, either all-African or multiracial, on which blacks would be represented. No black leader of any repute, if only for the sake of his own safety, was willing to serve on bodies such as these.

There was also the problem of consultation. Government spokesmen liked to say that they consulted black leaders regularly, but they had difficulties in coming up with names, except those of the homelands rulers, most of whom were in fact small-time despots shored up by South African arms. Black leaders who valued their credibility could not afford co-optation by the Government unless they could be seen to receive something of value in return. They never did. The release of Nelson Mandela would have been a relatively small price for getting African leaders with some standing in their own communities to enter into political discussions with the Government. Instead, P W Botha insisted that Mandela renounce violence as a precondition for his release.

When he refused, as indeed he had to, in order to retain his own standing with his followers, Botha tried to score a cheap debating-point by insisting that Mandela was actually responsible for his own imprisonment.

For the same reason Botha refused to unban the ANC and the PAC. They were after all 'terrorist' organisations committed to 'the armed struggle', however laughable that struggle may have been in practice. But even when facing a black leader with, at least at the time, a genuine mass following, committed to working within the system, hostile to sanctions and decidedly friendly to capitalist enterprise, Botha could not bring himself to negotiate except on his very own terms.

That black man was Mangosuthu Buthelezi, Chief Minister of the KwaZulu homeland and President of Inkatha, which described itself as a national liberation movement. Buthelezi had a proven following in Zululand and, in the early days of his fame in the 1970s, amongst non-Zulus as well. He had refused 'independence' from the Government because it would have meant accepting apartheid ideology; at the same time he saw KwaZulu as a base from which he could negotiate alliances with other anti-apartheid groups and promote non-racial alternatives to Nationalist policies.

Of course Buthelezi rejected apartheid. No reputable black leader could afford not to. But from the Government's point of view, and that of the white population, he was almost too good to be true. Buthelezi was a notoriously authoritarian figure on his home turf, where membership of Inkatha was essential for any ambitious black civil servant. He had a wafer-thin skin when it came to criticism of himself and his policies. But he rejected the violence of sabotage and terrorism in the pursuit of political change, he understood white fears and he did not advocate ruining the economy as a means of ending white rule. Buthelezi had succeeded in alienating the UDF and the ANC by his willingness to work within Government-created institutions. He was as 'moderate', in white terms, as any black leader who hoped to retain his credibility could be.

Even this was not enough for the State President. Over the years the Government attempted repeatedly to draw Buthelezi into negotiations, but for him there was to be no *quid pro quo* like the release of political prisoners or a commitment to end apartheid which would have enhanced his own prestige amongst South African blacks. Nor was it made clear to Buthelezi what they would be negotiating about. It seemed as if the Government was more interested in being seen talking to as high-profile a leader as Buthelezi than in actually going anywhere with him.

In 1986 the KwaNatal Indaba took place. It consisted of negotiations between a number of interest groups, including Inkatha, the Natal Provincial Council Executive and various business lobbies, in order to devise a joint regional alternative to apartheid. The cause of Natal devolutionism had been given new vigour by the failure of the tricameral system to deal with the issue of black participation. There had also been growing unrest in the province since the early 1980s as Inkatha faced rivals for the allegiance of blacks in the form of the UDF and Cosatu. Both Inkatha and Natal businessmen had a strong interest in a regional settlement favourable to social stability and a capitalist economy. The final Indaba proposals in 1987 were for a joint legislature on the familiar lines of consociationalism, but, unlike the tricameral Parliament, they appeared to be a genuine attempt to make multiracialism work. The legislature was to be elected by universal franchise; there were to be no saving clauses to preserve ultimate white control. There would still have been separate voters' rolls and segregation of land ownership, but it was strong stuff by the official standards of the day. The Government rejected the proposals instantly and without reservation.

In 1988 Buthelezi expressed his bewilderment and frustration to students at the University of Pretoria:

> When the Government behaves like this, how can I as a black leader believe that the State President is serious about his commitment to reform? What does he mean by reform? I just do not know. I do not believe South Africans know either.
>
> If the Government has a specific future in mind for South Africa, it is one of the best-guarded secrets. The chances are, however, that the South African Government has committed itself to a reform programme which has not yet been properly designed. The South African Government gives all the ap-

pearance of a government that does not know where it is leading the people.[11]

Buthelezi was right. The Government had lost whatever sense of direction it had. The tricameral Parliament was turning out to be a disaster, devoid of legitimacy amongst the two minority groups the Government had been striving to co-opt and the immediate cause of a black resentment so intense and encompassing that it could only be contained by what seemed a state of emergency made to last. Political disaster had led to economic disaster: a respectable rate of economic growth had now become the hostage of 'genuine' reform. Whatever the fine print, no one could doubt that it would have to involve political rights for blacks in the same state as whites. Under the current leadership it seemed further away than ever.

It was not only Buthelezi who found himself treated with public contumely by the State President. As he got older and as the exercise of autocratic power became second nature to him, P W Botha grew more prone to indulge a villainous temper and an inherent relish for confrontation with his critics. One of the most notorious instances was the 'Chris Ball affair' of 1987.

Chris Ball was the Managing Director of Barclays National Bank and a foremost critic of the Government's inadequacies in handling the economy and, not least, reform. He belonged to an increasingly familiar South African breed, namely nervous businessmen given to the demonstrative flaunting of their social conscience in public. Ball believed in reverse discrimination, or affirmative action, in his organisation. He was on friendly terms with the unspeakable Winnie Mandela, wife of the world's most famous political prisoner. But Ball made the mistake of giving ammunition to P W Botha. He provided bridging finance for a perfectly legal advertisement which appeared in newspapers countrywide calling for the unbanning of the ANC, much to the fury of the security establishment.

Botha found out about Ball's generosity from a tap on the telephone of Allan Boesak, the cleric well-known, amongst other things, for his leading role in extra-parliamentary opposition to apartheid. The State President had no scruples about exploiting information acquired by such dubious means. On 4 February he told the story to Parliament and demanded from Ball, as if he had committed a crime, a statement as to its truth. Ball's response was exceedingly foolish. He could have told Botha that neither the advertisement nor the provision of funds for its publication was an offence and that it was actually none of his business. Instead, he chose to go on the defensive by telling the press that he knew nothing about the advertisement.

Botha at once contacted an old friend, George Munnik, Chief Justice of the Cape Supreme Court, and asked him to head an inquiry. The judge apparently had no problems in taking on a task so glaringly political in its inspiration. In spite of Ball's denial at the inquiry that he was aware what the funds were for, Munnik found, on evidence hardly overwhelming in its persuasiveness, that he did know.

That was the end of Ball. He continued to deny knowledge, and he had the support of his board of directors, but Barclays had effectively been smeared as 'the ANC bank'. Ball resigned in 1989 and emigrated to Britain. As for Barclays, it became a South African-owned bank as its British parent company joined the scramble to disinvest. It changed its name to First National Bank and began to sponsor sport in a big way in an attempt to polish up its patriotic image.

For Botha the exercise must have been wholly satisfying. He had succeeded in discrediting one of his most irritating critics in the private sector. He had gone far in putting businessmen in their place. They now knew, if they did not before, that their views did not count for all that much with the State President. Nor could they doubt that if they overstepped some easily reached limits they would be facing a very rough and dirty fighter indeed.

The Ball episode had shown that P W Botha was willing and able to alienate one of the most important interest groups in the white community. The next episode, the Hendrickse affair, demonstrated Botha's preparedness to make enemies amongst the coloureds, whatever notions verligte Nationalists may have had of these people as a natural ally of the whites in offsetting the weight of black numbers.

As leader of the majority Labour Party in the House of Representatives, the Reverend Alan Hendrickse was a member of P W Botha's cabinet, as was the slippery Amichand Rajbansi, majority leader in the House of Delegates. Their position was inherently invidious. The principle of cabinet responsibility seemed to suggest that they were now party to the application of apartheid laws against their own people. Hendrickse, in particular, came in for plenty of criticism from younger members of the Labour Party. Although he was happy enough at first to receive Government patronage, Hendrickse came to realise that the Labour Party was liable to lose the little legitimacy it had amongst the people it was supposed to represent. This sobering thought persuaded him to get up from his knees, only to be faced by an evil-tempered State President plainly not willing to tolerate insubordination.

There was a series of confrontations which ended in Hendrickse's departure from the cabinet. There had been signs of Labour unrest before, as when members of the party called for the resignation of the Minister of Law and Order, Louis le Grange, after the Uitenhage shootings of March 1985. As a member of the cabinet Hendrickse had been much embarrassed, but he managed to talk his way out of that one. The first major confrontation, and easily the most bizarre, was the 'swimming incident' of 4 January 1987. On that day Hendrickse and a large Labour entourage went for a well-publicised swim at an exclusive 'whites-only' beach in Port Elizabeth. A fortnight later, after interviewing Hendrickse about his swimming habits, the State President went on television for nearly a half-hour to denigrate and humiliate his colleague. No one who saw the performance could have failed to be awed by the pettiness and downright meanness of the most powerful man in the country. But Hendrickse survived once more, at the cost of his remaining self-respect, when he apologised in a letter to Botha.

Clearly Hendrickse desperately wished to remain in the cabinet. Yet even worms turn, which is what Hendrickse was soon compelled to do. After the white election in May 1987 relations between the Government and the Labour Party deteriorated swiftly. As was predictable, P W Botha not only resented Labour attacks on the reforming zeal of the Government, but he responded in August with a scathing attack on the Labour Party in the House of Representatives. He pointed out to a surprised audience that they had 'no better friend in South Africa than the State President'. What was more, it was only Nationalist policy which made their presence possible that day: 'This is the nearest you have ever come in your lives to governing South Africa. This dispensation is the nearest the Coloured population has ever come to governing South Africa'.[12]

It was remarkably offensive, even by Botha's own high standards. Three days later on Saturday, 22 August, Hendrickse finally burnt his boats when he told a Labour Party congress that Botha's behaviour in Parliament was like that of 'a rat trapped in a corner'.[13] Hendrickse also announced that the Labour Party would not agree to extending the term of the current Parliament to 1992. Botha had not been keen on facing the Conservative Party again so soon, but all three Houses of Parliament had to give their consent. This was a straightforward reneging on an agreement Hendrickse had assented to in the cabinet.

Botha read the report of Hendrickse's address two days later. He wrote to Hendrickse informing him that his membership of the cabinet was 'unacceptable'. After receiving the letter Hendrickse attempted to make it appear that he had resigned from the cabinet, but the blunt truth was that he had been sacked. From now on the majority party in the House of Representatives went into opposition. It made a virtue of obstruction; a year later the coloured and Indian Houses adjourned for a fortnight rather than debate punitive amendments to the Group Areas Act. Strictly speaking, the white House could continue on its own when this happened, that was where the real power resided, but any credibility the tricameral system had depended on the co-operation of all three Houses.

By 1987 Botha was coming across as a man on the rampage, eager to confront and intimidate at the slightest provocation. Some of his actions were probably carefully calculated. The public rubbishing of Chris Ball brought tangible rewards: he had silenced a vocal critic from the private sector and other businessmen would think again before they shouted the odds about the Government's efforts at reform. But Botha's alienation of an organisation like the Labour Party, led by somewhat conservative men only too willing to benefit from and dispense official patronage, was sheer folly.

Botha did not have the temperament of a negotiator and conciliator, but his indulging of his tantrums at the public expense cannot simply be explained as the workings of a flawed personality increasingly out of control. He was operating in an institutional framework which made such behaviour only too possible. In the tricameral system effective power lay with the white House of Assembly. It was the National Party which controlled that House. P W Botha had long before hijacked the National Party and made it his creature. If the man at the top did not feel like winning friends and influencing people, there was really nothing to compel him to do so. Botha did not look for new allies because he saw no reason to do so. All that he needed was to command the ruling party, which he well and truly did.

The Government had not abandoned reform officially by 1987. It simply believed that restoring law and order came first. The state of emergency had led to a conspicuous decline in overt unrest and public violence. There was the obvious risk that the prominence of the security apparatus would give it a veto power over any reforms the Government could decide to proceed with. The fear was apparently confirmed on 22 February 1988 when the Government prohibited seventeen organisations from engaging in politically-related activities. They included such obvious candidates as the United Democratic Front and the Congress of South African Trade Unions. Ostensibly the organisations were restricted because they were promoting a 'revolutionary climate' and encouraging 'civil disobedience and revolt' as the Minister of Law and Order, Adriaan Vlok, put it.[14]

Yet such accusations were nothing new. These extra-parliamentary bodies had supposedly been doing that all along, over the years. Also, the timing was odd as the security forces had been achieving some success in curbing activities designed to promote a 'revolutionary climate'. Later events suggest that the Government was trying to set its own version of reform on course again. In October municipal elections were due throughout the Republic. The ANC would quite naturally call on Africans to vote with their feet and stay away. In 1984 the UDF had staged a highly effective boycott campaign of the Indian and coloured elections. It was important to the Government that blacks should register strong support for local institutions. Once they did so, 'consultation' would once more become a plausible option.

In 1985 the Government had introduced a new system of local government. By then black municipalities had the same status as white ones. It amounted to a further admission that Africans had more than just temporary rights outside the homelands. Now regional service councils made their appearance. These councils were joint metropolitan representative bodies on which the racially autonomous municipalities were represented on the basis of the proportion of municipal services they consumed, determined by complex formulas. It meant that the wealthier white local authorities dominated the RSCs. However, they were multiracial and they had more than advisory functions, another break with traditional Nationalist ideology. RSCs were also designed as redistributive bodies: the funds they raised through taxes were to be reallocated to the 'neediest' local authorities. The 1988 local elections would be a major test of the legitimacy of these new institutions. Significant support at the lowest level would then provide the foundation for blacks to be drawn into 'consultation' on one of those national councils the Government kept seeing as a substitute for one man, one vote. If there were those who did not wish to participate, it would then be their own bad luck. They would simply be excluding themselves.

The strategy was based on some obviously shaky assumptions. Whatever the turn-out at the municipal level might be, the problem of central participation for Africans seemed insoluble, given the Government's continued hard line on the release of Mandela and the unbanning of the ANC. Black leaders would still not want to place their persons and their reputations at risk by dealing with a government which desired to pick and choose those with whom it would negotiate.

Nor was there any reason to believe that tough action by the security forces would maintain 'law and order' indefinitely. In the Government's own thinking repression was a disagreeable interim necessity. Clearing away the 'agitators' would allow the majority of blacks who were either 'moderate' or undecided to participate in institutions which brought real benefits. Yet recent experience had been that after relaxation invariably came a resurgence of unrest. Africans, it seemed, were more susceptible to radical propaganda than the Government liked to believe.

Then there was the state of the economy. It had to provide the goods if redistribution through RSCs were to induce blacks to give strong support to local authorities. Yet recession continued and inflation remained high. There was an inherent constraint on economic expansion during the late 1980s: any revival in spending by investors and consumers ran into trouble because of higher levels of imports which could not be sustained in the absence of foreign capital inflows. There was another constraint: spending itself had to be restrained by higher interest rates as capital flowed out to repay foreign debt.

The picture was not entirely bleak. The informal sector of the economy had been growing, largely because of deregulation of black economic activity in the urban areas.[15] Much of this was not recorded in the official statistics, but it seems clear that it contributed substantially to black incomes in the cities. Also, many Africans had difficulties getting jobs in the formal sector of the economy, partly because of slow growth and partly because of the presence of increasingly powerful trade unions quite willing to pursue higher real wages for their members at the expense of the employment of non-members. The informal sector provided an alternative for people like these. Even so, it could only help reduce the impact of economic recession, which had to find its cure elsewhere.

The Government's own actions did little to help. In June 1988 it gave added thrust to the international sanctions campaign by renewing the state of emergency. In the same month it introduced group areas legislation which satisfied no one and antagonised all too many. There would now be areas of mixed occupation, but it would become still more difficult for members of other races to own or occupy property in white residential areas. There was the usual outcry, both at home and abroad. In the end more sensible courses prevailed and the Government withdrew the legislation, but by then familiar kinds of damage had been done.

The results of the municipal elections on 26 October were a mixed bag. Both the Government and its enemies managed to find grounds for optimism, at least in public. In Soweto the turn-out was exceptionally low, eleven per cent. In the townships of the radicalised Eastern Cape there was a similar lack of enthusiasm. But in other areas, further removed from the main economic centres and the unrest and violence, larger numbers voted. Overall it seemed that 27 per cent of registered voters went to the polls, which was less than 6 per cent of those eligible. This was still close on half a million Africans, a fair number, especially as municipal elections are nowhere regarded as great occasions of mass involvement. The Government could claim support for black local authorities which was not quite negligible. Yet, even on the most optimistic interpretation, it was plainly far from being an overwhelming mandate.

The Nationalists could at least console themselves that in the white municipal elections they had cut the Conservative Party down to size. The new Official Opposition in the House of Assembly could not consolidate its gains of the previous year. Its power base remained confined to the Transvaal; CP claims to be an alternative government qualified as one of the better jokes of the year.

The National Party in late 1988 had nowhere to go. Its schemes for drawing blacks into central government while retaining ultimate white veto power had made no progress. Revamped local authorities which would throw up black representatives to talk to the Government at the central level had not really risen to expectations. They would take time to do so – if they ever did. The only course appeared to be the maintenance of 'law and order'. Perhaps something would turn up.

The Nationalists were showing all the signs of having overstayed their time in power. After four decades of rule the National Party had degenerated into an alliance of opportunists, careerists, parasites and sometimes just plain petty crooks. Standards of public morality became a general casualty. A member of the cabinet took early retirement after he and his son were investigated for feathering their own nests at the taxpayer's expense. The Nationalist MP for Hillbrow resigned and later went to prison after he was found guilty of fiddling postal votes in his own favour in the 1987 election. The Nationalist MP for East London City resigned and was later found guilty of corruption; amazingly he got off with only a stiff fine. In the civil service top officials were exposed for their own corrupt practices. The leader of the Indian House of Parliament, Amichand Rajbansi, was dismissed from office by P W Botha after a commission of inquiry had exposed him as a gangster-like figure who habitually intimidated his political enemies.

The State President himself was displaying no capability whatever of leading the country out of its dead-end or of being able to rejuvenate his party. Fellow-Nationalists had become increasingly concerned over his fits of bad temper, his unwillingness to listen to any but a small circle of time-servers and sycophants who told him what he wanted to know, and his vituperative attacks on critics. In particular, his relationship with the Nationalist press had been going downhill fast. At the November congress of the National Party in the Transvaal, Botha referred to some journalists as 'dirty fellows' (*lunsrieme*) who liked dropping their loads on the country on Sundays.[16] The worst news was that Botha was showing no inclination to depart. On 12 January 1989 he turned 73 but still he gave not the least sign that retirement from public life was preying on his mind.

It required an act of God. On 18 January 1989 Botha was suddenly taken ill in Cape Town. He was taken to the Wynberg Military Hospital, where it was diagnosed that he had suffered a mild stroke. Speculation about his successor at once became intense. Botha himself had told a reporter who interviewed him on 27 September 1988 after ten years as head of the Government: 'If I must be honest, I must say that one can only do this work as long as one is healthy. If my health does not allow it, then I will myself decide to go'.[17]

Botha returned home on 24 January. The public heard nothing, except from his doctors, who on 1 February made an upbeat announcement that he was making 'unusual progress'. The next day Botha caused a sensation. He sent a letter to the Nationalist caucus in which he resigned as leader of the National Party and requested that his successor be chosen. He did not, however, resign as State President. Botha's decision to split the offices was the biggest mistake of his life.

The caucus was stunned when its chairman read out the letter. It could not let that interfere with the choice of a new leader, who had to be elected on the spot. There were four candidates: Chris

Heunis, the constitutional obfuscator and Cape leader of the National Party, who was acting as State President in P W Botha's absence; Pik Botha, the longstanding Minister of Foreign Affairs; F W de Klerk, Minister of National Education and Transvaal leader of the party; and Barend du Plessis, the Minister of Finance.

Pik Botha was eliminated in the first round. In spite of his high public profile he had never bothered about ingratiating himself with rank-and-file Nationalist MPs: he managed a mere 16 votes out of 130. Heunis was the next to go: high seniority in the party and cabinet was not enough to compensate for the severe blow to his prestige when he nearly lost Helderberg to Denis Worrall in 1987. In the final round De Klerk beat Du Plessis by the remarkably small margin of 69 votes to 61.

The leader of the Transvaal National Party had been widely regarded as the most likely successor to P W Botha. The surprise was that his victory over the 49-year old and relatively junior Barend du Plessis was such a close-run thing. The most likely explanation was that younger MPs, dissatisfied with the pace of reform under P W Botha, wanted more rapid advance, but did not see De Klerk as the man who could bring it.

They had reason for their pessimism. De Klerk came from a highly political background. His father, Jan de Klerk, had been one of the ablest members of the cabinets of Strijdom and Verwoerd. Strijdom had been his uncle by marriage. Both were notably right wing. His elder brother, Willem, however, was a leading verligte. It was he who had originally coined the famous expressions 'verlig' and 'verkramp'. But there was no sign that F W de Klerk had strong verligte tendencies himself. He represented a conservative constituency, Vereeniging, in a conservative province. De Klerk came across as a grey man, intent as leader on balancing the views of verligtes and conservatives, with personal inclinations towards the right. To many younger Nationalists he was a poor choice to lead the country away from apartheid.

But De Klerk's election brought huge and instant relief to a country heartily sick of P W Botha and his autocratic ways. The new Nationalist leader had a conciliatory personality; he did not believe in browbeating and intimidating others into agreement. He was accessible and did not surround himself with flunkeys. Also, the mere fact that he had no strong ideological commitments made for pragmatism. De Klerk suddenly began to sound far more critical of apartheid than he had before. It began to seem as if perhaps there could still be room for compromise and a negotiated political settlement between the Republic's conflicting groups.

The major problem of course was P W Botha. It soon became clear that he fully intended to continue as State President. He wrote to his stand-in, Chris Heunis, to inform him that he would resume office on 15 March. This was truly bad news for his fellow-Nationalists. They, and the rest of the country, had been expecting that the relinquishing of one office would inevitably, and soon, lead to departure from the other.

They had much mistaken their man. Botha had fallen into the error of so many autocratic rulers before him, also too long in office: he genuinely came to believe that he was indispensable. He could not trust lesser men to take over the running of the country. He was even more out of touch than that. In his letter of resignation as Nationalist leader he wrote: 'The State Presidency would then in a particular degree become a binding force in our country'.[18] It was an astonishing statement from a man who had thrived on divisiveness and confrontation and had aroused the deepest animosities in his own party. P W Botha was, in truth, detested throughout the Republic, but his judgement had become so warped as a result of self-induced isolation from everyday affairs and the unavoidable effects of a stroke, that he had no inkling how far he had removed himself from being a 'binding force'.

Yet, even if it was Botha who proposed, it was the National Party which would dispose. A split between party leadership and supreme executive authority was unprecedented in the history of Nationalist rule, as it was in the history of South Africa. Although Botha had made the National Party his docile tool, and he could virtually do with it what he wanted, he could not do without it. Once he abandoned the Nationalist leadership, the foundation of all his power, he was lost. His constitutional powers were not enough to save him. The Party was at last free to abandon him. It wasted little time in doing so.

F W de Klerk swiftly called a meeting of the Federal Council of the National Party for 13 March, two days before Botha was due to return to office. As the highest decision-making body of the party the council called for the reunification of the two offices which had just been separated. Immediately afterwards, the Nationalist Parliamentary caucus endorsed the appeal unanimously.

The Party itself was prepared to go through all the public face-saving motions. The Federal Congress of the National Party was to meet on 29 June. The evening before, a banquet was to be held at which the Party would say farewell to Botha and his wife. Gradually the news leaked out that the Bothas would not be there. It turned out to be correct. No amount of persuasion could induce Botha to attend, nor did he give any explanation in public. Compared with what was to come, it was a triviality.

F W de Klerk had picked up kudos with a trip to Europe, where he met the heads of government of West Germany, Britain, Portugal and Italy. He was seen as a man with an open mind with no fixed agenda for South Africa. He would try to repeat the performance with a visit to Zambia on 28 August when he and Pik Botha would meet President Kenneth Kaunda.

On 11 August P W Botha issued a statement in which he denied any knowledge of the planned visit. It was an outright contradiction of the announcement by Pik Botha the previous evening that the visit had been agreed upon after consultation with the State President.

The much surprised F W de Klerk knew that Botha opposed the visit strongly but had no doubt that he was aware of it. He issued a statement in which he diplomatically referred to 'a misunderstanding'.[19] The next day De Klerk held a meeting of Nationalist ministers; he received their unanimous support. On Monday, 14 August, the cabinet met in Cape Town under the chairmanship of the State President. He was given the choice which had been agreed upon two days before: he could cease to act as President on grounds of ill health. As earlier in the year, an acting President would be appointed; after the election Botha could retire formally. He replied that he would rather resign. His ministers did not attempt to change his mind.

That evening Botha explained his decision on television. It was a repetition of what he had already said, with some embellishments.

He claimed that he had first heard about the visit on 10 August when Kaunda was quoted on television to that effect. Botha knew Kaunda as a bitter enemy of South Africa, as witnessed in the massive assistance he gave the ANC for its 'terrorist actions' against the Republic. Hence Botha asserted that he could not approve the visit and had no choice but to resign. The next day F W de Klerk was sworn in as acting State President.

By any count, it was an appalling performance. The reasons given by Botha for his resignation were transparent nonsense. He had himself sent cabinet ministers to confer with Kaunda in Lusaka; Zambia's enthusiasm for the ANC had then been no problem. As for not being told about the visit, it is difficult to imagine that De Klerk and Pik Botha would have failed to inform a man who was so touchy about his prerogatives and so swift to lose his temper. The most charitable explanation is that Botha's stroke had done nothing to improve his memory. Even if his objections were valid it is still extraordinary that Botha should have chosen to make so public an issue of them at a time when it could only have damaged the National Party in an election a mere three weeks away. In spite of his lifelong enforcement of the party line, he now abandoned all restraint in his efforts to harm the party which had so recently told him to go. Nothing in his public life became him like the leaving it.

It was clear by then that the Government would lose seats both to the right and the left. The only question was how many. The economy was still performing poorly: a low gold price and pressure on the balance of payments kept interest rates high and growth low. The Conservative Party was talking confidently about coming within striking distance of forming a government as white rejection of reform acquired momentum. The Democratic Party, the supposedly more broadly-based party which had emerged from the ashes of the PFP, was hoping for a 'hung Parliament' in which no party would have an absolute majority and the Nationalists would therefore be compelled to look for support on the left.

The National Party took a clearer stand on 'reform' than in any previous election, although it did not much bother with spelling out the details. It would dearly have liked to smear the Democratic Party as soft on security, but in view of De Klerk's visit to the

ANC's patron, Kenneth Kaunda, it had to tone down that familiar tune. Although it did lose seats to the right and the left, as predicted, the National Party did not do as badly as many commentators expected. It lost seventeen seats to the Conservatives and twelve to the Democratic Party. The final result was 93 seats for the Nationalist, 39 for the Conservative Party and 33 for the Democratic Party. Of the votes cast, 48 per cent went to the Nationalists, 31 per cent to the CP and 20 per cent to the DP.

Although the two opposition parties had advanced at the Nationalist expense, there was little indication that they could go much further. The Democratic Party showed that, like the PFP, its greatest support came from English-speaking urban voters; in spite of pre-election propaganda about youthful Afrikaners looking for a verligte alternative to the Nationalists, on 6 September there were not many around voting for DP candidates. The Conservative Party made its first gains in the Cape and the Orange Free State, but did not advance much in the Transvaal.

As winning parties do, even if their majorities are down, the Nationalists interpreted the result as a mandate for their policies. It was even more favourable than it appeared at first sight, they now argued. As F W de Klerk, who at last became State President on 14 September, expressed it: 'It is very clear that an overwhelming majority of about 70 per cent of the white voters supported renewal and reform, as well as a policy which aims at giving full political rights in one way or another to all South Africans'. What was more, it was the National Party which had overwhelming support for its own particular brand of reform.[20]

One thing at least had changed. The former fence-sitter was now taking an outspoken verligte line. Whether events pushed him that way, whether it was a matter of intense soul-searching, or whether it was both, F W de Klerk had emerged as the Nationalist leader who would finally have to dismantle white supremacy. He was an unlikely choice as a man of destiny, but from unpromising origins he had travelled a long way. De Klerk had now embarked on a course that would take him even further from his beginnings and into a future that was overpowering in its uncertainty.

Notes

Chapter 1
1. J. Lawrence, *Harry Lawrence* (Cape Town, 1987), p. 221.
2. S. Pienaar, *Getuie van Groot Tye* (Cape Town, 1979), p. 16.
3. N.M. Stultz, *Afrikaner Politics in South Africa, 1939–1948* (California, 1974), pp. 57–8.
4. M. Roberts and A.E.G. Trollip, *The South African Opposition, 1939–1945* (Cape Town, 1947), p. 160.
5. Stultz, p. 157.
6. Ibid., p. 156.
7. Quoted in W.K. Hancock, *Smuts: The Fields of Force, 1919–1950* (Cambridge, 1968), p. 146.
8. Quoted in D. and J. de Villiers, *Paul Sauer* (Cape Town, 1977), p. 87.
9. Ibid., pp. 86–7.

Chapter 2
1. T.P. 1/1922, para 267.
2. W.M.M. Eiselen, 'Harmonious Multi-Community Development', *Optima*, March 1959, p. 10.
3. Personal communication from Eiselen (July, 1972).
4. Communication to G.D. Scholtz, *Dr Hendrik Frensch Verwoerd, 1901–1960,* 2 vols. (Johannesburg, 1967), v. 1, p. 213.
5. Senate Debates, 1948, col. 246.
6. A. Luthuli, *Let My People Go* (London, 1963), p. 63.
7. Quoted in Eiselen, p. 6.
8. U.G. 28/1948, p. 19.
9. *Senate Debates*, 1952, col. 3611.

Chapter 3
1. *House of Assembly Debates*, 1952, cols. 587–98.
2. Luthuli, p. 97.

3. R. van der Ross, *The Rise and Decline of Apartheid* (OUP, 1986), p. 252.
4. Quoted in Van der Ross, p. 258.
5. Quoted in M. Benson, *The African Patriots* (London, 1963), p. 63.
6. Luthuli, p. 99.
7. T. Lodge, *Black Politics in South Africa since 1945* (Johannesburg, 1983), p. 44.
8. J. Robertson, *Liberalism in South Africa, 1948–1963* (OUP, 1971), pp. 148–9.
9. H. Adam and H. Giliomee, *The Rise and Crisis of Afrikaner Power* (Cape Town, 1979), p. 61.
10. M. Olson, *The Rise and Decline of Nations* (Yale, 1982), pp. 43–7.

Chapter 4
1. De Villiers (1977), pp. 86–7.
2. U.G. 61/1955 (hereafter Tomlinson), p. xviii.
3. Ibid., p. 194.
4. W.P.F./1956, p. 3.
5. Tomlinson, p. 48.
6. T. Bell, *Industrial Concentration in South Africa* OUP, 1973), p. 16.
7. Tomlinson, p. 114.
8. Ibid., p. 49.
9. Ibid., pp. 140–1.
10. Ibid., p. 184.
11. A.N. Pelzer (ed.), *Verwoerd Speaks* (Johannesburg, 1968), pp. 92, 99–100.
12. Tomlinson, p. 192.
13. *House of Assembly Debates*, 1956, cols, 5306–7.
14. Ibid., 1958, col. 4164.
15. Senate Debates, 1951, col. 2894.
16. Quoted by M. Horrell, *A Decade of Bantu Education* (Johannesburg, 1964), p. 4.
17. *House of Assembly Debates*, 1953, col. 2894.
18. *Senate Debates*, 1954, col. 2599.
19. C.W. de Kiewiet, *A History of South Africa, Social and Economic* (OUP, 1941), p. 79.

Chapter 5
1. Ben Schoeman, *My Lewe in die Politiek* (Johannesburg, 1978), pp. 202–3.
2. Ibid., p. 203.
3. Quoted in Luthuli, p. 211.
4. Benson, pp. 226–7.
5. *The Cape Times*, 17 September 1958.
6. Quoted by J. Botha, *Verwoerd is Dead* (Cape Town, 1967), p. 22.
7. B. Schoeman, p. 224.
8. Ibid., p. 239.

Chapter 6
1. B. Schoeman, p. 178.
2. Pelzer, p. 161.
3. Die Transvaler, 7 November 1958.
4. B. Schoeman, p. 288.
5. Ibid., p. 208.
6. Ibid., pp. 246–7.
7. *The Cape Times*, 2 September 1958.
8. Botha, p. 44.
9. Pienaar, p. 60.
10. Ibid., p. 60.
11. Eiselen, p. 8.
12. *House of Assembly Debates*, 1959, col. 62.
13. Ibid., cols. 63–4.
14. Ibid., col. 6221.
15. Ibid., col. 62.
16. S.L. Barnard and A.H. Marais, *Die Verenigde Party – Die Groot Eksperiment* (Durban/Pretoria, 1982), p. 109.
17. B.M. Schoeman, *Van Malan tot Verwoerd* (Cape Town, 1973), p. 228.

Chapter 7
1. F.A. van Jaarsveld and G.D. Scholtz (eds.), *Die Republiek van Suid-Afrika* (Johannesburg, 1965), p. 6.
2. G.D. Scholtz, v. 2, p. 60.
3. B.M. Schoeman, pp. 185–6.
4. G.D. Scholtz, v.2, p. 61.
5. Pelzer, p. 323.
6. Van Jaarsveld and Scholtz, p. 6.
7. *The Cape Argus*, 10 March 1960.
8. *The Cape Times*, 3 February 1960.
9. Ibid., 3 February 1960.
10. Ibid., 12 February 1960.
11. Pelzer, p. 367.

Chapter 8
1. R. Segal, *Into Exile* (London, 1963), p. 63.
2. *House of Assembly Debates*, 1960, col. 3759.
3. Ibid., col. 3875.
4. *The Cape Times*, 23 March 1960.
5. Quoted by Scholtz, v.2, p. 153.
6. Pelzer, p. 375.
7. Quoted by Botha, p. 66.
8. *Die Burger*, 20 April 1960.
9. J. Lewin, *Politics and Law in South Africa* (London, 1963), pp. 107–115.

10. S.R. Lewis, Jr., *The Economics of Apartheid* (New York, 1990), pp. 23, 39.
11. E. Hoffer, *The True Believer* (New York, 1951), p. 29.

Chapter 9
1. Botha, p. 67.
2. J.J.J. Scholtz, *Die Moord op Dr Verwoerd* (Cape Town, 1967), p. 81.
3. Pelzer, p. 397.
4. Ibid., p. 395.
5. *The Cape Times,* 1 June 1960.
6. *Die Burger,* 16 March 1960.
7. *House of Assembly Debates*, 1960, col. 3769.
8. Pelzer, p. 408.
9. *Rand Daily Mail*, 9 September 1960.
10. Ibid., 10 September 1960.
11. Quoted in A. Hepple, *Verwoerd* (Penguin, 1967), p. 178.
12. B.M. Schoeman, p. 196.
13. Pelzer, pp. 410–12.
14. Quoted by G.D. Scholtz, v.2, p. 107.
15. Quoted by A. Sampson, *Macmillan* (Penguin, 1967), pp. 190–91.
16. *The Cape Times*, 16 March 1961.
17. Pelzer, p. 604.
18. K. Heard, *General Elections in South Africa, 1943–1970* (OUP, 1974), p. 134.
19. *The Cape Times,* 17 August 1961.

Chapter 10
1. S.R. Lewis, p. 24.
2. *House of Assembly Debates*, 1951, col. 3797.
3. Quoted in J. Kantor, *A Healthy Grave* (London, 1967), p. 223.
4. *House of Assembly Debates*, 1965, cols. 252–67.
5. Quoted in J. D'Oliveira, *Vorster–The Man* (Johannesburg, 1977), p. 215.
6. Quoted in Kantor, p. 225.
7. *The Cape Argus*, 31 August, 1961.
8. Quoted in Kantor, p. 224.
9. Pienaar, p. 60.
10. *Die Burger*, 24 November 1960.
11. Ibid., 1 December 1960.
12. Pienaar, p. 60.
13. Ibid., p. 53.
14. Quoted in D'Oliveira, p. 215.
15. Cf. A.D. Lowenburg, 'An Economic Theory of Apartheid', *Economic Inquiry*, January 1989.
16. E.g. Olson, op. cit., and M. Lipton, *Capitalism and Apartheid* (London, 1985).

17. Lowenburg, p. 60.
18. Ibid.
19. Quoted in Adam and Giliomee, p. 222.
20. Quoted in G.D. Scholtz, v. 2, p. 171.
21. A. Boshoff, *Sekretaresse vir die Verwoerds* (Cape Town, 1974), p. 228.
22. B. Schoeman, pp. 278, 308.
23. J. Butler, R.I. Rotberg and J. Adams, *The Black Homelands of South Africa* (California, 1977), p. 2.
24. Ibid.
25. Quoted in G.M. Carter *et al.*, *South Africa's Transkei: The Politics of Domestic Colonialism* (London, 1967), p. 186.
26. E. Munger, *Afrikaner and African Nationalism* (OUP, 1967), pp. 111–2.
27. Cited by S. van der Horst, 'The Economic Problems of the Homelands', in N.J. Rhoodie (ed.), *The South African Dialogue* (Johannesburg, 1972), p. 186.
28. S. Greenberg, *Legitimating the Illegitimate* (Yale, 1989), p. 47.
29. Lipton, pp. 45–6.
30. *Race Relations Survey, 1965* (Johannesburg, 1966), p. 2.
31. Pienaar, p. 63.
32. *Die Burger*, 26 September 1962.
33. *Die Burger*, 27 April 1964.
34. Pienaar, p. 65.

Chapter 11
1. B. Schoeman, p. 320.
2. B.M. Schoeman, p. 14.
3. Giliomee and Adam, p. 202.
4. Ibid., pp. 202–3.
5. D'Oliveira, p. 233.
6. Ibid., p. 232.
7. Ibid., pp. 205–6.
8. Ibid., p. 233.
9. Pienaar, pp. 74–5.
10. B. Schoeman, p. 244.
11. Ibid., p. 342.
12. J.H.P. Serfontein, *Die Verkrampte Aanslag* (Cape Town/Pretoria, 1970), p. 22.
13. Pienaar, pp. 46–7.
14. Serfontein, p. 56.
15. B. Schoeman, p. 324.
16. Ibid., p. 338.
17. Quoted in D'Oliveira, pp. 220–1.
18. B. Schoeman, p. 334.
19. Ibid., pp. 334–5.
20. Serfontein, p. 157.

21. B. Schoeman, p. 360.
22. Serfontein, p. 214.
23. *Race Relations Survey, 1970,* p. 1.
24. F.A. van Jaarsveld, 'Die Afrikaner se Groot Trek na die Stede 1886–1976', in P.G. Nel (ed.), *Die Kultuurontplooiing van die Afrikaner* (Pretoria, 1979), pp. 227–9
25. D. O'Meara, *Volkskapitalisme* (Cambridge, 1983), p. 251.

Chapter 12
1. *House of Assembly Debates,* 1969, col. 3883.
2. Quoted in D'Oliveira, p. 251.
3. G.C. Olivier, 'South Africa's Relations with Africa', in R. Schrire (ed.), *South Africa: Public Policy Perspectives* (Cape Town, 1982), pp. 280–1.
4. Quoted in D'Oliveira, p. 214.
5. H. Giliomee and L. Schlemmer, *From Apartheid to Nation-Building* (Johannesburg, 1989), p. 72.
6. Lipton, p. 46.
7. Ibid., p. 35.
8. W.A. Lewis, *Racial Conflict and Economic Development* (Harvard, 1985), p. 44, 121.
9. S.R. Lewis, p. 135.
10. *Race Relations Survey, 1973,* p. 114.

Chapter 13
1. Quoted in D. Woods, *Biko* (London, 1978), p. 114.
2. Ibid., p. 118.
3. Ibid., p. 123.
4. Ibid., p. 124.
5. Quoted in B. Hirson, *Year of Fire, Year of Ash* (London, 1979), p. 85.
6. Ibid., p. 107.
7. Ibid., pp. 110–11.
8. S.R. Lewis, p. 24.
9. Quoted in *Race Relations Survey, 1975,* p. 285.
10. Ibid., p. 284.
11. Ibid., p. 286.
12. Hirson, p. 133.
13. Ibid., pp. 155–6.
14. Lodge, p. 329.
15. Quoted in A. Ries and E. Dommisse, *Broedertwis* (Cape Town, 1982), p. 73.
16. Hirson, p. 260.
17. J. Suckling, quoted in C.R. Hill, *South Africa* (London, 1981), p. 47.
18. T. Lodge, p. 333.

Chapter 14
1. Quoted in *Race Relations Survey, 1972,* p. 2.

2. Ibid., pp. 2–3.
3. Cited by Van Jaarsveld, p. 188.
4. Adam and Giliomee, p. 184.
5. Op. cit., pp. 163–4.
6. S.R. Lewis, p. 23.
7. Ibid., p. 39.
8. Lipton, p. 408.
9. F. de Villiers, 'Hutt Revisited: Capitalism and Apartheid' in *Apartheid – Capitalism or Socialism?* (London, 1986), p. 24.
10. Quoted in *Race Relations Survey, 1973* (Johannesburg, 1974), p. 218.
11. Quoted by H. Giliomee, 'Afrikaner Politics 1977–1987: From Afrikaner Nationalist Rule to Central State Hegemony', in J. Brewer (ed.), *Can South Africa Survive?* (London, 1989), p. 118.
12. *Race Relations Survey, 1971*, pp. 199–200.
13. Quoted in *Race Relations Survey, 1973*, p. 259.
14. Ibid., p. 219.
15. Giliomee and Schlemmer, p. 105.
16. Lipton, pp. 65–6.
17. S. Marks and S. Trapido, 'South Africa since 1976: An Historical Perspective', in S. Johnson (ed.), *South Africa: No Turning Back* (Indiana, 1989), p. 30.
18. Cited by Lipton, p. 407.
19. Quoted by Lipton, p. 170.
20. Summarised in *Race Relations Survey, 1979* pp. 275–79.
21. Ibid., pp. 394–97.
22. Adam and Giliomee, p. 182.

Chapter 15

1. A. Paton, *Save the Beloved Country* (Johannesburg, 1987), p. 26.
2. Quoted by Olivier in Schrire, p. 286.
3. R.S. Jaster, *The Defence of White Power* (London, 1988), p. 27.
4. J.J.J. Scholtz (ed.), *P.W. Botha – Vegter en Staatsman* (Cape Town, 1987), p. 34.
5. Quoted in K.W. Grundy, *The Militarization of South African Politics* (London, 1986), p. 11.
6. Ibid., p. 35.
7. M. Rees and C. Day, *Muldergate* (Johannesburg, 1980), p. 167.
8. Ibid., 165.
9. B. Pottinger, *The Imperial Presidency* (Johannesburg, 1988), p. 10.
10. H. Adam, *Modernizing Racial Domination* (California, 1971), pp. 181–2.

Chapter 16

1. Grundy, p. 35.

2. Pottinger, p. 22.
3. Quoted by Pottinger, p. 22.
4. *Race Relations Survey, 1979,* p. 8.
5. Quoted by Munger, p. 67.
6. J.J.J. Scholtz (ed.), p. 38.
7. Ibid., pp. 37–8.
8. S.P. Huntington, 'Reform and Stability in a Modernizing, Multi-Ethnic Society', *Politikon,* December 1981.
9. S.P. Huntington, 'The trouble with reform', *Financial Mail,* 24 October 1986.

Chapter 17
1. Quoted in D. and J. de Villiers, *PW* (Cape Town, 1984), p. 181.
2. Quoted in ibid., p. 168.
3. Ries and Domisse (1982), p. 86.
4. Quoted in ibid., p. 191.
5. Quoted in Pottinger, p. 139.
6. Ibid.
7. A. Ries and E. Dommisse (1982), p. 108.
8. Quoted in De Villiers, p. 192.
9. *Financial Mail,* 26 February 1982.
10. C. Charney, 'Class Conflict and the National Party Split', *Journal of Southern African Studies,* April 1984, p. 210.
11. Ibid., p. 211.
12. O'Meara, p. 255.

Chapter 18
1. D. Worrall, 'The Constitutional Committee of the President's Council', *Politikon,* December 1981, p. 33.
2. Cf. Huntington (1981), Giliomee and Adam, chap. 10.
3. Op. cit., p. 14.
4. Quoted in J. Barber and J. Barratt, *South Africa's Foreign Policy* (Cambridge, 1990), p. 288.
5. Slabbert, p. 108.
6. Pottinger, p. 101.
7. Ibid., p. 104.
8. *Race Relations Survey, 1982,* p. 7.
9. *Race Relations Survey, 1983,* p. 30.
10. Slabbert, p. 106.
11. Ibid., p. 111.
12. *Race Relations Survey, 1983,* p. 80.
13. Ibid.
14. Slabbert, p. 112.
15. *Race Relations Survey, 1983,* p. 80.

Chapter 19
1. *Race Relations Survey, 1983,* p. 91.
2. Quoted in A. Sampson, *Black and Gold* (London, 1983), pp. 152–153.
3. *Race Relations Survey, 1983,* p. 57.
4. S.R. Lewis, Jr., p. 24.
5. Slabbert, p. 121.
6. *Race Relations Survey, 1984,* p. 64.
7. S.M. Davis, *Apartheid's Rebels* (Johannesburg, 1987), pp. 150–156.
8. Quoted in Barber and Barratt, p. 309.
9. *Race Relations Survey, 1986,* p. 485.
10. Quoted in Pottinger, p. 314.
11. Sampson, p. 32.
12. Ibid., p. 31.
13. Botha, p. 19.
14. G.J. Stigler, *Memoirs of an Unregulated Economist* (New York, 1988), p. 196
15. Paton, p. 7.
16. Botha, p. 19.
17. Huntington (1981), p. 16.
18. Huntington (1986).
19. Pottinger, p. 348.
20. Cf. Pottinger.

Chapter 20
1. G.F. Kennan, *American Diplomacy, 1900–1950* (London, 1952), p. 93.
2. E. Lourens and H. Kotzé, 'The South African White General Election of 1987: Shifting deck-chairs or burning boats?', *International Affairs Bulletin*, v. 11, no. 2, 1987.
3. Cited in H. Zille, 'The right wing in South African politics', in P.L. Berger and B. Godsell (eds.), *A Future South Africa: Visions, Strategies and Realities* (Cape Town, 1988), p. 59.
4. Cited in L. Schlemmer, 'South Africa's National Party Government', in Berger and Godsell, p. 20.
5. Charney, p. 271.
6. Schlemmer, p. 22.
7. H. Giliomee, in Brewer, p. 122.
8. Ibid., p. 121.
9. Cited in Lourens and Kotzé, p. 25.
10. Giliomee, in Brewer, p. 121.
11. Pottinger, p. 230.
12. Ibid., pp. 412–3.
13. Quoted in A. Ries and E. Dommisse, *Leierstryd* (Cape Town, 1990), p. 33.
14. Quoted in Barber and Barratt, p. 339.
15. B. Kantor, 'Challenge to South African Industrialists', *Intercom*, December 1989, p. 6.

16. Ries and Dommisse (1990), p. 74.
17. Ibid., p. 86.
18. Ibid,. p. 91.
19. Ibid., p. 229.
20. Ibid., p. 257.

Index

Adam, Heribert 269, 288
African education 79–82, 246–52,
    261–2, 275, 361
African housing 229
African living standards
    1946–60 148
    in 1970's 258–9
    1970–82 262
African local government 348–9,
    389–91
African National Congress (ANC)
    3–4, 15–18, 62–3, 64–6, 93–8,
    123–4, 137, 140–1, 149, 165, 173,
    176, 237, 341, 344–5, 350–1, 354,
    382, 384
African Resistance Movement (ARM)
    175–6
African trade unions 12, 264–6,
    267–71, 303, 345–6
African urbanisation 11–12, 15, 30–1,
    42–3, 50–1
    government restrictions 77–8
    increase in numbers, 1951–60 99
    legislation concerning 190–2,
        219, 229–32, 238, 256
    freehold rights, 1986 360
African workers
    advancement 258–9
    strikes 242–5, 262–3
    wages 249–50, 262–3
Afrikaanse Handelsinstituut 264, 270

Afrikaanse Pers 209
Afrikaner Broederbond 34, 212
Afrikaner nationalism 7–8, 22, 26–7,
    36–7, 66–7, 106–7
Afrikaner Orde 208, 213–15
Afrikaner Party 27, 29, 32, 34, 85
Afrikaner Weerstandsbeweging 351,
    372–3
Afrikaners, urbanisation of 183–4,
    218, 220, 269–71, 321–2
agriculture, decline in 1970's 256–7
Alexandra township, bus boycott
    95–6
Angola 250, 273, 280–2
Apartheid policy
    6–12, 23, 30–2, 38–9, 41, 68–70,
    117–119, 185–6, 275–7, 362
    see also neo-apartheid
arms embargo 359
Atlantic Charter 148–9
Azanian People's Organisation
    (AZAPO) 345, 352

Ball, Chris 384–5, 387
Ballinger, Margaret 53–4
Banda, Hastings 226
banning of persons 174–5
Bantu Affairs Administration Act,
    1971 230
Bantu Authorities Act 48–9, 79,
    99–100

Bantu Education Act, 1953 80–2, 95
Bantu Education, Department of
  enforcement of Afrikaans as a
  medium of instruction 246–7
Bantu Labour Regulations, 1965 229
Bantu Labour Relations Regulation
  Amendment Act, 1973 244
Bantu Self-Government Act,
  1959 121
Barclays National Bank 384–5
Barnard, Fred 133
Basson, Japie 116, 167, 168, 204
Beeld Die (newspaper) 207, 209, 210,
  214
Biko, Steve 238–40, 282
black activism in the 1980's 345–6
Black Consciousness Movement
  238–40, 245, 345
Black People's Convention 240–1
black reserves *see* reserves
black voters, removal from Cape
  common roll 40–2, 56
Boesak, Allan 343
border areas, industrialisation of
  73–5, 260
Botha, Fanie 303, 309, 318, 319, 338
Botha, P W 2, 12–14
  Minister of Coloured Affairs 295
  Minister of Defence 213, 254, 271,
    281–3, 286
  Cabinet Committee to investigate
  constitutional amendments, August
    1976 278–9
    Prime Minister 287–9, 296–8,
      300–3, 310–13, 318–30
    Executive President 328–330,
      336–7, 342, 347, 352–7,
      360–1, 380–2, 386–7
    illness & resignation 392–6
Botha, R F (Pik) 5, 288, 294, 303, 356,
  393, 396
Botswana 226, 342
Brakpan by-election, 1972 253–4
Bretton Woods system of fixed
  exchange rates 241

Britain, trade with South African in
  1960's 193
Broederbond 34, 212
Brown, S E D 214
Burger, Die (newspaper) 8–9, 126–7,
  138, 180, 209, 214
Butcher, Willard 355
Buthelezi, Mangosuthu, Chief G
  16, 352–3, 335

Cape Province
  African franchise 40–2
  apartheid measures 56
  coloured franchise 54–7, 210, 233–4
Cape Times (newspaper)
  discussion of South African
  exclusion from the
  Commonwealth 163–4
Carletonville strike, 1973 244
Carmichael, Stokely 239
Carter, Jimmy 279, 282–3
Cato Manor, massacre of policemen
  139
Chase Manhattan Bank, New York
  355, 358, 360
Christian Institute, banning of 235
churches, opposition to Native Laws
  Amendment Bill 101–2
Cillié, Piet 9
Citizen (newspaper) 285–6
civil service, growth of 52, 59, 93, 184,
  222, 296–7
Coloured Labour Preference Policy
  101
coloured parliament 278–9, 312, 327,
  331, 333, 347
coloured people
  franchise 54–7, 60–1, 88–92, 210,
    233–4
  Group Areas Act 234
  national income 258
  political rights 12, 54–7, 60–1,
    88–92, 129, 179–82, 210, 233–4,
    278–9
  training 260

409

Coloured Persons' Representative
   Council 234, 278, 333–4
coloured representation in President's
   Council 312–13
coloured university 122
Commonwealth Prime Ministers'
   Meeting, London March 1961
   159–63
Commonwealth, South Africa's
   exclusion from 161–3
Communism
   collapse of, in Eastern Europe 15
   influence on ANC party 17
   official propaganda concerning 223
Comprehensive Anti-Apartheid Act,
   October 1986 369
'comrades' in townships 349, 353
Congo, independence of 156, 158
Congress Alliance 97–8
Congress of Democrats 97
Congress of the People, Kliptown,
   25 June 1955 97–8
Congress of South African Trade
   Unions 388
Conservative Party 3, 13, 320, 331,
   335, 338, 351, 372–3, 378–9, 391,
   396
consociational democracy 326–7, 330
Constitutional Commissions of 1976
   tricameral parliament 278–9, 312
constitutional reform, committee
   report on 325–30
Craven Week, school rugby 310
Criminal Law Amendment Act
   94, 96
Crocker, Chester 342
Cuba, intervention in Angola 281–2
Cuito Cuanavale, battle of 359

Dagbreek (newspaper) 209, 214
De Klerk, F W 3, 5, 14–15, 18, 319,
   320, 333, 393, 395, 397
De Klerk, Jan 104, 206, 393
De Klerk, Willem 206, 393
De Kock, Gerard 355

De Villiers Graaff, Sir *see* Graaff, Sir
   David Pieter de Villiers
Defiance Campaign 62–6, 147, 149
Delius, Anthony 140
Diefenbaker, John 162
diplomats, black 213
District Six, Cape Town 39
Dönges, T E 57, 103, 144, 201
Du Plessis, Barend 393
Durban
   strikes 242–3, 260
   unrest 1984 349
Dutch Reformed Church, opposition
   to State interference 102

East Rand, unrest of 1984 349
Eastern Cape, unrest of 1984 349
Economic Development Programme,
   1972 258–9, 270
Eerste Ekonomiese Volkskongres 34
Eiselen, Werner, Dr 44–5, 79–80,
   101, 114, 118, 184
elections
   1948 7, 21–3, 33–5
   1953 59
   1958 103
   1961 166–9
   1970 217, 253
   1974 254–5
   1979 and
   1980 by-elections 304
   1987 377–80, 396–7
Eminent Persons Group (EPG) 364–5
English speaking population
   role under Vorster's government
   222
   support for P W Botha 306, 323, 376
Erasmus, F C 174
Erasmus, Rudolf
   investigation into Information
   Department 292–5
European Economic Community,
   sanctions against South Africa 368
Extension of University Education
   Act 121–2

410

Fagan, Henry, Native Laws Commission, 1946 9–10, 49–50, 70, 268
Fanon, Frantz 239
farmers, preferential treatment 52
Federasie van Afrikaanse Kultuurverenigings 34
Federation of South African Trade Unions (FOSATU) 350
First National Bank 385
Fischer, Abram 176
'floating colour bar' 260–1
FNLA (Angola) 281
Fort Hare University 122
Freedom Charter 96–8, 344
From Union to Apartheid (book) 53–4
funerals, political activity at 353

Garment Workers' Union 62
General Laws Amendment Act of 1962, 1963 and 1964 174
Gesuiwerde Nasionale Party 23
gold mines, labour demand 263
gold price
　fluctuations in 1970's 241, 259, 263
　weakness of, after 1981 371
Graaff, Sir David Pieter de Villiers 127, 131, 159, 167, 210
Group Areas Legislation 3, 8, 38–9, 275–6, 390
Grundy, Kenneth 284

Hammarskjöld, Dag 194
Harris, John 175
Havenga, Klaas 27, 29, 32, 56, 85–6
Hendrickse, Allan, Revd 334–5, 385–7
Herenigde Nasionale Party 26, 28–9
Herstigte Nasionale Party 217–18, 222, 255, 304, 309, 332, 351, 372
Hertzog, Albert 126, 201, 207–9, 211, 213–17, 221, 274, 308
Hertzog, J B M, Gen 23, 25–7, 41–2, 84, 90, 92
Hertzogites 207, 212–15, 218, 225

Heunis, Chris 328–31, 333–4, 336, 378, 393, 394
High Court of Parliament Act 57
Hirson, Baruch 240, 245, 249, 251
Hoffer, Eric 150
Hofmeyr, J H 41
homelands 114–19, 187–90, 230–1, 260, 301–2
Hoofstad (newspaper) 214, 216, 308
Horwood, Owen 294
Howe, Geoffrey 340
Huntington, Samuel 304–6, 326, 362–3

Immorality Act, 1950 39
　Abolition of Section 16 361
immigration policy 37, 178–9, 260
Indian Council 278
Indian parliament 12, 32, 278–9, 312, 327
　boycott of elections for 347
Indian representation on President's Council 312–13
Indians
　Group Areas Act 234
　national income 258
　training of 260
Industrial Conciliation Act
　Amendment to, 1956 and 1959 92–3
Industrial Concialiation Amendments Act, 1979 265, 303
Industrial Court 265
influx control 191–2
　abolition of, 1986 360
informal sector of the economy 390
Information Department, investigation of irregularities 292–5
Information scandal 273, 284–9, 290–1
Inkatha Freedom Party 16
Ivory Coast 227

Jansen, E G 70
Japan, sanctions against SA 368

job reservation 52
   abolition of 261
Joint Management Centres 296
Jonathan, Leabua, Chief of Lesotho
   198, 225–6

Kaunda, Kenneth 280, 368, 396
Kennan, George 369
Kerkbode (newspaper) 308
Kgosana, Philip 141–2
Koornhof, Piet 309–10
Kotze Commission 230
Kruger, Jimmy 282
KwaNatal Indaba, 1986 383

Labour Party 234, 333–5, 347, 385–7
Land Acts 1913 and 1936 42
   repeal of 3–4
Landman, Willem, Revd 113–14
Langa township, Uitenhage 139, 142, 353
Langley, Tom 338
Last White Parliament (book) 327–8
Lawrence, Harry 22
Lekoa, murder of Deputy Mayor, September 1984 348–9
Lesotho 226, 227, 342
Lewin, Julius 146–8
Lewis, Arthur 231–2, 359
Liberia 227
Lijphart, Arend 326
Lipton, Merle 191, 262
Lodge, Tom 251
Louw, Eric 119, 192
Luthuli, Albert 48, 54, 63, 123, 141, 151

Machel, Samora 341–2
Macmillan, Harold 131–5, 150, 155, 158, 162–3, 192
Malan, D F, Dr 22, 23, 26, 28–9, 32, 54, 56, 60–1, 84–6, 107, 126
Malan, Magnus 305
Malan, Wynand 377–8
Malawi 226, 228

Mandela, Nelson 1–2, 172–3, 175–177, 364, 381–2
Mandela, Winnie 384
Marais, Jaap 207, 211, 216–7, 274, 308
Marks, S 262
marriages, mixed, prohibition of 39, 275, 361
Matanzima, Kaiser, Chief 188–9
Matthews, Z K, Prof 96, 97
Maud, John, Sir 132
media censorship 234, 366
Meyer, Piet 212
military establishment, influence of 297, 364–6
Mine Workers' Union 261, 266, 303
mine workers' strike
   1946 32
   1979 303
Mitchell, Douglas 120, 135, 159–60
Mixed Marriages Act, abolition of 361
Modernizing Racial Domination 288
Mostert, Anton, investigation of exchange control irregularities 292–3
Mozambique 250, 280, 341, 365
Mozambique National Resistance (Renamo) 341–2
MPLA (Angola) 281
Mugabe, Robert 368
Mulder, Connie 284–8, 290–4
Muller, Hilgard 192
Muller, Louwrens 298
Munger, Edwin 190
municipal elections 1988 389–1
Munnik, George 385

Nasionale Pers 209–10
National Action Council 97
National Convention, 1908–9 39–40
National Education Finance Act, 1945 45
National Forum 344–5
National Party
   Afrikaner nationalism 7, 17–18, 36–8, 222

412

apartheid policy 41, 276–9
corruption 391
election victory, 1948 7, 21–3, 33–5
election victory 1953 59
elections 1958 103
elections 1961 166–9
elections 1970 217, 253
elections 1974 254–5
by-elections 1979 and 1980 304
electoral support in 1980's 373–6
elections 1987 377–80
election manifesto 1989 5
formation under D F Malan 23–5
immigration policy 37, 178–9
membership of the Commonwealth 38, 163–4
Natal Congress. P W Botha's speech 1985 356–7
1984 constitution 12
Orange Free State Congress 1962 185
power sharing policy 12, 14–15, 300–1, 312–18, 324
sympathy towards right wingers 205–6
Transvaal Congress, Pretoria 1969 216, 274
National People's Party 347
National Security Management System (NSMS) 296
National Union 167–8
National Union of South African Students (NUSAS) 235, 238–9
nationalisation policy 18
Native Education Commission 79–80
Native Land Act, 1913 42
repeal 3–4
Native Laws Amendment Act, 1937 42
Native Laws Amendment Act 1952 50–1
Native Laws Amendment Act 1957 101–2
Native Laws Commission, 1946 9–10, 49–50, 70, 268

Native representation in Parliament, abolition of 116
Native Representative Council 46–7
Native Resettlement Act 94–5
Natives (abolition of passes and co-ordination of documents) Bill 51
Natives (Urban Areas) Act of 1923 41–2
Natives (Urban Areas) Consolidation Act of 1945
Section 10 rights 191, 229, 268
Naudé, Beyers 235
Ndlwana v Hofmeyr (court case 1937) 56
Nehru, Jawaharlal 162
New Order 28–9
neo-apartheid 269, 271, 346
New Zealand rugby tour of South Africa 196–7, 211, 215
90 day detention 174–5
Nkomati Accord 341–2
Nkrumah, Kwama 162
No Revolution round the corner (article in *Africa South*) 146–8
non-statutory forum for blacks 352–3
non-white university colleges, conversion to universities 119
Nyanga township 142

oil price, rise in 259
Olson, Mancur 257
Olympic Games, exclusion of South Africa 195
Operation Palmiet 349–50
Oppenheimer, Harry 100, 260, 338, 341
Orange Free State National Party Congress 1962 185
Ossewa Brandwag 27–8, 33
Organisation of African Unity
call for sanctions 195
rejection of dialogue with South Africa 227–8

413

Othello (film), Verwoerd's reaction to 185
Oudtshoorn by-election 253–4

Pan Africanist Congress (PAC) 3, 16, 96, 124, 137–8, 140–2, 165, 173, 237, 345, 382
pass laws
 campaign against, March 1960 137–42
 interdepartmental inquiry into 191
Paton, Alan 273, 359
Philippi, campaign against pass laws 138
Physical Planning and Utilisation of Resources Act, 1967 229–30, 243
Pienaar, Schalk 23, 182, 191–2, 199, 206–7, 210
Pirow, Oswald 28
political parties, opinion poll on, February 1986 373–4
Political Science Association, Johannesburg
 Samuel Huntington's address, 1981 304
Pondoland, rural violence 99–100
Population Registration Act 38
 repeal of 3–4
Poqo 173, 175–6
Portugal, withdrawal from Angola and Mozambique 280
Poto, Victor, Chief 188
power sharing with coloureds and Indians 300–1, 312–18, 324
Pratt, David 143–4
President's Council
 creation of 312–13, 331
 report of Constitutional Committee on Constitutional Reform 325–30
press control 234
Pretoria, unrest of 1984 349
Prime Ministers' Economic Advisory Council, Pretoria 1972
 Economic Development Plan 258–9, 270

Progressive Federal Party (PFP) (later Democratic Party) 4, 10, 12, 14, 16, 120, 127, 166–8, 233, 255, 304, 332, 377, 378, 38
Prohibition of Improper Interference Bill 1966 210
Prohibition of Mixed Marriages Act 1949 39
Prohibition of Political Interference Act 233
Promotion of Bantu Self-Government Bill 1959 115–17
public amenities, segregation of 276
Public Safety Act 1953 94, 96
Publications Control Board 234

Rajbansi, Amichand 386
Reagan, Ronald 342, 352
referendum, November 1983 336–9, 340–1
regional service councils 389–90
Relly, Gavin 337
Republic of South Africa Constitution Act 1983 160, 336
republic referendum 125–7, 152–9, 160, 165
Reserves (*see also* Homelands) 71–9
Rhodesia (*see also* Zimbabwe) 195–6, 223, 227, 228, 280
Rhoodie, Eschel 285–7, 291, 294
Riekert, Piet, Commission of Utilisation of Manpower 264, 267–70
Rise and Decline of Nations (book) 257
Rivonia arrests 175–6

SA Suicide Squad 353
Sabotage Act *see* General Laws Amendment Act of 1963
Sachs, Solly 62
sanctions, post 1985 period 12–13, 357–60, 368–70
Sauer, Paul, Committee 1947 31–2, 69, 144
Schlebusch, Alwyn

Commission to investigate 4 organisations 1972–3 235
Constitutional Commission, 1979 312
support for P W Botha 287, 294
Schlemmer, Lawrence, survey of white political attitudes, 1982 333
Schoeman, Ben 84, 100, 104, 107, 110, 111–12, 186, 200–1, 203, 208, 211–17, 274
Schoeman, Hendrik 319–20
Schreiner, Olive 89
Section 10 rights *see* Natives (Urban Areas) Consolidation Act of 1945
security forces, action in townships 1985 353
Sekhukuneland, rural violence 99
Senate Act 89, 205
Senghor, Leopold 239
Separate Representation of Voters Act 1951 57
Separate Representation of Voters Amendment Act 1968 233
Serfontein, J H P 210, 215
Sharpeville
　anti-pass law campaign and massacre 138–9, 140–6, 151, 155, 158
　unrest, 1984 348
Slovo, Joe 15
Smith, Ian 196, 223, 227, 280
Smuts, Jan Christian 22, 23, 25, 29, 32, 33, 92, 149
Sobukwe, Robert 124, 137–8, 141, 151
socialism, collapse of in Eastern Europe 15
Solidarity Party 347
Sophiatown removals 94–5
Sotho-Tswana university 122
South Africa
　defence spending 190
　economic growth, 1950–1980 148, 170–2, 177, 346–7
　economic recession 1970's 13, 18, 242

　economic recession after 1985 355, 370–1, 396
　population statistics 14–15, 257
　rescheduling of debt repayments 360
　sanctions 357–60, 368–70
South African Broadcasting Corporation 174, 337, 378
South African Bureau of Racial Affairs (SABRA) 180–2
　Youth Congress, October 1966 206
South African Coloured People's Organisation 97
South African Communist Party 3, 62–3, 97–8, 176
South African Confederation of Labour 266
South African Congress of Trade Unions 97
South African Indian Congress 64, 97
South African Observer (newspaper) 214–16
South African Party 23
South African Students' Movement (SASM) 247–8, 251
South African Students Organisation (SASO) 238–40, 251
South West Africa/Namibia 55–6, 131, 193–5, 223, 227–8, 283
South West African People's Organisation (SWAPO) 282
Soweto Students' Representative Council (SSRC) 248–9
Soweto uprising 1976 12, 245–7, 249–52, 283
sports policy under Vorster 275–6
Stallard Doctrine 31, 41
State (Executive) President, creation of position 327–30
state of emergency,
　July 1985 353–5
　June 1986 365–6
　June 1988 390
State Security Council 296
stay-aways 248–9
Stigler, George 358

415

Strijdom, J G 26, 32–3, 61, 84–8, 103, 130–1, 393
strikes 242–5, 260, 303
Stultz, Newell 29–30
Suid-Afrikaanse Akademie vir Wetenskap en Kuns 212
Suppression of Communism Act 62, 94
Suzman, Helen 4, 168, 233
Swart, C R 27, 62, 103–4, 165–6
Swaziland 226

Terre'Blanche, Eugene 372–3
Thatcher, Margaret 359, 364, 368
There are no South Africans (book) 11
Theron Commission 1976 278
Tomlinson, F R Prof, Commission Report 1954 10, 70–80
Torch Commando 57–9
Trade Union Council of South Africa (TUCSA) 267
Transkei 48, 117, 187–8
Transkei Constitution Act 1963 188–9
Transkei Territorial Authority, independence demand 1961 188–9
Transvaal Champer of Industries, support for referendum 1983 337
Transvaal National Party Convention, August 1961 179
Transvaler (newspaper) 26, 44, 106, 209
Trapido, S 262
Treason trial 1956–60 98–9
Treurnicht, Andries 214–17, 246, 274, 293, 297–8, 302, 308–11, 318–20, 322, 335, 338
tribal government, creation of 149–51
tricameral legislature 12, 327, 330–1
 boycott of elections for 347
 achievements of 361
Trollip, Alfred 178
True Believer, The (book) 150
Tsafendas, Demetrio 198–9
Turnhalle constitutional conference 1975 283

Tutu, Desmond, Bishop of Johannesburg 352, 359

Umkonto we Sizwe 173, 175–7
Unita (Angola) 281
United Democratic Front (UDF) 343–5, 349–52, 354, 388
United Nations Charter 1945 149
United Nations Security Council arms embargo 193
United Party 10, 21–3, 29–35, 59, 112, 115, 120–1, 127–9, 149, 166–8, 204–5, 217, 253–5, 377
United States of America 193, 281–3, 342, 369–70
universities, segregation of 121–2, 238
University College of the North South African Students' Organisation Conference 239
University Colleges, conversion to universities 119
University of Cape Town 121–2
University of Natal 121
University of the Witwatersrand 121–2
Unlawful Organisations Bill 140
 strike in protest against 63

Vaal Triangle, unrest 1984 349
van den Bergh, Hendrik, Gen 294–5
van der Merwe, Daan 318
van der Merwe, Willie 318
van der Ross, Richard 55
van Jaarsveld, F A 218–19
van Rensburg, Hans 27–8
van Rooyen, Retief 287–8
van Zyl Slabbert, Frederick 327–8, 336–8, 347
Veg (newspaper) 215–16
Verkrampte Aanslag, Die (book) 210
Verwoerd, Hendrik
 early career 43–4
 editor of *Transvaler*, 1937 26, 44
 opposition to Afrikaner Party 32–3

Minister of Native Affairs, 1950
43–9, 50–1, 71–82, 87–8, 100–2
Prime Minister 1958 104, 108–119,
121, 125–31, 133–6, 139–40,
142–5
  attempted assassination 1960 143
  broadcast, May 1960 152–3
  Republic referendum 21 Sept 1960
152–9
  Commonwealth Conference 1961
160–4
  October 1961 election 166
  race policies 8, 78–9, 178, 180–2,
185–6, 188, 197
  foreign policy 192–4, 224–5
  Rhodesian policy 195–6
  sports policy 197
  assassination 1966 198
  attitude to Albert Hertzog 208
  attitude to liberal Afrikaans press
209
  comparison with Vorster 210
Verwoerd, Mrs H F 142, 164
Victoria Falls Conference,
August 1975 280
Viljoen, Marais 298
Vlok, Adriaan 388
Volkskongres 1944 31
Voortrekkers (scout organisation) 34
Vorster, Balthazar Johannes
  Minister of Justice 174–7
  Prime Minister 200–3, 210–16,
221, 223–8, 260, 271–5, 283–7

  State President 292–4
  resignation 294

Wage Act 241
Waring, Frank 178, 182, 202–4
Western Cape, unrest 1984 349
Western Transvaal, protest against
passes 99
white farmers, decline in political
influence 256–7
white labour
  influence of 257–8
  decline in 1970's 262
white miners' strike 1979 303
white trade unions 261, 266–7
Wiehahn, Nic, Commission of Inquiry
into Labour Legislation 264–5, 270,
303
World Alliance of Reformed
Churches 343
World Health Organisation, exclusion
of South Africa 195
World War II, effect on South Africa
25–6
works committees 263–4
Worrall, Denis 325–8, 331, 337–8

Young, C B 188

Zambia 342, 365, 368–9, 395–6
Zimbabwe (*see also* Rhodesia) 342,
365, 368–9
Zulu university 122